READINGS IN EARLY DEVELOPMENT
For Occupational and Physical Therapy Students

READINGS IN
EARLY DEVELOPMENT
For Occupational and
Physical Therapy Students

Compiled and Edited by

CLAIRE B. KOPP, Ph.D., O.T.R.
Department of Pediatrics
University of California at Los Angeles
Los Angeles, California

CHARLES C THOMAS · PUBLISHER
Springfield · Illinois · U.S.A.

Published and Distributed Throughout the World by
CHARLES C THOMAS • PUBLISHER
BANNERSTONE HOUSE
301-327 East Lawrence Avenue, Springfield, Illinois, U.S.A.
NATCHEZ PLANTATION HOUSE
735 North Atlantic Boulevard, Fort Lauderdale, Florida, U.S.A.

With THOMAS BOOKS *careful attention is given to all details of
manufacturing and design. It is the Publisher's desire to present books
that are satisfactory as to their physical qualities and artistic possibilities and appropriate for their particular use.* THOMAS BOOKS *will
be true to those laws of quality that assure a good name and good will.*

Printed in the United States of America
N-1

Preface

THIS IS A BOOK about the development of infants and children
—how the intact organism interacts with his environment. Development is a complex process; the scope of behavior is broad, and
individual variations are enormous. Yet, within the limitations
placed upon us by the very nature of being human and humane,
we are beginning to understand how early development affects
later behavior, what experiences may be crucial for healthy growth,
and the enormous adaptability of the human system.

We have been able to reach some of these conclusions because
the last decade has been a period of unprecedented research in
early development. Formulation of new theories, recasting older
theories in new perspectives, and more sophisticated instrumenta-
tion have led to new approaches in the study of the child and
changing conceptualizations about him. There has been a shift
from merely describing the behavior of the child to explaining
the "how" of development. Focus has been directed towards these
areas of investigation: the nature of early experiences for perceptual, cognitive, and social development; the interaction of heredity and environment as well as the interaction of learning and
maturation; individual differences observed very early in life; the
dyadic nature of parent-child interaction; the nature of early
learning experiences; and the structure of the human organism
which allows for language and complex thought processes. The
readings in this book are chosen to give you some of the flavor of
these recent studies and ideas. Three other considerations influenced the choice of selections. These were to provide some descriptive analysis of the child, to expose you to a wide range of research
techniques, and to present some provocative formulations about
the development of certain systems.

Many of you in the allied health professions will be working
with adults and children with various kinds of problems. You
might ask whether it is valuable to devote time and energy to the

study of development when you have so much to learn about the neuromuscular system, or abnormal behavior, or disease entities. There is no doubt in the editor's mind that in order to understand the person with a problem we must understand the intact system. The focus of attention, particularly with children, should be the whole child and the total process of development, even when the dominant problem seems to be disease or disability. To bring you knowledge, ideas, and questions about human development in the *raison d'être* for this book; to stimulate your thinking, to set in motion your own inquiries about children.

The readings, many dealing with the infant and young child, are grouped according to subject areas: learning, language, emotional and social development, etc. The student should keep in mind that these are just names that have been ascribed to a specific process, but in reality all of these systems interact and develop concomitantly. The articles also reflect what is now readily apparent, that many disciplines contribute to the study and understanding of the child. Most of the articles chosen have extensive references so you may pursue a topic in more detail.

A short introduction, written by the editor, prefaces each article. Generally, the introduction focuses on an area of interest in development and at the same time relates to the particular topic of the reading selection. It should be helpful to read the introduction both before and after reading the article.

Claire B. Kopp

Acknowledgments

APPRECIATION IS EXTENDED to the authors and publishers who permitted reproduction of the articles. Appropriate citation is listed with each article.

Appreciation is also extended to my mentors, past and present, who understand children so well, and whose knowledge has made the study of development stimulating and rewarding.

Finally, gratitude to my family, for their forbearance, and an additional thanks to my husband for being listener and critic.

Contents

PART VII
THE DEVELOPMENT OF BODY IMAGE AND LATERALITY

PART VIII
EMOTIONAL AND SOCIAL DEVELOPMENT

READINGS IN EARLY DEVELOPMENT
For Occupational and Physical Therapy Students

PART I

NEUROPHYSIOLOGICAL DEVELOPMENT

THE NEWBORN INFANT is not a totally nondiscriminating and defenselesss organism; he is able to see, hear, smell, and respond to pain, touch and position changes. Some of his basic reflexes include sucking, rooting, grasping, stepping, Moro, etc. Volitional behaviors include lifting the chin from a prone position and head turning. Within days after birth, infants demonstrate the ability to modify, in a small way, a basic response such as frequency of sucking which indicates a primitive form of learning has occurred. However, the newborn's behavior, to a large extent, is reflexive and is primarily under the control of subcortical processes. Cortical predominance is necessary for fine, controlled movement and of course for perception, memory, and cognition. Inhibition of many reflexes occurs, at various times, in the first few months due to the increasing development and integration of the cortex. The following two papers are concerned with developmental changes in postural reflexes. In the first paper Dr. Geoffrey Rushworth explains postural reflexes and their level of innervation. In the second paper Dr. Richmond Paine and his associates report their findings on the evolution of postural reflexes based on an extensive study of normal and abnormal infants. As you read, note that neither paper discusses the state of the infant (continuum from sleep through wakefulness) while discussing reflexive maturation. However, in the past few years it has been shown that state has a noticeable effect on the intensity of a response. Generally speaking, stronger responses are obtained when the infant is awake and quiet.

Chapter 1

On Postural and Righting Reflexes

Geoffrey Rushworth

Posture follows movement like a shadow; every movement begins
in posture and ends in posture.—C. S. Sherrington.[14]

In order to understand the disordered muscular activity of cerebral palsy, a knowledge of the postural reflexes is essential. The postural reflexes are automatic reactions which maintain the characteristic orientation of the body with respect to gravity, both during movement and at rest. Certain sensory organs are responsible for signalling any deviation from the normal posture, and the most important ones are appropriately situated within muscles themselves,[13] within the muscles and joints of the neck, and within the head (the labyrinth of the inner ear). When a normal voluntary movement is begun, the postural reactions accurately adjust themselves; the movement arises out of a posture which is itself gradually and sufficiently inhibited in the prime movers and antagonists to allow smooth and coordinated movement to occur, until finally, on ceasing the movement, a suitable posture is reattained. Meanwhile, more general postural reflexes have maintained body balance as a whole and an attitude most suitable for visual control of movement, if need be.

One of the disorders of function in cerebral palsy is a failure of the correct interaction of postural reflexes and voluntary movement, a failure that is partly due to a loss of the higher inhibiting mechanisms which normally damp down the postural re-

From *Cerebral Palsy Bulletin (Developmental Medicine and Child Neurology)*, 3:535-54, 1961. Reprinted by permission of the author and publisher.

Acknowledgements: I wish to thank my secretary, Miss G. E. Clark, for her careful and accurate transposition of a difficult manuscript. I am more than grateful to my wife, Dr. Elizabeth Martin, for her illuminating sketches, and she in turn wishes to thank Glinka and her other patient subjects.—G. R.

6

actions and allow movement to be superimposed on them. This loss of cerebral inhibition may cause the postural reflexes to be greatly exaggerated in cerebral palsy, and may reduce the patient's movement almost to a marionette state, the guiding force being gravitation. Voluntary activity may then be very restricted, but the patient can be taught how to initiate postural adjustments of limbs which are not themselves under direct voluntary control. This is an interaction of local and general static reactions which will be discussed later.

Much of our knowledge of postural reflexes stems from the inspiration of Sherrington and his pupils, Denny-Brown and Liddell in Oxford. It was they who contributed so much on the basic reflexes of the spinal cord and their linkage with posture. Since then, physiologists of many nations, including Magnus, Rademaker, de Kleijn, Schoen, Barraquer-Bordas, André-Thomas and Bard, have investigated successively higher centers of the nervous system, in which more general and often dominating postural reactions are organized and integrated with the spinal reflexes. Animals such as cats, dogs, rabbits, and monkeys were used to elucidate these various reflexes, but there is no doubt that in man the postural reflexes follow a similar pattern and distribution of organization, and are of a similar nature. In quadrupeds the head is the leading segment, bearing special sense organs which can register events at a distance, namely, the nose, ears and eyes, and it is hardly surprising that the postural reactions of the limbs and body are subjugated to the position of the head in relation to them.[15] Though in man the head is not usually the leading segment, the presence there of the eyes—now the dominant distance receptors—endow it with even more special significance, particularly in the performance of skilled movements under binocular visual control.

For the sake of convenience the postural reflexes will here be discussed under subdivisions determined by their centers of organization, but it must be remembered that there is interaction between these centers in the various levels of the nervous system to maintain balance and posture as a whole and to allow smooth and coordinated voluntary movement against this background.

THE SPINAL LEVEL

The isolated spinal cord has a large repertoire of limb reflexes including postural and stepping reflexes, yet a spinal animal is unable to stand unsupported and cannot initiate nor maintain walking. It lacks the organized facilitatory and inhibitory balance provided by higher levels of the nervous system.

Local Static Reactions of the Spinal Cord

These are confined to a single limb and are concerned with standing, though in a wider setting they provide the background for voluntary movement and the coordination of muscles.

The Stretch Reflex

When a muscle is stretched, very sensitive sensory organs within the muscle (muscle spindles) are stimulated, and they discharge a volley of impulses to the spinal cord. Here they excite, with the least possible delay, motoneurones of only that muscle which was stretched. A stretched muscle, then, tries to contract in order to prevent lengthening, and this is the stretch reflex.[8,9] Some muscles normally show a well-marked stretch reflex, and these are muscles which, in the normal attitude of the animal, oppose the force of gravity. The weight of a limb will stretch certain muscles, and their lengthening will tend to be prevented by the stretch reflex of these muscles (Fig. 1-1). Similarly, the weight of the body and head will stretch muscles connecting the limbs with the body and the head with the neck, as well as the extensor muscles of the back, and stretch reflexes will be evoked in all these, thus fixing posture against gravity by means of a single local reflex in each individual antigravity muscle.[4]

The stretch reflex is well designed to maintain posture for long periods, for muscle spindles do not readily fatigue but will discharge whenever the muscle is lengthened. Furthermore, antigravity muscles contain a large proportion of small, dark-red muscle fibers which are packed with myoglobin (an oxygen-carrying pigment), have contraction times of about 1/10 second, and may be fully tetanized at less than 30 impulses per second. This is

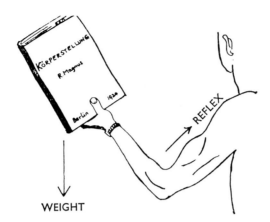

Figure 1-1. A stretch reflex.

a great economy in comparison with the paler, faster muscle fibers found predominantly in the muscles concerned with eye movements, running, and other swift alternating movements, for they may require 100 to 300 impulses per second to tetanize them and they can maintain their tension only for a very short time.[5]

It should be mentioned that the discharge of muscle spindles has a wider local effect than that described above, for not only does it excite its own motoneurones but it also inhibits the motoneurones of the antagonistic muscles. This is the basis of reciprocal innervation—a necessary accompaniment of all alternating movements.

The stretch reflex is a simple monosynaptic spinal reflex which is, nevertheless, limited and controlled from other centers within the brain. This is through descending pathways which either inhibit or facilitate the motoneurones themselves, or, less directly, the gamma motoneurones. The latter innervate small muscle fibers within muscle spindles which allow an adjustment of the sensitivity of this sensory organ and thus have control over the intensity of the discharge in response to stretch.[7,13]

The Positive Supporting Reaction

This consists of simultaneous contraction of opposing muscles so as to fix joints.[10,11,12] It is not designed for the prolonged maintenance of posture but is the basis of such attitudes as the poise before springing or standing to attention. It is a reflex capable of supporting a great weight and is particularly marked in the hind limbs. The stimulus for the reflex is a combined one of tactile and proprioceptive components (stretching the toe muscles), resulting from pressure on the sole of the foot near the toes.

This reaction is completely inhibited by plantar flexion, so that the limb can be rapidly transformed from a supporting pillar to an active moving member.

Segmental Static Reactions of the Spinal Cord

These reactions provide a wider coordination of posture between all four limbs and the body.

The Flexion and Crossed Extension Reflex

This provides support and the maintenance of balance whenever a limb is withdrawn from an injurious agent (Fig. 1-2). The

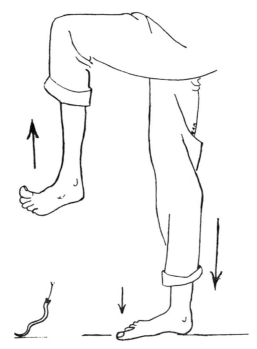

Figure 1-2. The reflex of flexion and crossed extension.

noxious stimulus is more effective if it is applied to the sole or to the palm, but reflex flexion of the limb, as a result of stimulation of the limb at other sites, may occur if the stimulus is strong enough. The extension of the contralateral limb, in the intact animal, may be strengthened further by the positive supporting reaction. The reflex of crossed extension long outlasts the brief stimulus which excites the flexion reflex.

The reflex pattern of flexion and contralateral extension may provide one of the phases of reflex stepping, though here the stimulus is clearly of a different nature.

Long Spinal Reflexes

These coordinate the relative postures of the fore and hind limbs, and they assume great importance during quadrupedal walking.

General Static Reactions of the Spinal Cord

These reflex responses are more widespread than the ones already mentioned, and they determine the posture of all four limbs and the body in relation to the relative position of the neck.

The Tonic Neck Reflexes

These are integrated in the upper cervical segments of the spinal cord and are very powerful mechanisms for coordinating the limb postures with the neck.[10,11] The reflexes depend on sensory impulses which are derived from the muscles and joints of the neck. They were intensively studied by Magnus and de Kleijn, who described five components. When the neck was rotated, the fore limb, on the side pointed to by the jaw, tended to extend, while the opposite fore limb flexed (Fig. 1-3). Bending the neck towards one shoulder produced the same result. These are the so-called asymmetrical tonic neck reflexes. When the neck was dorsiflexed, both fore limbs extended and the hind limbs flexed—the attitude of an animal looking upwards (Fig. 1-4). Flexion of the neck produced flexion of the fore limb and extension of the hind —the posture assumed by many quadrupeds while sniffing the ground (Fig. 1-5). These, like the next, are symmetrical tonic

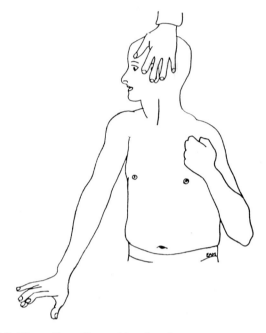

Figure 1-3. The reflex effects of head and neck turning on the arms.

neck reflexes. Finally, some quadrupeds show a "vertebra prom-
inens" reflex which consists of the flexion of all four limbs in response to a pressure stimulus in the region of the lower cervical
spine. This clearly serves to adjust the posture of a quadruped
while passing under an obstruction.

Sensory impulses from the neck can also produce compensatory movements of the eyes in such a way as to secure central binocular vision in the direction of turning.

THE POSTURAL REFLEXES OF THE MEDULLA

The decerebrate animal, in which the brain above the medul-
la has been destroyed, shows all the postural reflexes that we have
so far described, though in an exaggerated state due to the loss of
inhibitory control from the brain.[15] It can stand unsupported, although it cannot right itself if displaced, and, in addition, it ex-

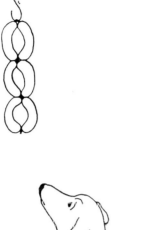

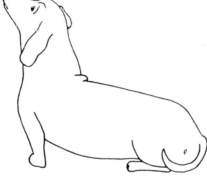

Figure 1-4. The reflex effects on the limbs of extension (dorsiflexion) of the neck.

Figure 1-5. The reflex effects on the limbs of flexion of the neck.

hibits further general static reactions which are derived from sensory impulses originating in the otolith organs in the labyrinth of the inner ear. An animal in its natural posture, with its head at 45 degrees snout down, has minimal labyrinthine effects on its four-limb musculature; but if it is placed in the supine position, with the head at 45 degrees snout up, then maximal extension of all four limbs occurs in response to the otolith stimulation.[10,11] Intermediate positions of the head, between the two extremes described, are thought to have intermediate effects on the extensor musculature.

In addition to these effects on limb musculature, the neck muscles are excited or relaxed by impulses arising in the otolith organs. Neck turning so produced may then secondarily enforce postural changes in the limbs through the tonic neck reflexes.

Some influence on the eye musculature is also exerted from the otolith organs to ensure that the visual fields are kept reasonably constant.

THE CEREBELLUM

It has been generally believed that the cerebellum is little concerned with the postural reflexes, and this may well be so in acute experimental animals undergoing cerebellectomy. However, the profound effect on postural reflexes of chronic cerebellar lesions in man and animals, can leave no doubt that the cerebellum plays an important rôle in a general way.[6,12] In more recent years, it has become clearer that the cerebellum may provide a center for the coordination and interaction of postural reflexes and voluntary movements in relation to sensory impressions coming from moving muscles, the eyes, and possibly other sense organs.[7]

THE MIDBRAIN AND THALAMUS

An animal whose brain has been destroyed as far back as the thalamus can stand in a normal posture and shows appropriate compensatory postural changes on turning the head and neck. In addition, it can now right itself if pushed over.

Righting Reflexes

The sites of the centers within the nervous system concerned with the elaboration of the righting reflexes have not been adequately worked out. However, the sensory impulses which determine the outcome are known to originate in the otoliths of the labyrinth, from tactile receptors in the trunk in particular, from the neck, and from the eyes. The optical righting reflexes will be considered later as they depend on the occipital cortex of the cerebral hemispheres.

Labyrinthine Righting Reflexes

Provided the otolith organs of both labyrinths are normal, then the head will be righted with respect to gravity, irrespective of the position of the body and independent of other sensory impressions.[10,11] Since movements of the head are linked with neck movements, which by the powerful tonic neck reflexes influence limb and body posture, the labyrinthine head-righting reflex is of great importance in restoring head—neck—limb—body posture with respect to gravity.

Body Righting Reflexes Acting on the Head

Asymmetrical stimulation of tactile or pressure receptors on one side of the body (such as the weight of the body lying on a table) can provide the cue for the muscular sequence which results in righting of the head in a labyrinthectomised animal. Under normal conditions this reflex must facilitate the labyrinthine righting reflexes.

Neck-righting Reflexes

Impulses arising asymmetrically from the neck muscles in a rotated position result in compensatory reflexes which tend to right the body in relation to the head.

POSTURAL REFLEXES DEPENDING ON THE CORTEX

It is currently believed that in normal primates and in man the postural reactions of lower levels of the nervous system are controlled and inhibited by the motor regions of the cerebral cortex and their outflow through the basal ganglia.

Optical Righting Reflexes

These require the mediation of the occipital cortex and probably need reasonable vision and visual orientation in space in the absence of other sensory cues. In normal individuals it probably has a dominant role, though facilitated and added to from other receptors.

Placing Reactions[1]

These consist of postural adjustments of the limbs in response to a moving tactile stimulus which allows the foot to be placed and weight supported on a solid object. They are usually tested by drawing a blindfolded animal's foot gently over the edge of a table, when the foot will at once be placed firmly and squarely on the table. This reaction depends on both the motor and sensory areas of the cerebral cortex.

Hopping Reactions[1]

These are compensatory movements which tend to bring a limb back from a displaced position. They are largely of tactile and proprioceptive origin, but depend on the motor area of the contralateral cerebral cortex.

STATOKINETIC REFLEXES

So far we have considered the various mechanisms that maintain posture in the static state or at repose and the means whereby posture is regained and retained if the animal or subject is displaced. Statokinetic reflexes, however, are produced by movement of the head or limbs and not by an abnormal orientation.

The Reactions of Movements of Limbs

We have already described the reflex adjustments of posture that are possible when a limb is moved either voluntarily or reflexly. There is an interplay of inhibition and excitation at the spinal level (reciprocal innervation), and, depending on the nature of the movement, flexion and crossed extension reflexes, positive supporting reactions, and stretch reflexes may all play an important part in adapting posture to movement.

Reactions to Movement of Progression (Linear Acceleration)

When a quadruped is suddenly lowered through the air, its limbs rigidly extend and its head also extends, even when blindfolded (Fig. 1-6). This response is similar to that which might be seen when an animal lands after jumping from a high place. In man, it is a common experience to notice strong extension of the legs while travelling up in a lift, and slight flexion at the hips and knees while travelling down. Forward progression in man tends to extend arms, legs, head, and neck; backward progression produces the reverse.

Figure 1-6. Extension of head and neck and all four limbs follow sudden lowering of an animal in space.

Reactions to Rotation (Angular Acceleration)

Reactions of the Head and Eyes

If the head is rotated about a vertical axis, the head and neck and eyes will turn to the opposite side as if to keep the gaze on a fixed point, but as the body turns further the head and eyes make a quick adjustment as if seeking a new fixation point, and then drift again in the direction opposite to the accelerating movement. This is head and ocular nystagmus, and when the movement ceases there is nystagmus in the opposite direction owing to the time lag in the movement of the labyrinthine fluid on deceleration.

Reactions of the Body

With rotation around the vertical axis there may be bending of the trunk towards the direction of movement with extension of the limbs on that side and a tendency to flexion on the opposite side.

ROLE OF PROPRIOCEPTORS WITHIN THE EXTRAOCULAR MUSCLES

From what has been said, the head is all-important as the bearer of the distance receptors, particularly the eyes, and through its proprioceptors (the labyrinths of the inner ear) it exerts a powerful influence over the body musculature. Posture of the head is closely linked with the eye muscles, and compensatory movements are all designed to provide central binocular vision, in a direction of orientation to gravity, which is the usual plane for our visual experiences and interpretation. It is of some interest to enquire whether the eye muscles themselves contribute, by means of proprioceptors, to this postural control. Receptors which respond to stretch have been demonstrated in the external ocular muscles, and fairly simple muscle spindles are to be found in histological sections.[17] There is no local stretch reflex; but instead, the afferent impulses from the stretch receptors are distributed to the motoneurones of antagonistic eye muscles (possibly not directly but through the superior colliculus). They also pass up the brain stem to the superior colliculus and even to the cerebral cortex. Reciprocal innervation and strict coordinate control of binocular adversive movements may be partly mediated through this sensory influx from muscle spindles, for they are so particularly sensitive (and can be made more or less so by the discharge of gamma motoneurones) that tiny deviations from the visual axis could be accurately signalled. Physiological experiments have, so far, elucidated only a relatively few bare facts on this subject. Some workers, such as von Tschermak,[16] believe that proprioceptors within the eye-muscles are responsible for judgment of visual space, but this view seems to dismiss some of the purely visual aspects of binocular vision and the role of previous experience and learning in almost every judgment we make.

CONCLUSIONS

Many postural mechanisms and centers for muscular co-ordination are located in the spinal cord. What is missing there is a mechanism for initiating movement and motor behaviour appropriate to the whole sensory influx, which requires integration with the needs of the head—the bearer of the distance receptors. Because of the important part played by the eye, not only for species survival but in man for the performance of skilled visual tasks, the head and neck contain sensory organs—centers which collect and distribute information and which dominate and mould the spinal centers into a modulated pattern of activity, initiated, controlled, coordinated, and integrated by suitable afferent influx.

Owing to the widespread distribution within the nervous system of centers controlling posture and tracts interconnecting them, it is little wonder that spasticity, flaccidity, increased positive supporting reactions, increased tonic neck reflexes, and other postural disorders are so commonly seen with almost any lesion of the brain and spinal cord. When, however, the postural disorder is established, it should be studied to enable the level of the lesion to be roughly localized and also to determine what reflex manoeuvers can convert it into predictable, controlled, and therefore useful movement.

The Bobaths have already explored this fundamental approach to the understanding and therapy of cerebral palsy.[2,3]

REFERENCES

1. Bard, P. Studies in the cortical representation of somatic sensibility. *Harvey Lect., 33*:143-169, 1938.
2. Bobath, K. The nature of the paresis in cerebral palsy. 2nd N.S.S. International Study Group on Child Neurology and Cerebral Palsy. *Little Club Clin. dev. Med.,* 1961.

3. Bobath, K. The long term results of treatment. *Ibid.*
4. Denny-Brown, D. On the nature of postural reflexes. *Proc. Roy. Soc. B., 104:*252-301, 1929.
5. Denny-Brown, D. The histological features of striped muscle in relation to its functional activity. *Proc. Roy. Soc. B., 104:*371-411, 1929.
6. Denny-Brown, D. Motor mechanisms—the general principles of motor integration. *Handbook of Physiology.* Neurophysiology II. Washington, D.C., American Physiological Society, 1960, Ch. 32, pp. 781-786.
7. Granit, R. *Receptors and Sensory Perception.* New Haven, Yale University Press, 1955.
8. Liddell, E. G. T., and Sherrington, C. S. Reflexes in response to stretch (myotatic reflexes) . *Proc. Roy. Soc. B., 96:*212-242, 1924.
9. Liddell, E. G. T. Further observations on myotatic reflexes. *Proc. Roy. Soc. B., 97:*267-283, 1925.
10. Magnus, R. Animal posture. *Proc. Roy. Soc. B., 98:*339-353, 1925.
11. Magnus, R. Some results of studies in the physiology of posture. *Lancet, 2:*531-536, 585-588, 1926.
12. Rademaker, G. G. J. Experiences sur la physiologie du cervelet. *Rev. Neurol., 1:*337-367, 1930.
13. Rushworth, G. Muscle sense organs and disorders of movement. *Cerebral Palsy Bull., 1*(No. 3):1-5, 1958.
14. Sherrington, C. S. Postural activity of nerve and muscle. *Brain, 38:*191-234, 1915.
15. Sherrington, C. S. The integrative action of the nervous system. London, Cambridge University Press, 1947.
16. von Tschermak, A. Introduction to physiological optics. Translated by P. Boeder, Springfield, Thomas, 1952.
17. Whitteridge, D. *Handbook of Physiology.* Neurophysiology II. Washington, D.C., American Physiological Society, 1960, ch. 42, pp. 1089-1109.

Chapter 2

Evolution of Postural Reflexes in Normal Infants and in the Presence of Chronic Brain Syndromes

RICHMOND S. PAINE, T. BERRY BRAZELTON, DESMOND E. DONOVAN, JAMES E. DRORBAUGH, JOHN P. HUBBELL, JR., AND E. MANNING SEARS

IN CONNECTION WITH a study of the evolution of postural reflexes in neurologically abnormal infants, it became apparent that existing information about the ages at which various changes take place in these reflexes in normal children needed to be amplified. Particularly, the range of variation of normal was not clear from reports in the literature, and it is clearly essential to know the outer limits of normal in order to interpret apparent abnormalities.

METHODS

Some of the infants for study, already well documented as to obstetrical and neonatal normality, were drawn from the Collaborative Study of Prenatal and Perinatal Factors in the Causation of Cerebral Palsies and Congenital Anomalies conducted at the Boston Lying-In Hospital and the Children's Hospital Medical Center in cooperation with the National Institute of Neurological Diseases and Blindness. Other babies, born at Boston Lying-In Hospital or Richardson House but not participants in the Collaborative Study, were included after review of their records by the same eight criteria to be described. Detailed information was available about the mothers' pregnancies, the babies' births, and their neonatal periods at the Boston Lying-In Hospital.

Babies were excluded from the study initially or after a subse-

From *Neurology, 14*:1036-1048, 1964. Reprinted by permission.

Supported in part by grants B-2400 and BP-2372 from the National Institute of Neurological Diseases and Blindness, National Institutes of Health, U.S. Department of Health, Education, and Welfare.

quent review of records for any of the following reasons: (1) maternal history of German measles, major surgery, x-ray therapy, anoxia, toxemia during pregnancy, or maternal diabetes; (2) any other reason for which the pregnancy was classified as abnormal by the reviewing obstetrician; (3) multiple birth, prematurity (birth weight under $5\frac{1}{2}$ lb.), placenta praevia, abruptio placentae, prolapse of the cord, cephalopelvic disproportion, a diagnosis of dystocia, cesarean section, or instrumental delivery other than uncomplicated low forceps; (4) a recorded interval of more than one minute from birth to the first breath (by study protocol this was timed by a trained observer not participating in the delivery itself) ; (5) other circumstances which were classified by the reviewing obstetrician as an abnormal delivery; (6) a diagnosis of "abnormal" or "suspect" on the neonatal pediatric or neurological examinations or in the review of neonatal records by a senior project pediatrician (history of neonatal convulsions, cyanosis, hyperbilirubinemia, or other abnormality) ; (7) diagnosis of neurological or other abnormality at any subsequent visit, and (8) postnatal history of convulsions, developmental retardation, or major postnatal illness or injury as evaluated by the responsible pediatrician.

It was recognized that the serial examinations would have to be conducted in a standardized manner with comparable gradation of interpretations and at sufficiently frequent intervals. The infants in the abnormal group (approximately 200) had been followed at intervals of three months to the age of 3 years, but it was believed that the evolution of postural reflexes took place much more rapidly in normal infants. Examinations of the normal group were to be carried out at intervals of four to six weeks; this coincided with visits for routine well child care. One hundred infants were started in the study; all were born on the ward service of the Boston Lying-In Hospital and subsequently received their general pediatric care in the Child Health Unit of the Children's Hospital Medical Center or in the private practices of four participants in the Collaborative Study who were trained in the neurological examination of infants and had jointly reviewed the examination protocols to agree on standardization.

Because of losses by moving away, diagnosis of abnormality, or failure to complete regularly scheduled visits, only sixty-six of the original group were available for review.

In addition to a conventional pediatric examination, the function of the nervous system was evaluated with special attention to the postural reflexes and automatisms peculiar to infancy. Methods used are described elsewhere.[1]

RESULTS AND DISCUSSION

Muscle Tone

The question of muscle tone was considered too subjective to be suitable for numerical gradation for statistical analysis. It was generally agreed that the predominant flexor tone of the limbs in normal full-term infants is lost in the upper extremities by not later than the age of 4 months and shortly thereafter in the lower extremities; this is in accord with other reports.[2] The availability of certain reflexes such as the triceps jerk and the posture assumed in vertical suspension in space changes with the subsidance of flexor tone; this will be discussed subsequently.

Reflexes

The biceps and knee jerks were present continuously from birth. The ankle jerks tended to be suppressed by hypertonus but were usually obtainable if the infant were placed in the prone position. The triceps jerk was usually difficult or impossible to obtain until the flexor tone of the upper extremity had diminished, at 2 to 4 months. The knee jerk of the newborn is normally followed by contraction of the adductors of both hips (crossed adductor spread). Our findings agree with those of Boll[3] who found crossed adductor spread in the majority of infants under 8 months of age but rarely above that (Boll reported 96% under 6 months and 60% at 7 months). Six percent of our patients showed adductor spread at 9 months, and a single patient did so at 12 months.

The plantar reflex (Babinski) is universally agreed to be extensor in young infants, usually with some degree of fanning of the toes as well. Unless unusually strong or asymmetric it is not of major diagnostic value in the first year of life. Its interpretation is highly subjective and the response itself quite variable in time with older infants; thus, detailed analysis by age was not attempted. In another study of normal infants from the same collaborative project, 75 percent were found to have extensor plantars at the age of 12 months but there was no statistical correlation with the ability to walk independently (70% also walked without aid at 12 months).[4] The age of conversion of the plantar reflex is probably later than often supposed. (Brain and Wilkinson[5] reported it still extensor in one normal child of 27 months and in 3 of an original 35 at 24 months).

Up to 8 or 10 beats of ankle clonus are acceptable as normal in the newborn period, but this phenomenon is soon lost. As many as 3 beats were obtainable consistently from only four of our patients at 2 months of age (2 at 3 months, 1 at 4 months, and none at a later age). It should be noted that this refers to consistently obtainable clonus and not to the pseudoclonus which is occasionally obtained from an older infant if a voluntary plantar flexion of the foot chances to coincide with the upward thrust of the examiner's hand.

Moro Reflex

The Moro reflex can be elicited by a considerable variety of methods including slapping one's hand onto the mattress beside the baby (Moro's original method[6]), pulling the baby's hands outward and releasing them, jerking the baby's feet, producing a startle by sudden light or sound, or dropping the baby's head backward about 30 degrees in relation to the trunk. The last mentioned method, suggested by Sanford,[7] has proved the most effective in our experience and in that of Westphal and Kennedy,[8] but other methods were tried if it produced no response. The common denominator of all of these methods would appear to be a change of position of the head relative to the trunk. If the head is dropped backward and its posture relative to the neck and trunk maintained unchanged, the Moro reaction is not obtained.[9] Although astonishingly little is known about the anatomic pathway of the Moro reflex, this observation would suggest that its origin may be in proprioceptive impulses from the neck muscles and the joints of the cervical vertebrae and that it is not primarily a vestibular reflex as often stated.[10] (Karlsson[11] recently reported a child with congenital absence of function of the vestibular as well as acoustic nerve who had had a normal Moro reflex as a newborn.) The reader is referred to the recent review of Mitchell[12] for a more detailed discussion.

The dissolution of the Moro reflex in the normal infants studied is shown in Figure 2-1. Approximately 20 percent of normal infants still show some response at 5 months if the reflex is reinforced by pressure against the baby's knees with the examiner's finger. We found no persistence of flexion or extension of the upper extremities at the age of 6 months or later, although flexion of the femora against the reinforcing finger may normally

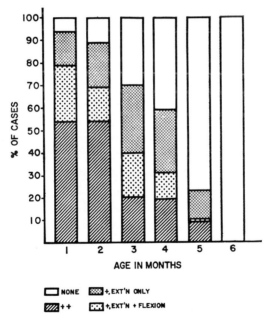

Figure 2-1. Dissolution of Moro reflex with increasing age: 2+ refers to complete response of normal newborn and 1+ to incomplete extension of upper extremities (separated according to presence or absence of subsequent flexor phase).

be felt until 6 or 7 months.[13] The persistence of the Moro reflex beyond 5 months will be discussed in a subsequent report on the abnormal group of infants. It is occasionally a useful diagnostic sign of delayed maturation of motor function (a "cerebral palsy" if due to a chronic nonprogressive lesion of the brain) but is usually of much less practical value than the tonic neck reflex. This is in contrast to the position of the Moro reflex as the paramount reflex peculiar to earliest infancy. It should universally be present in normal full-term newborns.

Tonic Neck Reflexes

The tonic neck reflex is diagnostically the most valuable of the infantile postural responses after 1 month of age. Historically speaking, it is the "asymmetric tonic reflex" of the head or neck on the body, according to Magnus,[14] and consists in extension of the upper extremity on the side toward which the face is rotated with flexion of the corresponding limb on the side of the occiput. The lower extremities often also participate but usually less consistently. Distinction must be made between assumption of this posture on active rotation of the head by the infant itself as opposed to the extent to which the pattern can be imposed by passive rotation of the head by the examiner. The pattern is usually assumed within a few seconds. Magnus[14] reported a reflex time usually under one second but occasionally up to six seconds. The response is usually held to originate with proprioceptive impulses from the neck muscles, perhaps more importantly from the atlantooccipital and atlantoaxial joints,[15] and to have an afferent path through the upper cervical roots. The pattern cannot be imposed on a normal infant of any age to a completely obligate extent (that is, to the degree that the baby cannot escape the pattern, which is maintained indefinitely so long as the head is held to the side). The response was tested by rotating the head to each side on 10 trials and holding the shoulders horizontal; it was classified as positive if obtainable on six occasions. Vassella and Karlsson[16] have calculated the probability of an apparently positive response by chance alone at 3:16 and the likelihood of obtaining this on 6 out of 10 trials by chance alone at only 0.4 percent.

Minkowski[17] reported obtaining the tonic neck reflex in fetuses and abortuses, the frequency increasing with age. Pollack[18] reports it in more than two thirds of normal newborns from 2 hours to 7 days of age. Our own experience indicates, however, that an imposable tonic neck reflex is quite rare in the immediate neonatal period, even in abnormal infants, and agrees with the reports of Peiper[19] and Vassella and Karlsson[16] who found it in only 8 percent of infants in the first week of life.

Tonic neck patterns become imposable on the majority of trials with almost all normal infants at some time during the first month of life. They are not sustained indefinitely. Since our first serial examination was made at approximately 1 month of age, the exact time of appearance cannot be evaluated in this study. As shown in Figure 2-2, a definite imposable reflex was obtained from 60 percent of normal month-old infants with gradual decline in frequency thereafter. If more equivocal responses are accepted, the peak incidence is at 2 months (80%). A definite tonic neck pattern could be imposed on none of our patients after 6 months of age, and not even an equivocal one could be imposed after 7 months. This is in accord with other reports such as Gesell and Amatruda[20] who give 24 weeks as the age at which the response is abnormal. It appears plausible that a tonic neck pattern may be actively assumed at a later age than it remains imposable, but Gesell and Ames[21] later report that normal infants of 20 weeks and above spend an equal fraction of their day in actively assumed tonic neck patterns and the reverse position. Landau[22] stated that 10 percent of normal babies show a tonic neck pattern up to 9 months of age, but this is probably an excessively late estimate. Six of our normal infants showed no imposable tonic neck reflex subsequent to 6 weeks of age; the relatively early disappearance of the response is probably of no significance. No normal infant showed an indefinitely sustained imposable response, but the pattern was sustained for more than thirty seconds in a small number of infants under 3 months of age. Magnus and de Klejn[23] accepted a sustained pattern as normal up to $3\frac{1}{2}$ months. We found the imposable tonic neck reflex to be comparable whether the head was rotated toward the left or toward the right in all but one instance, that of a single baby on one occasion at age 3 months. A tonic neck reflex which is consistently stronger with the head to one side than to the other is abnormal and is often followed by the emergence of a motor deficit (such as a cerebral palsy) which is usually more severe on the side of the greater tonic neck pattern.

Neck-righting Reflexes

To test the neck-righting reflex, the head is turned toward either side with the infant supine and the shoulders unrestrained. A positive response consists in rotation of the shoulders and then of the trunk and pelvis toward the side to which the face is turned. In older infants this is followed by turning onto the abdomen and getting up to stand in the quadripedal fashion. A variety of righting reflexes exist, having origin in the otoliths, tactile impulses from the trunk, and proprioceptive impulses from the neck muscles and the joints of the cervical spine as well as optical righting reflexes depending on visual cues. Optical righting reflexes require cortical function, but the others are obtainable in thalamic animals.[24] The neck-righting response considered here is present even with the eyes bandaged and was accepted as positive if imposable on 6 out of 10 trials. The neck-righting reflex gradually emerges during the disappearance of the tonic neck reflex which it replaces (Fig. 2-2) and was obtainable in all infants by 10 months of age. The neck-righting reflex is gradually covered up by voluntary activity and its age of disappearance is thus difficult to define. The present study has not been carried beyond the age of 12 months, but our experience has been that a neck-righting response can no longer be demonstrated once the infant is able to get up directly from the supine posture without first rolling over onto the abdomen and getting up on all fours. It should be added that a neck-righting reflex which is much stronger with the head to one side than to the other is not seen in normal infants nor is the response at any age so completely invariable that the baby could be rolled over and over across the floor like a log.

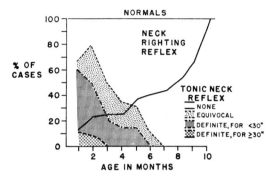

Figure 2-2. Gradual loss of imposable tonic neck reflexes with increasing age and emergence of neck-righting reflex.

Placing Reaction

The placing response is tested by suspending the infant vertically and drawing the dorsa of the feet up to touch the underside of a table, following which the feet are placed on top of the table. The placing is frequently asymmetric and should usually be so if cutaneous contact is made with a single foot initially (stereotyped simultaneous placing of both feet to initial contact by one is probably abnormal). Tactile impulses play a role in initiating the placing reaction, but traction on the ankle joint and lower extremity may be more important. It is usually considered to be a cortical reflex but is demonstrable with almost all normal newborns.[24,25] A complete, automatic, and highly stereotyped placing reflex in a baby with a spinal cord transection due to injury at birth recently has been observed. The latter finding suggests that placing may be a spinal automatism.

The placing reaction does not have a clear-cut disappearance at any specific age but is gradually suppressed or covered up by voluntary activity toward the end of the first year of life in most instances. We suspect that the placing reaction can be obtained as a withdrawal response at any age if traction is exerted against the ankle to the point of discomfort. However, in older babies it is never so uniform or so consistent as with newborn infants or a normal cat.

Stepping

The automatic stepping or walking of the normal newborn infant when supported in the standing position and inclined forward is gradually lost during the early months of life. It is sufficiently variable not to be obtainable on every trial, even with newborns, and it is even more variable from occasion to occasion in later months. Failure to obtain stepping at a single examination cannot be accepted as proof of its absence, and a timetable of disappearance cannot be constructed from the present study. We believe, however, that the stepping reaction usually declines or is lost in parallel with the supporting reaction which is more consistently either obtainable or absent.

Supporting Reaction

The supporting reaction (positive Stutzreaktion of Rademaker[25]) is elicited by supporting the infant vertically and allowing its feet to make firm contact with a tabletop or other flat surface. A positive response consists in simultaneous contraction of opposing muscles so as to fix the joints of the lower extremities. Its origin is partly tactile but probably more importantly based on pressure and proprioceptive impulses. It is not intended for prolonged maintenance of posture (unless perhaps in the case of a soldier standing at attention) but more as a posture preparatory for motion (Sprungbereitschaft); it is often followed by automatic stepping in young infants. Rademaker[25] reported the supporting reaction to be absent in spinal or thalamic animals, but Rushworth[24] considers it a spinal mechanism.

The maneuver described results in the case of a normal newborn in an increase of tone in the lower extremities so as to support a portion of the body weight. However, an important difference from the response obtainable with older infants and from normal standing is that the fraction of weight supported is less in the case of the newborn. Further, the posture of "standing" in the newborn includes a degree of flexion of the hip and knee. The newborn does not stand upright and does not extend and lock the knee joint. The response is difficult to quantitate but has been classified by arbitrary standards of good, fair, poor, or none, agreed on among us (in terms of fraction of weight supported, regardless of extension or partial flexion of the knee). It appears from Figure 2-3 that the neonatal supporting reaction with the lower extremities in a semi-crouching position gradually diminishes during the first four months of life to be followed by a subsequent increase so that all normal infants will support a substantial proportion of their weight by 10 months of age. One may suspect from Figure 2-3 that the graph represents the sum of two curves and that the semicrouching supporting reaction of the newborn period disappears to be replaced by a more mature form with locking of the knee. Ingram[26] places the disappearance of the neonatal form at 6 to 8 weeks. The stronger supporting reaction of later infancy may become demonstrable prior to the disappearance of the neonatal form, however, and fifteen (24%) of our patients never supported weight at a level evaluated as less than "fair." Ninety-six percent showed a "good" response by 9 months, although other authors have placed the lower limit of this at younger ages (Gesell and Amatruda[20] at 8 months and Illingworth[27] at 6 months).

Twenty-four of our 66 normal infants showed a tendency to stand in an equinus posture at one time or another. This indicates

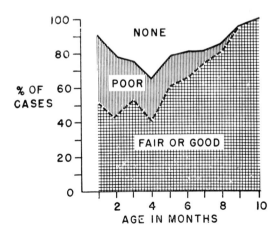

Figure 2-3. Supporting reaction of lower extremities with feet in contact with tabletop while body is suspended vertically about chest. Gradation as good, fair, or poor refers to proportion of body weight supported by infant.

that a tendency to stand on the toes is not confined to premature infants (in which it is the usual posture, probably because the predominant tone of the lower extremities is extensor rather than flexor as in full-term infants). Consistent supporting in equinus suggests future spasticity but occasional or variable standing on the toes is not abnormal. Crossing the lower extremities in the "scissor" posture is rare among "normal" infants, however. Scissoring was observed in only four of our normal infants and not consistently on every trial even with these. It was not seen after the age of 4 months.

The disappearance of the supporting reaction cannot be tabulated. With older infants it is positive if the infant desires to stand or to begin to walk. If he is not so inclined, he flexes the lower extremities or may put them out in front of him. It is our impression that subsequent to 10 months a clear supporting reaction is less easily demontrable and difficult to distinguish from voluntary standing. Balduzzi[28] stated that supporting was less clear after the age of 6 months.

Parachute Reflex

The parachute reflex, variously referred to as the precipitation or airplane reflex, corresponds to the response of the upper extremities or forelimbs in the optische Stehbereitschaft of Rademaker.[25] It is best elicited by suspending the infant horizontally in space, face down, and plunging it toward a tabletop or other flat surface. The arms extend and separate somewhat, and the fingers extend and spread as if to break the fall. Magnus[14] described a similar phenomenon when a baby was held vertically and allowed to tip forward at the waist toward a table. Rademaker considered the reaction to depend chiefly on visual stimuli, but the characteristic posture is obtainable (although with a less sharp end point) in response to linear acceleration with a blindfolded infant; previous experience of the tabletop is not needed.[2,24]

Rademaker[25] placed the development of the response in the upper extremities at 6 months and described a comparable phenomenon with the lower extremities at 9 to 12 months. Among our normal patients (Fig. 2-4) an incomplete extension of the upper extremities was first obtainable in some instances at 2 months. However, it was not until the age of 9 months that virtually all patients showed such a reaction, and the complete response of full extension of the upper extremities with spreading of the fingers was obtained from 100 percent only at 12 months.

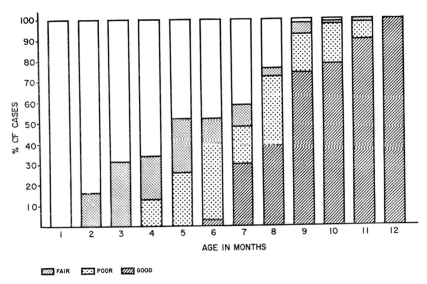

Figure 2-4. Emergence of parachute reaction in normal infants. Single striping represents complete response, dotted area is complete extension of upper extremities without spreading of fingers, and double cross-hatching is incomplete extension of arms.

The parachute reaction is a valuable physical sign in demonstrating a deficit of integration of movement at a suprasegmental level which affects the upper extremities, especially in distinguishing paraparesis from tetraparesis. However, it is not clearly known whether its anatomic locus is in the brain stem or at a higher level. Asymmetric participation of the two upper extremities was never seen in our normal group and would have to be considered an indication of abnormality.

Posture in Horizontal Suspension (Landau)

Landau's original paper[29] referred to elevation of the head followed by an increase of tone in the extensor muscles of the back when an infant is suspended horizontally in space with the face down. Schaltenbrand[30] described it clearly: "A child, lifted up with one hand under its trunk, face downward, will lift up the head and reflexly also the legs, while the spine is curved concavely upward." It is common experience that the lower extremities are partially extended and lifted upward toward the horizontal. Passive flexion of the neck is followed by loss of whatever extensor tone has been obtained in the back and lower extremities, but it is historically improper to call this the Landau reflex. The Landau reflex refers rather to the assumption of the posture originally. Andre-Thomas and associates[2] report that passive extension of the head with the infant in horizontal suspension will result in elevation of the lower extremities, but Landau[22] and Peiper and Isbert[10] did not obtain this. In our own experience, it is at least doubtful and variable as well as difficult to distinguish from the response to position in space as such.

The origin of the Landau posture is probably labyrinthine, as it is present in blind or decorticate animals[31] and in blindfolded infants.[10] However, it is probably reinforced optically since it is obtainable in seeing labyrinthectomized monkeys.[31] Mitchell[32] suggests that the raising of the head is a response to labyrinthine stimuli and that extension of the legs and back depends on a symmetric tonic neck reflex acting on the extensors of the back and limbs.

McGraw[33] and Mitchell[32] considered the response to be normally present at 3 months. Mitchell states that it is consistently present at 6 months but frequently difficult to obtain and inconsistent after that. We have graded the posture in horizontal suspension as follows: (1) elevation of the head well above the horizontal with arching of the spine to be concave upward, (2) elevation of the head above the horizontal with a straight spine, (3) head and spine both horizontal, (4) head slightly below horizontal and spine slightly convex upward (normal neonatal posture), and (5) collapse limply over the examiner's hand in the shape of an inverted letter U (never seen in normal infants).

The sixty-six normal infants studied are presented graphically in Figure 2-5. It will be seen that the head was above the horizontal in 55 percent at 4 months and in 95 percent at 6 months. (Illingworth[27] expects this at 3 months in most normal infants.) We found that the spine was at least slightly concave upward in approximately half of the 8-month-olds, but upward concavity was seen universally only at 10 months. Passive depression of the head always resulted in loss of whatever extensor tone of the back and lower extremities had been elicited. In the case of the Landau reaction, it is also impossible to tabulate the age of normal dissolution. André-Thomas and his colleagues[2] place this at 7 months, but it is more accurate to suggest that it is gradually covered up by struggling or other voluntary activity.

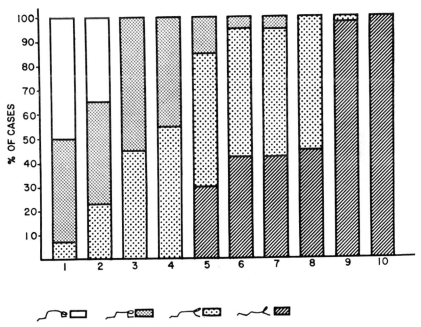

Figure 2-5. Posture in horizontal suspension as described by Landau. Figures under columns give age in months. Complete collapse into inverted U shape over examiner's hand was never seen with normal infants.

Vertical Suspension in Space

If a newborn infant is gradually brought to the vertical posture, being suspended in space by the examiner's hands about the
chest, the predominant flexor posture of the extremities is maintained during spontaneous movement during the major fraction
of time. If the baby has been drawn upward from the supine
position, the head lags behind and then falls forward when the
vertical posture is reached, but this is followed by some degree of
recovery and an unsteady maintenance of the head with the chin
off the chest. This degree of head control was universally present
among our normal patients at the age of 1 month and at subsequent examinations. Gesell and Amatruda[20] place strong and
steady head control at 12 weeks.

Our experience agrees with that of André-Thomas and associates[2] that the predominant flexion of the upper extremities
gradually disappears by 3 or 4 months and that of the lower
extremities by 4 to 5 months. However, this is difficult to quanti-

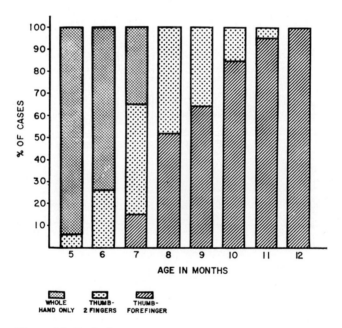

Figure 2-6. Evolution of handgrasp in reaching after object.

tate as the posture then varies more and more during time. Brief adduction of the lower extremities is normal, but consistent adduction in extension or scissoring is never seen among normal infants; consistent adduction in extension or scissoring suggests future spasticity.

A somewhat curious posture which infants sometimes assume in vertical suspension involves extension of the lower extremities which are separated at an angle of 30 degrees or more and semiflexed at the hips. This produces a forward extension of the lower extremities, and there is usually an accompanying avoidance of foot contact with a tabletop and a reluctance to bear weight. Various abnormalities of the lower extremities themselves can be responsible, but it also has been suggested that the posture is characteristic of atonic or ataxic diplegia or of abnormal development of affect. However, 6 of our 66 normal patients showed this posture at least once between ages 3 and 9 months and two of them, who are normal insofar as can be detected at one year, did so over a five-month period.

Handgrasp

It is usually stated as a rough guide that a baby can be expected to reach and grasp with the whole hand at 4 or 5 months, to grasp with the thumb and two fingers at 7 months, and to pick up a small object with the thumb and forefinger at 9 months. Among the sixty-six normal infants (Fig. 2-6) grasp was usually inconsistent or unreliable until 5 months. Gesell[20] places it at 20 weeks. Thumb to two-finger grasp was seen in 64 percent at 7 months and in all at 8 months. Pincer grasp with the thumb and forefinger was obtainable in 52 percent at 8 months but in all only at 12 months; the tabulation is based only on infants who reached and attempted to demonstrate grasp, excluding apparent refusals. Athetosis and consistent avoiding reflexes were never seen nor were they encountered in a previous unpublished study of 150 normal infants up to 15 months of age.

The automatic (reflex) palmar and plantar grasps of the normal newborn disappear gradually, not by a sharp end point but more by becoming inconsistent and variable from one examination to another and by merging into voluntary ability to release an object held in the hand (sometime after age 2 months). Illingworth[27] mentions the palmar grasp reflex as largely lost by 8 weeks of age, but Peiper[19] placed the palmar grasp as disappearing at 6 months and the plantar at 9 months, both being retained during sleep to a later age. The apparent discrepancy may reflect varying standards of consistency required for acceptance of the response as present. The inconsistency of grasp reflexes after 2 months of age appeared to us to preclude evaluation of the dissolution of this response in a series of single cross-section examinations.

Developmental Milestones

The age of first sitting when placed, acquisition of sitting posture, and standing and walking would have to be evaluated more from maternal statements than from cross-section examinations at four- to six-week intervals; cross-section examinations could give only an approximation. They correlate, of course, to a considerable degree with the changes in the postural reflexes which take place at corresponding ages. Tonic neck reflexes were in all instances no longer imposable by the time the infant acquired secure unsupported sitting balance when placed. The presence of imposable tonic neck reflexes is often considered an indication of lack of standing balance at that time in consideration of orthopedic surgery or bracing for patients with cerebral palsies. However, while imposable tonic neck reflexes appeared always to be lost by the time of sitting or standing in normal infants, there are occasional exceptions to this rule with abnormal children, as will be discussed in a subsequent report of that group.

It is possible to construct a graph of evolution of tonic neck and neck-righting reflexes; supporting, placing, stepping, and parachute reactions; and acquisition of posture in a typical normal infant. Such a presentation implies a more exact quantitative measurement of these phenomena than is available, however, and would be unjustified except that this type of study may be useful with abnormal children if its limitations are recognized. Possibly useful comparisons also can be made with the changes in muscle tone and tendon reflexes, as, for example, the persistent and increasing hyperreflexia of a spastic baby who is initially hypotonic and subsequently develops hypertonus in the extremities much earlier than in the trunk and neck.

Comparative Evolution of Infantile Reflexes

Comparison of the normal sequence of dissolution of those infantile reflexes which disappear with age and the emergence of those which appear with increasing age is best made in tabular form (see Table 2-I). The percentage figures will indicate that age at which all or any chosen majority of normal infants should have lost or acquired the response in question.

SUMMARY

The evolution of neurological signs, with special attention to the postural reflexes of infancy, was studied serially during the first year of life with sixty-six normal infants examined at four- to six-week intervals. The infants were participants in a collaborative study with the National Institute of Neurological Diseases and Blindness and were well documented as to gestational, obstetrical, and neonatal normality.*

The evolution of muscle tone, tendon reflexes, and special postural responses are discussed, with some of the major conclusions as follows:

1. The normal predominant flexor tone of the limbs of the newborn is overcome or lost by 3 to 4 months of age in the upper extremities and soon afterward in the lower.

2. While the biceps and knee jerks are obtainable in the newborn and the ankle jerk with some difficulty in the prone posture, the triceps jerk is first uniformly and easily elicited with the diminution of flexor tone of the limb at 3 months. Bilateral contraction of the adductors of the hips is a normal phenomenon after testing the knee jerk but is usually lost by 8 months of age. It cannot definitely be held abnormal after that age, however,

---

*The patients studied were born and spent their neonatal periods at the Boston Lying-In Hospital where Dr. Duncan E. Reed, chief of staff, and Dr. Stewart H. Clifford, pediatrician in chief, kindly made available pertinent records.

TABLE 2-I

Percent of Normal Babies Showing Various Infantile Reflexes with Increasing Age

| | Signs Which Disappear | | | | Signs Which Appear with Age | | | |
| Degree of Sign Tabulated | Moro | Tonic Neck Reflex | Crossed Adduction to Knee Jerk | Neck-righting Reflex | Supporting Reaction | Landau | Parachute | Hand Grasp |
Age (mo.)	Extension Even Without Flexor Phase	Imposable Even <30° or Inconstant	Strong or Slight	Imposable but Transient	Fair or Good	Head Above Horizontal and Back Arched	Complete	Thumb-to-Forefinger Alone
					Percentages			
1	93	67	?*	13	50	0	0	0
2	89	80	?*	23	43	0	0	0
3	70	50	41	25	52	0	0	0
4	59	34	41	26	40	0	0	0
5	22	31	41	38	61	29	0	0
6	0	11	21	40	66	42	3	0
7	0	0	12	43	74	42	29	16
8	0	0	15	54	81	44	40	53
9	0	0	6	67	96	97	76	63
10	0	0	3	100	100	100	79	84
11	0	0	3	100	100	100	90	95
12	0	0	2	100	100	100	100	100

*Divergence of experience and opinion between different examiners

since 6 percent of normal infants showed crossed adductor spread of the knee jerk at 9 months and a single patient even at 12 months.

3. The plantar reflex continued to show at least extension of the great toe (fanning of the other toes is more variable) up to the age of 1 year in 75 percent of normal babies. Conversion of the plantar reflex to the flexor response shows no correlation with ability to walk independently; 70 percent of normal 12-month-old infants in the study were able to walk independently.

4. The normal neonatal ankle clonus rarely persisted beyond 2 months of age and was never seen at 4 months or later.

5. A Moro reflex, which is comparable to that of the newborn (with flexion of the arms as well as initial extension), persisted up to 5 months in 9 percent of babies, but no Moro response of the arms was seen at 6 months or later.

6. It is rarely possible to impose a tonic neck reflex on a newborn, but tonic neck patterns appear in the early weeks of life and reach their peak at 2 months of age. No tonic neck pattern could be imposed on normal infants by passive rotation of the head at 7 months of age or later.

7. The neck-righting reflex gradually emerges as the tonic neck reflex disappears. It has no definite age of disappearance but is gradually covered up by struggling or other voluntary activity.

8. The placing reflex is present continuously from the newborn period but is gradually suppressed or covered up by other activity toward the end of the first year.

9. The positive supporting reaction of the lower extremities of the normal newborn includes partial flexion at the hip and knee and differs from the response of the older infant in which the knee is locked in full extension. In 76 percent of babies, the neonatal supporting reaction was lost or became significantly diminished and was subsequently replaced by the more mature form, but the transition may be unbroken. Occasional supporting of weight with the feet in equinus position was seen in 24 of 66 normal infants on one or another occasion. Scissoring of the lower extremities was rare in contrast; it is always inconsistent and transient.

10. The parachute reflex may be suggestive at 2 months but is first seen in complete form at 6 months. It was complete in 76 percent of normal 9-month-old infants but in 100 percent only at 12 months.

11. When normal infants are suspended horizontally, face down, in the Landau posture, the head is elevated above the horizontal in 55 percent at 4 months and in 95 percent at 6 months. However, consistent concavity of the spine upward is still obtained in under 50 percent at 8 months and in 100 percent only at 10 months. By 12 months the posture is less consistent and is often distorted or suppressed by struggling.

12. In vertical suspension in space, the normal flexor posture of the limbs of the newborn is lost or variable by 4 to 5 months. Consistent adduction in extension or scissoring of the lower extremities is not seen in normals.

13. All of the normal infants showed thumb to two-finger grasp at least by age 8 months. Thumb-to-forefinger pincer grasp was present in 84 percent by 10 months but in 100 percent only at 12 months.

The range of variation in the evolution of postural reflexes of normal infants furnishes a background for the serial study of 200 abnormal infants over a three-year period. The substance of the findings may be summarized as follows:

1. Of 129 infants who completed serial examinations at three-month intervals, the majority proved to have motor disabilities associated with nonprogressive chronic brain syndromes and classifiable as cerebral palsies. Seventeen showed only a general and comparable retardation of mental and motor development without specific abnormalities of muscle tone, reflexes, or involuntary movement.

2. Several sequences of evolution of muscle tone were encountered. These include persistent hypertonus from the neonatal period; hypertonus followed by hypotonus, with or without later increase in tone to abnormal levels; and early hypotonus followed by spasticity or dyskinesias, the latter with or without increase in muscle tone.

3. Infants who later developed spastic tetraparesis were often

hypotonic in the first year of life, especially in regard to the neck and trunk. Hyperreflexia, prolongation of the adductor spread of the knee jerk after the normal age, and ankle clonus were early clues to future spasticity as these phenomena were seldom striking in patients who later developed choreoathetosis or dystonia.

4. The Moro reflex was rarely retained past 6 months of age in any of the abnormal groups.

5. Delayed retention of an imposable tonic neck reflex and its presence in an abnormally obligate sustained degree were the major and most diagnostically useful abnormal postural responses in both spastic and dyskinetic tetraparesis. Tonic neck reflexes were retained slightly later than normal in 7 of 17 infants with general psychomotor retardation who showed no other abnormal motor signs, but in only 1 of these were tonic neck patterns imposable after the age of 9 months.

6. An important early clue to future spastic tetraparesis was that the positive supporting reaction of the lower extremities was more effective than the placing reaction, the reverse usually being true of infants who developed dyskinesias later.

7. The ability to reach after and grasp an object was delayed in acquisition in both types of tetraparesis, and early strong preference for one hand was characteristic of hemiparesis or asymmetric tetraparesis. Athetosis appeared earlier than is often stated: A few patients showed it as early as 9 months of age and just over half of the patients who were eventually athetotic demonstrated some abnormal movement of this type by 15 months. However, early athetosis is more likely to be followed by mild eventual disability of hand function than by severe disability, probably because the patients who later developed severe athetosis were unable to use the hands at all under 18 months of age.

8. The parachute reflex appears late and is stiff or disorganized in spastic and dyskinetic tetraparesis. Its asymmetry is a useful early diagnostic sign of hemiparesis.

9. Extension of the spinal column and elevation of the head and lower extremities in horizontal suspension in space, the Landau reflex, appear later than normal in almost all dyskinetic cerebral palsies and in the majority of spastic tetrapareses. Ex-

tension and adduction or scissoring of the lower extremities in vertical suspension are early characteristics of spastic tetraparesis.

10. Seven infants presented a variety of definitely abnormal motor signs on initial examination and were thought at that time to have cerebral palsies (future spasticity was expected in 6) ; these later lost all evidence of motor abnormality although at least three are mentally retarded. Five of the seven had clear histories of cerebral insults at birth, and it is suggested that the clinical courses of these patients reflect potential for cerebral recovery, at least in regard to motor function.

REFERENCES

1. Paine, R. S.: Neurologic examination of infants and children. *Pediat. Clin. N. Amer., 7:*471, 1960.
2. Thomas, A., Chesni, Y., and Ste. Anne Dargassies, S.: *The Neurological Examination of the Infant.* London, National Spastics Society, 1960.
3. Boll, F.: *Der gekreutzte Patellarsehnenreflex.* Diss. Greifswald, 1944.
4. Donovan, D. E., and Paine, R. S.: Prognostic implications of neurological abnormalities in the neonatal period. *Neurology (Minneap.), 12:*910, 1962.
5. Brain, W. R., and Wilkinson, M.: Observations on the extensor plantar reflex and its relationship to the functions of the pyramidal tract. *Brain, 82:*297, 1959.
6. Moro, E.: Das erste Trimenon. *Münch. Med. Wschr., 65:*1147, 1918.
7. Sanford, H. N.: The Moro reflex in the newborn. *Amer. J. Dis. Child., 54:*240, 1937
8. Westphal, M., and Kennedy, C.: An Evaluation of the Moro Reflex. Presented at American Academy of Neurology, Detroit, 1961.
9. Andre-Thomas, and Hanon, F.: De la naissance à la marche; quelques modes d'activité du nouveau-né. *Presse Med., 56:*229, 1948.
10. Peiper, A., and Isbert, H.: Über die Körperstellung des Saüglings. *Jb. Kinderheilk., 115:*142, 1927.
11. Karlsson, B.: Disorders of Labyrinthine Function in the Newborn. Presented at Third International Study Group on Child Neurology, Oxford, 1962.
12. Mitchell, R. G.: The Moro reflex. *Cerebr. Palsy Bull., 2:*135, 1960.
13. Lamote De Grignon, C.: La dissolution du réflexe de Moro et son integration dans la conduite du nourrisson. *Rev. Neurol., 93:*217, 1955.
14. Magnus, R.: Körperstellung, *Monographien aus dem Gesamtgebiet der Physiologie der Pflanze u. der Tiere,* 6 Band. Berlin, Springer, 1924.
15. McCouch, G. P., Deering, I. D., and Ling, T. H.: Location of receptors for tonic neck reflexes. *J. Neurophysiol., 14:*191, 1951.

16. Vassella, F., and Karlsson, B.: Asymmetric tonic neck reflex. *Develop. Med. Child Neurol., 4:*363, 1962.

17. Minkowski, M.: Sur les mouvements, les réflexes, et les réactions musculaires du foetus humain de 2 à 5 mois, et leurs rélations avec le système nerveux foetal. *Rev. Neurol., 37:*1105, 1235, 1921.

18. Pollack, S. L.: The grasp response in the neonate; its characteristics and interaction with the tonic neck reflex. *Arch. Neurol. (Chic.), 3:*574, 1960.

19. Peiper, A.: *Die Eigenart der kindlichen Hirntätigkeit,* 2nd ed. Leipzig, Georg Thisme, 1956.

20. Gesell, A., and Amatruda, C. S.: *Developmental Diagnosis,* 2nd ed. New York, Hoeber, 1947.

21. Gesell, A., and Ames, L. B.: Tonic neck reflex and symmetro-tonic behavior. *J. Pediat., 36:*165, 1950.

22. Landau, A.: Über die motorische Besonderheiten des zweiten Lebenshalbjahres. *Mschr. Kinderheilk., 29:*555, 1925.

23. Magnus, R., and De Klejn, A.: Die Abhängigkeit des Tonus der Extremitätenmuskeln von der Kopfstellung. *Pflügers Arch. Ges. Physiol., 145:* 455, 1912.

24. Rushworth, G.: On postural and righting reflexes. *Cerebr. Palsy Bull., 3:* 535, 1961.

25. Rademaker, G. G. J.: Das Stehen. Statische Reaktionen Gleichgewichts Reaktionen, u. Muskeltonus unter besonderer Berücksichtigung ihres Verhaltens bei Kleinhirnlosen Tieren. Berlin, J. Springer, 1931.

26. Ingram, T. T. S.: Muscle tone and posture in infancy. *Cerebr. Palsy Bull., 1:*5, 1959.

27. Illingworth, R. S.: *An Introduction to Developmental Assessment in the First Year.* London, National Spastics Society, 1962.

28. Balduzzi, O.: Die Stützreaktionen beim Menschen in physiologischen und pathologischen Zuständen. *Z. Neurol., 141:*1, 1932.

29. Landau, A.: Über einen tonischen Lagereflex beim älteren Saügling. *Klin. Wschr., 2:*1253, 1923.

30. Schaltenbrand, G.: The development of human motility and motor disturbances. *Arch. Neurol. Psychiat. (Chic.), 20:*720, 1928.

31. Magnus, R.: Some results of studies in the physiology of posture. *Lancet, 2:*531, 585, 1926.

32. Mitchell, R. G.: The Landau reaction (reflex). *Develop. Med. Child Neurol., 4:*65, 1962.

33. McGraw, M. B.: *The Neuromuscular Maturation of the Human Infant.* New York, Columbia University Press, 1943.

THE DEVELOPMENTAL PROGRESSION of psychophysiologic processes from the newborn period through early childhood is one of dramatic and complex changes. One cannot consider either maturation of the system or environmental influence as the sole determinant of the changes; rather each system interacts with the other. Heart rate, respiration, and electroencephalographic activity are measured frequently and used to indicate changes in function and ongoing processes. However, data from these indices may, at times, be difficult to interpret because the organism is dynamic and patterns of response may change without specific external stimulation. Moreover, researchers may not use the same methods to obtain their data or to analyze their results. In the following paper Drs. Lipton and Steinschneider report on several techniques used to obtain information on infant psychophysiological systems. Their results indicate considerable individual variation in the neonatal period in response capabilities. Developmental trends in cardiac response were noted as was the stability of response patterns in older infants. Currently Dr. Steinschneider and many other researchers are in the process of refining measurement techniques. The challenges will continue to be the integration of these data and the interpretation of their implications for behavior.

Chapter 3

Studies on the Psychophysiology of Infancy

EARLE L. LIPTON AND ALFRED STEINSCHNEIDER

U NDERSTANDING THE LABILE and seemingly disordered behavior of the infant's autonomic nervous system has been one of our major tasks for many years. This prolonged and concentrated study has resulted in an experimental model which we feel may lead to a better understanding of early infant behavior and its relationship to personality and disease in later life. The following discussion relates primarily to the methodologic approaches in three problem areas: individuality of neurophysiologic behavior in early life, stability and maturational trends, and autonomic end organ and skeletomuscular responsivity to various exteroceptive stimuli.

How, one might ask, did a group of research-oriented pediatricians come to investigate problems which have almost exclusively in past years occupied the attention of psychologists and child development specialists? The answer rests in the curiosity which accrued from years of attending to clinical medical problems for which there were no simple or direct answers. Whenever a so-called psychosomatic problem was investigated, whether it was a case of peptic ulcer, enuresis, or rumination, there always remained the question of constitutional predisposition within the

From Merrill-Palmer Quarterly of Behavior and Development, 10:103-117, 1964. Reprinted by permission.

The illustrations for this paper are from articles published previously by the authors (in collaboration with J. B. Richmond, M.D.) , being reproduced here with proper permission. Figure 3-1 has appeared in the *Journal of the American Academy of Child Psychiatry* for January, 1962. The others have appeared in *Psychosomatic Medicine*—Figure 3-2 in the January-February, 1960 number Figures 3-3 to 3-6 in the November-December, 1961 number. The courtesy extended by the editors of those journals in this respect is much appreciated. The studies reported here were supported, in part, by grants from the Ford Foundation, the Commonwealth Fund, and USPHS research grants MHO 4065, and I-K3-HD-21,852-01.

affected organ system.[17] Psychologic factors alone did not seem adequate to explain the course of events, since many individuals with comparable problems and personalities either did not manifest psychosomatic disease or demonstrated pathology involving other organ systems. It was the search for possible predisposing factors that initiated our studies of the autonomic nervous system in early life.[6,19]

The first task was to demonstrate that infants shortly after birth manifested individual traits with respect to autonomic end organ function.[10,11] If this were also demonstrated in premature infants and even in fetuses, one would accept the likelihood that such characteristics are congenital and possibly hereditary. Some of the evidence concerning individual differences in early life will be described later in this paper.

We next investigated whether such subject-specific visceral control mechanisms continued to characterize the individual infant as he matured, and/or whether there were developmental trends.

Once some of the techniques for data collection and analysis were established, it was possible to explore other pertinent questions. One that has preoccupied us has been the description of the neonate's capacity to sense stimuli in the world about him. Our initial explorations confirmed previous studies which demonstrated that he does not react in an "all or none" fashion to all forms of stimulation.[19] It has been even more fascinating to discover the relatively sophisticated nature of the infants' sensory-response system: an example is the study of sound discrimination which will be described briefly herein.[12] The possible applications of these techniques in problem areas such as conditioning and adaptation will hopefully become evident to the reader.

TECHNIQUES: PAST AND PRESENT

Pratt's comprehensive chapter on the neonate[18] describes the attempts, which date back many decades to study visceral and somatic responsivity in early life. Much fascinating and productive work resulted from those attempts to record objectively cardiac, respiratory, and muscular responses to varied stimuli. Pulse waves from the anterior fontanel sometimes provided the only means for recording cardiac rate. Tambours and smoked drums captured much of this information. The most objective and accurate measures of responsivity involved motor reaction times derived from various stabilimeters. Movement, an inescapable "enemy" of the neonatal investigator, often precluded studies of visceral activity during varied behavioral states.

Later, in the thirties, electronic devices offered some relief but, as with adult studies, the extraction of data even from electrocardiographic (ECG) tracings was so time consuming that simple averaging techniques were generally used. This allowed a limited vantage point for interpreting complex changes. However, a few of these studies included laborious measurements of cardiac cycle lengths to allow descriptions of responses in greater detail.[23]

When we first began these studies our major tool was the ECG. However, it was soon apparent that other devices would facilitate an understanding of the data. The cardiotachometer became available[4] and has been responsible for the elaboration of cardiac responses in detail. Such a device electronically transforms cardiac cycle durations ("interbeat" intervals) into cardiac rate, allowing for a readily interpretable visual display of the successive changes in rate (Fig. 3-1). One can easily understand the problems inherent in trying to analyze just the accompanying ECG tracing.

Upon our becoming proficient at obtaining artifact-free tracings of moving neonates, it was then possible to study cardiac rate control under even the most adverse conditions. Furthermore, extremely subtle changes which would have remained hidden within the maze of the ECG tracings could readily be detected. The detailed aspects of this technique are described elsewhere.[10]

Respiration has been recorded in these studies[7] by means of a tiny thermistor bead placed beneath the nares (Fig. 3-2). The thin wire leads are taped to the skin and lead to a circuit including a battery which, in turn, supplies the changing signal recorded via an A.C. coupled electronecephalographic preamplifier, amplifier, and oscillographic recorder. Modifications of the nose lead have been detailed elsewhere.[16]

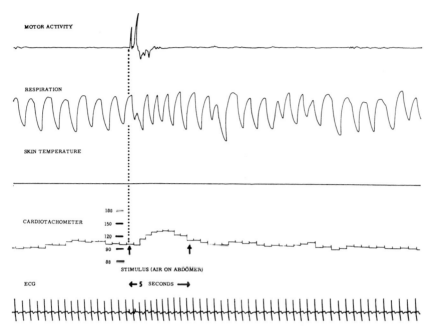

Figure 3-1. Polygraph record with stabilimeter tracing on top, indicating rapid startle response. During stimulation, the respiration rate increased and amplitude decreased. The heart rate, shown rising in the cardiotachometer record within less than one second, achieved a peak of 135 beats per minute, returning then to prestimulus levels. Changes were not so readily discernible in the EEG tracing at the bottom.

A more recent development by our Bioelectronic Laboratory is a device we have facetiously labeled the "peak-picker." This instrument detects the precise moment at which inspiration and/or expiration begins, and allows a recording of respiratory cycles in a fashion analogous to the recording of heart rate by the cardiotachometer. Unlike previous devices, it precisely measures each and every cycle and should markedly facilitate our current laborious data reduction of respiratory responses.

CURRENT ANALYTIC METHODS

A detailed description of the techniques underlying our analyses would be far beyond the scope of this paper. It has, in fact,

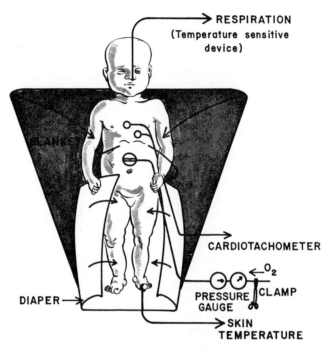

Figure 3-2. The drawing shows an infant subject with electrodes attached and a plastic cone attached above the umbilicus for delivery of an airstream stimulus. The diaper holds the legs in extension. The light recieving blanket restricts movements of the other body parts as desired.

been the major content of a series of recent papers[10,11,20,22] to which the reader is referred. Nevertheless, a brief description is necessary for an understanding of what is to follow.

The cardiac rate of an infant or child generally increases within a second or more after the onset of a suprathreshold external stimulus. Typically the rate accelerates and then gradually peaks to form an ogive. The peak is usually followed by a response curve of a similar nature, but in the opposite direction, which attains a reasonable stable rate termed the return level. The various parameters are shown in Figure 3-3. Occasionally responses are

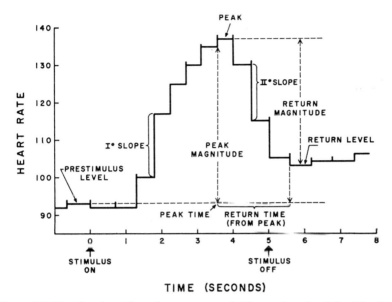

Figure 3-3. Simulated cardiotachometer record, illustrating the "physiological" parameters employed in the studies described by the authors.

flat (relatively unchanging rate), in a downward direction, or sometimes are erratic and not analyzable.*

The flat or downward responses (decreases in heart rate) are usually associated with high heart rates prior to stimulation. In fact, the magnitude measures of these responses (primarily slope, peak, secondary slope, and return magnitudes) are all negatively correlated with their respective prestimulus rates. Thus the largest changes in rate are associated with low cardiac rate levels before stimulation.[7,10,11,19] As a consequence, we have utilized a regression model which takes into account all the response measures of a given parameter. It allows estimates of average responses

_____

*These parameters have been programmed for a 7070 IBM computer, so that the measures can be extracted from digital information recorded on magnetic tape during the experiment. These machine definitions of the parameters were used in the extraction of data in the "white noise" study described later.

obtained at various points on the best fit line. The lowest prestimulus rate is associated with the average *maximal* response, while
the mean prestimulus heart rate predicts the most stable point on
the line—the *mean* responses. These statistical estimates, among
others, can be used to compare conditions either within a subject
or between infant subjects.

Fortunately, not all the analyses are so complicated. Each of
the parameters can be measured with respect to its timing and,
since these values are largely unrelated to the prestimulus level of
activity, means and variances, can be directly obtained for comparisons. As with much biological data, however, both prestimulus heart rate and these time measures assume a log normal distribution and must be so transformed before analysis.

The primary slope parameter represents simply the greatest
change between two adjacent cardiac cycles. With few exceptions
it is readily identifiable on the polygraphic record. Despite its
seeming simplicity and its representation of but a microscopic
piece of the cardiac response, it potentially affords important information.

Excluding the slope parameters, the remaining magnitude and
time measures are extracted from the respiratory tracings. They
are analyzed in a similar fashion.[14]

Experimental Variables

Many elements must be considered in designing and later interpreting any studies involving nervous system activity. When
stimulating the infant it is important to eliminate, insofar as possible, concurrent external stimulation or stimulation resulting
from physiologic change within the organism. Some dramatic cardiac changes often occur during such activities as hiccoughs,
yawning, and defecation.[13] Our laboratories are made relatively
sound proof, with temperature and humidity controlled and with
constant illumination to minimize external stimulation. Most experiments are conducted with the infant isolated in the laboratory
and observed through a window.

Included in a previous discussion of this problem[21] were such
other variables as habituation to the stimulus, changes in state of

consciousness, and interactions between musculoskeletal and autonomic end organ activity. These can, to some extent, be controlled in the analysis and experimental design. The latter interaction was the target of several studies which utilized swaddling to restrict motor activity.

Swaddling

In two separate studies we confirmed the impressions of experienced nursery nurses that tight "bundling" of newborns decreases motor activity and crying, and promotes sleep.[7,15] When the subjects were completely or partially (arms-free) swaddled, there were fewer stimulus trials during which a motor response was detected to the 5-second abdominal airstream stimulus.

In the later analysis of autonomic responsivity in these eighteen neonates, only the motor change trials were included.[5] This provided an independent estimate that the infant had sensed and responded to the stimulus. These studies demonstrated that the cardiac and respiratory responses, both with respect to magnitude and timing, were generally comparable under all conditions of motor restraint. Since the *degree* of motor activity was attenuated by the restraints, this indicated that autonomic responses are not wholly dependent upon motor activity. These relationships will be explored further in future studies.

The restraint technique enhanced the collection of data. The infant subjects were more "cooperative"; thus it was possible to maintain them at lower heart rate levels and obtain a larger number of maximal responses to stimulation. As a result of this experience, the subjects in our subsequent studies have always been at least partially, if not completely, swaddled.

These data are discussed elsewhere in detail within the framework of swaddling as an infant care practice.[15] Also included in that monograph are some neurophysiologic interpretations of these findings and a review of the history of swaddling in various cultures.

Individual Differences in Neonates

In attempting to demonstrate consistent differences in autonomic function between subjects, sixteen neonates were studied between the second and fifth days of life. The stimulus in these early experiments was a stream of air on the abdomen of 5 seconds duration administered under standard pressure (Fig. 3-2). The resultant cardiac responses were studied by means of the techniques previously alluded to, and the results confirmed the hypothesis that even neonates manifest individualistic patterns of autonomic behavior.[11] Figures 3-4 and 3-5 present two examples of the results: peak magnitude and time. It is clear that certain infants (e.g. *Ox*) may be exceedingly labile in their responses, yet they may manifest rapid reactivity. Others (e.g. *Wi*) may show relatively small, yet rapid, responses. The correlation in the sixteen infants between these two parameters was close to zero, indicating that time and magnitude probably provide different information. Furthermore, the various other magnitude and time parameters also were, in large measure, independent.

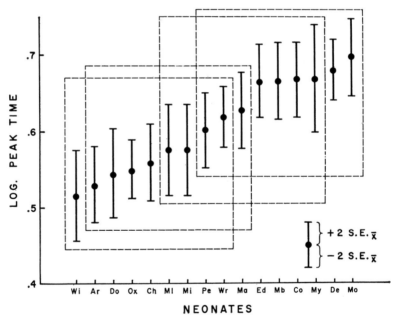

Figure 3-4. Means and the respective standard errors for log peak time for individual subjects. Each box encloses a group of infants whose means *cannot* be differentiated (e.g. *Wi* is significantly different from *Ma* and all other infants with greater mean log peak time).

The capacity of these infants to return to prestimulus levels was also explored and significant differences were found.[20] This was also the case with respect to variability of response.[22] These latter measures have particular pertinence to the question of the homeostatic capacity of an individual's visceral response system. They relate to a subject's capacity to maintain a reasonably steady state despite stimulation and whether he registers a stereotyped or a varied response to presumably identical stimulations. It seems clear from these studies that Lacey's concepts of "labile" and "stable" adult reactors applies equally well to younger subjects.[5]

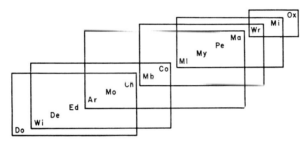

PEAK MAGNITUDE

Figure 3-5. Rank order of infant subjects in terms of peak magnitude. The boxes have the same meaning as in Fig. 3-4.

Developmental Trends

Fifteen infants who were studied as neonates returned to the laboratory at approximately two and five months of age. The same experimental techniques were used at all ages. The infants when older were sometimes uncooperative during the procedure, and swaddling was unsuccessful in pacifying most of them.

Two findings appear to be of primary importance. First, whether asleep or awake, the cardiac rate response curves, in most older infants, are modified as compared to the newborn responses. Characteristically the peak occurs more rapidly and is attenuated in magnitude at two and five months. Furthermore, the return phase begins very early in the response and the heart rate not infrequently drops below prestimulus levels even during the five seconds of stimulation.[8,14] These responses at two and five months are often less variable than the neonate measures. Between the second and fifth months there were no consistent trends toward further modification of the response curve.

A classical example of this phenomenon is found in Figure 3-6. The data were obtained during the first four months of life in a premature infant weighing $2\frac{1}{2}$ pounds at birth. These are the maximum response curves, reconstructed from estimates derived at the respective lowest prestimulus cardiac rates. On the left, one can see the *increase* in the heart rate *level* several weeks after birth and the subsequent decrease in later months. These changes in level are also found as term infants mature. On the right, the same response curves are presented as starting from a comparable baseline of zero. This more clearly demonstrates the changing response curve with age. This premature infant showed the more typical "mature" response pattern at four months, whereas term infants often manifest this change within the first two months of life. Some premature and term infants show no such trend.

Second, in the study of fifteen full-term infants, correlations were generally nonsignificant between measures in the newborn and the later months. However, significant correlations were dem-

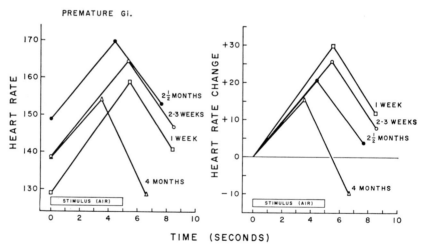

Figure 3-6. Reconstructed maximal cardiac responses of a small premature infant to an abdominal airstream during early months of life.

onstrated between the 2- and 5-month values. Thus evidence was provided to indicate that the responses of individuals maintain their relative ranking within a group of infants *after* the newborn period.

The first finding is significant in that it demonstrates that basic changes in autonomic control mechanisms do occur in humans during the early months of life. Such evidence is consistent with other studies of man and animals. The demonstration of some stability after two months suggests that many of these findings are stable and that they may have predictive value for later behavior both in and out of the laboratory. This is not to deny, however, that even the early newborn findings may allow predictions and prove to be of heuristic value.

We have recently been exploring techniques for studying children between the ages of one and five years. It has been reassuring to note that cardiac response curves to repetitive "white noise" stimulation in this age group can also be analyzed employing identical techniques. We are attempting now to restudy children who were previously tested as infants in the autonomic laboratory as well as others who have been followed primarily in the longitudinal study of personality development described by Drs. Caldwell and Hersher in their paper.

SENSORY CAPACITY

Describing the responses of infants at one or more age periods to essentially the same stimulus represents a step toward understanding individual characteristics. Of potentially greater importance is the description of the differential sensitivities and response capacities of infants to a wide variety of stimuli. One might hypothesize that infants, for example, vary in their sensitivities to *different stimuli*—some being relatively more responsive to sound as compared to tactile stimulation, and vice versa. Furthermore, it is likely that the capacity to discriminate between *qualities within a given sensory modality,* such as intensities of sound, is a congenital characteristic. Escalona and Bergmann[3] provided clinical descriptions of behaviorally disturbed children who appeared to be hypersensitive to certain stimuli, such as sound, and hypothesized distorted perceptivity as a precursor or concomitant feature of childhood psychoses.

As exploratory study involved ten neonates exposed to repetitive sound (85-decibel buzzer), tactile (abdominal airstream), and light (flashing 1/sec 100-watt bulb at 2 feet) stimulation. Each stimulus was of five seconds duration.[9]

The intensities of these stimuli were chosen arbitrarily, except for some previous observations which suggested that they were all well above threshold. Each of the stimuli resulted in cardiac response curves having the same general characteristics.

We were somewhat surprised to find that the ten infants manifested essentially no differences in the magnitude and timing aspects of the cardiac response curves when stimulated with either the sound or the airstream. In contrast, the response to the light was attenuated in all but one of the eight infants so tested. (Two subjects were identical twins and stimulated only with sound and the airstream.) The motor responses to the light often consisted only of eye blinks, although one very light, red-haired infant could not be included in the study because he startled and became hyperirritable with almost every exposure to the light!

Of considerable interest was the finding that the latencies of the motor responses, as recorded by a strain-gauge stabilimeter, demonstrated significant differences between the sound and airstream responses in 6 of the 10 infants. Two reacted significantly faster, on the average, to the airstream stimulus and the other four to the 85-dB sound. Again, as in all our experiments thus far, there were consistent differences between infants with respect to both cardiac and motor responsivity.

It is apparent, then, that human infant behavior cannot be *arbitrarily* assessed with any measuring device that happens to be available. The choice of the instrument is often fortuitous and the resultant measures cannot be considered as representative of the overall reactivity. There are complex interrelationships between autonomic end organs as well as between these and skeletal-motor and biochemical systems. It is essential ultimately to tap into many systems simultaneously, but this might best be accomplished only after probing at some depth into each, so as to avoid accepting arbitrary and superficial relationships.

One of our recent studies was designed to measure the capacity of neonates to discriminate between graduated intensities of "white noise." Would certain infants manifest "better" discrimination than others and could thresholds be established by this technique? We were interested in determining whether infants who were relatively more responsive to the high-intensity sound (100 dB) would likewise respond more when exposed to the lower intensities (85, 70 and 55 dB). These four sounds of five seconds duration were presented in random fashion, along with non-stimulated control periods during three separate sessions. This totalled 180 stimulus trials for each of nine subjects.

The results are most stimulating but, unfortunately, too complex for detailed presentation here.[12] Essentially, it was found that the percentages of startle and "motor change" responses tended to differentiate the stimulus levels in all subjects. Motor latency decreased with increasing stimulation even when startle trials were eliminated from the analysis.

Autonomic "reaction time" (primary slope time) also decreased progressively with increasing stimulus intensity. Conversely, the durations of the primary (peak) and secondary (return) phases of the response increased with intensity.

Analysis of the magnitude responses predicted from the *mean* prestimulus heart rate in most infants revealed that there was a progressive increase in all of the parameters (primary slope, peak, and return magnitudes) as the stimulus intensity increased. We were intrigued to find that the use of the *maximal* response capacity (response predicted at the subject's lowest prestimulus heart rate) resulted in fewer such trends. There was less tendency for differences to be found even between higher intensity levels. Thus, at mean heart rate levels when the infant tends to be more active and aroused, discrimination was more discernible in the cardiac responses.

However, the maximal response estimates were extremely stable, as demonstrated by high correlation coefficients across intensity conditions. This again supports the hypothesis of individual differences in responsivity. Furthermore, the capacity to discriminate (as measured by autonomic and musculo-skeletal responses) between the four intensity levels appeared to vary between infants.

These data showed no evidence of adaptation during a given session when the measures were transformed to standard scores. We have, however, witnessed the waning of a cardiac response even to 100 dB white noise when the stimulus was presented at lessened intervals. In this experiment, as in the others, the trials were never less than forty seconds apart.

We are currently studying responses of infants during the first two months of life to smaller gradations of intensities. This is an attempt to describe the discrimination curves in more detail and to delineate possible trends or stability over time. Concomitantly, higher and lower frequencies are being presented as a first approximation to the problem of pitch discrimination.

Besides the theoretical importance of such studies we recognize, as pediatricians, the limited skills now available for evaluating hearing in early life. This experimental model appears to have clinical implications. Recently this was demonstrated in a case tested in the laboratory. It was predicted with reasonable confidence that this severely jaundiced newborn infant had profound, if not total, hearing loss, presumably due to brain damage from the bilirubin pigment. This was confirmed clinically and on testing some eight months later.

CONCLUDING REMARKS

The experiments outlined in this paper have focused largely upon individual infants and small groups. Nevertheless, the amount of data and information obtained has been at times overwhelming and, but for the use of large computers, would have precluded the analytic approach which has been described. The problems, in a sense, necessitate an understanding of *individual* subjects, for the characteristics of visceral and somatic behavior in the human species are extremely varied and interactive.

Initially it would seem propitious, then, to study human infants in some depth and over long periods of time. The experiments thus far attest to the individuality of response capacity in early life and to some degree of stability of these measures. Simultaneous investigations of psychological characteristics and life experiences would seem rewarding.[2] At this point in time, we can only evaluate the visceral responsivity of a group of children who have been subjects in a longitudinal study of personality over the past five years.

It is planned to study a new group of children who will be followed both physiologically and psychologically from early infancy. If there are specific physiologic responses attending certain emotional states as suggested in adult studies, the earlier counterparts of these might be discovered during childhood. It might also be possible to demonstrate an association between autonomic behavior and overt emotional characteristics such as impulsivity, hyperactivity, emotional lability, and so on.

A somewhat more remote possibility would be the demonstration of organ predisposition to psychosomatic disease, since this would probably require a larger population to obtain enough cases. A recent, apparently successful, study along these lines demonstrated that a certain number of children from a sizeable population developed hypertension as adults.[1] This disease was statistically related to their hyperreactivity to the cold pressor test during early adolescence.

The studies described in this paper indicate a detailed approach for "tapping" into the world of the infant. They seem to contain the ingredients for developing other techniques to allow even deeper future probing into the intricate behavior of the young child. Where else these studies may lead—in the arbitrary divisions of our knowledge termed physiological, medical, psychological, and the like—is a question which only the future can resolve.

REFERENCES

1. Barnett, P. H., Hines, E. A., Jr., Schirger, A., and Gage, R. P. Blood pressure and vascular reactivity to the cold pressor test. Restudy of 207 subjects 27 years later. *J.A.M.A., 183*:845-848, 1963.

2. Darrow, C. W., and Heath, L. L. Reaction tendencies relating to personality. In K. S. Lashley (Ed.), *Studies in the Dynamics of Behavior.* Chicago, Univer. Chicago Press, 1932.

3. Escalona, S. K., and Bergmann, P. Unusual sensitiveness in very young children. *Psychoanalyt. Stud. Child, III.* New York, Internat. Univer. Press, 1949.

4. Lacey, J. I., Bateman, Dorothy E., and Van Lehn, Ruth. Autonomic response specificity. An experimental study. *Psychosom. Med., 15*:8-21, 1953.

5. Lacey, J. I., and Lacey, B. C. Verification and extension of the principles of autonomic response-steretotypy. *Amer. J. Psychol., 71*:50-73, 1958.

6. Lipton, E. L., Richmond, J. B., and Lustman, S. L. Autonomic function in the neonate and psychosomatic disease. *Amer. J. Dis. Child., 90*: 491, 1955. (Abstract)

7. Lipton, E. L., Steinschneider, A., and Richmond, J. B. Autonomic function in the neonate. II. Physiologic effects of motor restraint. *Psychosom. Med., 22*:57-65, 1960.

8. Lipton, E. L., Steinschneider, A., and Richmond, J. B. The maturation of autonomic nervous system function in the early months of life. *Psychosom. Med., 22*:325-326, 1960. (Abstract)

9. Lipton, E. L., Steinschneider, A., and Richmond, J. B. A study of the sensitivity of newborn infants to stimulation. Evaluation by means of autonomic and somatic responses. *Amer. J. Dis. Child., 102*:537, 1961. (Abstract)

10. Lipton, E. L., Steinschneider, A., and Richmond, J. B. Autonomic function in the neonate. III. Methodological considerations. *Psychosom, Med., 23*:461-471, 1961.

11. Lipton, E. L., Steinschneider, A., and Richmond, J. B. Autonomic function in the neonate. IV. Individual differences in cardiac reactivity. *Psychosom. Med., 23*:472-484, 1961.

12. Lipton, E. L., Steinschneider, A., and Richmond, J. B. Auditory discrimination in the newborn infant. *Psychosom. Med., 25*:490, 1963. (Abstract)

13. Lipton, E. L., Steinschneider, A., and Richmond, J. B. Autonomic function in the neonate. VIII. Cardio-pulmonary observations. *Pediatics, 33*:212, 1964.

14. Lipton, E. L., Steinschneider, A., and Richmond, J. B. Autonomic function in the neonate. VII. Maturational changes in cardiac control (MS.)

15. Lipton, E. L., Steinschneider, A., and Richmond, J. B. Swaddling: Historical, cultural, and experimental observations. (MS) .

16. Lipton, E. L., Walsh, L., Mueller, W., and Salamy, B. A respiratory alarm for infants. *J. Pediat.,* 1964.

17. Mohr, G. J., Richmond, J. B., Garner, Ann, and Eddy, Evelyn. A pro-

gram for the study of children with psychosomatic disorder. In G. Caplan (Ed.), *Emotional Problems of Early Childhood*. New York, Basic Books, 1955.

18. Pratt, K. C. The neonate. In L. Carmichael, *Manual of Child Psychology*. New York, John Wiley, 1954.

19. Richmond, J. B., and Lipton, E. L. Some aspects of the neurophysiology of the newborn and their implications for child development. In Lucy Jessner and Eleanor Pavenstedt (Eds.), *Psychopathology in Children*. New York, Grune & Stratton, 1959.

20. Richmond, J. B., Lipton, E. L., and Steinschneider, A. Autonomic function in the neonate. V. Individual homeostatic capacity in cardiac response. *Psychosom. Med., 24*:66-74, 1962.

21. Richmond, J. B., Lipton, E. L., and Steinschneider, A. Observations on differences in autonomic nervous system function between and within individuals during early infancy. *J. Amer. Acad. Child Psychiat., 1*:83-91, 1962.

22. Steinschneider, A., Lipton, E. L., and Richmond, J. B. Autonomic function in the neonate. VI. Discriminability, consistency, and slope as measures of an individual's cardiac responsivity. *J. Genet. Psychol.* 1964.

23. Sontag, L. W., and Wallace, R. F. Changes in the rate of the human heart in response to vibratory stimuli. *Amer. J. Dis. Child, 51*:583, 1936.

PART II

THE ROLE OF SENSE SYSTEMS IN DEVELOPMENT

For years mothers were told that their babies would not have functional vision until two months of age. But, frequently a mother would report that her baby, a week or two of age, seemed to be looking at her face. Mothers were more perceptive than some pediatricians and psychologists, for research has shown that the newborn is sensitive to intensities of light, fixates more on patterned than unpatterned stimuli, and tracks a moving stimulus. However, the infant is limited in his ability to accommodate to objects of varying distances but can focus on an object 8 to 9 inches from his face. Binocular fixation occurs about seven weeks of age. The point, though, is that infants do have a functioning, albeit immature, visual system, almost from birth. The auditory system, while not investigated as thoroughly as the visual system, shows the newborn can do some simple auditory discrimination. Obviously these findings have enormous implications for perceptual, cognitive, and social development, for the infant can actively use his vision and hearing early in life. In the following paper Dr. Richard Walters and Dr. Ross Parke discuss the development of social responsiveness in relation to vision and audition.

Chapter 4

The Role of the Distant Receptors in the Development of Social Responsiveness

RICHARD H. WALTERS AND ROSS D. PARKE

DURING THE past 25 years, the development of social responsiveness in infancy and childhood has most frequently been structured in terms of the establishing of dependency habits and the emergence of a dependency drive (e.g. Dollard and Miller, 1950; Sears *et al.,* 1953, 1957). In a recent discussion of the relationships among such variables as dependency, social deprivation, and various measures of social influence, Walters and Parke,[139] after pointing out that the concept of dependency, like many other social "variables" employed by child psychologists, is semievaluative in nature, offered an alternative analysis of the learning of social behavior in terms of the eliciting and modification of orienting and attending responses. This analysis led to the suggestion that the role of the distance receptors is of paramount importance in the development of social responsiveness in infancy and early childhood. In this paper, the authors attempt to marshal evidence, most of it of very recent date, that lends support to this suggestion.

CARETAKING AND NURSING SITUATIONS

An amalgam of psychoanalytic and Hullian learning theory led to an emphasis on the mother-child feeding relationship as the crucial context within which the infant develops its capacity

From L. Lipsitt and C. Spiker (Eds.). *Advances in Child Development and Behavior,* vol. 2. New York, Academic Press, 1965. Reproduced by permission.

The preparation of this paper was made possible by grants from the Ontario Mental Health Foundation (Grant No. 42) and the Defense Research Board of Canada (Grant No. 9401-24). The authors are grateful to Alice Winkelman for assistance in bibliographic and related work. They wish also to express their appreciation to the colleagues and friends who read the original draft of manuscript and made many valuable and constructive criticisms.

70

for social responses (e.g., Sears *et al.*[125]) . This relationship supposedly provided an unique opportunity for the association of the mother's presence and activities with the reduction of the frequently occurring primary drive of hunger, as a result of which these maternal characteristics were endowed with acquired secondary-reward value. Although the alleviation of infant distress other than that caused by hunger was seen as contributing to the mother's reward value, the Freudian influence (e.g. Freud,[43] originally published in 1905) channeled attention to the oral behavior of the infant to such an extent that orality and dependency have sometimes been utilized as overlapping, if not precisely equivalent, terms.[99]

Recent research indicates that the feeding agent is not invariably the primary object of the infant's early social responses. Harlow,[58] using as subjects infant rhesus monkeys, demonstrated that "contact comfort" was considerably more important than feeding as an antecedent of attachment behavior. The infants had access to two inanimate mother surrogates; one surrogate was constructed from a block of wood, covered with sponge rubber and soft terrycloth and warmed by radiant heat, while the other was constructed from wire-mesh and unheated. Half the infants were fed on the cloth mother and the remainder on the wire-mesh mother. Infants fed on the lactating wire mother spent decreasingly less time in contact with her and increasingly more time with the nonlactating cloth mother, "a finding completely contrary to any interpretation of derived drive in terms in which the mother-form becomes conditioned to hunger-thirst reduction" (p. 676). Subsequent reports from Harlow's laboratory[59,60] confirmed the initial findings. Moreover, they indicated that in the presence of a fear stimulus infant monkeys will seek the proximity of a cloth mother in preference to that of a wire mother and will also favor the cloth mother as a safe base from which to explore the environment; these preferences were manifested even when the wire mother was the source of nutrition.

Harlow emphasizes the role of contact comfort in the establishment of affectional behavior; while this variable may be of primary importance for the development of social responsiveness in subhuman mammals, in which motor responses are relatively well developed early in infancy, there is reason to believe that it is of far less importance in human social development.

Schaffer and Emerson[116] collected data concerning the attachment behavior of human infants during the first year and a half of life. Mothers were interviewed at four-week intervals from the time that the infants were 2 to 5 months old until they reached the age of 1 year and once again when the infants were 18 months old. Protest behavior (whining, moaning, crying) in seven different situations in which the infant's contact with other persons was interrupted provided indices of age of onset, intensity, and breadth of attachments. The investigators found that specific attachments were formed to individuals who never participated in routine caretaking activities and consequently questioned the view that social behavior arises primarily in the context of the feeding situation. "Satisfaction of physical needs does not appear to be a necessary precondition to the development of attachments, the latter taking place independently and without any obvious regard to the experiences that the child enocunters in physical care situations" (p. 67).

Schaffer and Emerson report several findings that support their conclusion. Attachment behavior is at first indiscriminate; during the first six months of life the infant protests the withdrawal of anyone's attention, familiar or strange, and it is only around the seventh month that specific attachments are manifested. Not all infants initially develop a single specific attachment; over a quarter of the infants observed displayed multiple attachments as soon as any specificity was apparent. Moreover, even at the onset of the formation of specific attachments, the mother was not inevitably the single, or sole principal, object of attachment.

Data collected when the infants had reached 18 months of age indicated that neither rigidity of feeding schedule nor age of weaning was related to the strength of attachment to the mother; however, there were fairly strong relationships between two variables relating to the mother's social responsiveness—the mothers' responsiveness to the children's crying and the extent to which they interacted with the children—and the degree of the children's attachment to their mothers. Three modes of interaction were distinguished: a personal approach involving a great deal of physical contact with the child, a personal approach primarily involving stimulation by the mother's voice and facial expressions, and an impersonal approach in which the mother diverted attention from herself through providing the child with toys, food, and other objects when he demanded attention. Infants whose mothers used physical contact as their preferred mode of interaction were no more intensely attached to their mothers than infants whose mothers preferred one of the other two modes. In addition, intrafamily comparisons indicated that a child's principal object of attachment tended to be a person who interacted intensely with him and was highly responsive to his demands for attention, but not necessarily the person who was most available to him or who performed the caretaking routines. For twenty-two of the infants, the principal objects of attachment had not participated at all in any aspect of the caretaking process.

The breadth of the children's attachment behavior at 18 months was positively related to the number of persons with whom they interacted, whether in a caretaking capacity or otherwise, but was not related to the number of persons with whom they interacted solely in a caretaking capacity. This finding lent further support to the investigators' contention that it is stimulation in general, and not simply the satisfaction of physical needs, that develops attachment behavior.

In view of the failure of Schaffer and Emerson to find any relationship between socialization variables related to early feeding experiences and infants' attachment behavior at 18 months, it is not surprising that attempts to relate such experiences to later dependency behavior have met with little success. Sears *et al.*,[125] in a report based on mother-interview data, found no relationship between the warmth of mothers toward their infants, defined essentially as a physical-contact variable, and the children's dependency behavior at age 5; breast-fed children were no more dependent than bottle-fed children; duration of breast or bottle feeding, age at commencement and termination of weaning, and

duration of weaning were all similarly unrelated to later dependency behavior. Equally negative results were reported in an
earlier study by Sears *et al.*[124]

The mounting evidence against the widely held view that
gratification of an infant's "oral needs" is necessarily the principal
antecedent of social responsiveness does not, however, imply that
the feeding situation itself is not of considerable importance for
the development of attachment to the mother. During feeding,
the majority of human mothers provide their infants with considerable auditory and visual stimulation, as well as with physical
contact. Haynes *et al.*[62] discovered that alert infants in the early
weeks of life have a fixed point of clearest vision at eight or
nine inches and that objects either closer or farther away cannot
be brought into sharp focus. Under normal feeding and other
caretaking conditions the mother's face is frequently exposed at
this optimal distance for patterned vision. Consequently, in caretaking situations, the infant has many opportunities for the development of social responsiveness on a purely perceptual basis.[37,102]

Moreover, the human face is demonstrably an object complex
and mobile enough to hold the infant's attention. The relationship between complexity and infant attention has been the subject of several investigations. In a pioneering study, Berlyne[11]
presented infants of 3 to 9 months with stimuli of varying degrees
of complexity. The stimuli were presented in pairs, and an observer recorded which stimulus in each pair was fixated first.
Stimuli containing a relatively large amount of contour were
more likely to attract initial fixations than were less complex
stimuli. A more recent experiment by Spears,[130] who employed
a wider range of stimuli of varying forms and colors, provided
further evidence of the importance of complexity as a determinant of infant attention. Analogous findings have been reported
for preschool children by Cantor *et al.*[26]

Fantz's investigations are more directly relevant to the issue
under discussion in this paper. In his initial study, Fantz[35] recorded the times that infants spent looking at stimuli of varying
complexity; records were obtained at weekly intervals from the
first to the fifteenth week of life. At all ages tested, the infants

were able to discriminate the different patterns and showed preferences for the more complex stimuli. In a later study, Fantz[36] utilized three flat objects, similar to a head in size and shape. On one stimulus was painted a schematic face pattern; on the second stimulus, facial features were presented in a scrambled pattern; the third, control stimulus retained the brightness value of the other stimuli but contained no facial features. Most infants within the age range of 1 month to 6 months exhibited a preference for the schematic face. Subsequently, Fantz assessed the preferences of infants in relation to six test objects, three patterned and three plain. The patterned objects—a face, a bull's eye, and a patch of printed matter—were all preferred to the plain objects; moreover, the face was overwhelmingly preferred to the other patterned stimuli.

Fantz[37] next compared the effectiveness of a life-size model of the human head and that of a flat form of the same outline for eliciting infant attention. During the first two months of life infants preferred the flat form; however, in the third month there was a marked shift to a preference for the three-dimensional head. These preferences were apparent even when the test objects were viewed monocularly.

Fantz's investigations were designed to determine the relative contribution of innate factors, maturation, and learning to the development of form perception. However, his findings also seem to have important implications for social development. The infant's visual preferences may facilitate the early nonspecific attachments that infants display to other humans; in addition, they may promote the recognition and discrimination of facial features and thus contribute to the formation of specific attachments.

Kagan and Lewis[70] recently reported preliminary results of an important longitudinal investigation of attention in infants. At 6 months of age, the infants were presented with two types of visual patterns—pictures of faces and geometrical designs—and three patterns of blinking lights. In addition, five auditory stimuli were presented: an intermittent tone, a selection of unusual jazz music, and three human voices each reading the same paragraph of English—a female voice, a male voice, and the voice of each child's own mother. The experimenters recorded the time for which the infants fixated each of the visual patterns; in addition, changes in the infants' motor activity and the vocalizations that occurred during the presentations of each of the visual and auditory stimuli were recorded. On the basis of previous findings with children and adults,[71,80,81] cardiac deceleration was selected as an additional, physiological index of attention.

Kagan and Lewis found that photographs of male and female faces elicited more sustained attention than nonhuman visual stimuli, which included a nursing bottle. Moreover, the female face elicited more vocalizations than the male face, suggesting that 6-month-old infants were able to differentiate between male and female faces. Of the three light patterns, the most complex appeared to elicit maximum attention, a finding that may be interpreted as supporting Fantz's claim that the attention value of the human face for infants is due, in part at last, to its complexity.

As he interacts with a caretaker, the infant not only experiences a constantly changing configuration of facial features but also frequently receives stimulation from the human voice. The role of auditory stimulation both within and without the caretaking situation has not yet been sufficiently explored. Kagan and Lewis found that on first being presented with human voices, especially that of a strange female, infants exhibited cardiac deceleration and quieting, followed by vocalization. On the basis of this findings, Kagan and Lewis suggest that human speech acquires psychological significance by the time an infant has attained the age of 6 months. Their suggestion is supported by Wolff's observations on infant smiling,[153] which are reviewed in the following section.

The conclusion that may be drawn from the limited available evidence is that visual and auditory stimulation occurring during caretaking plays an important role in the development of social responsiveness. This conclusion does not, however, imply that physical-contact and need-reduction variables do not contribute to this development. Igel and Calvin,[68] in a study that paralleled in some respects Harlow's original experiment with mother surrogates, found that infant puppies preferred a lactating "comfortable" surrogate to an equally "comfortable" surrogate on which they were not fed. Similarly, one would expect a human infant to form a stronger attachment to a caretaker who feeds, provides contact-comfort, and visual and auditory stimulation than to one who supplies a similar amount of stimulation through the distance receptors but provides little contact comfort or participates minimally in the feeding situation.

ELICITING OF SMILING RESPONSES

Smiling has frequently been employed as an index of social responsiveness. In the first two weeks of life, most smiling is more dependent on the infant's internal state than on the occurrence of external stimulation and is, therefore, of little social significance. By the third week, however, the infant smiles differentially to various kinds of external stimulation while wide awake. At this stage, smiling may be regarded as a social response.[153]

On the basis of repeated observations in standard situations, Washburn[140] reported that a smiling human face was the most effective stimulus for eliciting smiling and laughing in infants during the first year of life. Kaila,[72] working under the influence of Gestalt theory, presented evidence in support of the view that infant smiles are evoked by the stimulus configuration of a frontal view of the human face though not by a profile configuration. The effectiveness of the sight of a human face for eliciting infant smiles is also evident from Dennis' observations[30] on two infant girls. Dennis noted that practically all smiles occurring after the first month and a half of an infant's life were evoked before the experimenter had made physical contact with the infant. Moreover, very few smiles occurred during or after feeding.

Spitz[133] studied the effectiveness of a variety of human and nonhuman objects for evoking smiling responses in infants. He reported that whereas human objects, such as the experimenter's face, masks, and a scarecrow, effectively elicited smiling, nonhuman objects were incapable of eliciting smiles. Moreover, Spitz claimed that movement of all or part of a specific configuration consisting of two eyes, a nose, and a forehead was essential for evoking a smile. Spitz did not present adequate data in support of this claim, which subsequent investigators have failed to substantiate. While these investigators have generally agreed that the human face in movement is a very effective elicitor of smiles, their data indicate that the sight of a moving human object is not a necessary antecedent of infant smiling.

Recent evidence suggests that sounds are at first more effective than visual stimuli for evoking social smiles in infants. In a longitudinal study, Wolff[153] found that, as early as the third week, social smiles were more frequently evoked by a high-pitched human voice than by a variety of other auditory stimuli. Very shortly afterwards, visual stimulation contributed to the eliciting of smiles; by the end of the third week, the sight of a nodding human head, accompanied by the sound of the voice, was for some infants a more effective stimulus than the voice alone. During the fourth and fifth weeks, the sight of a silent human face was a sufficient condition for the eliciting of smiles, provided that there was eye-to-eye contact between infant and observer or the observer's face was moving.

Wolff's observations, although based on a sample of only four subjects, provide fairly convincing evidence of the effectiveness of stimulation through the distance receptors for eliciting social smiling. Unfortunately, Wolff did not test the effectiveness of proprioceptive-tactual stimulation until the third week when he introduced a game of "pat-a-cake," involving contact of the observer's and the child's hands. During the game the child could not see or hear the observer or any other adult. Proprioceptive-tactual stimulation of this kind failed to evoke smiles until between the fourth and sixth weeks. The later emergence of smiling to proprioceptive-tactual than to auditory or visual stimulation provides some evidence in favor of the view that social responsiveness is primarily based on stimulation through the distance receptors. It is possible, however, that if Wolff's infants had experienced the "pat-a-cake" stimulation from the first week, they would have responded to it earlier. According to J. B. Watson,[142] tactual and kinaesthetic stimuli, such as light touches on sensitive areas of the body, blowing on the body, tickling under the chin, and gentle jogging or rocking are capable of eliciting smiling of a nonsocial nature as early as the fourth day of life; the exact age at which tactual and kinesthetic stimuli of these kinds become capable of eliciting social smiling has yet to be established.

Wolff's study indicated that the human head was effective for eliciting smiles in the fourth and fifth weeks only if it was in movement or there was eye-to-eye contact between infant and observer. Ahrens[1,2] and Ambrose[5] have also emphasized the importance of movement and eye-to-eye contact. The available data suggest that very few infants commence to smile at a stationary, immobile human face before they are 6 weeks of age, but that most infants will smile at such a stimulus by the eighth or ninth week of life (e.g. Ambrose[5]; Gewirtz[49]).

Salzen[112] investigated the responses of an 8-week-old infant to a variety of nonhuman visual stimuli. Smiling was induced by cardboard ovals—white, black, or black and white—and also by a light source with a reflector. Rotation increased the effectiveness of the cardboard stimuli and flashing increased the effectiveness of the light source. Similarly, the normal mobility of the human face may contribute immensely to its potency as a social stimulus for infants.

Ambrose[5] studied the response strength of smiling to a stationary unsmiling human face in institution infants, 8 to 26 weeks old. The stimulus was presented for 30-second periods, separated by 30-second intervals that were utilized for recording the infants' responses to the stimulus; the series was continued until either smiling ceased or twelve successive presentations had been made. The infants' total smiling time during a series of presentations served as the dependent measure. Infants of 8 to 11 weeks of age did not respond at all to the stationary face, and very little smiling occurred among infants between 11 and 14 weeks of age. From 14 weeks on, all infants smiled; smiling time was at a maximum in the 17-20-week period, and declined thereafter. These findings are corroborated by data secured by B. L. White.[148]

A comparison of home-reared and institution infants indicated a similar pattern of responsiveness among the two groups; however, smiling occurred to the stationary face as early as 6 to 10 weeks among home-reared infants and reached a peak within the age range of 11 to 14 weeks. Ambrose[5] suggests that smiling is more frequently elicited and more often reinforced among home-reared infants than among infants reared in institutions. Consequently, through more rapid instrumental conditioning, the smiling response reaches peak strength earlier among home-reared infants. At the same time, "with maternal care conditioning of the classical variety probably also takes place more rapidly than with institutional care, with the result that there is a more rapid learning of the characteristics of the face or faces which elicit smiling" (p. 195). Ambrose proposes that on account of this more rapid classical conditioning, home-reared infants learn sooner than institution infants to discriminate the faces of strangers from those of caretaking adults; consequently, the home-reared infants show an earlier decline in smiling to a relative stranger.

The difference in timing of smiling-response patterns among home-reared and institution infants may be in part due, as Ambrose notes, to a difference in the difficulty of the discriminations that home-reared and institution infants have to make. The former infants, generally speaking, experience more intensive and continuous interaction with a very limited number of adult figures, whereas the latter are usually cared for by a number of adults of varying degrees of familiarity. The institution infant may therefore take longer to learn to discriminate familiar from relatively strange faces. One may suspect that infants from different institutions vary considerably in the timing of the emergence of indiscriminate and discriminative smiling, with the time-patterns depending on the caretaking arrangements of the various institutions.

Data recently secured by J. S. Watson,[143] using as stimuli both the experimenter's face and the faces of infants' mothers, suggest that the development and waning of the smiling response among home-reared infants is contingent on the presentation of the face stimulus in an upright position. With upright face stimuli, Watson obtained results comparable to those reported by Ambrose. In contrast, face stimuli that were presented upside down or at a 90-degree angle were relatively ineffective for eliciting smiles from infants ranging in age from 7 to 26 weeks. If, as Watson believes, caretaking activities, such as feeding and diaper changing, tend to be carried out with a 90-degree presentation of the caretaker's face, his data provide further evidence that the development of smiling as a social response is relatively independent of primary-drive reduction.

Watson's finding that smiling waned to the mother's, as well as to the experimenter's, face after the infants had attained the age of 13 to 14 weeks led him to call in question Ambrose's interpretation of waning as an indication that discrimination of strangers had been achieved. This finding may, however, result from Watson's use of a smiling, but otherwise completely unresponsive, maternal face, which may well constitute an "unfamiliar" stimulus for most infants.

Ambrose[5] noted that for both home-reared and institution infants the response strength of smiling waned over a single series of presentations of the experimenter's face in a single day. Smiling commenced at a relatively high level on the first presentation and gradually declined as the presentations were continued. This finding is not surprising in view of the fact that the experimenter's face was stationary and nonresponsive. A similar phenomenon of habituation (or extinction) was observed by Wolff,[153] who noted, however, that smiling could be readily reelicited if the stimulus pattern were changed through movement, for example, of the tongue, or through the addition or removal of a stimulus component such as a pair of sunglasses.

Data from various cultures[3,47,49] indicate that the speed at which smiling and other infant social responses develop is profoundly influenced by caretaking arrangements. Generally speaking, social development appears to be most rapid when these arrangements permit a great deal of sensory stimulation in a wide variety of social interaction situations. The remarkable precociousness of Ganda infants,[47] who lift their heads and smile by 1 month and whose social development through the first year of life is generally accelerated, may be due to their being carried in a seated position on the mother's back, a vantage point that provides them with a considerable amount of visual and auditory stimulation as the mother carries out her daily activities.

Brackbill[17] investigated the instrumental conditioning of the smiling response in eight infants between the ages of $3\frac{1}{2}$ and $4\frac{1}{2}$ months. During the baseline period and again during an extinction period that followed the conditioning, the experimenter stood motionless and expressionless with her face about fifteen inches away from the infant's. During the baseline period, smiles were emitted by all eight infants who were subsequently exposed to the conditioning procedure; data from a ninth subject for whom the baseline procedure was extended for a period of nineteen 5-minute intervals indicated that smiling declines and eventually ceases to a nonresponsive face. These findings are substantially in agreement with those reported by Ambrose.[5]

After securing operant rates of response, Brackbill placed four infants on a continuous reinforcement schedule and the remaining four infants first on a continuous, then on an intermittent, schedule. Reinforcement consisted of the experimenter's smiling in return, speaking softly to the infant, picking it up, patting it, and talking to it. All infants were reinforced for every smiling response until they gave no fewer than four responses during each of ten consecutive five-minute intervals. After criterion had been reached, one group of infants was reinforced first on a 2:1 variable-ratio schedule, then on a 3:1 variable-ratio schedule, and finally on a 4:1 variable-ratio schedule, while the second group continued to receive reinforcement for every response. Infants placed on the intermittent-reinforcement schedule markedly increased their rates of smiling as reinforcements were less and less frequently given. During thirteen 5-minute extinction intervals, there was a decline in the mean number of responses given by both groups of infants; however, the infants who had been intermittently reinforced responded at a significantly higher rate.

Brackbill recorded the incidence of protest (crying and fussing) responses. As smiling increased, protests decreased, and vice versa. Brackbill[17] (p. 123) conceptualized her results in terms of a habit hierarchy of two responses (smiling and protest) "for which the initially differing habit strengths were first reversed by selectively reinforcing only the weaker response, and then reversed again by extinguishing that response, allowing for recovery of the first."

The major significance of Brackbill's study lies in its demonstration that the smiling response may be strengthened or weakened according to well-established learning principles. Brackbill's reinforcer involved physical contact, auditory, and visual stimulation; consequently, the relative importance of these components cannot be assessed. It is probable that conditioning would have occurred if physical contact or auditory and visual stimulation had been separately employed as reinforcers.

Investigators are in disagreement concerning the genesis of smiling responses. Some writers have regarded smiling as innately determined,[20,55,133] while others have laid emphasis on the role of instrumental or classical conditioning.[17,30,49,137,140] Smiling occurs so soon after birth that there can be little doubt that smiling, as a physiological response, is innately determined. The question remains whether there is an unconditioned stimulus or "releaser" that evokes a *social* smile. Recent evidence[153] suggests that certain auditory or visual stimuli may be "releasers" of this kind. While no definite conclusion can be reached on this point, there is no doubt that social smiles are to a large extent elicited, maintained, and modified through the presentation of visual and auditory stimuli.

STIMULI ELICITING VOCALIZATIONS

There has been no systematic study of the kind of social events that elicit infant vocalizations, other than distress signals, or of the ages at which infants first vocalize to different classes of social objects or events. Ainsworth,[3] in a study of Ganda infants, reported that from the sixth month infants vocalized more readily and more frequently when interacting with their mother than when they were in interaction with other persons. As Ainsworth points out, differential vocalization is one of the means by which infancy attachment can be maintained through a middle distance. "The implication is that however important actual physical contact may be to the human infant, many of the components of attachment and much important interaction between the infant and a loved figure involve distance receptors rather than tactual and kinesthetic modalities" (p. 102).

Modification of infants' vocal responsiveness through social reinforcement has been reported by Rheingold *et al.*[104] who successfully utilized an operant-conditioning technique to increase the frequency of vocalizations among 3-month-old infants. A baseline level of response to a silent, expressionless face was established over sessions occurring on two successive days; during the subsequent conditioning period, the experimenter smiled, make three "tsk" sounds, and touched the infant's abdomen on most of the occasions on which he vocalized. The infants' responses increased in frequency during two reinforcement sessions, which occurred on the third and fourth days of the study. On the fifth and sixth days the experimenter behaved in precisely the same manner as she did on the first and second days. During this extinction period, there was a marked decrease in vocalizations and also an increase in the infants' emotional behavior, including vocalizations indicative of distress.

Rheingold *et al.*[104] suggested that some part of the reinforcing stimulus could have acted as a social "releaser." This possibility was investigated by Weisberg,[144] who employed six groups of infants in an experimental design which also permitted a test of the relative effectiveness of a social and a nonsocial reinforcer. The presence of a nonresponding adult, social stimulation similar to that employed by Rheingold *et al.* but not contingent on the infants' vocalizing, and both contingent and noncontingent nonsocial stimulation (a door chime) all failed to produce a increase in infant vocalizations. In contrast, social stimulation contingent on the infants' vocalizing resulted in a marked increase in rate of responsiveness over a previously established baseline level. During two extinction sessions, in which the experimenter was present but nonresponsive, the socially reinforced infants' rates of vocalization decreased, though not to the baseline level.

In the Rheingold *et al.* and Weisberg studies, the social stimulus included visual, auditory, and tactual elements. Further studies in which visual, auditory, and tactual stimuli are independently presented would be of value in determining the relative importance of stimulation mediated by the distance receptors and of physical contact stimuli in modifying infant vocalizations. Moreover, investigations into the relative potency of social and nonsocial stimulation should attempt to control the complexity variable; a major defect of Weisberg's study is that his social stimulation involved three sense modalities, whereas he utilized a nonsocial stimulus that had auditory components only.

Vocalizations indicative of distress (crying, whimpering, and whining) occur immediately at birth and may be elicited by a variety of stimuli, including sudden, intense auditory or visual changes.[69,136] The fear response as delineated by J. B. Watson,[141] is elicited by sudden noises and loss of support, as well as by physically painful stimulation.

Kessen and Mandler[77] have effectively criticized theories that present all infant distress as originating from a single archetypical event or class of events producing physical pain. They point out, for example, that the startle and distress responses of infants occur to stimuli that are not physically painful and that interruption of highly practiced and well-organized responses frequently provides an occasion for the expression of distress. The observation that human beings afflicted with congenital analgesia exhibit a normal development of anxiety to nonpainful events[34,146] affords particularly strong support for the viewpoint expressed by Kessen and Mandler. Further instances of eliciting of infant distress by nonpainful stimulation are provided in the studies by Brackbill,[17] Rheingold *et al.*,[104] and Schaffer and Emerson.[116]

Kessen and Mandler[77] make the suggestion that: "in addition to the classical mechanisms of escape and avoidance of danger, anxiety is brought under control (that is, diminished or removed) by the operation of *specific inhibitors*" (p. 400). These inhibitors, according to Kessen and Mandler, need have no relation to a specific state of discomfort, privation, or pain. The authors cite nonnutritive sucking,[76] physical contact with the mother,[58] rocking, and the sight of the adult face as possible congenital or early developed inhibitors of distress.

There is considerable evidence in favor of the view that the human face serves as an inhibitor of distress (e.g. Brackbill,[17]). Other visual and auditory stimuli also seem to have this capacity. There is, in fact, a possibility that any complex novel stimulus that is capable of eliciting smiles from infants can, under certain circumstances, act as a distress inhibitor.[112]* Perhaps most of the apparently congenital inhibitors of distress produce their effect through the eliciting of responses incompatible with crying and other manifestations of distress.

Evidence of the effectiveness of a very specific kind of auditory stimulation for reducing infant distress is provided by Salk.[111] Salk measured the weight change, food intake, amount of crying, and average time taken to fall asleep of 102 neonates who were exposed to a normal heartbeat sound, recorded on tape, and of a control group of 112 neonates under ordinary hospital conditions. The infants exposed to the heartbeat cried less and took a shorter time to fall asleep than the control infants. They also gained more weight over a four-day period, in spite of the fact that the two groups of infants consumed approximately the same amount of food, a finding indicating that the experimental group probably exhibited less restless activity. Other sounds—a metronome set at 72 beats a minute and continuously recorded lullabies—were not effective in inducing sleep; moreover, when a gallop heart rate and a heartbeat of 128 beats a minute were introduced into the nursery, there was an immediate increase in the infants' crying and restlessness. Salk suggests that there is auditory imprinting to the mother's heartbeat in the human fetus during prenatal life. Whether or not Salk's suggestion receives further support, his initial findings definitely indicate the importance of some kinds of auditory stimulation for both inducing and reducing infant distress. Further evidence to this effect is provided by Weiss,[145] who found that infant activity, probably indicative of distress, was reduced through auditory stimulation by tones of

---

*B. L. White[148] agrees with this point of view on the basis of some of his unpublished research findings. He considers, however, that the factor of familiarity is also involved.

75 and 50 dB, with the louder tone producing the greater reduction.

A study with monkeys, reported by Seay *et al.*,[126] has some relevance to the issue under discussion. The experimenters separated 6- to 7-month-old monkeys from their mothers for a three-week period; the infants were placed in pairs in a cage with Plexiglass® sides through which they could see their mothers. The investigators reported that the infants showed increases in crying and in visual contacts with their mothers during separation and increases in clinging behavior when they were returned to them. The findings support Harlow's view that contact comfort is an important socialization variable, at least for monkeys. In the absence of a third experimental group of infants, not permitted visual contact with their mothers, it is impossible to tell whether the infants' distress was alleviated by permitting visual contact during the separation period. This possibility deserves exploration.

At the human level, Schaffer and Emerson[116] provide data concerning the relative potency of different kinds of social-interruption sequences for eliciting protest behavior at different ages. Changes in relative potency occurred in the course of the first eighteen months of life. In the early months of life, interruption of physical contact was more likely to evoke protest than interruption of visual contact; after the first six months, interruption of visual contact became increasingly important as an evoking stimulus. This shift in the relative potency of physical and visual contact may perhaps be attributed to an increase in the range of the infant's vision. Until vision is sufficiently developed for the form of more distant objects to be clearly perceived, separation events that commence at some distance from the infant and provide no auditory cues (for example, a mother's quietly leaving the room) can have no significance for the child.

In socializing their children, the majority of parents rely heavily on the production of distress. The view that has predominated in the child-training literature is that the effectiveness of "disciplinary" procedures derives from events that are associated with physical pain during the early stages of the child's life. Just as the alleviation of physical discomfort caused by hunger has been regarded as the crucial factor in establishing attachments, so the occurrence of physical pain in the absence of the parent has been presented as a crucial factor in the development of fears of abandonment and loss of love. An excellent example of this kind of theorizing is provided by Dollard and Miller:[32]

> Let the child get very hungry when it is alone, let it cry and not be heard or attended to, but let the quantity of stimulation in its body from hunger and from crying continue to rise. When the child is finally fed, these very strong terminal responses are reinforced and can be attached to all the stimuli which were present during the period of its intense hunger. These responses can produce stimuli of drivelike strength. Similarly responses which produce strong drives can be attached to the darkness, to the immobility of objects, to quietness, to absence of parental stimuli. Once the child has inadvertently learned to fear darkness and quietness and immobility, it will also learn to escape from the darkness into the light, from the quietness into noise, and from immobility into the presence of others (pp. 133-134).

According to this theoretical orientation, the association of isolation with physical pain gives rise to fears that later enable parents to discipline their children through techniques that threaten withdrawal of supportive parental interaction. Since there are sources of distress other than physical pain, this theorizing is of doubtful validity. In presenting their critique of traditional accounts of the development of anxiety, Kessen and Mandler[77] make the suggestion that the removal of specific inhibitors of distress or the threat of their removal may have a disinhibitory effect. The efficacy of many parental disciplinary maneuvers—isolation, threats of withdrawal of affection, ridicule, and deprivation of privileges, which often symbolize withdrawal of parental approval and affection—may well be due to disinhibition of distress. Such procedures can be effectively used by parents who have never or very rarely physically punished their children; when these procedures have not been paired with the infliction of physical pain, their effectiveness cannot be attributed to a pain-signaling function.

In this section we have presented evidence that certain kinds of auditory and visual stimulation serve to quiet a distressed infant and that the interruption of such stimulation evokes distress reactions. The efficacy of many disciplinary techniques may therefore originate from the child's visual and auditory, as well as contact comfort, experiences and have little or nothing to do with experiences of physical pain. Physical punishment is not a preferred technique of discipline in most North American homes;[125] in fact, parents who physically punish infants in the first few months of life are generally regarded as "abnormal." Consequently, opportunities for the infant's associating parent-produced pain with threats of loss of parental affection and attention are extremely limited. On the other hand, opportunities abound for the association of parental threats implying withdrawal of physical, visual, and auditory contact (affection or love) with the actual withdrawal of contact. The threat may then serve to disinhibit anxiety or distress and initiate behavior designed to reinstate parental contact.

EXPLORATORY BEHAVIOR AND PLAY PATTERNS

Investigations of the affectional systems and attachment behavior of human and monkey infants[3,59] have revealed that once a secure infant-mother attachment has been formed, the infant will use the mother as a base from which to explore its environment. A similar observation was made years ago by Arsenian,[8] who observed preschool children's reactions in a strange room in the mother's presence or absence. When left alone in the room, the children showed little exploratory activity, tending instead to remain in the vicinity of the door; in contrast, if the children were accompanied by their mother on the first session, they moved around the room and played freely with available toys.

The importance of exploratory locomotor behavior in the development of social responses is most clearly evident from research with infant monkeys.[61,110] Harlow and his co-workers observed that infant monkeys raised on mother surrogates were markedly retarded, in comparison with normally raised infant monkeys, in the development of social-play patterns. Even greater retardation was found in infant monkeys reared together in the absence of a mother.

The form that early exploratory behavior of young organisms takes is necessarily species-specific. In comparison to human neonates, newly born subhuman primates and mammals, such as dogs and cats, have relatively well developed manipulative and locomotor responses.[105] Apart from the grasping reflex, the first prehensory responses of human infants occur some time after following responses to visual and auditory stimuli have made their appearance, and integrated reaching and grasping behavior appears only in the fifth to sixth months of life.[149] Contrast this with the prehensile development of the infant monkey who can, within the second week of life, approach and grasp other monkeys and cling to its mother without assistance, even when the latter is moving rapidly.[110]

Psychologists who have sought to trace the genesis of social responses in infancy have focused on the following response to a tactual stimulus—the turning of the neonate's head to make oral contact with an object placed against its cheek.[125] In contrast, relatively little weight has until recently been given to the tracking of a moving object or head-movement directed toward sources of sound, which has been observed to occur as early as the first day of life, provided that the infant is in a state of alert inactivity.[152] The infant's visual capacities, although developed to a greater extent in respect to form perception than has customarily been supposed,[38] are admittedly restricted for the first few weeks of life;[37,62,149] nevertheless, the early occurrence of head-turning responses to visual and auditory stimulation is probably of as much importance for later social development as is the sucking reflex. Certainly, the capacity for visual and auditory responses, however rudimentary, is present soon after birth in the form of the orienting reaction.[12,90] This response, may, in fact, be the primary foundation for the infant's social development, since it is accompanied by modifications of attention that frequently bring the infant into contact with the social agents who, at the commencement of his life, provide him with most of his visual and auditory stimulation. These modifications of attention also seem to be the forerunners of responses that have been variously labeled as "curiosity" and "exploration," of which attention is an essential component.[29]*

There is some evidence that the orienting response may have considerable strength very early in an infant's life. Bronshtein et al.[18] reported that the nonnutritive sucking of neonates could be inhibited by a loud tone; however, this finding was not replicated in a subsequent study by Kaye and Levin.[75] Kasatkin and Levikova[73] conditioned the sucking response of infants, 14 to 48 days old, to a colored light by pairing the light with a bottle of milk; on the initial conditioning trials, the light stimulus evoked an orienting response which required habituation before conditioning could proceed. Demonstrations that orienting responses to auditory and visual stimuli may, very early in a child's life, interrupt or suppress the sucking reflex present a challenge to theories of social development that depict the infant's behavior as controlled almost exclusively by internal stimulation.

Most of the following responses that an infant remains capable of making during the first few months of life consist of head and eye movements in response to visual or auditory stimulation. By means of these responses he is able to explore objects at a moderate distance for some months before he can approach them through locomotion, and he can thus establish and maintain contact with his social environment. Impressed by the manner in which an infant follows social objects, particularly the mother, with its eyes, Caldwell[25] has suggested that the oculomotor following response of infants may be a human equivalent of the locomotor following response of "imprinted" birds.

The manner in which environmental factors may modify the development of visual exploratory behavior in very young infants is neatly demonstrated in a series of ongoing studies by B. L. White.[147] Institutionally reared infants who were provided with twenty minutes of daily handling over and above that received in normal caretaking situations showed, in comparison to control

---

*Wolff and White[154] have recently demonstrated that 4- and 5-day-old normal infants are capable of visually pursuing a $7\frac{1}{2}$-inch bright red circle through an arc of approximately 60 degrees.

infants, accelerated development of visual exploratory activity. Infants who were provided with a very large amount of visual stimulation, in addition to handling, exhibited initial retardation of exploratory behavior; however, after several weeks of exposure to this extra stimulation, these infants' activity increased well beyond the point reached at the same age level by control infants and by those who had received only the additional handling. In addition, pilot data suggested that salient objects, placed at a distance designed to facilitate maximum attention from infants, would greatly accelerate the development of visually directed reaching. White's data strongly support the view that stimulation in general, provided that the amount is not excessive, facilitates the development of classes of responses that are undoubtedly important for later social development.

Even when locomotor skills have been developed, the infant's exploratory behavior is stimulated and guided by input through the distance receptors. In addition, the development of adequate locomotor skills may be highly dependent on visual feedback from components of motion of the body.[149] Thus, visual and auditory stimuli are of primary importance in facilitating and maintaining locomotor exploratory activities, without which the infant's social interactions would be necessarily limited.

Moreover, an infant's contact with a mother or other familiar adult, who may serve as a secure base from which it may explore, may be maintained primarily through vision and hearing. Schaffer and Emerson[117] compared a group of infants who resisted any form of physical contact involving restraint ("noncuddlers") with infants who actively sought out physical contact ("cuddlers"). Both groups of infants used their mothers as "a haven of safety" during exploratory activities, but the groups differed in their typical mode of response to fright. Noncuddlers, rather than seeking close contact with the mother, established proximity by looking away from the frightening object and turning toward the mother or made only limited physical contact through holding the mother's skirt or hiding their faces against her knee. There may well be constitutional or early established differences among infants that are reflected in the extent to which their social attachments are developed and maintained by distance-receptor stimulation. For some restless, hyperactive infants, contact is apparently not comforting;[117] these infants may develop attachment behavior primarily on the basis of distance-receptor stimulation, which may then suffice to maintain their contact with caretakers during early exploratory activities.

Whereas Schaffer and Emerson seem to emphasize constitutional factors as a basis for individual differences among infants in the extent to which physical contact is sought during exploratory activity or play, Kagan and Lewis[70] place more weight on the role of early experiences involving maternal reinforcement of infants' physical-contact behavior. Kagan and Lewis observed the behavior of 13-month-old children in a free-play situation in the presence of their mothers; following the free-play session, the children were frustrated by being separated by a barrier from their mothers and from previously accessible toys. Children who frequently made physical contact with their mothers during play also tended to exhibit distress when frustrated: this pattern of behavior was much more characteristic of girls than of boys. Parent data indicated that mothers of these "high-touch, high-cry" children had tended to employ child-training practices involving close physical contact between mother and child. However, the precise significance of the data is difficult to determine since, according to Lewis,[86] mothers who provided much physical contact and reinforced touching behavior also tended to provide frequent distance-receptor stimulation. Like many recent multivariable studies bearing on the development of social responses in infancy and early childhood, the Kagan and Lewis experiments require and merit replication with improved dependent measures and additional controls.

Some evidence has been provided by Rheingold[103] that exploratory responses in infants as young as 3 months may be reinforced by visual and auditory feedback. Infants placed in a specially designed crib[106] were able to touch a ball that, by means of an electrical circuit, activated brief motion-picture sequences, accompanied by music. When the appearance of a motion-picture sequence was contingent on the infants' touching the ball, rates of ball touching were higher than those obtained when presentations of the visual and auditory stimuli were not contingent on the infants' responses. Preliminary investigations appeared to indicate that exploratory behavior may be strengthened merely through the visual and auditory experiences that this behavior produces, but that the behavior is more adequately maintained when the sensory feedback is complex and varied than when the stimuli presented are relatively simple and unvarying. Further data in support of the view that infants' exploratory and operant play responses can be shaped by perceptual reinforcement produced by the infants' own activities are provided by Friedlander[45] and Friedlander and Kessler.[46] Comparable findings were obtained in Butler's studies on the exploratory behavior of monkeys.[22,23]

Reports of controlled observations on the social development of blind, deaf, and deaf-blind infants, whose exploratory activities are necessarily curtailed, are conspicuously lacking in the literature on physically handicapped children. Nevertheless, it is generally agreed that defects of vision and hearing are associated with social retardation.[48] Careful comparisons of the development of infants with visual and auditory defects with that of infants with normal vision and hearing could throw considerable light on the role of the distance receptors in social development. Admittedly, there are methodological difficulties, including that of early diagnosis;[137] nevertheless, comparative studies of this kind would be worthwhile projects.*

IMITATIVE BEHAVIOR

The tendency for a person to reproduce, with a greater or lesser degree of exactness, the actions, attitudes, or emotional responses of others has generally been labeled "imitation" by experimental psychologists and "identification" in theories of

---

*Ongoing research, recently reported by R. A. Scott,[121] confirms the view that congenitally blind children tend to be socially retarded. Such children, according to Scott, display little social interaction and tend to engage in autoerotic activities involving self-stimulation. In Scott's terminology, borrowed from Mead,[94] these children fail to develop realistic "I-thou" relationships.

social and personality development. However, the various distinctions between "imitation" and "identification" that have been proposed by social scientists[97,100] are of little theoretical or practical value since both concepts refer essentially to the same behavioral phenomena.[10] The importance of imitation for the topic under discussion lies in the undeniable fact that it is almost always mediated by the distance receptors.

According to Freudian theory,[44] the relationship between a child and the person who cares for, feeds, and protects him ("anaclitic object choice") provides the foundation both for the development of imitative behavior and for the establishment of subsequent social-emotional attachments. This point of view, which has greatly influenced learning theory approaches to the problem of imitation,[97,98,125,151] ignores the possibility that the occurrence of imitative behavior may precede the formation of specific attachments and may therefore itself contribute to the development of a child's responsiveness to others.

There is considerable dispute concerning the age at which imitative responses first appear in a child's repertory. To a large extent, the issue is a semantic one, with proponents of apparently opposed views using different criteria for labeling a response as imitative. Shirley,[127] for example, reported an almost complete absence of imitative behavior among a group of fifteen infants, 54 to 74 weeks of age, when the criterion of imitation was the exact copying of complex manipulative or verbal behavior. Such a criterion is, however, far too stringent; precise and detailed copying of a model is the exception rather than the rule even among older children and adults.[79] Moreover, the development of imitative behavior is probably a continuous process in which the simpler approximate reproductions, observable in infants, are the precursors of the more exact copying that is characteristic of early childhood.

Detailed data on imitative behavior in early infancy are largely limited to records of observations on individual infants, often secured by professionally interested parents and usually focused on the imitation of adult speech.[87,101,134,138] In the absence of adequate normative data on a wide range of responses, these observations can provide only a rough indication of the times at which imitative behavior first makes its appearance.

According to Piaget,[134] the earliest precursor of imitation, the cry of a child in response to another child's cry, may occur in the first few days of an infant's life. However, the crying of another infant rapidly becomes ineffective as an eliciting stimulus,[21] and it thus seems probable that Piaget is mistaken in regarding crying in response to a cry as anything more than a distress reaction to a loud sound.* On the other hand, there is considerable evidence that infants will reproduce a variety of adult responses, at least in an approximate manner, well before attachment behavior is apparent. Zazzo[158,159] has provided records (some filmed) of imitative tongue protrusions among infants less than 1 month of age, and several observers have noted the occurrence of imitative vocalizations and mouth and hand movements well within the first half year of an infant's life.[28,101,134] While many of these investigators[87,101] agree that this early imitative behavior occurs only if the response is already in the child's repertory and the adult imitates the child first, this limitation does not reduce the significance of the behavior for early social development.

The social significance of the imitative responses of early infancy resides largely in their capacity for fostering adult-child interactions. Piaget's description[101] of an interaction sequence between his daughter and her mother provides an excellent illustration of this function:

> At 0:6 (25) J. invented a new sound by putting her tongue between her teeth. It was something like *pfs*. Her mother then made the same sound. J. was delighted and laughed as she repeated it in her turn. Then came a long period of mutual imitation. J. said *pfs*, her mother imitated her, and J. watched her without moving her lips. Then, when her mother stopped, J. began again, and so it went on. (p. 19)

J's imitative behavior evidently served to prolong and intensify the visual and auditory stimulation which her mother was

---

*J. B. Watson[142] strongly repudiates the view that the sound of an infant's crying will elicit crying from another child. The majority of writers, however, appear to disagree with Watson. Possibly there are individual differences among infants in respect to sensitivity to sounds, and disagreements arise from sampling limitations.

providing. If Schaffer and Emerson[116] are correct in their claim that stimulation of this kind is of paramount importance for the development of social attachments, the infant's capacity for approximate reproduction of adult responses assumes theoretical significance as a child-initiated contribution to the attachment process. As Church[28] points out, "imitation early becomes a vehicle of playful communication between child and adult" (p 34).

The available data on imitation in early infancy, although admittedly scanty, suggest that the infant's capacity to reproduce actions and sounds made by others manifests itself some time before specific attachments are formed. Moreover, the infant's imitative responses may prolong adult-child interactions and thus facilitate the development of attachment behavior. Since mutual interaction sequences involving imitation are, especially in the first months of a child's life, largely, if not entirely, mediated by vision and hearing, the data provide additional evidence for the importance of the role of the distance receptors in the development of social responsiveness.

RELATED THEORETICAL PROBLEMS
Arousal and Attention

In the preceding sections it has been suggested that the infant's attentiveness to socially significant stimuli may have its origin in the orienting reaction and may be facilitated by the complexity and constantly changing characteristics of the stimulation provided by the faces and voices of human caretakers. The orientation reaction is accompanied both by changes in arousal level and by modifications of attention;[12,13] moreover, there is evidence from studies with animals, children, and human adults that changes in arousal influence cue utilization and perceptual organization.[19,33,74,128] The relationships between arousal, attention, and social responsiveness are undoubtedly complex and at the present time not well understood. However, the classes of infant responses that have been discussed in this paper—smiling, vocalizations, exploration, and imitation, as well as attending responses—have all been linked in one way or another with variations in arousal. Some brief comments on research on arousal and attention are consequently in order.

One of the few well-established facts relevant to arousal responses in infants is that there are marked individual differences in autonomic reactivity and related behavioral indices, for example, activity level and crying, even among neonates,[4,57,78,109,152] and that these differences are relatively stable, certainly over the first few months of life.[89,116,135] One may speculate that individual differences in reactivity influence the extent to which attention is paid to socially relevant stimuli and consequently the rapidity with which attachment behavior develops. This suggestion is consonant with research findings on older subjects (summarized by Bandura and Walters,[10] pp. 200-203), indicating that emotional lability facilitates social learning, a process that can be achieved only if attention is given to the responses of other persons.[139]

Many observers have commented on the increased salience of attachment behavior when infants are physically or perceptually separated from a familiar adult. In fact, Schaffer and Emerson[135] employed various indices of "separation upset" as measures of attachment formation. The protest responses recorded by the investigators, varying from whimpering and lip trembling to loud consistent crying, may perhaps result from the disinhibition of "primitive" distress responses[77] that tend to terminate when a person is seen or heard by the child. Protest responses, as Salzen[112] has noted, may also be alleviated by complex, varying, nonhuman stimuli that can capture and arrest the attention of a child. It thus seems that the withdrawal of certain kinds of external stimulation may be associated with heightened arousal,[7,82] while the provision or reinstatement of external stimulation may, under some circumstances, have a quieting effect, which is often reflected in a smile. Smiling and protest may, in fact, be conceptualized as responses that are linked with different arousal levels.[17] Generally speaking, social smiling accompanies the focusing of attention on some environmental object and a lessening of general activity, whereas protest behavior, at least during early infancy, is characterized by diffuse, restless activity, as well as by crying, and a lack of prolonged attention to any single environmental event.

According to Wolff,[153] smiling becomes socially significant only when the response has acquired a certain degree of autonomy from variations in arousal state. By this, Wolff means that the smiling must occur when the infant is awake and "bright-eyed" and not when it is drowsy or in a light sleep. The sense in which Wolff employs the term "arousal" is, however, different from that which it has acquired in the writings of psychologists such as Berlyne,[12] Hebb,[66] Lindsley,[88] and Malmo,[92] whose interests have focused on the functioning of the reticular activating system. According to these latter writers, an organism's level of arousal *increases* as the organism changes from a drowsy state to one of alertness. Wolff's observations appear, therefore, to indicate not that social smiling is independent of the infant's arousal state, as this concept is generally employed, but that the infant must be in a sufficiently aroused state to attend selectively to environmental stimuli. The conclusion that may be drawn, on the basis of observations of smiling and protest behavior, is that positive social responses are most likely to occur when an infant's arousal level is within a moderate range that permits the focusing of attention on objects in its environment.

Kagan and Lewis[70] reported positive relationships between fixation times and cardiac deceleration for highly attentive 6-month-old infants, i.e. those with long fixation times, but no relationship between these variables for infants who were minimally attentive. These findings suggest that infants who are most responsive to auditory and visual stimuli also display parasympathetic effects which may have reinforcing properties.[93] The direction of any cause-and-effect relationships that may be involved are far from clear; the Kagan and Lewis findings nevertheless suggest that a relatively high degree of attention to visual and auditory stimuli is accompanied, and perhaps sustained, by modifications of neurophysiological states.

The relationships between arousal level and exploratory behavior or stimulus seeking has been discussed by a number of psychologists.[12,13,40,65-67,83,84,129] Although the relevant theories differ considerably in detail, all attempt to identify some optimal condition, either of arousal or of stimulus input or patterning, which the organism strives to maintain. Among infants, exploration seems to occur most readily when the infant is alert and active, but not overwhelmed by a large amount of intense novel stimulation;[148] "no observant parent will question the fact that babies often act in this way [i.e. manipulate and perceptually explore objects] during those periods of their waking life when hunger, erotic needs, distresses, and anxiety seem to be exerting no particular pressure"[150] (p. 320).

Any detailed discussion of theoretical approaches to the problems of "intrinsic motivation" and of the relationship between arousal level, external stimulus properties generating arousal changes or conflict, and modifications of attention cannot be undertaken within the context of the topic of this paper. It may, however, be tentatively concluded that observations of infants are consistent with the view that perceptual functioning, including the functioning of the distance receptors, is facilitated by a moderate degree of emotional arousal and that stimulation provided by the distance receptors is, in some way, rewarding for the infant. Most of the infant's visual and auditory stimulation initially occurs within the context of social-interaction sequences; consequently, evidence that there are important interactions between stimulation through the distance receptors and emotional-arousal states tangentially supports the view that this kind of stimulation can play a critical role in the development of human attachments.

Imprinting and the Critical-period Hypothesis

Several investigators[6,16,25,56,120] have been impressed by apparent similarities between "imprinting" phenomena in precocial birds and the formation of attachments by human infants. Gray[56] defined imprinting as "an innate disposition to learn the parent, or parent-surrogate, at a certain early period in life" (p. 156) and proposed that "the smiling response in human infants is the motor equivalent of the following response in animals below the higher primates" (p. 160). Caldwell[25] offered the alternative proposal that the visual following response is the human equivalent of the locomotor following response of birds, while Salk[111] has suggested that the human fetus is imprinted to its mother's heartbeat. A somewhat different point of view, mainly based on studies of the attachment behavior of dogs, is expressed by Scott,[120] who holds that, during a critical early period of development, a young animal will become attached to any animal or object with which it comes into long contact.

The value of attempting to identify parallels between specific responses of human infants to other members of its species and imprinting phenomena in birds is highly questionable. Nevertheless, the observation that imprinting in ducks normally occurs before feeding takes place has lent strength to the view that attachment behavior is not necessarily generated within the context of the feeding situation. Support for this view also comes from an experiment by Fuller (cited by Scott[120]), who demonstrated that dogs who had contact with a human being but were otherwise socially isolated became attached to this person even though he was not associated with the feeding situation. Perhaps even more significant is Fisher's finding[39] that puppies display attachment to a human with whom they have only painful physical interaction if no other social contact is available to them. Studies with animals provide evidence, then, that birds and dogs form attachments that neither originate in a hunger-reduction context nor are mediated by contact-comfort experiences. It therefore seems safe to conclude that stimulation through the distance receptors—through vision, hearing, and possibly, in the case of dogs, through smell*— may be a sufficient basis for the development of attachment behavior in some subhuman species. In view of the rapid development in human infants of distance-receptor functioning and the importance of these receptors for later human behavior, there is little reason to doubt that early distance-receptor experience may

---

*The important role of olfactory stimuli in the genesis of attachment behavior in kittens has been noted by Schneirla and Rosenblatt.[118]

not sometimes also suffice for the development of human attachment behavior.†

Research on precocial birds and dogs has led to the theory
that there is a relatively short period early in life which is critical
for the development of attachment or filiative behavior. Caldwell[25] has distinguished two, not necessarily unrelated, aspects of
this critical period hypothesis: (1) There is a critical period *beyond* which attachment behavior will not develop; and (2) there
is a critical period *during* which an organism is maximally susceptible to influences that promote attachment behavior. While the
first of these aspects has received considerable attention and support in studies of subhuman species,[119] it has received relatively
little attention in discussions of the formation of attachments by
human infants, among whom there are remarkable individual
differences in respect to the time at which specific attachments
first appear.[116] Applications of the critical period hypothesis to
human infants have, in fact, focused on the relative harmfulness
of *disruptions* of infant-caretaker relationships at different stages
of infant development. "The present evidence indicates that while
the period of 6 weeks to 6 months is a critical one for the formation and determination of social relationships, the later ages are
also *critical* with regard to psychological damage resulting from
breaking off these relationships" (Scott,[120] p. 34; italics not in
original). In this context, the term "critical" appears to lose much
of the apparent significance with which it has been endowed by
research findings on critical periods in subhuman species.

Obviously, the disruption of a specific attachment can have
no particular significance until a specific attachment has been
formed. Evidence that infants under 6 months of age are not
greatly disturbed by separation from their mothers, whereas older

---

†Cairns[24] has now provided evidence in favor of the view that an animal will
develop a relative preference for any perceptually prominent object with which it
has been continuously brought into proximity. Lambs confined with canines showed
increasing preference for their cohabitants, as opposed to members of their own
species, over a nine-week period. A similar, though less marked, increase in preference for the cohabitant was demonstrated for lambs confined with a continuously
operating television set. In a later phase of the study, lambs failed to develop
preferences for a nonoperative, perceptually dead, television set.

infants show much more disturbance,[156] provides support of the hypothesis that most infants do not develop specific attachments until the second half of the first year of life but does not have a crucial bearing on the critical-period hypothesis. Moreover, the data provided by Schaffer and Emerson[116] more directly support the former hypothesis than do clinical observations on reactions to "traumatic" separation events. The severity of a reaction to a disruption of an established affectional relationship, at any stage of life, is probably a function of the deprived person's competence to seek out and secure alternative sources of rewarding experiences. In this respect, infants are probably little less handicapped than elderly persons, for whom separation may also have both acute and relatively long-term deleterious effects.[14]

Admittedly, there is considerable evidence that the age of an infant when separation occurs and the duration of the separation period are highly significant variables in relation to both the immediate effects of the disruption of the relationship and its long-term effects on the child's social-emotional development.[15,50-54,91, 113,115,131,132,155-157] However, this evidence in no way demonstrates that disruption of a caretaker-child relationship at a particular stage of development *inevitably* proves detrimental to the infant's subsequent social adjustment. In fact, research findings indicate that the effects of separation are highly dependent on the infant's experiences during and following the separation period[156] and can, under some circumstances, have long-term beneficial effects.[85]

While the critical period hypothesis appears to receive little support from research on human infants, it seems possible that there are *events* that are critical for the development of human social behavior.[25] Under the influence of Freudian theory, clinically oriented research workers have sometimes assumed that these critical events are biologically based concomitants of "mothering."[107] The alternative view, favored in this paper, is that the events in question are not intrinsically related to the nurturant activities of a need-reducing, comfort-producing adult, but rather consist of frequent associations of the infant's own species with exteroceptive stimulation. From this latter point of view, perceptual-cognitive development, largely fostered by exteroceptive

stimulation, is essential for social development; attachment behavior occurs because certain individuals, usually of the same
species as the infant, are associated more often than others with
the perceptual-cognitive stimulation provided by environmental
events. This point of view is not purely speculative; it is supported by the evidence provided in previous sections of this paper
as well as by some of the findings concerning the effects of separation and institutionalization, cited below.

After a thorough, careful review of studies of the effect of
separation from parents in early childhood, Yarrow[156] concluded
that many of the apparently harmful effects of separation experiences can be attributed to general deprivation of stimulation—
sensory, social, and affective—which characterizes many institutional environments, rather than to the disruption of a specific
parent-infant relationship. If some consistency in caretakers and a
reasonably stimulating environment are provided, institutional
living does not appear seriously to hamper the social development
of children.[42,102] Three studies, in particular, seem to confirm the
importance of exteroceptive stimulation, particularly through
vision and hearing.

In a classic study, Dennis[31] and his wife reared twins under
conditions of minimal stimulation, avoiding the customary affectional interactions that occur between caretakers and child. In
spite of the experimenters' avoidance of fondling and other social
responses directed toward the children, the twins exhibited no
social-emotional retardation. Judging from Dennis' description
of the procedures, it seems reasonable to assume that the infants
received a considerable amount of exteroceptive stimulation both
during observation periods and while routine caretaking activities
were being carried out in an "impersonal" manner. The experimenters talked within the hearing of the infants, even if they did
not talk to them; they spent a good deal of time within sight of
the infants while recording the infants' behavior. In fact, they
may have provided as much distance-receptor stimulation for the
infants as do many natural parents. From the point of view expressed in this paper, the Dennises' findings are therefore less
paradoxical and puzzling than they have appeared to be to some

psychologists who have not favored the maturational interpretation advanced in the report of the study.

Rheingold[102] compared the social responsiveness and exploratory behavior of institutionalized infants of 3 to 4 months of age with those of home-reared infants of the same age. Contrary to expectations, she found that the institution infants were more socially responsive to the examiner than the home-reared infants and that they were in no way deficient in their exploratory responses. Rheingold was led to the conclusion that the institution provided sufficient stimulation in general to evoke visual exploration of the environment, which, she suggested, formed the basis of human sociability.

Schaffer[114] has provided a preliminary report of a comparative study of two groups of infants temporarily separated from their mothers. One group, the hospital group, had regular contact with their mothers but received little total stimulation, social or otherwise, during the separation period. The second group, the baby-home group, had no contact with their mothers during separation but received a considerable amount of social and other stimulation. On their return home, the baby-home infants established specific attachments to their mothers much more rapidly than infants in the hospital group. "In the Hospital group all but one infant took at least four weeks to establish a specific attachment, two took approximately three months to do so, and one infant had still not shown any specific attachment behavior by the time he reached the end of the first year. In the Baby-Home group, on the other hand, five of the nine infants developed a specific attachment within five days of returning home and two others did so within the second week . . . These data suggest that a prolonged acquaintance with the individual (s) with whom a specific attachment is eventually formed is less essential than the total amount of prior social stimulation received by the infant, irrespective of the source" (p. 191). Schaffer concluded by offering the hypothesis that attachment behavior is a three-stage process: ". . . an early phase in which optimal arousal is sought from all parts of the environment precedes a phase where the infant, having learned that social objects provide the best sources of such stimulation, shows indiscriminate attachment behavior to all human beings, and this finally gives way to the phase with which we are best acquainted, namely the phase of specific attachments" (p. 196).

The previous discussion has omitted consideration of an important phenomenon of human behavior—the appearance of fear of strangers, which has sometimes been regarded as the homologue of the flight response of many subhuman species.[41] In what sense, it may be asked, is this a critical event in the genesis of attachment behavior? Gray[56] has suggested that the emergence of fear of strangers marks the end of the critical period during which attachment behavior must be established, if it is to be established at all. Some support for this view has been found in Moltz's discussions of the mechanisms of imprinting in ducklings.[95,96]

According to Moltz, attachment to an imprinting object occurs in precocial birds because modifications in sensory input accompanying the approach response are associated with a parasympathetically governed organic set. The approach response is thus incompatible with sympathetically governed anxiety or fear states. Once fear has been acquired through a recognition of the distinction between familiar and strange aspects of the environment,[64] the approach response is maintained because it is accompanied by anxiety reduction. Establishment of an approach response therefore occurs during an early critical period in which the imprinting object is salient and other subsequently strange aspects of the imprinting situation are not yet noticed.*

Data on human infants[116] indicate that, generally speaking, specific attachments are evident before fear of strangers is manifested. Moreover, it is common knowledge that human infants will often exhibit intensified attachment behavior when first confronted by a strange person or environment. However, human caretakers differ in the extent to which they reduce or induce anxiety in the course of their interactions with infants.[6] If the principal caretaker frequently induces anxiety in the infant, this anxiety may generalize to other individuals in the early months

---

*Moltz's theorizing has, of course, important implications for the relationship between arousal and attention, which was discussed in the previous section.

of an infant's life; in this case, generalized anxiety may have to be extinguished before attachment behavior that is maintained by anxiety reduction can occur. Under such circumstances, prolonged attachments to a specific object may not be manifested until after the discrimination between familiar and strange has been achieved and fear of strangers has developed. Wide individual differences in the timing of the first appearance of specific attachments[116] seem to support the view that the achievement of familiar-strange discriminations does not preclude the emergence of an initial specific attachment.

Extensions to the attachment behavior of human infants of theorizing concerning imprinting and the critical period hypothesis have raised more problems than they have solved. The identification of analogies can suggest useful cause-effect hypotheses only if differences, as well as similarities, between phenomena are taken into account. However, analogical thinking concerning imprinting phenomena and the formation of human attachments has at least encouraged some developmental psychologists to break away from traditional lines of thinking concerning the origins of social responsiveness and has helped to focus attention on the possible role of distance-receptor stimulation in the genesis and maintenance of human social behavior.

A COMMENT ON DEPENDENCY

In this discussion of the development of human sociability, we have substituted the term "attachment" for the concept of dependency, which has been generally favored in the child-training literature.[9,10,27,125,151] In the first place, as we have argued elsewhere,[139] "dependency" has functioned as a semievaluative, rather than a descriptive, concept and will therefore probably prove to be of little ultimate value in conceptualizing social phenomena. Secondly, we agree with Bowlby[16] that to be dependent on someone and to be attached to someone are not the same thing. "The terms 'dependence' and 'dependency' are appropriate if we favour the theory of Secondary Drive, which has it that the child becomes oriented towards his mother because he is dependent on her as the source of physiological gratification. They are, however, inappropriate terms if we believe that dependence on physiological satisfactions and psychological attachment, although related to one another, are fundamentally different phenomena" (p. 371).

Much effort has been devoted to accounting for the manner in which a child gives up its physical dependence on its mother and substitutes interactions largely mediated by the distance receptors for the clinging, physical contact "dependency" responses of infancy and early childhood years. We maintain that attention and approval seeking are not entirely derivates of early physical dependency gratifications but are habits that are developed from the beginning of life in the course of the infant's perceptual transactions with its environment, most of which involve visual and auditory stimulation. In this connection, it is interesting to note that Sears[123] has recently provided some evidence in favor of a two-factor theory of dependency which suggests that physical contact behavior develops relatively independently of responses such as attention and approval seeking. One may speculate that whereas positive and negative reinforcement, as well as modeling,[10] of physical contact responses may be highly important in the formation of later patterns of sex behavior, the formation of psychological attachments is primarily fostered by distance-receptor experiences. Certainly, in later life the majority of social attachments are developed and maintained in the context of visual and auditory interactions and are accompanied by relatively little physical contact stimulation.

REFERENCES

1. Ahrens, R. Beitrag zür Entwicklung des Physionomie und Mimiker-kennens. *Z. Exp. Angew. Psychol.,* 2:599-633, 1954.
2. Ahrens, R. Das Verhalten des Säuglings in der Zeit zwischen erstem únd siebentem Monat. *Z. Exp. Angew. Psychol.,* 2:412-454, 1954.
3. Ainsworth, M. D. The development of infant-mother interaction among the Ganda. In B. M. Foss (Ed.), *Determinants of Infant Behaviour,* II. New York, Wiley, 1963, pp. 67-104.
4. Aldrich, C. A., Sung, C., and Knop, C. The crying of newly born babies: II. The individual phase. *J. Pediat.,* 27:89-96, 1945.
5. Ambrose, J. A. The development of the smiling response in early infancy. In B. M. Foss (Ed.), *Determinants of Infant Behaviour.* New York, Wiley, 1961, pp. 179-196.

6. Ambrose, J. A. The concept of a critical period for the development of social responsiveness in early human infancy. In B. M. Foss (Ed.), *Determinants of Infant Behaviour*, II. New York, Wiley, 1963, pp. 201-225.

7. Amsel, A. The role of frustrative nonreward in noncontinuous reward situations. *Psychol. Bull., 55*:102-119, 1958.

8. Arsenian, J. M. Young children in an insecure situation. *J. Abnorm. Soc. Psychol., 38*:225-249, 1943.

9. Bandura, A., and Walters, R. H. *Adolescent Aggression.* New York, Ronald Press, 1959.

10. Bandura, A., and Walters, R. H. *Social Learning and Personality Development.* New York, Holt, Rinehart, and Winston, 1963.

11. Berlyne, D. E. The influence of the albedo and complexity of stimuli on visual fixation in the human infant. *Brit. J. Psychol., 49*:315-318, 1958.

12. Berlyne, D. E. *Conflict, Arousal, and Curiosity.* New York, McGraw-Hill, 1960.

13. Berlyne, D. E. Exploratory and epistemic behaviour. In S. Koch (Ed.), *Psychology: A Study of a Science,* vol. 5. *The process areas, the person, and some applied fields: Their place in psychology and in science.* New York, McGraw-Hill, 1963, pp. 284-364.

14. Birren, J. E. *The Psychology of Aging.* Englewood Cliffs, N. J., Prentice-Hall, 1964.

15. Bowlby, J. *Maternal Care and Mental Health.* Geneva, World Health Organization, 1952 (WHO Monogr. Ser., No. 2).

16. Bowlby, J. The nature of the child's tie to his mother. *Int. J. Psycho-Anal., 39*:350-373, 1958.

17. Brackbill, Y. Extinction of the smiling response in infants as a function of reinforcement schedule. *Child Develpm., 29*:115-124, 1958.

18. Bronshtein, A. L., Antonova, T. G., Kamenetskaya, A. G., Luppova, N. N., and Sytova, V. A. On the development of the functions of analyzers in infants and some animals at the early stage of onto-genesis. In *Problems of Evolution of Physiological Functions.* Acad. Sci., U.S.S.R., 1958 (Dept. of Hlth, Educ., and Welf., U.S.A., Translation Service, 1960, pp. 106-116).

19. Bruner, J. S. Matter, J., and Papanek, M. Breadth of learning as a function of drive level and mechanization. *Psychol. Rev., 62*:1-10, 1955.

20. Bühler, C. *The First Year of Life.* New York, Day, 1930.

21. Bühler, C., and Hetzer, H. Das erste Verständnis für Ausdruck im ersten Lebensjahr. *Z. Psychol., 107*:50-61, 1928.

22. Butler, R. A. Incentive conditions which influence visual exploration. *J. Exp. Psychol., 48*:19-23, 1954.

23. Butler, R. A. The differential effect of visual and auditory incentives on the performance of monkeys. *Amer. J. Psychol., 71*:591-593, 1958.

24. Cairns, R. B. The Attachment Behavior of Mammals. Unpublished paper, Indiana University, 1964.

25. Caldwell, B. M. The usefulness of the critical period hypothesis in the study of filiative behavior. *Merrill Palmer Quart. Behav. Develpm.*, *8*:229-242, 1962.

26. Cantor, G. N., Cantor, J. H., and Ditrichs, R. Observing behavior in preschool children as a function of stimulus complexity. *Child Develpm.*, *34*:683-689, 1963.

27. Child, I. L. Socialization. In G. Lindzey (Ed.), *Handbook of Social Psychology*, Vol. II. Reading, Mass, Addison-Wesley, 1954. pp. 655-692.

28. Church, J. *Language and the Discovery of Reality*. New York, Random House, 1961.

29. Dember, W. N., and Earl, R. W. Analysis of exploratory, manipulatory, and curiosity behaviors. *Psychol. Rev.*, *64*:91-96, 1957.

30. Dennis, W. An experimental test of two theories of social smiling in infants. *J. Soc. Psychol.*, *6*:214-223, 1935.

31. Dennis, W. Infant development under conditions of restricted practice and minimum social stimulation. *Genet. Psychol. Monogr.*, *23*:143-191, 1941.

32. Dollard, J., and Miller, N. E. *Personality and Psychotherapy*. New York, McGraw-Hill, 1950.

33. Easterbrook, J. A. The effect of emotion on cue utilization and the organization of behavior. *Psychol. Rev.*, *66*:183-201, 1959.

34. Fanconi, G., and Ferrazzini, F. Kongenitale Analgie: Kongenitale generalisierte Schmerzindifferenz. *Helv. Paediat. Acta.*, *12*:79-115, 1957.

35. Fantz, R. L. Pattern vision in young infants. *Psychol. Rec.*, *8*:43-47, 1958.

36. Fantz, R. L. The origin of form perception. *Scient. Amer.*, *204*:66-72, 1961.

37. Fantz, R. L. Pattern discrimination and selective attention as determinants of perceptual development from birth. In A. H. Kidd and J. L. Rivoire (Eds.), *Perceptual Development in Children*. New York, International Universities Press, 1965.

38. Fantz, R. L., Ordy, J. M., and Udelf, M. S. Maturation of pattern vision in infants during the first six months. *J. Comp. Physiol. Psychol.*, *55*:907-917, 1962.

39. Fisher, A. E. The Effects of Differential Early Treatment on the Social and Exploratory Behavior of Puppies. Unpublished doctoral dissertation. Pennsylvania State Univer., 1955.

40. Fiske, D. W., and Maddi, S. A conceptual framework. In D. W. Fiske and S. Maddi (Eds.), *Functions of Varied Experience*. Homewood, Ill., Dorsey Press, 1961, pp. 11-56.

41. Freedman, D. G. The infant's fear of strangers and the flight response. *J. Child Psychol. Psychiat.*, *1*:242-248, 1961.
42. Freud, A., and Burlingham, D. *Infants Without Families*. New York, International Universities Press, 1944.
43. Freud, S. Three essays on the theory of sexuality. In J. Strachey (Ed.), *Standard Edition*, vol. 7. London, Hogarth Press, 1953, pp. 125-243. (First published in German, 1905.)
44. Freud, S. On narcissism: An introduction. In E. Jones (Ed.), *Collected Papers*, Vol. IV. London, Hogarth Press, 1925, pp. 30-59. (First published in German, 1914.)
45. Friedlander, B. Z. Techniques for Attended and Unattended Studies of Human Infants' Operant Play for Perceptual Reinforcement. Unpublished manuscript, Mental Development Center, Western Reserve University, 1964.
46. Friedlander, B. Z., and Kessler, J. W. Extended Automatic Monitoring of Infants' Spontaneous Play for Perceptual Reinforcement. Unpublished manuscript, Mental Development Center, Western Reserve University, 1964.
47. Geber, M. Problèmes posés par le développement du jeune enfant Africain en fonction de son milieu social. *Travail Hum.*, *23*:97-111, 1960.
48. Gesell, A., and Amatruda, C. S. *Developmental Diagnosis: Normal and Abnormal Child Development*. New York, Hoeber, 1941.
49. Gewirtz, J. L. The course of infant smiling in four child-rearing environments in Israel. In B. M. Foss (Ed.), *Determinants of Infant Behaviour*, III. London, Methuen, 1965.
50. Goldfarb, W. Infant rearing and problem behavior. *Amer. J. Orthopsychiat.*, *13*:249-266, 1943.
51. Goldfarb, W. Effects of psychological deprivation in infancy and subsequent stimulation. *Amer. J. Psychiat.*, *102*:18-33, 1945.
52. Goldfarb, W. Psychological privation in infancy and subsequent adjustment. *Amer. J. Orthopsychiat.*, *15*:247-255, 1945.
53. Goldfarb, W. Variations in adolescent adjustment of institutionally reared children. *Amer. J. Orthopsychiat.*, *17*:449-457, 1947.
54. Goldfarb, W. Emotional and intellectual consequences of psychologic deprivation in infancy: A revaluation. In P. H. Hoch and J. Zubin (Eds.), *Psychopathology of Childhood*. New York, Grune & Stratton, 1955, pp. 105-119.
55. Goodenough, F. L. Expression of the emotions in a blind-deaf child. *J. Abnorm. Soc. Psychol.*, *27*:328-333, 1932.
56. Gray, P. H. Theory and evidence of imprinting in human infants. *J. Psychol.*, *46*:155-166, 1958.
57. Grossman, H. J., and Greenberg, N. H. Psychosomatic differentiation

in infancy: I. Autonomic activity in the newborn. *Psychsom. Med.,* *19*:293-306, 1957.

58. Harlow, H. F. The nature of love. *Amer. Psychologist, 13*:673-685, 1958.
59. Harlow, H. F. Primary affectional patterns in primates. *Amer. J. Orthopsychiat., 30*:676-684, 1960.
60. Harlow, H. F. The development of affectional patterns in infant monkeys. In B. M. Foss (Ed.), *Determinants of Infant Behaviour.* New York, Wiley, 1961, pp. 75-88.
61. Harlow, H. F. The maternal affectional system. In B. M. Foss (Ed.), *Determinants of Infant Behaviour,* II. New York, Wiley, 1963, pp. 3-33.
62. Haynes, H. M., White, B. L., and Held, R. Visual accommodation in human infants. *Science,* 1965.
63. Haynes, H. M., White, B. L., and Held, R. Visual Accommodation in Human Infants. Unpublished paper. Massachusetts Institute of Technology, Cambridge, Mass., 1964.
64. Hebb, D. O. On the nature of fear. *Psychol. Rev., 53*:259-276, 1946.
65. Hebb, D. O. Drives and the CNS (conceptual nervous system). *Psychol. Rev., 62*:243-254, 1955.
66. Hebb, D. O., and Thompson, W. R. The social significance of animal studies. In G. Lindzey (Ed.), *Hondbook of Social Psychology,* Vol. I. Reading, Mass, Addison-Wesley, 1954, pp. 532-561.
67. Hunt, J. McV. Motivation inherent in information processing and action. In O. J. Harvey (Ed.), *Motivation and Social Interaction.* New York, Ronald Press, 1963, pp. 35-94.
68. Igel, G. J., and Calvin, A. D. The development of affectional responses in infant dogs. *J. Comp. Physiol. Psychol., 53*:302-305, 1960.
69. Illingsworth, R. S. Crying in infants and children. *Brit. Med. J., 1*:75-79, 1955.
70. Kagan, J., and Lewis, M. Studies of Attention in the Human Infant. Unpublished manuscript, Fels Research Institute, Yellow Springs, Ohio, 1964.
71. Kagan, J., and Rosman, B. L. Cardiac and respiratory correlates of attention and an analytic attitude. *J. Exp. Child. Psychol., 1*:50-63, 1964.
72. Kaila, E. Die Reactionen des Säuglings auf das menschlichte Gesicht. *Annales Universitatis Aboensis, 17* (Ser. B. Humaniora): 1-114, 1932.
73. Kasatkin, N. I., and Levikova, A. M. The formation of visual conditioned reflexes and their differentiation in infants. *J. Gen. Psychol., 12*:416-435, 1935.
74. Kausler, D. H., and Trapp, E. P. Motivation and cue utilization in intentional and incidental learning. *Psychol. Rev., 67*:373-379, 1960.
75. Kaye, H., and Levin, G. R. Two attempts to demonstrate tonal suppres-

sion of nonnutritive sucking in neonates. *Percept. Mot. Skills, 17:* 521-522, 1963.

76. Kessen, W., and Leutzendorff, A. M. The effect of non-nutritive sucking on movement in the human newborn. *J. Comp. Physiol. Psychol., 56:* 69-72, 1963.

77. Kessen, W., and Mandler, G. Anxiety, pain, and the inhibition of distress. *Psychol. Rev., 68:*396-404, 1961.

78. Kessen, W., Williams, E. J., and Williams, J. P. Selection and test of response measures in the study of the human newborn. *Child Develpm., 32:*7-24, 1961.

79. Koffka, K. *The Growth of the Mind.* London, Kegan Paul, 1924.

80. Lacey, J. I. Psychophysiological approaches to the evaluation of psychotherapeutic process and outcome. In E. A. Rubenstein and M. B. Parloff (Eds.), *Research in psychotherapy.* Washington, National Publishing Co., 1959, pp. 160-208.

81. Lacey, J. I., Kagan, J., Lacey, B. C., and Moss, H. A. Situational determinants and behavioral correlates of autonomic response patterns. In P. H. Knapp (Ed.), *Expression of Emotions in Man.* New York, International Universities Press, 1963, pp. 161-196.

82. Lawrence, D. H., and Festinger, L. *Deterrents and Reinforcements: The Psychology of Insufficient Rewards.* Stanford, Stanford Univer. Press, 1962.

83. Leuba, C. Toward some integration of learning theories: the concept of optimal stimulation. *Psychol. Rep., 1:*27-33, 1955.

84. Leuba, C. Relation of stimulus intensities to learning and development. *Psychol. Rep., 11:*55-65, 1962.

85. Lewis, H. *Deprived Children.* London, Oxford Univer. Press, 1954.

86. Lewis, M. Unpublished research, Fels Research Institute, Yellow Springs, Ohio, 1964.

87. Lewis, M. M. *Infant Speech: A Study of the Beginnings of Language.* London, Kegan Paul, 1936.

88. Lindsley, D. B. Emotion. In S. S. Stevens (Ed.), *Handbook of Experimental Psychology.* New York, Wiley, 1951, pp. 473-516.

89. Lipton, E. L., and Steinschneider, A. Studies in the psychophysiology of infancy. *Merrill-Palmer Quart. Behav. Develpm., 10:*103-117, 1964.

90. Lipsitt, L. P. Learning in the first year of life. In L. P. Lipsitt and C. C. Spiker (Eds.), *Advances in Child Development and Behavior,* vol. 1, New York, Academic Press, 1963, pp. 147-195.

91. Lowrey, L. G. Personality distortion and early institutional care. *Amer. J. Orthopsychiat., 10:*576-586, 1940.

92. Malmo, R. B. Activation: A neuropsychological dimension. *Psychol. Rev., 66:*367-386, 1959.

93. Malmo, R. B. Slowing of heart rate after septal self-stimulation in rats. *Science, 133:*1128-1130, 1961.

94. Mead, G. H. *Mind, Self, and Society*. Chicago, University of Chicago Press, 1934.
95. Moltz, H. Imprinting: Empirical basis and theoretical significance. *Psychol. Bull., 57*:291-314, 1960.
96. Moltz, H. Imprinting: An epigenetic approach. *Psychol. Rev., 70*:123-138, 1963.
97. Mowrer, O. H. *Learning Theory and Personality Dynamics*. New York, Ronald Press, 1950.
98. Mowrer, O. H. *Learning Theory and the Symbolic Processes*. New York, Wiley, 1960.
99. Murphy, L. B. Some aspects of the first relationship. *Int. J. Psycho-Anal., 45*:31-43, 1964.
100. Parsons, T. *The Social System*. New York, Free Press, 1951.
101. Piaget, J. *Play, Dreams, and Imitation in Childhood*. London, Routledge & Kegan Paul, 1951.
102. Rheingold, H. L. The effect of environmental stimulation upon social and exploratory behaviour in the human infant. In B. M. Foss (Ed.), *Determinants of Infant Behaviour*. New York, Wiley, 1961, pp. 143-171.
103 Rheingold, H. L. Controlling the infant's exploratory behaviour. In B. M. Foss (Ed.), *Determinants of Infant Behaviour*, II. New York, Wiley, 1963, pp. 171-175.
104. Rheingold, H. L., Gewirtz, J. L., and Ross, H. W. Social conditioning of vocalizations in the infant. *J. Comp. Physiol. Psychol., 52*:68-73, 1959.
105. Rheingold, H. L., and Keene, G. C. Transport of the human young. In B. M. Foss (Ed.), *Determinants of Infant Behaviour*, III. London, Methuen, 1965.
106. Rheingold, H. L., Stanley, W. C., and Cooley, J. A. Method for studying exploratory behavior in infants. *Science 136*:1054-1055, 1962.
107. Ribble, M. A. *The Rights of Infants*. New York, Columbia Univer. Press, 1943.
108. Ribble, M. A. Infantile experiences in relation to personality development. In J. McV. Hunt (Ed.), *Personality and the Behavior Disorders*, II. New York, Ronald Press, 1944, pp. 621-651.
109. Richmond, J. B., and Lipton, E. L. Some aspects of the neurophysiology of the newborn and their implications for child development. In L. Jessner and E. Pavenstadt (Eds.), *Dynamic Psychopathology in Childhood*. New York, Grune & Stratton, 1959, pp. 78-105.
110. Rowell, T. The social development of some rhesus monkeys. In B. M. Foss (Ed.), *Determinants of Infant Behaviour*, II. New York, Wiley, 1963, pp. 35-49.
111. Salk, L. Mothers' heartbeat as an imprinting stimulus. *Trans. New York Acad. Sci., 24*:753-763, 1962.

112. Salzen, E. A. Visual stimuli eliciting the smiling response in the human infant. *J. Genet. Psychol., 102:*51-54, 1963.

113. Schaffer, H. R. Objective observations of personality development in early infancy. *Brit. J. Med. Psychol., 31:*174-183, 1958.

114. Schaffer, H. R. Some issues for research in the study of attachment behaviour. In B. M. Foss (Ed.), *Determinants of Infant Behaviour,* II. New York, Wiley, 1963, pp. 179-196.

115. Schaffer, H. R., and Callender, W. M. Psychologic effects of hospitalization in infancy. *Pediatrics, 24:*528-539, 1959.

116. Schaffer, H. R., and Emerson, P. E. The development of social attachments in infancy. *Monogr. Soc. Res. Child Developm., 29:* No. 3 (Serial No. 94), 1964.

117. Schaffer, H. R., and Emerson, P. E. Patterns of response to physical contact in early human development. *J. Child Psychol. Psychiat., 5:* 1-13, 1964.

118. Schneirla, T. C., and Rosenblatt, J. S. Behavioral organization and genesis of the social bond in insects and mammals. *Amer. J. Orthopsychiat., 31:*223-253, 1961.

119. Scott, J. P. Critical periods in the development of social behavior in puppies. *Psychosom Med., 20:*42-54, 1958.

120. Scott, J. P. The process of primary socialization in canine and human infants. *Monogr. Soc. Res. Child Develpm., 28:* No. 1 (Serial No. 85), 1963.

121. Scott, R. A. The Socialization of the Blind Child. Unpublished paper. Russell Sage Foundation, New York, 1964.

122. Sears, R. R. Identification as a form of behavioral development. In D. B. Harris (Ed.), *The Concept of Development.* Minneapolis, Univer. of Minnesota Press, 1957, pp. 149-161.

123. Sears, R. R. Dependency motivation. In M. R. Jones (Ed.), *Nebraska Symposium on Motivation.* Lincoln, Univer. Nebraska Press, 1963, pp. 25-64.

124. Sears, R. R., Whiting, J. W. M., Nowlis, V., and Sears, P. S. Some child-rearing antecedents of aggression and dependency in young children. *Genet. Psychol. Monogr., 47:*135-236, 1953.

125. Sears, R. R., Maccoby, E. E., and Levin, H. *Patterns of Child Rearing.* New York, Harper, 1957.

126. Seay, B., Hansen, E., and Harlow, H. F. Mother-infant separation in monkeys. *J. Child Psychol. Psychiat., 3:*123-132, 1962.

127. Shirley, M. M. *The First Two Years: A Study of Twenty-five Babies.* Vol. II. *Intellectual Development.* Minneapolis, Univer. of Minnesota Press, 1933.

128. Smock, C. D. Effects of motivational factors on perceptual-cognitive efficiency of children who vary in intellectual levels. Co-operative Research Project No. 790. Purdue University, 1962.

129. Smock, C. D., and Holt, B. T. Children's reactions to novelty: An experimental study of curiosity motivation. *Child Develpm., 33:*631-642, 1962.
130. Spears, W. C. Assessment of visual preference and discrimination in the four-month-old infant. *J. Comp. Physiol. Psychol., 57:*381-386, 1964.
131. Spitz, R. A. Hospitalism: An inquiry into the genesis of psychiatric conditions in early childhood. *Psychoanal. Study Child, 1:*53-74, 1945.
132. Spitz, R. A. Hospitalism: An inquiry into the genesis of psychiatric conditions in early childhood: A follow-up report. *Psychoanal. Study Child, 2:*113-117, 1946.
133. Spitz, R. A. The smiling response: a contribution to the ontogenesis of social relations. *Genet. Psychol. Monogr., 34:*57-125, 1946.
134. Stern, C., and Stern, W. *Die Kindersprache: eine psychologische und sprachtheoretische Untersuchung,* (4th ed.), Leipzig, Barth, 1928.
135. Thomas, A., Chess, S., Birch, H., and Hertzig, M. E. A longitudinal study of primary reaction patterns in children. *Comprehensive Psychiat., 1:*103-112, 1960.
136. Thompson, G. G. *Child Psychology.* Boston, Houghton Mifflin, 1952.
137. Thompson, J. Development of facial expression of emotion in blind and seeing children. *Arch. Psychol., No. 264,* 1-47, 1941.
138. Valentine, C. W. The psychology of imitation with special reference to early childhood. *Brit. J. Psychol., 21:*105-132, 1930.
139. Walters, R. H., and Parke, R. D. Social motivation, dependency, and susceptibility to social influence. In L. Berkowitz (Ed.), *Advances in Experimental Social Psychology,* I. New York, Academic Press, 1964, pp. 231-276.
140. Washburn, R. W. A study of the smiling and laughing of infants in the first year of life. *Genet. Psychol. Monogr., 6:*397-537, 1929.
141. Watson, J. B. *Psychology From the Standpoint of a Behaviorist.* Philadelphia, Lippincott, 1919.
142. Watson, J. B. *Behaviorism.* Chicago, Univer. of Chicago Press, 1924.
143. Watson, J. S. Unpublished study. The Merrill-Palmer Institute of Human Development and Family Life, Detroit, 1964.
144. Weisberg, P. Social and nonsocial conditioning of infant vocalizations. *Child Develpm., 34:*377-388, 1963.
145. Weiss, LaB. A. Differential variations in the amount of activity of newborn infants under continuous light and sound stimulation. *Univer. Iowa Stud. Child. Welf., 9:*9-74, 1934.
146. West, L. J., and Farber, I. E. The role of pain in emotional development. In *Explorations in the Physiology of Emotions (Psychiat. Res. Rep., No. 12,* 119-126, 1960).
147. White, B. L. The Development of Perception During the First Six Months of Life. Paper presented at the Annual Meeting of the

American Association for the Advancement of Science. Cleveland, Ohio, 1963.

148. White, B. L. Personal communication, 1964.

149. White, B. L., Castle, P., and Held, R. Observations on the development of visually-directed reaching. *Child Develpm., 35*:349-364, 1964.

150. White, R. W. Motivation reconsidered: The concept of competence. *Psychol. Rev. 66*:297-333, 1959.

151. Whiting, J. W. M., and Child, I. L. *Child Training and Personality: A Cross-cultural Study.* New Haven, Yale Univer. Press, 1953.

152. Wolff, P. H. Observations on newborn infants. *Psychosom. Med., 21*: 110-118, 1959.

153. Wolff, P. H. Observations on the early development of smiling. In B. M. Foss (Ed.), *Determinants of Infant Behaviour,* II. New York, Wiley, 1963, pp. 113-134.

154. Wolff, P. H., and White, B. L. Unpublished paper. Harvard Medical School and Massachusetts Institute of Technology, 1964.

155. Yarrow, L. J. Maternal deprivation: Toward an empirical and conceptual re-evaluation. *Psychol. Bull., 58*:459-490, 1961.

156. Yarrow, L. J. Separation from parents during early childhood. In M. L. Hoffman and L. W. Hoffman (Eds.), *Review of Child Development Research,* Vol. I. New York, Russell Sage Foundation, 1964, pp. 89-136.

157. Yarrow, L. J., and Goodman, M. S. *Effects of Change in Mother Figure During Infancy on Personality Development.* Progress Report, 1963. Family and Child Services, Washington, D.C., 1963.

158. Zazzo, R. In J. M. Tanner and B. Inhelder (Eds.), *Discussions on Child Development,* vol. 1. London, Tavistock Publications Ltd., 1956, p. 72.

159. Zazzo, R. Le problème de l'imitation chez le nouveau-né. *Enfance, 10*: 135-142, 1957.

A FRETTING INFANT ceases to cry when he is picked up; a newborn held to an adult's shoulder scans his surroundings. Both behaviors indicate the importance of contact to the young infant. Contact, in times of stress and nonstress, helps the infant to first differentiate himself from another, and later his caretaker from yet another person.

The sense of touch is also important for cognitive development as the infant manipulates and explores by handling objects. Touch, pressure, and kinesthesis are part of the near receptor sense system, whereas vision and audition are distance receptors. Early in life, incoming stimuli related to the near receptor system have more impact on infant behavior, but as the distance receptors mature the baby relies more on vision for learning than on any other sense. However, the sense of touch does not lose its importance. We touch to increase our sensory imput as an explanation or a reinforcement of what has been seen. In addition, we communicate affect by touch.

In the following paper, Dr. Lawrence K. Frank discusses the role of touch as a means of communication, and the formation of personality in relation to tactile experiences. In a thought-provoking analysis, Dr. Frank also discusses how simple tactual responses are elaborated into complex signal systems by the mechanism of language.

Chapter 5

Tactile Communication

LAWRENCE K. FRANK

INTRODUCTION

T HE SKIN is the outer boundary, the envelope which contains the human organism and provides its earliest and most elemental mode of communication. Despite its often crucial role in human behavior, touch or tactile experiences have been largely neglected, especially by those concerned with personality development and expression. In view of their pervasive role in human communication, this statement of what tactile experiences involve may offer clues to further study and provide some insights into the large significance of tactile communications.

This paper will attempt to outline the processes of tactile communication in terms of the following topics: (1) tactile-cutaneous processes; (2) tactile experiences in personality development; (3) cultural patterning of tactile processes; (4) pathology of tactilism; (5) need for further research.

Each of these topics, if adequately treated, would call for extended discussion exceeding the limits of this paper and the writer's competence. Therefore the following is offered to focus discussion and to evoke the contributions of others in helping to delineate this relatively neglected aspect of human experience and of communication. The references given in this paper are not to be taken as an exhaustive bibliography, but rather as suggestive of leads which the writer has come upon, but in many cases has not been able fully to explore.

As a theoretical basis for this exposition, it is assumed that there is a series of communicative processes, of recognition and response to signals, to signs and to symbols, initially received

Reprinted, and abridged, from *Genetic Psychology Monographs*, *56*:209-255, 1957. By permission.

through the various sensory processes. Thus the infant as an organism, with the wisdom of the body and its inherited neuromuscular, sensory, and physiological functional capacities, arrives with a repertory of signal recognition and response. He is sensitive, in greater or less degree, to the biological *signals* received from the environing world, including human beings and from his internal functioning, and he responds to these in the naïve inherited patterns of reflexes such as grasping, Moro, Babinski, coughing, yawning, sneezing, swallowing, regurgitating, lid and pupillary reflexes, and through various sensory processes, gustatory, olfactory, visual, auditory, taste, smell, light-dark, noise and especially tactile, through which he receives signals such as warm-cold, pain, pressures. These processes initially function with little or no discrimination, although there are obviously individual differences in thresholds which may vary from time to time as the infant's internal states are altered, especially when ill, fatigued, or emotionally disturbed.

When the infant receives two signals more or less concomitantly, as in conditioned reflex experiments, the second unconditional and previously indifferent signal may become a surrogate for the first, becoming a *sign* and evoking the response previously called out by the biologically adequate signal. Thus, the infant begins to enlarge his repertory of recognition and response, learning to exhibit responses to *signs,* signifying what is occurring or about to occur.

Later on, the infant learns to recognize various signals and signs as *symbols* which are defined by others. Not only are these *symbols* pointed out and made apparent to the child by an adult, but the response to these symbols is also defined and established by the adult so that the child learns to perceive and then to respond in patterns which are not the products of trial and error searching, or fixation by rewards and punishment; nor are they random, improvised activities or inherited gestalts.*

---

*"Symbols—in the proper sense of this term—cannot be reduced to mere signs. Signals and symbols belong to two different universes of discourse; a signal is a part of the physical world of being; a symbol is a part of the human world of meaning. Signals are operators; symbols are designators." Cassirier, E., *Essay on Man.* Anchor Edition, p. 51.

Each symbol is culturally defined in a context or field, and the response thereto is culturally patterned and prescribed so that the human child learns whatever tradition prescribes as appropriate for such symbols. Moreover, the child is usually eager to learn these culturally patterned symbols and to exhibit the prescribed responses thereto which he sees or hears others doing. As contrasted with the various theories of learning now current, we might say that this cultural learning, once started, continues like an autocatalytic process, insofar as the child, without specific immediate rewards and punishments, without reduction of tension or reenforcement in the usual sense, strives to live in the adult world, however difficult or frustrating he may find his attempts to master it. He learns to learn,† as symbols and concepts, especially language, provide entrance into the adult world and guides to its understanding. Thus the infant-child begins to recognize and to respond to *symbols* which are culturally patterned meanings; he learns to impute these meanings to the world and to human beings and to exhibit the appropriate conduct thereto. Nothing in the signal-sign before such learning can evoke this symbolic response which also is rarely or ever exhibited without such learning. Moreover, the response to a symbol may be a newly learned response not in his original repertory.

We may observe in this process how a basic biological awareness becomes selectively focused to include (and therefore to exclude) only that which is relevant in the multiplicity of events; how this selective awareness becomes patterned perception as the individual learns to perceive what he is ready to recognize and respond to, and to impute meaning to what he perceives.

Thus the person creates, as it were, his own stimuli by evoking from the world what has been established, for him, as meaningful and significant for eliciting the appropriate responses, as culturally patterned.[17] With the development of language the child begins to develop concepts and symbols as ways of organizing experience, as patterns for stabilizing the environment, maintaining a more steady threshold in the face of the continual flux of experience.[22] Then he interprets that version of experience in terms of

---

†Learning to learn has been termed deutero-learning by Gregory Bateson.[2]

his cultural patterns. The individual thereby is able to impose some order and meaning upon the world, relating himself to events and people through the cultural-social patterns which he has learned and uses, in his own idiosyncratic fashion.

This approach enables us to trace the sequential process whereby the organism transforms all of his biological needs and functional capacities into the purposive, patterned conduct and relations for living in a symbolic cultural world and then participating in the social world, while continuing to be and to function as an organism and to maintain his own idiomatic life space or private world.[17] Whatever the individual organism learns as he becomes a human personality may be viewed as an elaboration, refinement, transformation of his basic sensorimotor and biological functions which continue to operate, but in the patterns and in relations to the world as he has learned to perceive events and to code them and to deal with them in his patterned responses.

Thus, it is essential that we try to clarify the role of various functional and sensory processes as basic to all human communication and to recognize more clearly the significance of tactual experience, here termed tactilism.

Since the child must establish and maintain continual intercourse with the world, we may view this process of development and maturation in terms of communication. Beginning with the primary physiological functioning (eating, eliminating, etc.) and sensory awareness of, and naïve spontaneous responses to, the world, especially persons, the child may be viewed as learning to replace these initial modes of communication with patterned purposeful practices and relations which involve the establishment of signs and symbols for communication. As indicated, these signs and symbols serve as surrogates for the primary signals but also they function as uniquely human modes of communication, so that the individual increasingly lives in a symbolic world and increasingly seeks symbolical fulfillments, especially in his interpersonal relations. The extent and elaboration of these symbolic processes and the problems of communication they present reflect and express the cultural traditions of each people who may be found with different degrees of elaboration of communication.

As pointed out later, tactual sensitivity is one of the primary modes of communication and of orientation. While tactile communication is never wholly superseded, it is elaborated by the symbolic process. "Vocal language has a very great technical advantage over tactile language; but the technical defects of the latter do not destroy its essential use."* Thus in many interpersonal relations tactile "language" functions most effectively and communicates more fully than vocal language. Moreover, the meaning and full significance of many symbols depend upon prior tactile experiences which give the symbol both its meaning and its affective richness. "The direct animal intuitions aren't rendered by words; the words merely remind you of your memories of similar experiences".† Thus we may say that in all symbolic communications such as language, verbal or written, the recipient can decode the message only insofar as his previous experiences provided the necessary meaning and the affective, often sensory, coloring and intensity to give those symbolic messages their content.

The frequency of tactile figures of speech, for example, in English speech, illustrates this. Thus we repeatedly say, "I am touched," or "I feel" which implies both a tactile and an emotional response. Experiences are described as "touching," while many adjectives such as harsh, rough, smooth, tender, warm, cold, painful, imply a tactile sensation or experience even when used to describe nontactile events. Without prior tactile experiences, these adjectives would carry little meaning.

Since cultures differ in the use of symbolic communication, especially in use of written languages, the more highly elaborated symbolic cultures, which rely so largely upon written communication, assume that a person has had these early tactile experiences, which, as we may observe in our own culture, may be denied or curtailed in the infancy of some children. On the other hand, those cultures which provide rich and prolonged tactile experiences, carrying the baby next to mother's body and deferring weaning until late or keeping the baby swaddled or on a cradle board,

---

*Cassirier, E., *Essay on Man*. Anchor Edition, p. 56.

†Huxley, A., *After Many a Summer Dies the Swan*. Avon Edition, p. 130.

may by so much limit the development of many kinds of symbolic recognition and response. Another aspect of this may be to contrast these cultures which rely largely upon signal communication and utilize symbols and concepts to a limited extent, while another culture may subordinate signals and rely chiefly upon symbols and concepts. Again to quote Cassirier, "A sign or signal is related to the thing to which it refers in a fixed and unique way;" "A symbol is not only universal but extremely variable," so that communication through symbols enlarges the ambiguity of messages, increases the "noise" and calls for redundancy, all of which is enhanced when the traditional symbols become less clear and acceptable and so are either redefined with new meanings or superseded by new symbols which only slowly are accepted.

It seems necessary, if not desirable, in this discussion to accept a transactional conception.[10] This transactional process may be distinguished from the familiar action, reaction, and interaction of classical physics by recognizing that *action* implies self action, as in animism, or an autonomous clockwork which rarely or ever occurs except perhaps in the spontaneous emission of a quanta of energy; that *reaction* implies an alteration of the inertia of a particle or body under an impact from outside which moves it, changes its direction of movement or alters its motion; that *interaction* implies dual *reactions* where two bodies receive impacts from each other and react accordingly. In *transactions* we are concerned with the activity of an organism which evokes messages from the environment, including persons, and responds to those messages in terms of their meaning for him, with patterned activities that are not naïve reactions, but are the products of past experiences under adult guidance. Thus the transactional process involves reciprocal, circular relations, like a feedback, with the participating persons tuned or prepared for such circular, reciprocal communications. The messages are governed as much by the intended receiver as by the intent of the sender, and each message evokes a response from the other, as contrasted with a linear reaction or interraction.

The individual may be seen as actively participating in the communication process; he does not passively await a stimulus, but actively scans the world for the kind of messages he is ready to receive and often tries to evoke those messages. This goes beyond the familiar stimulus-response formula of a linear relation, necessitates a circular, reciprocal relationship in which the two persons communicating by their responses to each other evoke reciprocal responses as a dialectical process or as resonance.

Here we see what G. N. Mead described as "taking the role of the other," since the sender of a message assumes that the receiver, while having different ways of thinking and of symbol recognition and response, will receive that message, exhibiting some shared conceptions, and will respond. This response may not be what is expected or desired, but it is more or less responsive to the message because in turn the receiver of the message, partially at least, "takes the role of the other" when decoding or interpreting it and replying. Probably the "taking of the role of the other" becomes more significant, even crucial, in sending or receiving signals, such as direct tactile messages which may not have the culturally defined meanings of linguistic messages and other signs and symbols. If the symbols of each one are too divergent, neither can take the role of the other or communicate adequately except by gestures and other signals, as we discover when in another culture.[41]

While symbols are essential to interpersonal communication on a human level, they are also essential for communication with the self since we think of ourselves in images of the self and rely upon a variety of linguistic symbols to orient and guide our activities, especially in reveries, fantasy, inner speech and reflective thinking.[60]

The role of emotional reactions and persistent affective responses (anxiety, guilt, hostility) in communications needs to be more fully recognized and further clarified, especially since every message sent and received by a person evokes some physiological change which if of sufficient magnitude or persistence we call emotional or affective.[15] The communication between two persons may be governed more by these physiological emotional reactions than by the content of the message especially since the coding of a message may be warped or distorted by the emotional reaction of the sender. The *quality* or *intent* of a message, as contrasted with its content, may be conveyed by the emotional coloring-tone of voice, facial expression, gestures, or lightness or heaviness of touch and the recipient may respond largely to this intent or quality. Thus small children often respond more to quality than to content, hearing the tone of voice more than the words spoken by a parent, and responding to the kinesic messages.[5]

This suggests that in communications we may observe the transmission and reception of symbolic content *along with signals* so that the recipient of such dual messages may respond simultaneously to the content (as he has decoded it symbolically) and also to the signal which evokes the physiological responses we call emotional reaction or affection response. This ambiguity may be deliberate and indeed in some cultures it may be an accepted convention, as in joking, teasing, irony, sarcasm, especially among certain castes, classes, or in dealing with another age group, as parent to child, or the initiators to the pubertal boy or girl. As indicated later, there are various kinds of tactilism when an individual evokes direct tactile signals, as in masochism, or reassuring tactile contacts to confirm and reenforce verbal messages of affection, or gives contradictory tactile messages, in play and teasing.[1]

Tactile experiences considered as messages and responses are exceedingly diverse and capable of an amazing variety of transformations in human communication, where, as in language, we must recognize both the cultural patterning and the idiosyncratic deviations and elaborations.

The skin, according to the textbooks, is sensitive to warm-cold, pain, and pressure, with varying thresholds to stimulation. The awareness or perception of warmth or cold is, however, relative to the state of the organism, including emotional reactions, immediately prior experience and earlier experience, such as habituation (e.g. "chemical fingers"), also impairment of homeostasis. Pain likewise may be elicited in varying degrees, although Hardy *et al.* assert a constant threshold to pain produced by a heat lamp upon the forehead.[25] An altered awareness of pain has been observed in individuals under different circumstances, such as fighting, and especially strong sexual or emotional disturbances (which may be exhibited in higher or lower thresholds to pain). And as indicated later (Pathology), there may be acute hypersensitivity as well as anesthesias to pain or any tactile stimulation, a masochistic enjoyment of pain, and a variety of aberrant responses to experiences exhibited in and through the skin (stigmata).

Head suggested the two terms *protopathic* and *epicritic* sensory awareness; protopathic being the awareness of the undifferentiated, more or less massive, impacts of noxious, harmful or painful stimuli; epicritic being the capacity for discriminating through tactile contacts, especially in purposive seeking or skillful manipulations. This distinction, whether or not structurally present in the nerves, calls attention to the two phases or stages in tactile experiences which may be received as gross undifferentiated tactile contacts or pressures, and the finely differentiated contacts of varying intensity and tempo. The first often evokes avoidance although in some cultures close tactile contacts are frequently sought[3] and, of course, are present in sexual intercourse. The second involves not only discrimination of textures, shapes, elasticity, etc., but also manipulations of what is perceived tactually. Tactile perception always involves some kind of contact or impact and may be increased by training or decreased by habituation.

The skin is the largest organ of the body with a variety of functions,[48] including the crucial function of acting as a thermostat for regulating the homeostatic processes. Being exposed to the world it receives the direct impacts of the environment which it mediates to the organism. Also, the human skin is being continually renewed in the epidermis and is richly provided with sweat glands, except for a few surfaces, and with apocrine glands under the arm (which do not function until puberty), and with sebaceous glands at the roots of hair. The skin has both a taste and an odor. Thus sweat is salt and secretions from various areas of the body, especially the apocrine glands and the genital areas, may be considered as messages which have a highly stimulating effect on others. Unlike many other mammals, the human body has only vestigial body hair and therefore the human skin is more exposed to the world and is probably more sensitive. Moreover, movements of the hair of the body stimulate various cutaneous sensations by greater or less follicular displacements. Thus, stroking the hair "against the grain" may tickle or be painful, while "with the grain," as the hair lays naturally, may be pleasant, soothing, and reassuring.

There are sympathetic connections to the sweat glands and to the capillaries just under the skin, but until recently these have not been considered as conducting tactile stimuli.[33,52] As is well known, the sweat glands function not only in response to heat, but also as the human subject undergoes stress and emotional reactions of greater or less magnitude—the so-called psycho-galvanic reflex. The capillaries also dilate and contract under similar stimulation of heat-cold and of emotional reaction, as shown by blushing and pallor in various psychosomatic disorders, like Reynaud's disease.

Rats which have been gentled are better able to metabolize food and are less susceptible to surgical shock,[26] and various forms of experimentally produced convulsions, etc.[6] Licking, nuzzling, cuddling of young mammals by the mother is a form of tactual stimulation that apparently has an important function in the care and rearing of the young. Kittens cannot urinate or defecate unless the mother licks the anus or urethra and thereby elicits evacuation.[51] Rats raised from birth with a cardboard ruff around their necks to prevent licking their bodies were less capable as adults of caring for their own young by licking them.[4] Pavlov is reported to have induced sleep in dogs by applying rhythmic electrical simuli of low intensity to the skin of the animal.

While we think of the skin as the outer integument exposed to the world, the gut, from the mouth to the anus, is exposed to material from the environment and is lined with epithelial cells not unrelated to the skin and derived from the same embryological layer as skin and nervous system. It is also significant that end organs for tactile stimuli are richly provided in and around the mouth and anus, in the male and female genitals, and are apparently more numerous or sensitive in the skin adjacent to these parts, the so-called erogenous zones or areas. Apparently the human female is tactually sensitive all over her body.[43]

The tactile sensitivity of the body differs from location to location, as dramatically shown by the several erogenous zones, the specific areas sensitive to being tickled and the increased or decreased sensitivity produced by repeated experiences, such as shaving the face, plucking the beard, eyebrows or body hair, calloused hands, soles of feet, etc.

Years ago E. A. Bott at Toronto found that the third, or ring finger, was passively the most sensitive to a hair aesthesiometer *under controlled laboratory conditions,* while the forefinger was much more sensitive when being used purposefully to detect the presence of a hair concealed under a piece of cigarette paper. This indicates as in vision and hearing, that the individual has a highly selective and variable awareness and an idiosyncratically patterned perception especially when engaged in goal-seeking, purposive conduct. What the individual perceives is not a passive response to a stimulus but an active creating or evoking of the stimulus for which he is prepared, or to which he is expecting to respond.

Most motor activities are oriented by tactile stimulation: the hands, fingers, even the feet, are guided by touch. Thus the function of the opposed thumb-finger, which is uniquely human, is governed by tactile stimulation and discrimination, guided by visual cues.[47] As Wolfe has remarked:

> The *hand* as both a tool of learning about the outside world and as an organ of spatial sensibility can be considered the fundamental vehicle of the structure of thought. Spatial differentiation goes with physical as well as mental "balance," and gives to perception the tridimensional aspect essential to the orientation of man in the outside world and to its representation in his mind. One can therefore say that the hand as an organ of sensibility assumes spatial or tri-dimensional imprints of the outer world in the cortex of the brain.[67]

Since the adult or older child exhibits such an array of smooth, coordinated and often highly skillful motor activities, it is often forgotten how much prolonged learning and especially tactile experience were required earlier to achieve these motor patterns. Also, the individual rarely recalls how, in early life, he relied upon touch for his initial orientation to the spatial dimensions of the world and of people, being guided by varying pressures and resistances, bumps, mild or severe pain, and by warmth and cold, textures and elasticity for establishing his later coordinations in which visual signs (size, shape, appearance, colors, distances, etc.) function as surrogates for these primary tactile signals from which he learned initially.

We can say that the skin, as an organ of communication for both sending and receiving messages, is highly complex and versatile, with an immense range of functional operations and a wide repertory of responses. These can be understood only by assuming a more richly endowed sensory-nervous process than the warm-cold, pain-pressure categories. It is probable that sympathetic innervation, perhaps that of the sweat glands and capillaries, is also conductive to the viscera and to other organ systems, thereby accounting for the soothing effect of rhythmic patting and caressing on a baby, also of rough handling which may evoke emotional reactions.[33,35,52] In so far as capillary dilation and constriction by cold or warm either initiates or accelerates large alterations in circulation of the blood, with concomitant changes in respiration and glandular secretion, the skin may be regarded as one of the major components of the homeostatic process.[34] There are varying thresholds to tactual stimulation as when the subject being stimulated may respond to the same stimulation in different ways at different times, according to the time, place, and state of the individual when receiving or seeking such tactual contacts. There are also apparently alterations in sensitivity-response with age, as shown by the increased awareness of the skin and frequent attention (scratching, etc.).

A person who is strongly reacting emotionally, as in acute fear or pain, or grief, may be able to recover his physiological equilibrium through close tactual contacts with another sympathetic person. Thus, as will be discussed later, patting the baby rhythmically not only soothes him, but apparently promotes well being and metabolic efficiency. Babies and children especially require these contacts to recover from acute disturbances. Prolonged deprivation of such tactual contacts and soothings may establish in the baby persistent emotional or affective responses to the world, since his initial biological reactions to threats have not been allayed and hence may become chronic.

The human organism is engaged in continual intercourse with the environment. It continually receives and responds to messages coming as changing air pressures and breezes or winds of varying impacts, being warmed or cooled, exposed to light of varying intensity in the sun, etc., to ultraviolet and other radiations, including cosmic rays, to shorter waves, such as sound, to liquids, such as fog, rain, bathing. These impacts are all initially received by the skin, through which varying impulses and internal processes take place of large significance for organic well being. Caressing, again a rhythmic minimal tactual stimulation, not warm-cold or pain or pressure in the sense of eliciting deeper kinesthetic or muscle sense, also provides a sensitive mode of communication of immense significance in adult life as exhibited in intimacy and affectionate relations.

It has been found practical and effective to administer various medical treatments through the skin[65] by electrical conduction, by rubbing into the skin, such as sex hormones, to produce Vitamin D in the organism by exposure to ultraviolet light, and to soothe and relax disturbed and excited mental patients by prolonged immersion in warm water. These are elaborations and refinements of the ancient practices of applying poultices and other mixtures to the skin for the treatment of internal conditions, all indicating that the skin is a conductor of many different kinds of substances and energy transformations of which touch and the four classes of tactual sensation are only limited examples.

Tactual sensitivity is probably the most primitive sensory process appearing as a tropism, thigmotaxis, in lower organisms. Many infra-human organisms are oriented by their feelers or antennae by which they *feel* their way through life. It is also the primary mode of orientation to the world in organisms living underground, in fish and probably many reptiles. Tactual sensitivity operates before the appearance of other sensory processes, except perhaps the chemical sensitivity of organisms to alterations in their fluid medium (reaction to heat-cold, acidity-alkalinity), presence or absence of specific chemical substances, and later to odors. Even smell may be considered as a refined tactual response —the airborne particles impinging upon the olfactory organs.

Being such a primitive mode of reception and orientation, tactual sensitivity is of large significance in the early development of the infant, both as an embryo and as a foetus, and in the early years of life. Also, being the primary mode of infantile communication, tactile experiences are crucial in later learning, providing much of the basic experiences for developing symbolic recognition and response, as will be discussed later. In view of this, it is noteworthy that many theories of personality development have generally ignored or neglected tactile experiences to focus upon the sphincters and orifices—mouth, anus, urethra,[12] which, however, operate largely by tactual stimulation and the variations therein induced by experiences, largely tactile. The various orifices and sphincters, such as the mouth and lips, the anus and perineum, the genitals, the nose and eyelids, are all richly supplied with end organs for tactile reception with low thresholds normally.

TACTILE EXPERIENCES IN PERSONALITY DEVELOPMENT

Personality development will be discussed in terms of the ways an infant organism relates himself to the world, learning to transform his organic needs and functional capacities into the patterned, purposive conduct and prescribed relationships of his group while continuing to be and to act in his idiosyncratic fashion. This approach enables us to focus upon the circular, reciprocal processes in and through which the individual carries on his incessant intercourse with the world, relating himself transactionally as an organism in a geographical, cultural, social *field*.[17] Thus the personality process may be viewed as communication in which we may observe more closely how tactile experiences provide primary modes of communication which seemingly are essential to the development of the many forms of symbolic recognition and response for later learning and maturation.

Tactual sensitivity appears early in foetal life as probably the first sensory process to become functional.[8,28] During uterine life the foetus more or less floats in a liquid medium, the amniotic fluid, cushioned against impacts and the atmosphere, but continually stimulated by the events of his small world.

During the nine months of gestation, the embryo and fetus is continuously receiving the rhythmic impacts of the maternal heartbeat, transmitted through the amniotic fluid (and therefore magnified), impinging upon the skin of his whole body. His own heartbeats will later synchronize or be out of tune with the maternal heartbeats and so provide either a series of coordinated or dissimilar impacts upon his skin to which he develops a continuous response, as physiological resonance. Thus at birth the infant comes from a rhythmically pulsating environment into an atmosphere where he has to exist as a discrete organism and relate himself through a variety of modes of communication.[46] Probably the infants who are carried close to the mother on her back or hip receive some continuation of these rhythmic impacts upon the skin.

At birth the fetus passing through the birth canal undergoes a series of pressures and constrictions which involve sometimes intense tactual experiences. Moreover, the newborn is more or less suddenly exposed to the atmospheric pressures and altered temperature, evoking respiratory activity and presumably a number of tactile responses. The skin of the newborn is covered with a creamy substance which, if not interfered with, will be absorbed like a vanishing cream. Usually the newborn is bathed, dried, and often oiled, greased, or powdered.

The infant's need for contacts, for nuzzling, cuddling, patting, and his usually quick and accepting response to these tactile messages may be largely derived from his uterine experiences which have exercised his tactuality. Each infant differs in his "needs," his susceptibility and response and in the time when he will relinquish these infantile experiences and accept alienation from close contact with the mother. Putting fingers, thumb, food, objects or parts of another person's body in the mouth is a tactual experience. It may lead to chewing and swallowing or it may be retained and used as a source of gratification. Parental care and love may be largely tactual contacts and comforting, reassuring tactile experiences which give the infant encouragement and the confidence in the world as well as physiological assistance in achieving a more effective homeostasis, especially when under stress. Thus the kind and duration of early tactile experiences wherein the infant can send and receive messages outside his body have a large significance in early personality development as his first so-called "object-relations."[13] "No new external element gives rise to perceptive, motor or intelligent adaptation without being related to earlier activities."[49]

It is well recognized that the newborn mammal "needs" to be nuzzled and licked by the mother who, among infra-human species, performs these functions after biting the cord and often eating the placenta. The young remain close to the mother's body, receiving warmth and close tactual contacts, plus frequent licking and nursing. The human infant may receive a variety of treatments that conforms to this mammalian pattern or departs drastically therefrom. Some infants are kept close to the mother, may be given the colostrum (as do infra-human babies), allowed to nurse freely and as long as desired. Other infants may be isolated from the mother, as in most hospitals, fed at intervals and given a minimum of bodily contacts. The opossum young are extreme cases of pups born prematurely who can survive only by attaching themselves to a teat and remaining there close to the mother for the time necessary for maturation. Tactile experience is immediate, and transitory, operating only as long as contact is maintained. It is also a reciprocal experience in the sense that what a person touches also touches him, and often evokes emotional reactions of greater or less magnitude.[56] Tactile experience is ordinarily limited to two persons, a means to intimacy and expresson of affection or hostility and anger.

In his earliest experiences, the infant has a number of tactile experiences: close bodily contacts, being cuddled or patted rhythmically, touching the lips to the mother's body and more specifically to the nipple, increasingly fingering or handling the mother, especially the breast. These experiences may be viewed as early tactile communications which are carried on as transactional processes. The infant evokes from the mother the tactile stimulation which he "needs" and to which he responds in his own individual fashion as in sucking; the mother solicits from the infant this touching and sucking, which evokes milk from the breast.[12] Babies seem to differ widely in their "needs" for tactile experiences and in their acceptance and response to tactile ministrations. They are dependent upon the mother person who may provide these generously or may deny or largely deprive the infant of these experiences. A baby may become attached to a blanket, soft cuddly animal, or a rattle and begin to enjoy the tactile contacts, especially of textures. These early-found sources of satisfaction may serve as surrogates for contact with the mother's person.

It may not be unwarranted to assume that the infant initially has a primitive tactual sensitivity and capacity for response which is acute at birth in varying degrees in individual infants and which needs to be functionally operative and fulfilled as an essential stage in his development. Denial or deprivation of these early tactile experiences may compromise his future learning, such as speech, cognition, and symbolic recognition, and his capacity for more mature tactile communication, as we will discuss later. This initial or primary tactual sensitivity and need for tactile experiences may then diminish, or be incorporated in larger patterns as do the early reflexes (Babinski diminishing but retained in walking).

In these early tactile experiences we may see more clearly how the infant begins to communicate tactually and gradually enlarges his communications as he develops his capacities for other sensory awareness and perception and for other forms of response. Here the suggestion made earlier about signals, signs, and symbols finds application since in infant development, and indeed in personality development generally, we may observe this progression from signal to sign to symbol.

The baby begins to communicate with himself by feeling his own body, exploring its shape and textures, discovering its orifices and thereby begins to establish his body image which, of course, is reinforced or often negated by pleasurable or painful tactile experiences with other human beings. It seems highly probable that the continual physiological alterations internally, some of which he has such as colic or stomach ache or a full bladder or rectum, also enter into this evolving image of the body. Later on various visual cues may be established as he focuses his vision upon his fingers and feet and so begins to build up a visual image to supplement and to reinforce his tactile experiences.

The newborn infant with underdeveloped, inadequate capacity for homeostasis apparently requires these tactile experiences for maintaining his internal equilibrium. Thus, he keeps warm through bodily contacts. He maintains, or recovers, his internal equilibrium when disturbed by fear or pain (including digestive upsets—stomach ache, gas, etc.) , hunger, cold, through close contacts with the mother person and rhythmic tactual stimulation, as in patting, stroking, and caressing. It cannot be too strongly emphasized that the infant when disturbed emotionally* usually responds to patting or even vigorous, but rhythmic, slapping on the back with increasing composure. In an older child this patting may awaken or keep him awake, but it puts an infant to sleep; this age difference offers some support for the assumption of an early infantile sensitivity or need for rhythmic tactual stimulation which fades out or is incorporated into other patterns or becomes quiescent until puberty.

The baby responds to the signal(s) given by the nipple and the tactile contacts involved in nursing by sucking, which is a message to the mother; thereby he allays his hunger as she responds by lactation. The combination of two or more signals thus established a sign so that sooner or later the infant recognizes the mother and begins to respond to her with the set or expectation for consummation through feeding.[27]

Likewise, the infant is cuddled and patted by the mother when disturbed, frightened, or in pain. Usually she speaks or hums or sings to him at the same time. Thus he learns to recognize the sound of mother's voice as a sign, or surrogate for her touch. Later he may respond to her voice at a distance as a surrogate for her

---

*What we call emotional reactions may be viewed as physiological responses to messages, usually signals, such as pain, hunger contractions, loud noises, bright light, cold, etc.; these responses exceed the usual normal range of physiological variability exhibited in moment to moment, hour to hour, day to day alterations for maintaining a dynamic, internal equilibrium (homeostasis) .[15]

actual physical contact. This becomes clear when he has learned to recognize words, (although he may not be able to talk) and her reassuring words are accepted, although she is not present and touchable, as symbolic equivalents of tactile experience. Likewise, the child learns to recognize the mother's voice as a sign of her disappointment and may cringe at her harsh voice as to physical punishment which he has experienced previously when scolded or spanked. It seems clear that the child's reception of verbal messages is predicated in large measure upon his prior tactile experience so that facial expressions and gestures become signs and symbols for certain kinds of tactile communications and interpersonal relations. A person who is emotionally disturbed while holding or carrying an infant may communicate that disturbance to the infant through tactile contacts just as a calm, relaxed person may soothe a disturbed child by holding him, with or without patting. The close, tactual contact of being held firmly apparently reassures a child.

What seems to be involved in the infant's maturation is that the primary mode of tactile communication is replaced by auditory and kinesic messages[5] which are no longer signals but become signs which later become or are replaced by symbols to which the infant responds, both physiologically and symbolically.[40]

If the human child were limited to purely tactual communications, he could not fully develop his capacity for fantasy and imagination, and for building the conceptual framework required for living in a cultural world. Thus the learning of abstractions means literally developing the capacity to recognize and respond to various symbols as in words or designs which serve as surrogates for the concrete actuality of events, for the most part initially perceived tactually.[62]

The baby's initial orientation to the spatial dimensions of the world occurs through tactile explorations—feeling with hands and fingers, often with the lips, manipulating and testing out the qualities, size, shape, texture, density, etc., of whatever the infant can touch. The manipulations involve motor activities and increasingly skillful neuromuscular coordinations which are established through tactile messages that are gradually supplanted and replaced by visual cues in most children. Thus the baby's perception of the world is built upon and initially shaped by tactile experiences.[19] It is to be remembered that as in all symbolic processes, the meaning of the symbol derives from prior direct sensory awareness which may or may not be reinstated at a later time. However, as Margaret Lowenfeld has suggested, these early primary sensory experiences are increasingly overlaid by cognitive patterns of symbolic recognition and response so that they may become more or less inaccessible except through such experiences as in the World Game, finger painting, clay modeling, water play, etc., and certain esthetic experiences.[36]

The potency of music, with its rhythmical patterning and varying intensities of sounds, depends in large measure upon the provision of an auditory surrogate for the primary tactile experiences in which, as discussed earlier, rhythmic patting is peculiarly effective in soothing the baby, while tickling, a recurrent, more or less rhythmic, tactile message, may evoke a cumulative response of considerable intensity, as in sex orgasm, which comes as a climax to repeated tactile messages. It has been remarked that Wagner's *Liebestod* is a musical version of intercourse leading to orgasm and postcoital subsidence.

The way the blind learn through tactile explorations to build up a series of schemas, if not visual images, of the world, and to develop concepts and symbol recognition and response indicates that while visual symbols often become the surrogates for tactile, nevertheless the tactile may, as in finger language, become a symbolic process for complicated and subtle communications of concepts and highly differentiated meanings.[37] This is illustrated by the account of Helen Keller's initial learning of names, such as water, from tactile experience of running water, and the communication of that word by finger language. As Cassirier has pointed out (p. 56, Anchor Edition), learning names and meanings immediately enlarges the child's world and gives him new modes of communication, even when limited to tactile communication, as with Helen Keller and Laura Bridgman.

As indicated in the section on "Cultural Patterning of Tactile Processes," one of the basic experiences of a child is learning to respect the inviolability of things, animals, places, and persons which occurs when the child becomes mobile and explores the world. This involves the curtailment and prohibition of tactile experiences, forbidding the child to touch whatever is defined by adults as inviolable (property, sacred places, forbidden objects, persons). His naive approach to these inviting object-persons is blocked and prohibited, often with painful punishment, until they are perceived as not-touchable except when he has permission or has performed the necessary rituals, negotiations, buying, etc. Not only are these tactile experiences of crucial significance for social order, but the transformation of the child's naive impulsive response to the world into the learned observance of inviolability, usually involves emotional disturbances, conflicts with parents and often over-learning, so that the child may become inhibited and less capable of making tactile contacts, even those which he or she may seek as occasions for interpersonal relations, as in intercourse.

Here we see how tactile experiences undergo a second critical phase. Early, he has experienced primary tactile fulfillment or denial as a baby, and developed his idiosyncratic mode of tactile communication and its elaboration into other modes. Now he must undergo an often severe restriction upon tactile experiences in which the world around him is alienated from his touch so that he must learn to recognize almost everything visually[53] and auditorially, as a symbol of inviolability which he must recognize, inhibiting his spontaneous impulse to touch or strike. His own body, especially the genitals, may be defined as inviolable, not to be touched under penalty of punishment. This means the child must learn to impute inviolability to what was previously accessible and thereby he is inducted into the social world of respect for property and persons and of sex morals, according to the often highly elaborate codes of custom and law. Needless to say, children may learn to observe these inviolabilities through punishment and exhibit law-abiding conduct when watched or fearful of detection and punishment, but not develop the self-administered inhibitions for social order. Or, they undergo continual conflicts between the impulsive response to forbidden things and persons and the partially learned, but not fully accepted, prohibitions. A recognition of the basic tactile experiences in learning socially prescribed conduct and respect for the law offers clues to the genetic study of socialization and its vicissitudes

Tactile experiences and recognition of symbols for tactily accessible and nonaccessible things and persons therefore are highly significant in the development of personality. Thus we may say that initial tactile experiences provide the basic orientation to the world and especially the physiological signals which evoke the child's naive spontaneous responses. These are transformed, elaborated, refined, and increasingly discriminated through gestures, facial expressions, tones of voice and through language, into the most subtle modes of interpersonal communication. Indeed, the transactional processes of reciprocal, circular relations can become operative only as the child learns how to evoke, as well as to respond, through kinesics and language, and the amazing variety of ritual, ceremonies, and symbols of his group.

Tactile communications are also involved in interpersonal relations in a more direct manner, as we may observe in the infant and child. Through the earliest bodily contacts and other tactile experiences, the baby communicates in a reciprocal way, mother to baby, and baby to mother, one evoking from the other what will in turn evoke his or her response in a tactile dialectic. These experiences establish the individual's early pattern of intimacy and affection, his first interpersonal relations which apparently persist as a sort of template by which he establishes and conducts his subsequent interpersonal relations, using verbal and kinesic patterns, especially in more intimate sexual relations. The baby develops confidence in the world, trust in people, through these early tactile relations which reciprocally establish the meaning of the world for him and also his expectations and feelings toward that world.

Thus, how the baby is treated, what tactual experiences he has being bathed, clothed, tucked in bed, or in sleeping bag, how he is mothered and handled by others governs his initial tactual responses and by so much guides his subsequent learning and relationships. How the baby feels in his own skin, as treated according to the cultural patterns of his group, gives him an image of his body with feelings about it which reflect and express such experiences.[32] He may learn to expect, to evoke, tactual contacts or be passive or anesthetic, with little or no such contacts. When one remembers the diversity of patterns of infant care, being kept close to mother's body, or isolated and left alone, being free to kick and squirm and wave his arms, to play with objects, or parts of his own body, or to be tightly swaddled or bound to a cradle board, it is evident that babies can survive under a variety of treatments. But it also seems clear that their early tactile experiences enter into and largely govern their subsequent learning and their use of patterns of communication.[16]

If the baby is limited in his tactile experiences, denied much opportunity to send or receive tactile communications, he presumably must wait until his capacity for visual and auditory recognition and reception have developed sufficiently to permit him to enter into communication with others. Thus, such a child will not only have little tactile experiences upon which to develop his sign and symbolic communication, but will be expected to rely upon more or less arbitrary visual and auditory symbols and to accept their meanings, not as experientially learned, but as prescribed by others. This suggests that while children so reared can and do learn sign and symbol recognition and response, they may be more dependent than other children upon the authority of parents who define and impose these signs and symbols. These children, also being limited in early motor activities and manipulation therefore may be more willing to abide by authoritative pronouncements or more ready to rebel.

Symbols lacking primary tactile validation may be less clearly and less effectively established as basic codes for communication later. This offers one approach to the schizoid and schizophrenic personalities who have been unable to enter fully and effectively into the symbolic, cognitive world of ideas as accepted by others, and who are reported to be frequently rejected babies, or deprived of mothering. Also this may throw light upon the impairment of abstract thinking observed in children who have been separated from the mother.[20] Since living in a symbolic world of ideas and concepts is a most difficult and subtle achievement, denial or deprivation of primary tactile experiences may be revealed as crucial in the development of personalities and character structure, and also in the configuration of a culture.

One of the significant events in the development of personality has long been recognized in terms of the child's learning to distinguish between "me" and "not-me," often stated as his first "facing of reality." It seems more probable that the child's first recognition of "not me" is of highly specific, idiosyncratic "not-me" as contrasted with the consensual world of actuality ("reality"). The baby apparently quite early recognizes the "not-me" as *my* mother, *my* bottle, *my* crib, *my* rattle, etc., each being tactually experienced and accepted and responded to idiomatically. Only later does the child replace this idiosyncratic "not-me" with the more generalized concepts and symbols of the public consensual world of "reality." This transition occurs and is facilitated with the use of language and the acceptance of visual and auditory surrogates or signs and symbols.

The baby's initial communication with the world being largely tactile, the early recognition of the "not-me" probably comes as these tactual signals become signs of specific meanings, namely, of "my" familiar, reassuring, comforting mother, bottle, bed, etc., from which he receives the familiar, customary tactile messages, plus the reassuring auditory and visual cues (mother's voice and face and hands) which further distinguish and establish these as signs of "my" world. Language, first as recognizable signs and then as symbols and then as verbal messages he can send, provides the conceptual framework of ideas, concepts, and expectations for living in the common public world ("reality"). This requires the gradual replacement of the idiosyncratic "not-me" by the consensual "not-me," a transition from the largely tactile to linguistic and kinesic and symbolic communications. This transition to the symbolic world and acceptance of adult concepts is not always easy for children. Some may only partially give up their idiosyncratic "not-me" and try to live on two levels of communication, while others may be unable to attain even this degree of participation in the consensual world, continuing to rely upon signals.

It seems clear that only as the baby achieves some degree of internal stability (homeostasis) and develops more awareness of the external world can he begin to shift from dependence upon tactual to linguistic communication and thereby orient himself in the symbolic-cultural world. If we view learning as essentially a process of developing new ways of relating to the world *(knowing* as a transactional relationship as Dewey and Bentley have proposed), then learning to live in a symbolic world requires a firm base of physiological functioning and an initially adequate tactile orientation to the world that can be stabilized through patterned perception guided by concepts.[22]

While babies differ in their initial threshold to tactual stimulation, the provision of tactile experiences or their denial undoubtedly will accentuate or modify these individual differences. Thus, deprivation of early tactual experiences may evoke exploratory searches for surrogates such as masturbation, finger and thumb sucking, pulling or fingering the ears, nose, hair, a variety of autotactilism, or as indicated, reliance upon other modes of communication. The tactilly responsive baby, despite indulgence by parents, may seek further autotactile experiences to provide fulfillments. Each seeks to communicate with the world, and especially people, through tactile modes if allowed (the haptic type as V. Lowenfeld has described it), and also to communicate with the self through tactual manipulations if permitted. Here it is difficult to separate the motor, kinesic patterns from the tactile except to say that these motor activities seem to be guided by a tactile orientation, the hands and fingers acting like antennae or feelers which probe the surroundings for ensuing motor activities.[38]

This offers a clue to the schizoid and the schizophrenic personalities who quite early in life exhibit this partial or extensive resistance to accepting the ideas and concepts of their culture, which in turn may be viewed as arising from inadequate or distorted tactile experiences early in life, such as denial of tactile experiences or inability to establish and maintain tactile communication upon which conceptualization can be built.[7] There is some evidence that speech retardation and difficulties[9,61] and also reading disabilities may arise from early deprivation of or confusion in tactile experiences, since such children often exhibit peculiarities of tactual sensitivity and response.[11] Also it has been found that babies separated from their mothers frequently exhibit limited capacity for abstract thinking or conceptual formulation.[7,20] Hence it seems probable that in the genesis of these various kinds of personalities, there may be basic tactile deprivations and confusions, and also the emotional and affective disturbances arising from lack of adequate or effective tactile reassurance and comforting in early life.

Recently Bateson[1] has suggested that the schizophrenic is unable to distinguish between different kinds of verbal messages, literal and figurative, confusing what is metaphor with what is factual. This he attributes to the ambivalent relations and especially communication with the mother who cannot genuinely love her child but cannot accept her own rejection of the child. The role of tactual communications in early infancy may be highly significant therefore in this suggested development.

The tactile stimulation of the genitals, as in masturbation (or their manipulation by adults, siblings, etc.), seems to be almost universal, but may be curbed by parents, just as the infant and child's approaches and seeking of tactual contacts may be limited or denied. The child is often alienated from the mother around five or six (regarded as the peak of the Oedipus situation) when apparently this seeking and giving of tactual contacts begins to diminish in our culture. Thus we see boys increasingly evading or being denied such tactual contacts and tactual comforting, although girls may continue to enjoy it. If there is a diminution in tactual sensitivity and experiences in middle childhood, the so-called latency period, it abruptly ceases at puberty when the pubertal boy and girl usually become avid for tactual contacts, seeking to touch and to be touched. It may be found fruitful to consider the latency period as primarily a change in tactile sensitivity which, of course, includes the genitals. However, it should not be assumed that in this latency period there is no interest or concern for sex since curiosity about sex and intercourse may be intense, while mutual and self-masturbation often takes place, and boys and girls exhibit their nude bodies to each other to satisfy their curiosity about the other sex.

In adolescence we see the increasing frequency of tactile communication, at first between members of the same sex, as boys walk together with arms on each others' shoulders, girls with arms around each others' waists, and then the first tentative heterosexual explorations of caressing, petting, "necking," and frequently attempts at intercourse. Tactile communication in adult mating, both as foreplay and in intercourse, has been elaborated and refined by some cultures into the most amazing array of erotic patterns which through a variety of tactual stimulation of various parts of the body serve to arouse, prolong, intensify, and evoke communication. Here we see tactile communication, reinforced and elaborated by motor activities and language, by concomitant stimulation, visual, auditory, olfactory, gustatory, and the deeper muscle senses, combined to provide an organic-personality relationship which may be one of the most intense human experiences. It is, or can be, considered an esthetic experience in that there may be little or no instrumental, purposive, or cognitive elements, with greater or less loss of space-time orientation. But the elementary sexual processes of the human organism may be transformed and focused into an interpersonal love relationship with an identified person to whom each is seeking to communicate, using sex not for procreation, as in the mating of a female in heat ready to be fertilized, but as "another language,"[50] for interpersonal communication. Here we see how the primary tactile mode of communication, which has been largely overlaid and superseded by auditory and visual signs and symbols, is reinstated to function with elementary organic intensity, provided the individuals have not lost the capacity for communication with the self through tactile experiences.

In the development of the individual personality beginning in childhood and accelerated in adolescence, we may observe how the recognition and response to signs, as previously discussed, is eloborated into the symbolic process. But it should be emphasized that learning symbolic recognition and response for communication occurs only as the child or adolescent is indoctrinated and practiced in this by more experienced individuals who, as culture agents, define the meaning of symbols and direct the less experienced in performing the prescribed conduct responsive to those symbols.

Thus we can see the individual learning to respond, with patterns of various kinds and in different modes, tactual, kinesic, language (which are not naive organic responses), to biological signals or their learned surrogates; further, the individual develops responses, which are uniquely human, to symbols which have been created and established as the occasions for such learned symbolic responses.

For example, the individual may withdraw his hand when he touches fire or a hot object that serves as a *signal* to that withdrawal response, often a reflex withdrawal to pain. He may learn then to recognize the color of a hot object or its customary shape as a *sign* of its hazardous nature and thereafter avoid touching it. But when he learns to respond to the word "hot," he is acting symbolically, since his recognition of and response to that word, "hot," are not naive biological responses but recognition of a *symbol* with appropriate response to that symbol according to what others have taught him.

This emphasis upon the cultural patterning of symbolic processes seems justified because we have recognized that symbols are cultural, but have not given equal recognition to the necessity of learning these symbols from others. Thus, various infra-human organisms can be trained to recognize and respond to symbols of a fairly wide range, but no animal ever teaches its young to recognize and respond to symbols, although they do help the young to recognize signals and some signs. This points to the uniquely human capacity for maintaining its basic organic processes, including recognition of many signals, and also for superseding and replacing these primary modes of communication with signs and symbols, thereby enormously enlarging the range and subtlety of human communications and providing for the development of the highly individualized, idiosyncratic personality processes. We can observe how each person learns to use these processes in his own way for his own purposes as he relates himself to the world and other persons. The elementary, primary modes of communication may be overlaid, superseded, and incorporated in symbolic communication but under stress, may again become regnant.

There is little systematic observation of how tactile experiences and modes of communication function in the development of personality[37] and how the tactile are interrelated with the linguistic and kinesic modes where any one of the three may become a surrogate for one or two others, and all three may be partially or wholly superseded by visual symbols, as in the arts, especially graphical plastic art.[30] We can begin to realize the complexity when we gain more understanding of human communication.[60] For this we need to recognize that the human child has immense potentialities which give rise to his idiosyncratic awareness and perception of the world (life space-private world), always patterned by his tradition, with a highly idiomatic personal code for communicating and receiving and interpreting messages from the world and from other persons.

REFERENCES

1. Bateson, G. *A Theory of Play and Fantasy.* New York, Psy. Research Reports 2, December, 1955. Amer. Psychiat. Assoc.
2. Bateson, G. *Social Planning and the Concept of Deutero-Learning.* Conf. on Science, Phil. and Religion, 2nd Symposium. New York, Harper, 1942, pp. 81-97.
3. Bateson, G., and Mead, M. *Balinese Character.* New York, Academy of Sciences, 1941.
4. Birch, H. G. Personal communication.
5. Birdwhistle, R. *Introduction to Kinesics.* Louisville, Univ. Louisville, 1954.
6. Bovard, E. W., Jr. A theory to account for the effects of early handling on viability of the albino rat. *Science,* July, 187, 1954.
7. Bowlby, J. *Maternal Care and Mental Health.* Geneva, World Health Organization, 1951.
8. Carmichael, L. Behavior during fetal life. In *Encyclopedia of Psychology.* New York, Citadel Press, 1951.
9. Despert, J. L. Emotional aspects of speech and language development. *Int. J. Psychiat. Neurol., 105*:193-222, 1941.
10. Dewey, J., and Bentley, A. *Knowing and the Known.* Boston, Beacon Press, 1949.
11. Douglas, E. Personal communication.

12. Erikson, E. *Childhood and Society.* New York, Norton, 1950.
13. Fairbairn, W. R. *An Object-Relations Theory of the Personality.* New York, Basic Books, 1954.
14. Frank, L. K. Concept of inviolability in culture. *Amer. J. Sociol., 36:*607-615, 1931.
15. Frank, L. K. *Feelings and Emotions.* New York, Random House, 1953. (pamphlet)
16. Frank, L. K. Genetic psychology and its prospects. *Amer. J. Orthopsychiat., 21:*506-522, 1951.
17. Frank, L. K. *Nature and Human: Man's New Image of Himself.* New Brunswick, N.J., Rutgers Univ. Press, 1951.
18. Frank, L. K. *Individual Development.* New York, Random House, 1954. (pamphlet)
19. Frank, L. K. Role of play in personality development. *Amer. J. Orthopsychiat.,* vol. 25, 1955.
20. Goldfarb, W. *Am. J. Orthopsychiatry, 14:*441.
21. Goldstein, K. *Human Nature in the Light of Psychopathology.* Cambridge, Harvard Univ. Press, 1940.
22. Goldstein, K. *The Organism.* New York, American Book, 1939.
23. Goldstein, K. The sign of Babinski. *J. Nerv. Ment. Dis., 93:*281-296, 1941.
24. Hallowell, I. The self and the behavioral environment. In *Culture and Experience.* Philadelphia, Univ. Pennsylvania Press, 1955.
25. Hardy, J. D., Goodsell, H., and Wolff, H. G. *Pain, Sensation, and Reactions.* Baltimore, Williams & Wilkins, 1952.
26. Hammett, F. S. Studies of the thyroid apparatus. *Endocrinology, 4:*221-229, 1922.
27. Hendrick, I. Early development of the ego: Identification in infancy. *Psychoanal. Quart., 20:*44-61, 1951.
28. Hooker, D. *The Prenatal Origin of Behavior.* Lawrence, Univ. Kansas Press, 1952.
29. Kahn, T. C. Theoretical foundations of audio-visual-tactile rhythm induction therapy experiments. *Science,* July, 103-104, 1954.
30. Kepes, G. *Language of Vision.* Chicago, Theobold, 1951.
31. Kinsey, A. C., et al. *Sexual Behavior in the Human Female.* Philadelphia, Saunders, 1953.
32. Kubie, L. S. Body symbolization and development of language. *Psychoanal. Quart., 3:*1-15, 1934.
33. Kuntz, A., and Haselwood, L. A. Circulatory reactions in the gastro-intestinal tract elicited by local cutaneous stimulation. *Amer. Heart J., 20:*743-749, 1940.
34. Kuntz, A. Anatomic and physiologic properties of cutaneo-visceral vasomotor reflex arcs. *J. Neurophysiol., 8:*421-430, 1945.
35. Lloyd, D. P. C. Reflex action in relation to the pattern and peripheral source of afferent stimulation. *J. Neurophysiol., 6:*111-119, 1943.

36. Lowenfeld, M. World pictures of childhood. *Brit. J. Med. Psychol., 18:* 65-101, 1939.

37. Lowenfeld, V. *Nature of Creative Activity.* New York, Harcourt Brace, 1939.

38. Lowenfeld, V. *Creative and Mental Growth.* New York, Macmillan, 1947.

39. Martin, A. R. The body's participation in dilemma and anxiety phenomena. *Amer. J. Psychoanal.,* vol. 5, 1945.

40. Maslow, A. H. The expressive component in behavior. *Psychol. Rev., 56:* 261-272, 1949.

41. Mead, G. H. *Mind, Self, and Society.* Chicago, Univ. Chicago Press, 1934.

42. Mead, G. H. A behavioristic account of the significant symbol. *J. Philos., 19:*161, 1922.

43. Mead, M. *Male and Female.* New York, Morrow, 1949.

44. Mead, M. The swaddling hypothesis: Its reception. *Amer. Anthropol., 56:*395-409, 1954.

45. Mead, M., and MacGregor, F. C. *Growth and Culture.* New York, Putnam, 1951.

46. Meerloo, J. A. Archaic behavior and the communicative act. *Psychiat. Quart., 29:*60-73, 1955.

47. Montague, M. F. A. Sensory influences of the skin. *Texas Reports Biol. Med., 2:*291-301, 1953.

48. Montague, W. *The Structure and Function of Skin.* New York, Academic Press, 1956.

49. Piaget, J. *Play, Dreams, and Imitation in Childhood.* New York, Norton, 1951.

50. Plant, J. S. *The Envelope.* New York, Commonwealth, 1950.

51. Reyniers, J. A. *Germ-Free Life Studies.* Lobund Reports 1-2, 1948-1949.

52. Richins, C. A., and Brizzee, K. Effect of localized cutaneous stimulation on circulation in duodenal arterioles with capillary beds. *J. Neurophysiol., 12:*131-136, 1949.

53. Ruesch, J., and Kees, W. *Non-Verbal Communication.* New York, Basic Books, 1956.

54. Sechehaye, M. A. *Symbolic Realization.* New York, Internat. Univ. Press, 1951.

55. Sulzberger, M. B., and Zaidens, S. H. Psychogenic factors in dermatological disorders. *Med. Clin. North Amer., 32:*669, 1948.

56. Straus, E. W. Aesthesiology: Its significance for the understanding of hallucination. In *A New Orientation in Psychotherapy.* New York, Basic Books, 1957.

57. Tompkins, H. J. Veterans' administration. *New York Times,* July 21, 1953.

58. Travell, J., and Bigelow, N. H. Role of somatic trigger areas in pattern of hysteria. *Psychosomat. Med., 9:*353-363, 1947.

59. Travell, J., and Ringler, S. H. Relief of cardiac pain by local block of somatic trigger areas. *Proc. Soc. Exper. Biol., 63:*480-482.
60. Vigotsky, L. S. Thought and speech. *Psychiatry, 2:*29-54, 1939.
61. Wyatt, G. The Role of Interpersonal Relations in the Acquisition of Language. (Unpublished manuscript.)
62. Werner, H. *Comparative Psychology of Mental Development.* New York, Harper, 1940.
63. Waal, N. Special technique of psychotherapy with an autistic child. In G. Kaplan (Ed.), *Emotional Problems of Early Childhood.* New York, Basic Books, 1955.
64. Walter, G. *The Living Brain.* New York, Norton, 1953.
65. Weiss, S., and Davis, D. Significance of afferent impulses from the skin in mechanisms of visceral pain; skin infiltration as useful therapeutic procedures. *Amer. J. Med. Sci., 176:*517-532, 1928.
66. Weaver, W. Science and complexity. *Amer. Sci. 36:*536-544, 1948.
67. Wolfe, C. *The Hand in Psychological Diagnosis.* New York, Philosophical Library, 1952.
68. Zaidens, S. H. Dermatological hypochondriasis. *Psychosomat. Med., 12:* No. 4, 1950.

THE KINESTHETIC SYSTEM, innervated by receptors in the muscles, tendons, and joints, provides information about position and movement of the body. The posture of the body, walking, grasping, indeed all movements, are discerned because of the kinesthetic system. Many of these movements are almost automatic, as are the adjustments we make when we lift an object heavier than anticipated or when we change our walking pattern to accommodate to surface changes of the terrain. Kinesthesis and the other sense systems are integrated, that is they jointly operate in the input to, and the output from, the organism. The ontogenesis of kinesthesis has not been studied frequently as there are obvious experimental problems. A provocative clinical formulation about the system and its impact on infant behavior has been stated by Dr. Anna Kulka and her associates, who have a psychoanalytic perspective. They view kinesthesis as a drive which must be met, with motility representing tension discharge. Note that their explanation of kinesthesis is considerably broader than the neurophysiological definition. Also of interest is the emphasis the authors place on the nature of the maternal-child relationship as it evolves from tactual-kinesthetic contacts.

Chapter 6

Kinesthetic Needs in Infancy

Anna Kulka, Carol Fry, and Fred J. Goldstein

THIS PAPER is a preliminary statement of hypotheses which we formulated as a result of observation of normal infants, neonates, prematures, and disturbed children.

The *first* hypothesis is that there exist kinesthetic needs or drives which are separate from and of equal importance with the oral, anal, and phallic drives. By kinesthetic we mean all incoming sensory modalities: light, touch, pressure, temperature, visceral afferent, and also their central representations. By kinesthetic drive we refer to tension release, or pleasure derived through the above modalities.

Throughout this paper we use contact urge to include kinesthetic drives, as defined above, together with urges for gratification from other sensory modalities: smell, sight, hearing, oral kinesthetic, as distinct from oral tasting, together with their central representations.

The kinesthetic phase predates the oral, and as in the classical development phase, has its own primary and specific modality of expression. Similarly, this stage of development is never completely left behind but is modified and incorporated into highly complex and sublimated activities throughout life. Again, as in the other drives the kinesthetic drive can undergo vicissitudes, some of which we hope to deal with in some detail later in this paper.

The *second* hypothesis which we wish to postulate is that the modality of expression of the kinesthetic drives is motility. In the premature infant and normal neonate, motion is the first means of tension discharge.

At birth the myelinization of the pyramidal tracts is incom-

From *American Journal of Orthopsychiatry, 30*:562-571, 1960. Copyright, the American Orthopsychiatric Association, Inc. Reproduced by permission.

plete. The extrapyramidal system is the dominant functioning motor system. Cortical control is not yet established. Therefore, the dominant movement pattern available for tension discharge and the reestablishment of homeostasis is the mass reflex or so called mass movement. The more premature or immature the infant, the more this mass movement dominates and is only gradually replaced by the less primitive reflexes and coordinated motor activity.

In this paper motility will only be discussed as it is a modality of the kinesthetic drive. Motility as a drive in its own right is not in the scope of this paper.

A *third* hypothesis to be presented in its broadest form is that the kinesthetic development of an individual is influenced by events in his life, particularly those of the early mother-child relationship. What the norms are for this development have still to be determined. We believe that early extreme deprivation of kinesthetic needs may in some cases lead to hypermotility which in turn seems to be precursor of the syndrome of hyperkinesis in young children, Or, in other cases of severe deprivation, hypomotility may occur as in the state of "anaclitic depression" referred to by Spitz[25] in his familiar work on institutionalized children.

The *fourth* hypothesis, which needs to be included for completeness, is that, as with other basic drives, a range of normal variation, probably of constitutional nature, occurs in the intensity of the drive itself, in the capacity of the individual to tolerate various frustrations, and in the quantity and quality of individual motor activity.

The purpose of presenting these hypotheses is not merely a theoretical one. The senior author in her clinical experience has dealt with many conscientious mothers who wish to do well by their babies and who are not neurotically inhibited in their own knesthetic impulses toward their babies, but who need an intellectual framework in which to function. They feed their babies vitamins because they think that is what they should do, and they may not cuddle their babies because they think they should not do so, as it will "spoil" the baby, etc. Particularly with bottle feeding the infant's kinesthetic need may be ignored unless specifically recognized as such.

One of the most important normal satisfactions of mothering is the pleasure the mother derives from contact with her baby. We have seen babies who, having received too little cuddling, which has resulted in an accumulation of muscular tension in the baby, have become very hard for the mother to hold. The baby seems to want to squirm out of her arms and the mother is likely to report that the baby doesn't want to be held. This seeming rejection of the mother on the part of the baby is often distressing to the mother, making her feel inadequate or angry at the baby and thereby perpetuating a vicious circle between the two. In many instances the senior author has been able to prove to such mothers that with persistence and the right sort of handling and holding, the baby would respond to completely relaxing, which is, of course, the normal response to cuddling.

Though we do not wish to imply that there may not be some important dynamic reason why a given mother cannot handle a baby to their mutual satisfaction, still, owing to the "mutuality" of the relationship, the satisfaction the mother experiences if she can be taught to hold her baby comfortably may reinforce her positive feelings for the baby and materially improve the situation and perhaps prevent severe pathology later.

The senior author's experience with autistic children has impressed her deeply with the tremendous need of these children for physical contact even if at first they shrink away from it. This need for contact far exceeds the need for oral gratification. Such a conviction is shared by almost all workers in the field. L. Bender, for instance, told that she could make an autistic child write only if she would put her hands on his, and in a personal communication expressed the belief that the seriously emotionally disturbed child needs much physical contact with the therapist. Mahler[17] sees this intensive desire for body contact only in what she calls the symbiotic type: "They crave body contact and seem to want to crawl into you. . . ."

On the other hand, Waal[27] describes how she was able to achieve almost immediate response from a typical autistic, withdrawn child by taking him on her lap, carrying him in her arms, spoon-feeding him, stroking him, and massaging the most stiffened parts of his body. When she stroked his mouth, he opened his lips and licked her. While doing this, she interpreted to him his wish to be a baby and to have his mother all for himself. His response to this was amazing.

Rank[20] described the first phase of treatment with atypical children as the one in which one makes "restitution to the child for the frustrations of his past." "We meet the child's needs at whatever level he presents himself." Again, according to Putnam,[19] " . . . from the standpoint of differential diagnosis, etiology, and treatment, the early psychoses must be brought into close comparison with states of 'hospitalism,' 'anaclitic depression,' and all types of clinical conditions due to deprivation of mothering or affection. . . "

In England, O'Gorman[18] has capitalized on a hitherto unused resource. He assigned certain institutionalized mentally defective girls to autistic children, each to fondle, cuddle and sleep with a child under the nurses' supervision. Dramatic improvement in the autistic children was reported. They developed coordinated motor behavior and speech. The foster mothers also were very happy with their role. This constitutes a most intensive, round-the-clock form of kinesthetic restitutive therapy.

The third area of personal experience of the senior author is with hyperactive, or better called hyperkinetic, children of early school age, which will be discussed later in the paper.

We are currently engaged in a research project the aim of which is to develop an experimental technique for obtaining objective data which may be used to substantiate or refute our hypotheses. Simultaneous measurements (EMG) of muscle tension and relaxation, respiration and heart rate, etc., in both mothers and infants are being recorded. It is hoped that in a controlled experiment, variations in maternal handling may be correlated with infant reactions to acute kinesthetic frustration or satisfaction.

In reviewing the literature we found that the first reference is probably Freud,[5] in *Three Contributions to the Sexual Theory*, where the entire skin of the infant was considered erogenous.

Ribble,[21] an author most emphatic about the need for mothering and close bodily contact, says:

> Infants who do not get this sort of mothering show increasing and persistent muscular tension and the increasing tension is accompanied by inadequate breathing.
>
> Furthermore, in such cases, tension usually persists long past the period when it may be regarded as purely physiological. It becomes a kind of primitive anxiety.

However, in spite of this emphasis on the need for bodily contact and relief of tension, Ribble did not stress that there is libidinal gratification derived from it but attributes the *first pleasurable* experience to oral gratification.

Mahler[17] states that "bodily contact with the mother, that is, fondling and cuddling, is an integral prerequisite for the demarcation of the body ego from the nonself within the state of somatopsychic symbiosis of the mother-infant dual unity." Although Mahler, Spitz,[25] Goldfarb,[7] and others point out that lack of mothering can cause the most severe disturbance, they do not conclude that the disturbance of the infants was related to deprivation of kinesthetic needs.

Greenacre[9] stressed the fact that intrauterine life and early infancy form a continuum and that "the fetus reacts to discomfort with an acceleration of the life movements at its disposal," stating that these responses are an earlier form of anxiety-like response. Greenacre further postulates that the fetus derives some pleasure from moving and contact with the maternal body.

Greene[10] raised the question of the earliest object relations starting in the womb. He attributes the soothing quality of rocking and patting to their similarity to cardiac and respiratory rhythm in the womb. Sontag[24] recorded specific movements in the fetus when the mother was under emotional stress or hypertensive. Brody[3] states that among 4-week-old infants it was the maternal activity of "moving" that had the more central position over feeding; that the infant's first pleasurable responses were to being picked up, rocked, given a warm bath, as well as to being fed.

A. Freud[4] writes:

> There is, I believe, in the first weeks after birth, a phase where the body needs, such as the need for intake and output, breathing, sleep, skin comfort, movement, etc. reign supreme. . . . I do believe that the sensations which are connected with the arousal and fulfillment of these needs are the first mental representations of body, i.e. they form the first content of the mind. . . . Certainly the observation of maternal feeding behavior showed that save under conditions of body security and comfort, no infant, however hungry, appeared to enjoy his feeding.

Bowlby[2] has emphasized the pre-oral tie to the mother, using the phrase "primary object clinging."

In animal life, the importance of handling, or of not being reared in isolation from the mother has been noted.[12,14,22,23] Recently, Harlow[11] did some very striking experiments on the nature of love in monkeys. He writes: "These data make it obvious that contact comfort is a variable of overwhelming importance in the development of affectional responses, whereas lactation is a variable of negligible importance."

We should now like to outline briefly a postulated normal development of the kinesthetic drive.

Contact needs are probably gratified fully in intrauterine life, and a gradual transition in the postnatal period is mandatory for healthy development. Much of the earliest kinesthetic satisfactions must be supplied to the infant by the environment—cuddling, rocking, being kept warm, etc.

Different societies have evolved different patterns of supplying satisfaction for these kinesthetic needs. Most primitive mothers carry their small infants around with them during all their activities, with the help of straps, boards, baskets, and the like. More modern societies use cradles and buggies. Certain groups swaddle their babies with more or less restriction of motion.

Different treatment will undoubtedly result in different character structure. For example, the swaddled infant who is then carried on the mother's back receives the satisfaction of contact and the sensations of motion through her. This fate is very different from that of the infant who is swaddled and then left in isolation.

Gorer[6] concluded a causal relationship between Russian swaddling and Russian character. The baby was swaddled and left in isolation, then unswaddled and fed. The Russian character, he stated, was depressed, with heightened fantasy life on the one hand and periodic indulgence in extreme gaiety and feasting on the other.

The mode of tension release in the neonatal period is the mass reflex later replaced by more channelized and organized movements. As the infant grows the motor skills are rapidly acquired and are in part available to the service of the kinesthetic drive. The baby can more actively seek contact with the mother—grasping, crying purposefully, crawling toward her, calling her by name. Other situations are also sought. The baby bounces, rocks himself, splashes in the bath, all with obvious pleasure. He discovers the extent and content of his own body on a kinesthetic level. These discoveries are crucial to his early ego development.

Later, the toddler when in need goes to mommy to be picked up and comforted or wants someone to swing him in the air. Then there is the "dearly beloved" blanket or cuddle toy which is a part of almost every child's life. Kinesthetic satisfactions and loving care of the body more and more are taken over by the growing child himself.

With normal growth and development through latency and adolescence, kinesthetic needs are met in a number of ways. Many sports are engaged in because they feel good; part of the satisfaction of pals and friends and identification with a particular group is of a kinesthetic nature.

As adults, people work in jobs which afford a high degree of kinesthetic satisfaction: potters and other craftsmen, nurses, doctors caring for their patients' physical needs, masseurs, acrobats, to name but a few.

Kinesthetic gratification as part of forepleasure is an integral part of lovemaking. More sublimated forms of kinesthetic satisfaction for adults is the "mental closeness" of friends and of colleagues—the feelings of security and closeness through psychological identification with a group, club, community, family, etc.

Let us now touch upon some of the vicissitudes of the kinesthetic drive. Undoubtedly many await discovery.[1,13] It is hoped
that the word vicissitude used in this sense will convey the idea of
an interaction between an individual—with his unique constitution—and his particular environment dating back from infancy to
the time when pathology was observed.

In dealing with the kinesthetic drive in several different areas
pathology may be seen (1) in the primary kinesthetic area itself;
(2) in the central representation of kinesthetic impulses; (3) in
the motor area where the disturbance is postulated as secondary to
kinesthetic pathology.

Severe early deprivation of kinesthetic needs may lead to hypomotility or the "anaclitic depression" of Spitz,[25] with a low survival rate among the infants so afflicted. Hypomotility and retardation of lesser degrees are probably not often recognized as such:
we may wonder about the "too good" baby. On the other hand,
severe early deprivation of kinesthetic needs may lead to hyper
motility.

As we have said, in normal neonates acute deprivation leads to
increased muscle tension. Rocking and head banging and other
such rhythmic movements which are seen in infants with prolonged deprivation may be an attempt to gratify their own kinesthetic
needs. Premature infants are particularly vulnerable to increased
muscular tension. It may be postulated that for their particular
state of neuromuscular development, close cuddling and rocking
should be as constant as in the mother's womb. If this is so, the
modern incubator falls far short of a good environment for a premature infant.

Some infants and young children with hypermotility develop
what is called the syndrome of hyperkinesis.[8,16] As a psychiatrist
to city schools, the senior author has had many such cases referred
to her by teachers who find such children disruptive in the classroom. It is important that hypermotility or hyperkinesis be distinguished from hyperactivity or acting out. We consider the
former, hypermotility and hyperkinesis, to be a regression or fixation at an infantile motor level and not subject to cortical con-

trol; whereas the latter, hyperactivity or acting out, is under cortical control, though not under ego control. Of course, the two may
coexist.

By way of illustration, we shall present the following cases, in
which full bloom hyperkinesis was found, and where the history
of early deprivation of kinesthetic needs was clearly obtainable; as
with other regressive symptoms, hyperkinesis is often aggravated
by stress.

N, seven, was brought to the attention of the child guidance clinic
because she showed such irritability and contortion of her body during
school that the teacher finally had to exempt her because she was too
disturbing to the rest of the class. Apart from the hyperkinesis, the
teachers also felt that the child had lost any interest in work and complained that no one liked her. She couldn't make any friends and appeared to be unhappy. Rheumatic activity and brain pathology were
ruled out by all tests and neurological examination.

N was born prematurely and was thus more vulnerable to kinesthetic deprivation. She was born at a time when the mother was quite
upset because the father was called into the service and about to go
overseas. The mother's milk "didn't agree" with the baby, who was
bottle fed. When N was five weeks old, the mother had to go to work.
The father was already overseas. Mother could say almost nothing
about N's early infancy. The young infant was placed in different
homes. During this time she developed head shaking and rocking—a
form of attempted autogratification. As to training, the mother knew
nothing except that a maternal aunt "broke her in" within one week
before her second year. The mother admitted that she had not felt
ready for the child and could not bear physical contact with the baby.

When N was five years old, her mother gave birth to twins. N had
been prepared by having been told that *she* would have a baby to
play with. However, when the twins were brought home, they were
sick and N was not permitted even to see them and certainly not to
hold them. This constituted a further kinesthetic deprivation. The
mother too was invalided after the delivery and unable to give N
much-needed attention. Soon after this N developed rheumatic fever
and the family doctor put her to bed and kept her away from the
others in the family. After the acute illness was over, she had a ton-
sillectomy. Soon afterward, N developed the hyperkinesis which persisted until her referral.

This case responded to therapy. The mother was able to be more
understanding of N's bizarre jumpiness. The symptoms largely disappeared except at times of increased stress. She had high grades in
school, was outgoing and had many friends.

P weighed only two pounds at birth. She was kept on the ward for three months. There were no indications of any birth injury.

The mother was never close to this child nor to the two older children, who also showed behavior disorders.

When P was in the first grade, she was referred to a child guidance clinic because of destructiveness, hyperactivity, nail biting and enuresis, for being "oversexed," and because "nobody exists but her."

The mother was frank, admitting that she had not wanted another child, that she never could give her any affection and that she purposefully did not wish to baby her, since she did not want to spoil her.

After several sessions, the child became more expressive of her infantile needs for mothering. She would sit on the therapist's lap, nurse from the baby bottle, and ask to be rocked and wheeled around in a baby buggy. She used baby talk and asked for soft toys to cuddle.

During this time of restitutive therapy, she acted much less belligerent at home, was able to play with other children, and the relation with her mother improved.

K, six also was referred from school because he was too hyperkinetic and unmanageable. He would crawl on all fours like a dog and bark, or circle around like a horse in a corral.

He was unable to participate in any group and became a menace in the neighborhood. He would throw rocks, turn on sprinklers so that all passers-by would get wet, upset pets; or, he would upset a whole department store because he found out how to stop an escalator, or ride into the stores on his bicycle, etc. He was never still, but was in wild motion with his arms, or he would race from one place to another, throw, jump, roll on the floor. His face also was in constant mobility.

Yet he was an affectionate child, brilliant, with a tremendous fantasy life and full of charm.

K was full term. The parents were young, very immature, both the youngest in their families. The mother gave the history that she could not ever cuddle the baby and was always in doubt whether he was normal.

In his sessions he regressed to acting like a baby, wanted to be even diapered and permitted to wet, and demanded mothering.

During this time he became able to stay on for half a day, in a private school with only a few other children and a very understanding director. The parents could not leave him alone for a second, and when the second child was born, they felt K's unpredictable behavior too threatening to keep him at home. It also seemed clear that K needed a more stable environment than the one with his parents, in order to recover.

He was sent to New York. K was diagnosed as schizophrenic and placed in a residential treatment center.

These cases illustrate pathology in the motor area which we feel represents a vicissitude of the kinesthetic urge, in which regression to the mode of tension discharge of earliest infancy has taken place.

Many children under stress or when overtired become uncontrollably hypermotile. Nor is it uncommon for adults to have uncontrollable movements or twitches with fatigue. This is probably due to regression with decreased cortical control at such times. Not only may regression take place to earlier modes of motor expression but the primacy of the cortical control may never become established. Kinesthetic needs will then be expressed with immature motor patterns, as with some of the whirlings and posturings of the autistic children.

The primacy of cortical control may also never be established in certain cases of brain damage.

Overrestriction of motor outlet in children by overfearful or restrictive mothers leads to rhythmic stereotyped repetitive behavior.

Lastly, we wish to postulate that since the central representations of the kinesthetic drive form perhaps the earliest mental representation of the body image, inadequate ego development, inadequate differentiation of self from nonself, inadequate sense of reality may be in part attributable to early deprivation of kinesthetic needs. Further elaborations of this idea fall beyond the scope of this paper.

SUMMARY AND CONCLUSIONS

Four hypotheses were presented: (1) A kinesthetic drive exists in infancy separate from and of equal importance with the oral drive, and predates the oral drive. (2) Motility is the mode of expression of this kinesthetic drive. (3) The kinesthetic development of an individual is influenced by events in his life, particularly those of the early mother-child relationship. (4) Normal variation, probably of constitutional nature, exists in the drive itself, in the capacity for tolerating frustration.

The authors have postulated a normal development of this drive and have discussed vicissitudes it may encounter, the most clinically familiar at the present time being early severe deprivation leading to hypomotility or hypermotility. Some practical applications of these concepts for both prevention and treatment are suggested. The importance of additional theoretical formulations and further research is emphasized.

REFERENCES

1. Bergman, Paul, and Sibylle Escalona. Unusual sensitivities in very young children. In *The Psychoanalytic Study of the Child.* New York, Internat. Univ. Press, 1949, Vol. III/IV, pp. 337-357.

2. Bowlby, John. The Nature of the Child's Tie to His Mother. *Int. J. Psychoanal., 39:*350-373, 1958.

3. Brody, Sylvia. *Patterns of Mothering.* New York, Internat. Univ. Press, 1956.

4. Freud, Anna. Problems of infantile neurosis: a discussion. In *The Psychoanalytic Study of the Child.* New York, Internat. Univ. Press, 1954, Vol. IX, pp. 16-71.

5. Freud, S. *Three Contributions to the Sexual Theory.* New York, Putnam, 1910.

6. Gorer, G. *The People of Russia.* New York, Chanticleer, 1950.

7. Goldfarb, W. Infant rearing and problem behavior. *Am. J. Orthopsychiat., 13:*249-265, 1943.

8. Goldfarb, W. Effects of psychological deprivation in infancy and subsequent stimulation. *Am. J. Psychiat. 102:*18-33, 1945.

9. Greenacre, Phyllis. Predisposition to anxiety. *Psychoanal. Quart., 10:*66-99, 1941; also found in *Trauma, Growth and Personality,* New York, Norton, 1952.

10. Greene, Wm. A., Jr. Early object relations, somatic, affective, and personal. *J. Nerv. Ment. Dis., 126:*225-253, 1958.

11. Harlow, Harry F. The nature of love. *Am. Psychologist, 13:*673-685, 1958.

12. Kahn, M. W. Infantile experience and mature aggressive behavior of mice. *J. Genet. Psychol., 84:*65-75, 1954.

13. Leitch, M., and S. Escalona. The reactions of infants to stress. In *The Psychoanalytic Study of the Child.* New York, Internat. Univ. Press, 1949, Vol. III/IV, pp. 121-140.

14. Levy, D. M. On the problem of movement restraint. *Am. J. Orthopsychiat. 14:*644-671, 1944.

15. Levy, D. M. Experiments on the sucking reflex and social behavior of dogs. *Am. J. Orthopsychiat. 4:*203-224, 1934.

16. Lourie, R. The role of rhythmic patterns in childhood. *Am. J. Psychiatry,* *105*:653-660, 1949.
17. Mahler, M. S. On child psychosis and schizophrenia. In *The Psychoanalytic Study of the Child.* New York, Internat. Univ. Press, 1952, Vol. VII, pp. 286-305.
18. O'Gorman, Gerald. The halt and the blind. *Calif. Ment. Hlth. News,* Nov.-Dec., 1958, p. 2.
19. Putnam, Marian C. Some observations on psychoses in early childhood. In Gerald Caplan (Ed.), *Emotional Problems of Early Infancy.* New York, Basic Books, 1955, pp. 519-526.
20. Rank, B. Intensive study and treatment of pre-school children who show marked personality deviations or "atypical development" and their parents. In *Emotional Problems of Early Childhood,* op. cit., pp. 491-503.
21. Ribble, Margaret A. Infantile experience in relation to personality development. In J. McV. Hunt (Ed.), *Personality and the Behavior Disorders.* New York, Ronald Press, 1944, Vol. II, pp. 621-651.
22. Ruegamer, W. R., L. Bernstein, and J. D. Benjamin. Growth, food utilization and thyroid activity in the albino rat as a function of extra handling. *Science, 120*:184-185, 1954.
23. Scott, T. H., and W. R. Thompson. Whirling behavior in dogs. *Science, 123*:939, 1956.
24. Sontag, L. Some psychosomatic aspects of childhood. *Nerv. Child, 5*:296-304, 1948.
25. Spitz, R. A. Anaclitic depression. In *The Psychoanalytic Study of the Child.* New York, Internat. Univ. Press, 1946, Vol. II, pp. 313-342.
26. Spitz, R. The psychogenic diseases in infancy. In *The Psychoanalytic Study of the Child.* 1951, Vol. VI, pp. 255-275.
27. Waal, Nic. A special technique of psychotherapy in an autistic child. In Gerald Caplan, (Ed.), *Emotional Problems in Early Infancy.* New York, Basic Books, 1955, pp. 431-449.

PART III
MOTOR DEVELOPMENT

In our desire to understand the acquisition and process of man's cognitive functioning, man's other unique ability has often been overshadowed. That primates grasp and use simple tools is well documented, but only man has mastery of the differentiated components of the hand which afford great precision. The human infant, at birth, is limited to a reflex grasp and nondirected movements of the extremities. At one year of age, after a long, spasmodic period, grasp and release are coordinated, thumb and finger prehension is controlled. Although there is not agreement on a theoretical explanation for this transition, there are studies such as the one by Drs. White, Castle, and Held to chronicle, in detail, the ontogenesis of prehension. The paper is a report of a normative study on visually directed prehension in the first six months of life of institution-reared infants. General observations and specific test responses are described for each stage in the sequence. It is important to note that, in a later study, the authors were able to show that "top level reach" could be accelerated by offering considerably more general and specific stimulation to another group of institution-reared infants. This, they felt, demonstrated the plasticity of certain behaviors in the visual-motor sequence.

Chapter 7

Observations on the Development of Visually Directed Reaching

BURTON L. WHITE, PETER CASTLE, AND RICHARD HELD

T HE PREHENSORY abilities of man and other primates have long been regarded as one of the most significant evolutionary developments peculiar to this vertebrate group.[2,17] In man, the development of prehension is linked phylogenetically with the assumption of erect posture (thus freeing the forelimbs from the service of locomotion), the highly refined development of binocular vision, and the possession of an opposable thumb, among other specializations. One important accompaniment of the development of prehension is man's unique capacity to make and utilize tools. Considering the acknowledged importance of these developments in phylogeny, it is surprising how little is presently known about the ontogeny of prehension in man. The research to be presented here is focused on the behavioral ontogenesis of this vital function in the human infant during the first six months of life.

The detailed analysis of the development of a sensorimotor function such as prehension inevitably raises a classic theoretical problem. The human infant is born with a diversified reflex repertoire, and neuromuscular growth is rapid and complex. In addition, however, he begins immediately to interact with his postnatal environment. Thus we face the complex task of dis-

From *Child Development,* 35:349-364, 1964. Copyright 1964 by the Society for Research in Child Development, Inc. Reprinted by permission.

This work was supported by Grant M-3657 from the National Institute of Mental Health, U. S. Public Health Service, and Grant 61-234 from the Foundation's Fund for Research in Psychiatry.

The research was conducted at the Tewksbury Hospital, Tewsbury, Massachusetts. We are very grateful for the consideration and aid given by Dr. Lois Crowell and Head Nurses Helen Efstathiou and Frances Craig, among others.

tinguishing, to the extent that is possible, between those contributions made to this development by maturation or autogenous neurological growth and those which are critically dependent upon experience or some kind of informative contact with the environment. Previous work in the area of prehension has been variously oriented in regard to these polar alternatives, and it is important to note that the positions taken with regard to this theoretical problem have resulted in the gathering of selected kinds of data: namely, those kinds deemed relevant by each particular investigator to the support of his point of view on the development of prehension. Our own point of view is focused primarily around the role that certain kinds of experience have been shown to play in the growth and maintenance of sensorimotor coordinations.[11] Consequently, we have focused our attention on gathering detailed longitudinal data of a kind that would aid us in eventually testing specific hypotheses about the contributions of such experience to the development of prehension.

Halverson[7] studied the reaching performance of infants, beginning only after the onset of what we have come to consider a rather advanced stage in the development of prehension (16 weeks). Gesell[5] used the response to single presentations of a dangling ring and a rattle as items in his developmental testing procedures. These tests were designed to be used with subjects as young as 4 weeks of age, but prehension was of only peripheral concern to Gesell. Both of these workers subscribed to the theoretical position, championed by Gesell, that most if not all of early growth, including the development of prehension, is almost exclusively a function of progressive neuromuscular maturation: an "unfolding" process. This view undoubtedly contributed to their neglect of the possible significance of the role of input from the sensory environment and to their stress on normative level of performance per se, rather than the relation between a level of performance and its behavioral antecedents.

Piaget[20] made a number of original observations on the development of prehension, including the earliest stages of the process, which are prior to 3 months of age. His data are somewhat limited since his subject group consisted only of his own three children. And, as with Gesell, Piaget's interest in prehension was peripheral to another concern, namely, the sensorimotor origins of intelligence. Piaget's theoretical approach differs considerably from that of Gesell, being concerned primarily with the cognitive aspects of development. His work is focused on the adaptive growth of intelligence or the capacity of the child to structure internally the results of his own actions. As a result, he has formulated a theoretical point of view that centers around the interaction of the child with his environment, an approach similar to our own. This interaction is seen by Piaget as giving rise to mental structures (schemas) which in turn alter the way in which the child will both perceive and respond to the environment subsequently. This point of view avoids the oversimplified dichotomy of maturation versus learning by conceptualizing development as an interaction process. Without the aliment provided by the environment schemas cannot develop, while without the existence of schemas the environment cannot be structured and thus come to "exist" for the child.

Some primitive sensorimotor schemas are, of course, present at birth, the grasp reflex and visual-motor pursuit being two that are particularly relevant to prehension. Both Gesell and Piaget describe the observable development of the subsequent coordination between vision and directed arm and hand movements, part of which is clearly dependent on some kind of practice or experience. Gesell, however, contented himself with a vague acknowledgment of the probable role of experience in development, whereas Piaget attempted to determine in a loose but experimental fashion the role of specific kinds of experiences and structured his theorizing explicitly around the details of the interaction process.

Piaget takes the position that informative contact with the environment plays an important role in the development of spatial coordination and, in particular, prehension. The work of Held and his collaborators[11,13-16] on the development and maintenance of plastic sensorimotor systems in higher mammals, including human adults, has led to a similar point of view. These laboratory studies have addressed themselves to the question of which specific kinds of contact with the environment are required for the maintenance and development of accurate sensorimotor abilities such as hand-eye coordination. This work constitutes a more rigorous experimental approach to some of the same kinds of problems that Piaget has dealt with on the basis of his extensive observations and seems likely to be relevant to the ontogeny of prehension in particular.

It was with this general framework in mind that we undertook the study of prehension. In studies of animal development[21,22] the technique of selective deprivation of environmental contact has been successfully used to factor out critical determinants. Since human infants obviously cannot be deliberately deprived, other experimental strategies must be employed. One approach would be to enrich in selective fashion the environment of a relatively deprived group of infants, such as might be found in an institutional setting. The rate of development of such a group could then be compared with that of a similar group not receiving such enrichment. Under such conditions the differences might well be small and consequently the techniques of observation and measurement should be as precise and as sensitive as possible to detect systematic differences. Consequently, our first task was to determine in detail the normal sequence of behaviors relevant to prehension spanning the first six months of life. At the end of this time, visually directed prehension is well developed. This preliminary information would enable us to devise sensitive and accurate scales for the measurement of prehension. We could then proceed with an examination of the role of contact with the environment in the development of this capacity. In addition, we felt that a detailed normative study of prehension was an important goal in its own right and one that would help fill an important gap in the study of human growth. It should be noted, however, that the results of this study can only be considered normative for subject groups such as ours.

METHOD

Subjects

Our subjects were thirty-four infants born and reared in an institution because of inadequate family conditions. These infants were selected from a larger group after a detailed evaluation of their medical histories* and those of their mothers along with relevant data on other family members whenever available. All infants included in the study were judged physically normal.

Procedure

For testing, infants were brought to a secluded nursery room where lighting, temperature, and furnishings were constant from day to day. After diapering, the infant was placed in the supine position on the examination crib. We used a standard hospital crib whose sides were kept lowered to 6 inches above the surface of the mattress in order to facilitate observation.

Our procedure consisted of 10 minutes of observation of spontaneous behavior (pretest) during which the observers remained out of view. This period was then followed by a 10-minute standardized test session during which stimulus objects were used to elicit visual pursuit, prehensory, and grasping responses. For the purposes of this report, the prehension-eliciting procedure is most germane. On the basis of several months of pilot work we selected a fringed, multicolored paper party toy as the stimulus object since it seemed to produce the greatest number of responses in tests of a large number of objects. This object combines a complex contour field with highly contrasting orange, red, and yellow hues. We suspect that these qualities underlie the effectiveness of this stimulus. This speculation is consistent with the findings in the field of visual preferences of human infants.[1,4] The infant's view of the object consists of a red and orange display, circular in form, with a diameter of about $1\frac{1}{2}$ inches. He sees a dark red

*Infants' daily records were screened under the supervision of Drs. P. Wolff and L. Crowell for signs of abnormality using standard medical criteria. Mothers' records were examined for possible genetic pathology and serious complications during pregnancy or delivery.

core, 1 inch square, surrounded by a very irregular outline. Two feathers, one red and one yellow, protrude 1 inch from the sides. We presented the object to the supine infant at three positions for 30 seconds each. Presentations were initiated when the infant's arms were resting on the crib surface. The infant's attention is elicited by bringing the stimulus into the infant's line of sight at a distance of about 12 inches and shaking it until the infant fixates it. The infant's head is then led to the appropriate test posture (45° left, 45° right, or midline) by moving the stimulus in the necessary direction while maintaining the infant's attention with renewed shaking of the stimulus when necessary. The object is then brought quickly to within 5 inches of the bridge of the nose and held in a stationary position. Infants over $2\frac{1}{2}$ months of age do not require as much cajoling and the stimulus may be placed at 5 inches immediately. This entire procedure takes no more than 10 seconds with most infants, but occasionally it takes much more time and effort to get young subjects to respond appropriately. The order of presentation was changed from test to test. In certain cases it was necessary to vary the position of the object to determine whether a response was accurately oriented or not. All data were collected by the authors. No infant was tested if he was either ill, drowsy, asleep, or obviously distressed.[3,23] On the average, each infant was tested at weekly intervals. Generally, two observers were present during testing. However, both testing and recording could be handled by a single person.

RESULTS
The Normative Sequence

We found that under our test conditions infants exhibit a relatively orderly developmental sequence which culminates in visually directed reaching. The following outline, based upon a frequency analysis, describes briefly the spontaneous behaviors and test responses characteristic for each half-month interval from 1 through 5 months.

1 to 1½ Months

PRETEST OBSERVATIONS. The infant lies in the tonic neck reflex position so that his head is fully turned to the side. The hand towards which the eyes are oriented is often in the center of the visual field, but the eyes neither converge on it nor do they adjust to variations in its position. The infant maintains one direction of gaze for prolonged periods. The infant can be made to track a moving object with his head and eyes over an arc of 180 degrees given the proper stimulus conditions. We have obtained reliable responses using a $7\frac{1}{2}$ inch bright red circle against a 14 by 12 inch flat white background as a stimulus. This target is brought into the line of sight of the supine infant at a distance of 12 to 36 inches from the bridge of his nose. Optimal distance at this age is about 24 inches. Attention is elicited by low amplitude, rapid oscillation of the stimulus in the peripheral portion of the visual field. The same motion in the foveal area is ineffective in initiating fixation. Visual pursuit is then induced by moving the target at an approximate speed of 12 inches per second in a semicircular path above the infant's head and in front of his eyes. At this age, pursuit consists of a series of jerky fixations of the red circle which bring its image to the foveal area. As the target continues to move across the field, there is a lag in the following response of the eye until the image again falls on the peripheral region of the retina. At this point, the infant responds with a rapid recentralizing of the image. If the target does not continue its motion or is moving too slowly, and therefore remains in the foveal range for more than a few seconds, the infant's gaze drifts off. We have called this level of response "peripheral pursuit."

Retinoscopic studies[8] indicate that infants have not yet developed flexible accommodative capacities at this age: their focal distance when attending to stimuli between 6 and 16 inches appears to be fixed at about 9 inches. Visual stimuli closer than 7 inches are rarely fixated.

TEST RESPONSES. In view of the foregoing retinoscopic finding, it is not surprising that the test object fails to elicit the infant's attention. Since the infant's fixed focal distance to near stimuli is approximately 9 inches, the test object at 5 inches produces a badly blurred image on the retina. Usually, however, the infant looks away from the stimulus at this time. When he does attend to the object, he is considerably farsighted (at least three diopters) according to retinoscopic responses. It is clear then that, during this age period, the stimulus is not as effective as it is for older infants whose accommodative capacities are more advanced. This ineffectiveness is probably attributable in large part to loss of the complexity of patterning of the retinal image caused by poor focusing. Occasionally, a brief glance may be directed at the stimulus when it is presented on the side favored by the tonic neck reflex. Presentations on the other side are most always ineffective, since they are generally outside of the infant's field of view, as a result of the tonic neck reflex.

1½ to 2 Months

PRETEST OBSERVATIONS. The tonic neck reflex is typically present. The infant's eyes occasionally converge on and fixate his own hand (usually the extended hand in the preferred tonic neck reflex posture). The direction of gaze now shifts occasionally to various parts of the visual surround. The responses to the retinoscope indicate that the infant now has the capacity to focus a clear image on the retina when the stimulus is 6 inches above the bridge of the nose. Often, at this age, a new form of visual pursuit is seen. Attention may be elicited in the foveal region using the previously described technique, and tracking is continuous over wide sectors (up to 90°) of the stimulus path. During these periods the response seems to anticipate the motion of the stimulus rather than lagging behind as in peripheral pursuit. We have called this behavior "central" pursuit. This finding is in agreement with Gesell's observations.[6]

TEST RESPONSES. The infant glances at the test object in all presentations. However, sustained fixations are only present on the side of the favored tonic neck reflex. At best, fixation lasts only 5 to 10 seconds. Fixation is judged according to Ling's criteria.[18] As Wolff has noted,[23] shifts in activity level occur during these periods. At this time such shifts do not follow immediately upon fixation of the object, but appear gradually. Whether the infant becomes more or less active depends on his initial level of behavior. If an infant is alert and inactive, he usually becomes active; whereas if he is active, he becomes less so as he directs his gaze at the stimulus. The latter phenomenon is more common.

2 to 2½ Months

PRETEST OBSERVATIONS. The tonic neck reflex is still typically present although the head is now only half turned (45°) to the side. In contrast to the previous stages, the infant may shift his gaze rapidly from one part of his surround to another and he rotates his head with comparative ease and rapidity. He now shows a good deal of interest in the examiner. The hand in view in the tonic neck reflex posture is now the object of his attention much of the time that he is awake and alert. The viewed hand may be on the crib surface or held aloft. His eyes now occasionally converge on objects as near as 5 inches from his eyes and central pursuit is usually present. For the first time it is possible to elicit central pursuit of the test object placed as near as 5 inches and moving with a velocity of about 12 inches per second.

TEST RESPONSE. Typically, the infant exhibits immediate and prolonged interest in the stimulus, fixates the object, his activity level shifts, and he makes a swift accurate swipe with the near hand. Usually the object is struck but there is no attempt to grasp since the hand is typically fisted. The probability of a swipe response is greater when the test object is presented on the side of the commonly viewed hand which is the hand extended in the favored tonic neck reflex position.

2½ to 3 Months

PRETEST OBSERVATIONS. The tonic neck reflex is often present though less frequently than in earlier periods. The head is often near the midline position, and the limbs are usually symmetrically placed. Sustained hand regard continues to be very common. Sustained convergence upon objects as near as 3 inches from the eyes can now be elicited. The infant is more active than at earlier ages. According to retinoscopic examinations, the infant's accommodative capacities are fast approaching adult standards. They differ from the adult in that there is a slightly smaller range of accurate function (5 to 20 inches) and a slower rate of adaptation to the changing stimulus distances.

TEST RESPONSES. All presentations of the test object result in immediate fixation and an abrupt decrease in activity. Side presentations elicit either swiping behavior as described in the previous age range or else the infant raises the near hand to within an inch or so of the object (unilateral hand raising) and glances repeatedly from object to hand and back (alternating glances).

3 to 3½ Months

PRETEST OBSERVATIONS. The tonic neck reflex is now rare, and the head is mostly at the midline position. Sustained hand regard is very common, and bilateral arm activity is more frequent than in previous months, with hands clasped together over the midline often present. Occasionally, the glance is directed towards the hands as they approach each other or during their mutual tactual exploration. The infant's accommodative performance is now indistinguishable from that of an adult.

TEST RESPONSES. The typical response to a side presentation is one or both hands raised with alternating glances from the stimulus to the hand nearest the object. The middle presentation is more likely to elicit bilateral activity such as hands over the midline and clasped, or both hands up, or one hand up and the other to the midline where it clutches the clothing. Here too, alternation of glance from hand to object is common.

3½ to 4 Months

PRETEST OBSERVATIONS. The tonic neck reflex is now absent. Occasional sustained hand regard continues. Hands clasped over the midline is common, and visual monitoring of their approach and subsequent interplay is usually present.

TEST RESPONSES. The responses are similar to the previous group with bilateral responses predominating. Hands to the midline and clasped is a favored response at this time even to a side presentation. It is now sometimes combined with a turning of the torso towards the test object (torso orienting).

4 to 4½ Months

PRETEST OBSERVATIONS. Sustained hand regard is now less common, although examination of hands clasped at the midline is sometimes present. The infant is much more active. The feet are often elevated, and the body is occasionally rotated to the side.

TEST RESPONSES. Bilateral responses such as hands to midline, both hands up, or one hand up and the other to the midline are now the most common responses to all presentations. These responses are usually accompanied by several alternating glances from the stimulus to one or both hands and back to the stimulus. Torso orientation to the side presentation is now common. At times, the clasped hands are raised and oriented towards the stimulus. Occasionally, one hand will be raised, looked at, and brought slowly to the stimulus while the glance shifts from hand to object repeatedly. When the hand encounters the object it is fumbled at and crudely grasped. This pattern has been described by Piaget.[20] Towards the end of this stage, opening of the hand in anticipation of contact with the object is seen.

4½ to 5 Months

PRESENT OBSERVATIONS. At this age pretest findings are no different from those obtained during the previous stage.

TEST RESPONSES. The last stage of this sequence is signified by the appearance of what we call top level reaching.* This response is a rapid lifting of one hand from out of the visual field to the object. As the hand approaches the object, it opens in anticipation of contact. Hands to the midline with alternating glances and Piaget-type responses are still more likely than top level reaching, but within the next few weeks they drop out rather quickly.

The chronology of 10 response patterns is presented in Table 7-I. This chronology focuses on the test responses seen most consistently in our subject groups. The columns "Observed In" and "N" indicate that some of the responses are not shown by all subjects. Although 34 subjects were tested, the group size for each response is considerably smaller for several reasons. First, infants

---

*Halverson[7] has described the gradual refinement of visually directed reaching from this point on. Subsequent developments, however, concern modifications of the trajectory and posture of the hand rather than new categories of prehensile response.

TABLE 7-I
Chronology of Responses

Response	Observed In	N	Median and Range of Dates of First Occurrence
Swipes at object	13	13	(2:5)
Unilateral hand raising	15	15	(2:17)
Both hands raised	16	18	(2:21)
Alternating glances (hand and object)	18	19	(2:27)
Hands to midline and clasp	15	15	(3:3)
One hand raised with alternating glances, other hand to midline clutching dress	11	19	(3:8)
Torso oriented towards object	15	18	(3:15)
Hands to midline and clasp and oriented towards object	14	19	(4:3)
Piaget-type reach	12	18	(4:10)
Top level reach	14	14	(4:24)

(Timeline scale: 2m · 3m · 4m · 5m · 6m)

were not available for study for a uniform period of time. All of our subjects were born at the maternity section of the hospital. Usually they were transferred to the children's section at 1 month of age where they remained until they were placed in private homes. Aside from neonatal screening procedures, all tests and observations were performed at the children's section. Some infants arrived from maternity at 1 month of age and stayed through the next five or six months. Others arrived at the same age and left after a few weeks, and still others arrived as late as 3 months of age, etc. Since we were concerned with the time of emergence of the new forms of behavior, we were obliged to exclude a large number of data because we could not be sure that a late-arriving infant would not have shown the response had we been able to test him earlier.

Another factor which guided us in the analysis of our test protocols was the ease of detection of responses. Each of the ten items listed is relatively easy to pick out of the diverse behaviors shown by infants and therefore can serve as a developmental index. At times, the presence of a response was questionable. Such data were excluded from the analysis. It is likely therefore that the correct median dates are actually a few days earlier than those charted. A single clear instance of a response was considered sufficient for inclusion in the "observed" column, although multiple instances were by far more common. Another relevant consideration is the limiting effect of weekly testing. Although more frequent testing would have resulted in more accurate data, we felt the added exposure to test conditions might introduce practice effects into our subject groups.

Summary of the Normative Sequence

In summary, then, given the proper object in the proper location and provided that the state of the subject is suitable, our subjects first exhibited object-oriented arm movements at about 2 months of age. The swiping behavior of this stage, though accurate, is not accompanied by attempts at grasping the object; the hand remains fisted throughout the response. From 3 to 4 months of age unilateral arm approaches decrease in favor of bilateral patterns, with hands to the midline and clasped the most common response. Unilateral responses reappear at about 4 months, but the hand is no longer fisted and is not typically brought directly to the object. Rather, the open hand is raised to the vicinity of the object and then brought closer to it as the infant shifts his glance repeatedly from hand to object until the object is crudely grasped. Finally, just prior to 5 months of age, infants begin to reach for and successfully grasp the test object in one quick, direct motion of the hand from out of the visual field.

An Analysis of the Normative Sequence

When one examines the course of development of prehension, it becomes apparent that a number of relatively distinct sensorimotor systems contribute to its growth. These include the visual-motor systems of eye-arm and eye-hand, as well as the tactual-motor system of the hands. These systems seem to develop at different times, partly as a result of varying histories of exposure, and may remain in relative isolation from one another. During the development of prehension these various systems gradually become coordinated into a complex superordinate system which integrates their separate capacities.

During stages 1 and 2 (1 to 2 months), the infant displays several response capacities that are relevant to the ontogeny of prehension. The jerky but coordinated head and eye movements which are seen in *peripheral* visual pursuit are one such capacity. This form of pursuit is an innate coordination since it is present at birth.[19] However, another form of pursuit is seen during the second month. The smooth tracking response present in *central* visual pursuit is a more highly refined visual-motor coordination. The path now followed by the eyes appears to anticipate, and thus predict, the future position of a moving target. Whether this response is in fact predictive at this early age remains to be conclusively determined. But this growing capacity of the infant to localize and follow with both his eyes and head is clearly an important prerequisite for the development of visually directed prehension. It should be noted that motion seems to be the stimulus property critical for eliciting attention during this stage.

Arm movements show little organized development at this stage and are limited in the variety of positions that they can assume, in large part because of the influence of the tonic neck reflex. The grasp reflex is present and can be elicited if the palm of the hand encounters a suitable object. But neither of these capacities is yet integrated with the more highly developed visual-motor tracking capacity. Infants of this age do not readily attend to near objects, namely those less than 9 inches distant. Thus, it is not surprising that objects which the infant is able to explore tactually, including his own hands, are not yet visually significant. At this stage, the tactual-motor capacities of the hands remain isolated from the visual-motor ones of the eye and head.

During stages 3 and 4 (2 to 3 months), the isolation of response capacities begins to break down, in part because the infant's eyes can now readily converge and focus on objects that are potentially within his reach. Central pursuit can be elicited from as near as 5 inches. One important consequence of this is that the infant now spends a good deal of time looking at his own hands. In addition, visual interest, sustained fixation, and related shifts in activity level are now readily elicited by a static presentation of the proper stimulus object. This indicates a growing capacity for focusing attention which is no longer exclusively dependent on motion.

In keeping with the above developments, it is at this stage that we see swiping, the first prehensory behavior. The appearance of this behavior indicates the development of a new visual-motor localizing capacity, one which now coordinates not only movements of the eyes and head but also those of the arms. Swiping is highly accurate, although it occasionally overshoots the target. It does not include any attempt at visually controlled grasping. Such grasping would indicate anticipation of contact with the object and is not seen at this stage. Instead, grasping is exclusively a tactually directed pattern which remains to be integrated into the growing visual-motor organization of prehension.

The next prehensory response, which develops soon after swiping, is that of raising a hand to within an inch or so of the stationary object followed by a series of alternating glances from object to hand and back. The crude but direct swiping response has been replaced by a more refined behavior. The visual-motor systems of eye-object and eye-hand are now juxtaposed by the infant and seem to be successively compared with each other in some way. This is the kind of behavior that Piaget refers to as the mutual assimilation and accommodation of sensorimotor schemas.[24]

During stages 5 and 6 (3 to 4 months), the infant exhibits mutual grasping, a new pattern of spontaneous behavior. This pattern, in which the hands begin to contact and manipulate each other, is particularly important for tactual-motor development. In addition, the visual monitoring of this pattern results in the linking of vision and touch by means of a double feedback system. For the eyes not only see what the hands feel, namely each other, but each hand simultaneously touches and is being actively touched.

In keeping with these developments, hands to midline and clasped is now seen as a test response. This is a tactual-motor response pattern during which the infant fixates the object while the hands grasp each other at the midline. Grasping is thus coming to be related to the now highly developed visual-motor coordination of the head and eyes. At this time, however, grasping is not yet directed towards the external object but remains centered on the tactual interaction of the infant's own hands.

During stages 7 and 8 (4 to 5 months), the infant finally succeeds in integrating the various patterns of response that have developed and coordinating them via their intersection at the object. Thus, alternating glances now become combined with the slow moving of the hand directly to the object which is fumbled at and slowly grasped. The visual-motor schemas of eye-hand and eye-object have now become integrated with the tactual-motor schema of the hand, resulting in the beginnings of visually directed grasping. This pattern has been described by Piaget.[20] It is not until the attainment of the highest level of reaching at the end of this stage, however, that one sees the complete integration of the anticipatory grasp into a rapid and direct reach from out of the visual field. Here all the isolated or semi-isolated components of prehensory development come together in the attainment of adult-like reaching just prior to 5 months of age.

The Role of Contact with the Environment

Having made a preliminary analysis of the normative sequence of behaviors, we may proceed to a detailed consideration of the question that originally motivated this study. How can we test for the contribution made by conditions of exposure to the development of prehension? At what stages of growth and in what manner can experimental techniques be applied? Our findings, examined in the light of these questions, yield a projected program of experimental investigation.

Experimental research with both human adults[10-14,16] and with animals[15,21] has strikingly demonstrated the importance of motility for the development and maintenance of visual-motor capacities. This work has shown that the variations in visual stimulation that result from self-produced movements constitute a source of information to the growing nervous system that is required for the proper development of function. Two factors are critical for providing this information. They are certain natural movements of the organism and the presence of stable objects in the environment that can provide sources of visual stimulation that will vary as a consequence of these movements. Deprivation studies with higher infra-human mammals have shown that, in the absence of either one of these factors, vision does not develop normally.[15,21] No comparable systematic studies of the importance of such factors in the development of human infants are available. However, the complementarity of results between studies of adult rearrangement and of neonatal deprivation in animals[13] leads to specific suggestions as to the conditions of exposure essential for the development of the infant's coordination. For example, in the special case of eye-hand coordination, the work of our laboratory indicates the importance of visual feedback from certain components of motion of the arm, as well as from grosser movements of the body, as in locomotion. How shall we test the applicability of these findings to the development of the human infant? Obviously, we cannot experimentally deprive human infants, but the subjects of the present study are already being reared under conditions that seem to us deficient for optimal development. Thus, we are able to study the effects of systematic additions to the environments of our subjects. Moreover, since our research emphasis is on the importance of the exposure history of the human infant, the fact that our subjects are born and reared under uniform conditions is a distinct advantage. It assures us that previous and current extra-experimental exposure will not be a major source of variability as it might well be under conditions of homerearing.

The everyday surroundings of our subjects are bland and relatively featureless compared to the average home environment. Moreover, the infants almost always lie in the supine posture which, in comparison to the prone position, it much less conducive to head and trunk motility. Furthermore, the crib mattresses have become hollowed out to the point where gross body movements are restricted. We plan to provide a group of these infants with enriched visual surrounds designed to elicit visual-motor responses. In addition, we will place these infants in the prone position for brief periods each day and use plywood supports to flatten the mattress surfaces. These changes should result in significantly greater motility in the presence of stable visible objects. We will assess the effects of such procedures by comparing the sensorimotor capacities of our experimental group with those of a control group reared under currently existing conditions.

We recognize that any effects which may result from the exposure of infants to enriched sensory environments are contingent upon the state of maturation of their neuromuscular mechanisms. We do not, for example, expect visually directed reaching within the first six weeks of life, when the infant's hands are generally kept fisted and objects within reaching distance are inappropriate for sustained visual fixation. On the other hand, it is quite likely that some aspects of the development of prehension are critically dependent upon prior sensorimotor experience.

A preliminary study has confirmed our suspicion that the onset of sustained hand regard is in part a function of the alternative visual objects present in the infant's environment. For example, under the normal hospital routine where alternative visual objects are at a minimum, the control group of infants began sustained hand viewing at about 2 months of age. In contrast, a pilot group whose cribs were equipped with a variety of objects for viewing failed to exhibit sustained hand regard until 3 months of age. The reason for this marked delay appeared to be the presence of a small mirror placed some 7 inches above the infant's eyes. Invariably, within a week after being placed in the experimental cribs, each infant began to spend most of his waking time staring at his reflection in the mirror. This stimulus virtually monopolized the infants' visual exploratory efforts. This average delay of one month in the appearance of sustained hand regard seems to be clear evidence of the relevance of the visual surround for its development. Since the time of onset can be significantly delayed by a procedure which diverts the infant's attention from his hands, perhaps other procedures designed to direct the infant's attention towards his hands will result in the advanced onset of sustained hand regard. However, the normal hospital environment may already constitute the optimal condition for directing the child's attention to his hands, since there is virtually nothing else for him to look at. If so, our control group should not be considered deprived with respect to the visual requirements underlying the onset of this particular behavior.

Once sustained hand regard appears, swiping at the test object inevitably follows within a few days. On the average, our infants first exhibited swiping responses at 2 months and 3 days of age. We have called this behavior swiping rather than reaching since the hand is kept fisted, thereby precluding successful grasping of the object. Swiping, like visual motor pursuit and fixation, seems to be a stimulus-bound response. This means that the presence of stimuli appropriately designated and located guarantees repeated responses from the infants. The latter half of the path of the swiping response is often viewed by our infants. Moreover, this path is curved rather than direct and entails a rotation of the hand. Precisely this kind of experience has been found necessary for the compensation of errors in reaching caused by the wearing of prism-goggles by human adults.[9] We therefore plan to provide our infants with stimulus objects suitably designed to elicit such responses as soon as sustained hand regard appears. We suspect that the increased occurrence of these rotational arm movements and the feedback stimulation that results may facilitate the acquisition of eye-hand coordinations in infants. We cannot, however, expect visually directed prehension to occur at $2\frac{1}{2}$ months of age, even though it seems that we can elicit repeated swiping behavior almost at will. The missing element is the grasp, which is precluded by an innate reflex which keeps the hands fisted, or partially so, until at least 3 months of age.

As the tonic neck reflex drops out at about 3 months of age, the arms are released from their asymmetric posture and tend to move in more similar paths. The inevitable consequences of this development is the mutual discovery of the hands at some point near the middle of the infant's chest. This pattern is initially non-visual. It is usually several weeks before the infant begins to look at this tactual interplay of his hands. He then spends a great deal of time watching their mutual approach and departure as well as their contacts. Piaget[20] has suggested that this pattern may be conducive to the onset of visually directed prehension of external objects. We have found that this is sometimes the case, but, just as often, infants who exhibit this behavior early are either late in top level reaching or arrive at this stage at about the median age of the group. The prolonged observation of one hand approaching and grasping the other is a virtually innate guarantee of the visual-motor integration of the arm approach and the grasp. On the other hand, since swiping, which appears six weeks earlier, guarantees frequent contact of the hand with the prehensory object, and tactual exploration and the grasp reflex often result in closure, it seems reasonable to assume that integrated prehensory responses would develop through the introduction of suitable external objects at this earlier time. Perhaps it is the absence of such objects that accounts for the 81-day average gap between the onset of swiping responses and the attainment of successful visually directed reaching seen in our subject group.

In addition to the study of prehension, we plan similar tests of the role of exposure in the development of prerequisite behaviors such as accommodation, convergence, and visual motor pursuit.

REFERENCES

1. Berylne, D. The influence of the albedo and complexity of stimuli on visual fixation in the human infant. *Brit. J. Psychol., 49*:315-318, 1958.
2. Darwin, C. *The Descent of Man.* Modern Library, 1871.
3. Escalona, S. The study of individual differences and the problems of state. *J. Amer. Acad. Child Psychiat., 1*:11-37, 1962.
4. Fantz, R. L. A method for studying depth perception in infants under six months of age. *Psychol. Rec., 11*:27-32, 1961.
5. Gesell, A., and Amatruda, C. *Developmental Diagnosis.* New York, Hoeber, 1941.
6. Gesell, A., Ilg, F. L., and Bullis, G. F. *Vision: Its Development in Infant and Child.,* New York, Hoeber, 1949.

7. Halverson, H. M. An experimental study of prehension in infants by means of systematic cinema records. *Genet. Psychol. Monogr., 10:*110-286, 1932.

8. Haynes, H. Retinoscopic Studies of Human Infants. Unpublished manuscript.

9. Hein, A. Typical and Atypical Feedback in Learning a New Coordination. Paper read at Eastern Psychol. Ass., Atlantic City, April, 1959.

10. Held, R. Shifts in binaural localization after prolonged exposures to atypical combinations of stimuli. *Amer. J. Psychol., 68:*526-548, 1955.

11. Held, R. Exposure-history as a factor in maintaining stability of perception and coordination. *J. nerv. ment. Dis., 132:*26-32, 1961.

12. Held, R. Adaptation to rearrangement and visual-spatial aftereffects. *Psychol. Beiträge, 6:*439-450, 1962.

13. Held, R., and Bossom, J. Neonatal deprivation and adult rearrangement: complementary techniques for analyzing plastic sensory-motor coordinations. *J. Comp. Physiol. Psychol., 54:*33-37, 1961.

14. Held, R., and Hein, A. Adaptation of disarranged hand-eye coordinations contingent upon reafferent stimulation. *Percept. Mot. Skills, 8:*87-90, 1958.

15. Held, R., and Hein, A. Movement-produced stimulation in the development of visually-guided behavior. *J. Comp. Physiol. Psychol., 56:*872-876, 1963.

16. Held, R., and Schlank, M. Adaptation to optically-increased distance of the hand from the eye by reafferent stimulation. *Amer. J. Psychol., 72:*603-605, 1959.

17. Jones, F. W. *Arboreal Man.* London, E. Arnold, 1916.

18. Ling, B. A genetic study of sustained visual fixation and associated behavior in the human infant from birth to six months. *J. Genet. Psychol., 61:*227-277, 1942.

19. Peiper, A. *Die Eigenart der Kindlichen Hirntätigkeit,* 2nd ed. Leipzig, Thieme, 1956.

20. Piaget, J. *The Origins of Intelligence in Children,* 2nd ed. New York, International Universities Press, 1952.

21. Riesen, A. H. Plasticity of behavior: psychological series. In H. Harlow and C. Woolsey (Eds.) , *Biological and Biochemical Bases of Behavior.* Madison, Univer. of Wisconsin Press, 1958, pp. 425-450.

22. Riesen, A. H. Stimulation as a requirement for growth and function in behavioral development. In D. W. Fiske and S. R. Maddi (Eds.) , *Functions of Varied Experience.* Homewood, Ill., Dorsey Press, 1961, pp. 57-80.

23. Wolff, P. H. Observations on newborn infants. *Psychosom. Med., 21:*110-118, 1959.

24. Wolff, P. H. The developmental psychologies of Jean Piaget and psychoanalysis. *Psychol. Issues, 2:*1-181, 1960.

S EX, BODY SIZE, birth order, general health, race, social class and other cultural factors are variables which have been associated with motor abilities. Unfortunately, it is difficult to clearly interpret the interrelationship of the variables because of varying experimental results. The following large-scale study by Dr. C. B. Hindley and his associates is interesting because of its method, data analysis, and findings, although it offers no definitive solution. The authors assessed the age of walking in five European countries and also analyzed sex and social class differences within each sample group. Rather than use direct age units, the authors used a logarithmic scale which they felt better represented the fast-paced developmental changes which occur in the early months and the slower changes seen in the toddler period. Dr. Hindley reports significant variation in age of walking between the samples but no sex or class differences within each sample group. Suggested explanations used to account for the differences include genetic variation, differential maternal behaviors, and nutrition.

Chapter 8

Differences in Age of Walking in Five European Longitudinal Samples

C. B. HINDLEY, A. M. FILLIOZAT, G. KLACKENBERG,
D. NICOLET-MEISTER, AND E. A. SAND

INTRODUCTION

THE AIM OF THIS PAPER is to report data on age of first walking in five European longitudinal samples, with reference to the nature of the distributions, differences between them, and relationships to sex and social class. The five studies, in Brussels, London, Paris, Stockholm, and Zurich, have been collaborating with the help of the International Children's Centre. A base line of common methods has been used for the study of both physical and psychological development.[11] The methods of psychological enquiry have included common testing procedures and asking the same questions at the same ages, from infancy onwards.[20]

There have been a number of previous studies of age of onset of walking, the results of, which were summarized by Dennis and Dennis[8] in 1940, and Dennis[7] in 1943. Since then the subject does not appear to have received much attention, except by Pineau[36] and Shapiro,[40] and the more general studies of locomotor development by Pasamanick,[34] Knoblock and Pasamanick,[25,26] and Williams and Scott.[49]

Unfortunately, of the studies reviewed by the Dennis's, all but those of Bayley[1] and Pyles *et al.*[38] depended on mothers' long-term memories. The same applies to Pineau's study.[36] Pyles *et al.*[38] ob-

Reprinted from *Human Biology*, *38*:364-379, 1966, by permission of the Wayne State University Press. Copyright 1966, Wayne State University Press, Detroit, Michigan.

We wish to thank all our colleagues who have helped with the collection of the data; the International Children's Centre for making possible our collection; and Mr. Michael Healy, Dr. L. Martin and Dr. J. M. Tanner, for their helpful comments on the preparation of the data.

tained their information from mothers of infants of 21 months, but they showed that even over such a comparatively short interval mothers tended to underestimate age of onset of 0.4 months. Inaccuracies over longer intervals have been brought to light by McGraw and Molloy,[32] Robbins,[39] and Mednick and Schaffer.[33]

Until fairly recently the possible role of environmental factors in locomotor development had been rather discounted, largely under the influence of Gesell.[14] More generally, Weiss, as recently as 1955, concluded from his work in experimental embryology that "neither learning nor patterns of sensory stimuli have any basic part in the development of orderly cerebral functions"[47] (p. 392). Some of the difficulties entailed by the concept of maturation are discussed by McGraw[31] and Carmichael.[4] Regarding Gesell's evidence, coming primarily from his twin control studies, it has been suggested that Gesell and Thompson's conclusions[15] were rather sweeping, based as they were on twins both of whom had plenty of opportunity for general locomotor activity.[21]

Recent advances in the study of neural structures and chemistry have made it clear, contrary to Weiss' assertion, that differences of experience can have demonstrable effects on the central nervous system. Brattgard[3] was able to detect biochemical effects on individual retinal connecting neurones following the absence of normal stimulation, while Levine and Alpert,[29] Wase and Christensen,[46] and Tapp[44] have demonstrated changes in the gross chemical composition of young animals' brains, related to different degrees of postnatal stimulation.

From a rather different point of view, Widdowson and McCance and their colleagues have demonstrated the possibility of speeding up the processes of physical maturation of rats,[48,9] which are accompanied by behavioral precocity.[28] The authors attribute these effects to the more abundant diet of the accelerated animals. However, as the litter size of these animals was artificially reduced to three, compared with fifteen to twenty in the controls, some of the differences may have been due to this difference in mode of life.

Sufficient has been said to make it desirable to approach any differences to be found in locomotor development free from a priori assumptions and to be ready to consider the possible effects not only of heredity, but of nutrition, and mode of life.

With regard to differences in age of walking, Bayley's finding[1] of a high correlation between it and general measures of motor behavior at the age of 12 months (r = .88) provides justification for referring to results based on the more specific or the more general variable. This is particularly so when the latter has been "gross motor behavior" as in the Knoblock and Pasamanick study.[26]

The aspect of physical maturation which one would most like to be able to relate to locomotor behavior is that of the central nervous system. While in a general way there is evidence of a relationship between myelinization and function,[5,27,31,24,45] it has not as yet been possible to relate neural maturation to behavior in individual children. Such gross factors as prematurity[19,26] and illness[42] are of course associated with delay in locomotion. There seems little consistent relationship with birth weight[36] nor with weight around the age of walking.[35] On the relationship to perhaps the best index of physical maturity, ossification, evidence in the literature is scant.

Sex differences have seldom emerged as significant in any individual study, though girls have usually been reported as walking slightly earlier. Combining the results of ten samples, from Hawaii and the U.S.A., Smith et al.[41] reported a highly significant difference in favor of the girls. This remained so when account was only taken of the six Hawaiian subsamples from whom the data were collected in a comparable manner.[22]

Relationships to socioeconomic variables have not been clear-cut. Bayley and Jones[2] reported negligible correlations on their rather small and somewhat restricted sample. Knoblock and Pasamanick[26] reported significant social class differences among Negro infants in gross motor development at 40 weeks, in favor of the groups of higher status, but not among white infants. Williams and Scott[49] also found social class differences among Negro infants, but in an opposite direction. The greater permissiveness among mothers of the lower groups seemed to be a favorable factor.

Likewise, findings have been contradictory with regard to racial differences. Smith *et al.*[41] found none among their seven Hawaiian groups, whereas Pasamanick[34] found an advance in locomotor development among Negro infants of New Haven compared with white during the first and second year. Yet the later study of Knoblock and Pasamanick[26] on a much larger sample in Baltimore failed to confirm the earlier finding. Their work, that of Williams and Scott,[49] and of Geber[13] all suggest that differences which have been attributed to race can equally, or probably better, be accounted for by socioeconomic and particularly cultural factors.

Contrary to the earlier claims of Gesell, it would appear that stimulation affects locomotor development. Dennis[7] and Pretacznikowa[37] have found considerable locomotor retardation among children in institutions, associated with lack of handling and spending much of their time in cots. The well-known cradle-board study,[8] in which there were no differences according to use or lack of use of the board, is hardly very crucial, as even the cradle-board infants spent much of their day off the board, as the authors themselves made clear. Williams and Scott's findings[49] suggest that permissiveness of mothers is also likely to be of some importance.

SUBJECTS AND SOCIAL ASSESSMENTS

The manner of recruitment of the samples has been described in detail elsewhere.[23] Suffice it to say that in each of the five investigations the attempt was made to recruit a sample of newborn infants as typical as possible of the area in which it was located. Comparisons with the parent populations of the cities in question suggested that the Stockholm sample was the most representative, the Zurich and London samples reasonably so, and that of Brussels rather overweighted with children of the upper social groups. Adequate information on this point is not available for the Paris sample.

Social class was assessed by a summation of scores on the four criteria: parental occupation, parental education, source of income, and quality of dwelling.[16,17,23] The samples differ significantly in social class composition (P < .001). Those of Brussels and Zurich have relatively few cases in classes 4 and 5, and correspondingly more in classes 1, 2 and 3 (Table 8-II). By contrast, the other three samples have the largest numbers of cases in classes 4 and 5.

These differences may be a function of the representativeness of the samples, in some degree, and in interpreting them two other factors should also be taken into account. For one thing, despite efforts to the contrary, it is not unlikely that the application of the social criteria would to some extent be influenced by local standards. This would apply particularly to housing. Equally, the social connotations of a particular occupation, or type of residence, are likely to vary between different cultures. However, in a general way, the obtained differences in social composition may be regarded as probably reflecting the characteristics of the neighborhoods from which the samples were drawn and the mode of life of the inhabitants of the several cities.

METHOD

During the course of extensive interviews with mothers about the behavior of their children,[20] at 9 months, 12 months, 18 months, 2 years, 3 years, the following question was asked: "When did he first walk alone?" The criterion used was that the child could walk a few steps without support. It will be evident that as the bulk of children walk before two years, very few mothers were called upon to remember over a period longer than 6 months, and in most cases less than that.

The information was recorded in terms of calendar months, except at London where it was in weeks, which could readily be converted. As an example of the system used, 10 months was taken to be the midpoint of the category $9\frac{1}{2}$ months but below $10\frac{1}{2}$ months. In one case (Stockholm) 10 months was taken to mean from 10 months up to 11 months, and therefore for all purposes of calculation the midpoint of the category was regarded as 10.5 months. It is to be noted that this lack of uniformity in recording would tend towards overestimation of age of onset in the Stockholm sample, because mothers are more likely to reply in the round figures of 10, 11 etc., rather than $10\frac{1}{4}$, $10\frac{1}{2}$ etc. Thus, the reply "10 months" can be expected to include certain children who walked a little before 10 months, yet they will be included in the 10-11 month category. This will not apply to the other samples, be cause the reply "10 months" will be included in the 10 month category, whether the true age is $9\frac{3}{4}$ or $10\frac{1}{4}$ months.

Errors in estimation of age of walking would be of two main kinds: (1) *Random errors.* These would chiefly tend to occur in attempts at recall and would cancel each other out in any statistical comparisons. (2) *Systematic errors.* (a) Investigators may have used slightly different criteria of what constituted "a few steps." (b) The same may apply to mothers. (c) There may be systematic errors of recall among mothers.

It is conceivable that (b) and (c) may differ for different social and national groups. Certainly Emery-Hauzer and Sand[10] provided evidence that mothers of wanted children tended to overestimate their childrens' abilities, as compared with mothers of unwanted children. Fortunately, it was possible to compare the between-sample results at two ages (12 months and 18 months) when the children were seen by the investigators.

RESULTS

To minimize the effects of any possible variations in the application of the walking, or social criteria, analyses by sex and social class have been done separately for each sample.

Nature of the Distributions of Age of Walking

Smith *et al.*[41] reported that the combined distribution they obtained from Hawaiian and American children was not normal, and preliminary plots of the data from each of the present samples echoed this finding. A plot of age of walking against the logarithm of age yielded distributions which were approximately normal (Fig. 8-1) . However, only in the case of the Stockholm and Zurich samples could the hypothesis of normality be safely accepted. The other three samples yielded significant departures from it (Table 8-I)

To examine matters further, the cumulative distributions of

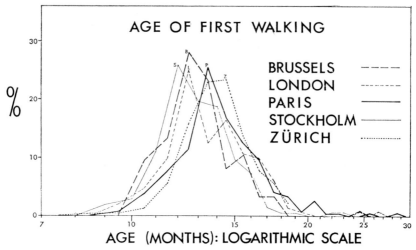

Figure 8-1. Age of first walking in the five samples: frequency distributions. Logarithmic scale of age.

logarithm of age of walking were plotted on probit paper. This results in straight line plots when the underlying distributions are normal.[12,30] As will be seen (Fig. 8-2), all the curves are very close approximations to straight lines between the 5th and 95th percentiles. Below, and particularly above these points, there are divergencies. This suggests that a log-normal type of distribution represent the data very satisfactorily except for a few anomalous children who walk particularly late. Smith *et al.*[41] suggested that they may constitute a special group.

TABLE 8-I

Significance of Departure from Normality of the Distributions of Logarithm of Age of Walking

	Brussels	London		Paris	Stockholm		Zurich	
χ^2	15.18	12.96		24.90	8.52		3.87	
d. f. (k—3)	5	6		9	5		6	
p	<.01	<.05	>.02	<.01	<.20	>.10	<.70	>.50

A lack of correlation between means and variances of the samples (rho 0.1) also suggests that further transformations were unlikely to be of value. Logarithm of age was therefore used as the basis for all further calculations.

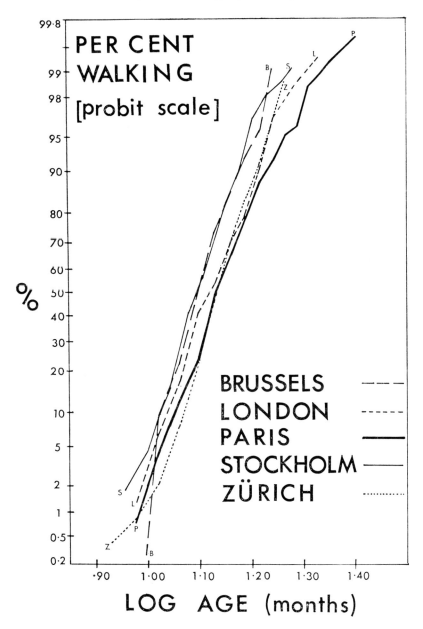

Figure 8-2. Age of first walking: Cumulative frequency distribution. Logarithmic scale of age, probit scale of percentages.

Relationship to Sex and Social Class, Within Samples

Two-way analyses of variance, by sex and social class, were carried out on the data from each sample, which are summarized in Table 8-II. In no sample could any significance be attached to either sex or social-class differences, nor was there any significant interaction between them (Table 8-III).

Considerable differences are to be found among the standard

TABLE 8-II

Age of Walking by Sex and Social Class in Each Sample*

All values are in terms of logarithm of age in months except the last two columns, which are in months (S.D.'s × 100)

	Social Class	Boys			Girls			Total Sample			
		N	Mean (×100)	S.D. (×100)	N	Mean (×100)	S.D. (×100)	Mean	S.D. (×100)	Mean (months)	Median (months)
Brussels	1 & 2	42	1.118	6.99	34	1.108	6.46				
N = 211	3	48	1.109	6.75	42	1.089	5.49	1.102	6.34	12.65	12.48
	4 & 5	25	1.089	5.50	20	1.095	5.76				
London	1 & 2	12	1.162	6.16	10	1.128	12.57				
N = 152	3	24	1.111	6.59	21	1.106	6.27	1.124	7.40	13.31	13.23
	4 & 5	39	1.121	6.51	46	1.131	7.78				
Paris	1 & 2	18	1.132	4.39	20	1.146	6.92				
N = 272	3	58	1.144	6.13	43	1.138	6.92	1.140	7.33	13.81	13.58
	4 & 5	71	1.138	8.01	62	1.141	8.63				
Stockholm	1 & 2	29	1.104	5.01	21	1.100	5.92				
N = 209	3	39	1.099	6.97	26	1.095	6.38	1.097	6.45	12.51	12.44
	4 & 5	52	1.096	7.02	42	1.093	6.70				
Zurich	1 & 2	32	1.122	6.65	25	1.142	5.06				
N = 233	3	81	1.136	5.54	78	1.132	5.52	1.134	5.65	13.59	13.63
	4 & 5	5	1.125	4.90	12	1.150	6.10				

Significance of Differences:

Social Composition of Five Samples $\chi^2 = 180.3$, d. f. 8, $p < 0.001$

Within Samples, Age of Walking Means:	No significant differences by sex or social class (See Table 8-III).
Between Samples, Age of Walking Variances:	Differ significantly ($p < 0.001$), by Bartlett test, (Snedecor, 1956, p. 287).
Means:	Differ significantly ($p < 0.001$) by between-within analysis of variance, taking account of heterogeneous variance (Snedecor, 1956, p. 288).
Modified t tests of all differences Snedecor, 1956, p. 98):	Stockholm and Brussels each differed significantly from the other three means ($p < 0.001$); London differed significantly from Paris ($p < 0.05$).

TABLE 8-III

Within Sample Analysis of Variance by Sex and Social C

Mean squares in units of logarithm of age in months × ·

		Sex	Social Class	Interaction	Resid
Brussels	d. f.	1	2	2	205
	mean square	5.020	10.520	3.750	3.955
	p	> .25	< .10 > .05	> .25	
London	d. f.	1	2	2	146
	mean square	0.450	11.490	4.210	5.449
	p	> .25	< .20 > .10	> .25	
Paris	d. f.	1	2	2	266
	mean square	0.023	0.143	1.415	5.460
	p	> .25	> .25	> .25	
Stockholm	d. f.	1	2	2	203
	mean square	0.578	0.839	0.021	4.247
	p	> .25	> .25	> .25	
Zurich	d. f.	1	2	2	227
	mean square	0.450	0.580	4.090	3.125
	p	> .25	> .25	> .25	

Values for sex, social class and interaction are unbiased estimates (method of fitting constants), to compensate for disproportionate subclass numbers (Snedecor, 1956).

deviations of the subgroups within some of the samples (Table 8-II). By the Bartlett test,[43] they proved to be significant for the Paris sample (P < 0.01), and nearly so for the London sample (P < 0.10). However, as no regular trends, according either to sex or social class are discernible (Table 8-II), no account was taken of these differences in further analyses.

Differences Between Samples

In view of the lack of relationship to age of walking of sex and social class, these factors could be ignored in a direct comparison of the overall data from the five samples.

A Bartlett test revealed highly significant differences in their variances (P < 0.001) (Table 8-II.). That this is not attributable simply to the low standard deviation of the Zurich sample was confirmed by a similar level of significance (P < 0.001) among the other four.

Mean age of walking differed considerably between the five samples (Table 8-II), and analysis of variance (taking account of heterogeneous variance,[43] indicated a high level of significance of these differences (P < 0.001). Their extent can perhaps be most directly compared in terms of medians, which ranged from 12.44 months in the Stockholm sample to 13.58 months in that of Paris. As a check on any systematic differences in errors on the part of mothers, numbers walking by $11\frac{1}{2}$ months were compared. This age immediately preceded the 12 month testing sessions, which therefore provided a check by the investigators on mothers' claims. This revealed similar differences (x^2 44.27, d.f. 4, P < 0.001), the sole change being reversal of order of the two latest walking samples, Zurich and Paris.

DISCUSSION

Nature of the Distributions

Rather surprisingly, a perusal of the literature yields no previous suggestion that distributions of age of walking approximate to normal form when logarithm of age is employed. The present results may be accepted with considerable confidence, insofar as reliance is not placed on the long-term memories of mothers, and as the curves from the five samples are reasonably consistent in form.

On the face of it, there is every reason for supposing that logarithmic measures of age may be more appropriate for studying the development of behavior than ordinary age units. They take account of the rapidity of early development, and gradual deceleration in rate, by giving equivalence, for example, to the interval between 2 months and 3 months, and that between 20 months and 30 months. A previous study of maternal practices which themselves are likely to depend partly on the infants' rate of development, suggested that age of weaning from bottle, and age of starting elimination training, could also best be represented in logarithmic units of age.[23]

Social Class Differences

In none of the samples did we find evidence of the kind of differences reported by Knoblock and Pasamanick[25] or Williams and Scott.[49] This suggests, that in these five samples the differences in mode of life of the social-class groups are not sufficient to affect

gross locomotor development. Such a supposition v
keeping with the comparison of physical growth d
five samples,[18] which, contrary to earlier studies, again ...
evidence of social class differences. To account for this Graffar
and Corbier call attention to the recent improvement of living
standards of the lower social-class groups in advanced industrial
countries. Apart from a diminution in nutritional differences,
more general differences in mode of life probably decreased.

Sex Differences

Unlike the Hawaiian study,[22,41] the present investigation not
only gives no evidence of a significant sex difference within any
sample, but there is no consistency of trend from one sample to
another (Table 8-II). Nor are there consistent trends of sex differences in variances.

The discrepancy between the two studies can, perhaps, be ac
counted for by reference to the hypothesis employed by Graffar
and Corbier,[18] to the effect that boys tend to be more affected by
adverse circumstances than girls. In that case, a difference in favor
of the girls would be expected in the less favorable socioeconomic
conditions of Hawaii around 1930, rather than in those of samples coming from the relatively favored circumstances of Western
Europe in the 1950's.

Differences Between Samples

In seeking possible reasons for the very significant differences
in onset of walking in the different samples, several possibilities
suggest themselves. If they are an artefact of slight differences in
the use of the criteria, it would primarily be on the part of the
investigators, as the check on numbers walking by $11\frac{1}{2}$ months
would on the whole eliminate the maternal factor. The possibility of the investigators using different criteria cannot be entirely
eliminated, but becomes less likely to be a serious factor as the
order of the samples in mean age of walking is identical with that
of their means on the Brunet-Lézine development test at one year,
and almost so with the order of their mean heights at one year.[18]
On balance, it seems justifiable to regard the differences as prob-

ably reflecting underlying population differences, especially as social class was not a significant factor.

The relationship to the infant-test scores and to height at one year, though it needs confirming by further within-sample studies, suggests that some samples are generally somewhat more advanced than others in general development at one year. This might conceivably reflect genetic differences, though this would not seem the most likely explanation in the light of the findings of Smith *et al.*[41] and Geber.[13] Further, although the Stockholm sample is likely to differ racially from the others, it is not at all obvious that the Brussels sample—which is near to that of Stockholm in age of walking—is more closely related racially to it, than to the other three samples.

Possible environmental factors would be those of nutrition, and of maternal handling. Evidence on neither of these is presently available, but there could be differences in the general approach of mothers of the type studied by Williams and Scott[49] and Geber.[13] The differences in height at one year suggest that a nutritional factor might be involved, consistent with the animal studies of Lát *et al.*[28] If it were, it would presumably differ more between the samples than between any of the social class groups within samples.

The significant differences in the variability of the samples* is something which does not appear to have been previously reported, but a reanalysis of the Smith *et al.*[41] data brings to light evidence of the same phenomenon among six racial subgroups. To what extent such differences may express genetic or environmental differences it is not possible to say. Were there any evidence of significant social class differences within the samples, one would suppose that the presence of relatively fewer cases from the less favored classes 4 and 5, in the Brussels and Zurich samples, might be responsible for their smaller variances.

Many of the points raised require further investigation, but the present study at least suggests that this would be worthwhile.

---

*We are indebted to Mr. M. J. R. Healy for pointing out that these differences must be accepted with some caution, as the Bartlett test is sensitive to the elongations of the tails of the distributions (Fig. 8-1) .

SUMMARY AND ABSTRACT

Previous studies of the relation of age of first walking to sex, social and racial factors, are reviewed, and attention is called to the limitations of long-term retrospective data. In this investigation ages of first walking are compared of children from five European longitudinal samples with N's ranging from 152 to 272. The data were analyzed in terms of logarithm of age of walking, which brought the distributions nearer to normality. There were no significant sex nor social class differences within any of the samples, contrary to findings of some other investigators. The five samples differed significantly in variances and in means. Possible reasons for these differences, including genetic, nutritional, and parental factors, are discussed.

REFERENCES

1. Bayley, N. The development of motor abilities within the first three years. *Monogr. Soc. Res. Child Develop., 1:*(No. 1), 1935.

2. Bayley, N., and Jones, H. E. Environmental correlates of mental and motor development: A cumulative study from infancy to 6 years. *Child Develop., 8:*329-41, 1937.

3. Brattgard, S. O. The importance of adequate stimulation for the chemical composition of retinal ganglion cells during early post-natal development. *Acta Radiol. Suppl. 96.*

4. Carmichael, L. The onset and early development of behavior. In L. Carmichael (Ed.), *Manual of Child Psychology,* 2nd ed. New York, Wiley, 1954, pp. 60-185.

5. Conel, J. Le R. *The Postnatal Development of the Human Cerebral Cortex:* Vol I. *Cortex of the Newborn* (1939), Vol. II *Cortex of the One-month Infant* (1941). Cambridge, Harvard University Press, 1939-1941.

6. Dennis, W. On the possibility of advancing and retarding the motor development of infants. *Psychol. Rev., 50:*203-218, 1943.

7. Dennis, W., Causes of retardation among institutionalized children: Iran. *J. Genet. Psychol., 96:*47-59, 1960.

8. Dennis, W., and Dennis, M. G. The effect of cradling practices on the age of walking in Hopi children. *J. Genet. Psychol., 56:*77-86, 1940.

9. Dickerson, J. W. T., and Widdowson, E. M. Some effects of accelerating growth: II Skeletal development. *Proc. Roy. Soc., B, 152:*207-217, 1960.

10. Emery-Hauzeur, C., and Sand, E. A. Enfants désirés et non-désirés. *Enfance, 15:*109-126, 1962.
11. Falkner, F. (Ed.) *Child Development—An International Method of Study.* Vol. 5 in *Modern Problems in Pediatrics.* Basel, Karger, 1960.
12. Finney, D. *Probit Analysis,* 2nd ed. Cambridge, Cambridge University Press, 1952.
13. Geber, M. Problèmes posés par le développement du jeune enfant Africaine en fonction de son milieu social. *Travail Hum., 23:*97-111, 1960.
14. Gesell, A. *The Ontogenesis of Infant Behaviour.* In Carmichael, L. (Ed.), *Manual of Child Psychology,* 2nd ed., New York, Wiley, 1954. pp. 335-373.
15. Gesell, A., and Thompson, A. Learning and growth in identical infant twins: An experimental study by the method of co-twin control. *Genet. Psychol. Monogr., 6:*1-124, 1929.
16. Graffar, M. Une méthode de classification sociale des échantillons de population. *Courr. Cent. Int. Enf., 6:*455-459, 1956.
17. Graffar, M. Social study of the samples. *In* Falkner (1960), pp. 30-42.
18. Graffar, M., and Corbier, J. Contribution à l'étude de l'influence socio-économique sur la croissance et le développement de l'enfant. *Courrier, 16:*1-25, 1966.
19. Hess, J. H., Mohr, G. J., and Bartelme, P. F. *The Physical and Mental Growth of Prematurely Born Children.* Chicago, Univ. of Chicago Press, 1934.
20. Hindley, C. B. The psychological investigations. *In* Falkner (1960), pp. 43-69.
21. Hindley, C. B. Learning theory and personality development. *In* R. MacKeith and J. Sandler (Eds.), *Psychosomatic Aspects of Paediatrics.* Oxford, Pergamon Press, 1961, pp. 71-102.
22. Hindley, C. B. Race and sex differences in age of walking—a re-analysis of the Smith *et al.* (1930) data. *J. Genet. Psychol.,* 1967.
23. Hindley, C. B.; Filliozat, A. M.; Klackenberg, G.; Nicolet-Meister, D., and Sand, E. A. Some differences in infant-feeding and elimination training in five European longitudinal samples. *J. Child Psychol. Psychiat., 6:*179-201, 1965.
24. Kennedy, C. Physiologic characteristics of growth of the human brain. *J. Pediat., 59:*928-938, 1961.
25. Knoblock, H., and Pasamanick, B. Further observations on the behavioral development of Negro children. *J. Genet. Psychol., 83:*137-157, 1953.
26. Knoblock, H., and Pasamanick, B. The relationship of race and socio-economic status to the development of motor behaviour patterns in infancy. *Psychiat. Res. Rep.,* No. 10, 1958.
27. Langworthy, C. *Development of Behavior Patterns and Myelinization in*

the Human Fetus and Infant. Carneigie Institute, Pub. No. 139, Washington, 1933.

28. Lat, J.; Widdowson, E. M., McCance, R. A. Some effects of accelerating growth: III. Behavior and nervous activity. *Proc. Roy. Soc. B., 153:* 347-356, 1960.

29. Levine, S., and Alpert, M. Differential maturation of the central nervous system as a function of early experience. *Amer. Arch. Gen. Psychiat., 1:*403-405, 1959.

30. Martin, L. *Etude biométrique de grandeurs somatiques recuellis sur les conscrits et recrues belges et de leur évolution.* Bruxelles, Institut National de Statistique, 1958.

31. McGraw, M. B. Maturation of behavior. *In* L. Carmichael (Ed.) *Manual of Child Psychology.* New York, Wiley, 1946, pp. 332-369.

32. McGraw, M. B., and Molloy, L. B. The pediatric anamnesis: Inaccuracies in eliciting developmental data. *Child. Develop. 12:*255-265, 1941.

33. Mednick, S. A., and Schaffer, H. R. Mothers' retrospective reports in child-rearing research. *Amer. J. Orthopsychiat., 33:*457-461, 1963.

34. Pasamanick, B. A comparative study of the behavioral development of Negro infants. *J. Genet Psychol., 69:*3-44, 1946.

35. Peatman, J. G., and Higgons, R. A. Relation of infants' weight and boby build to locomotor development. *Amer. J. Orthopsychiat., 12:*234-240, 1942.

36. Pineau, M. Développement de l'infant et dimension de la famille. *Biotypologie, 22:*25-53, 1961.

37. Pretacznikowa, M. Mental development of children in the first year of life in three kinds of educational environment. (English summary) *Psychol. Wych., 3:*32-46, 1960.

38. Pyles, M. K.; Stolz, H. R., and MacFarlane, J. W. The accuracy of mothers' reports on birth and developmental data. *Child Develop., 6:*165-176, 1935.

39. Robbins, L. C. The accuracy of parental recall of aspects of child development and of child rearing practices. *J. Abnorm. Soc. Psychol., 66:* 261-270, 1963.

40. Shapiro, H. The development of walking in a child. *J. Genet. Psychol., 100:*221-226, 1962.

41. Smith, M. E.; Lecker, G.; Dunlap, J. W., and Cureton, E. E. The effects of race, sex and environment on the age at which children walk. *J. Genet. Psychol., 38:*489-498, 1930.

42. Smith, S. Influence of illness during the first two years on infant development. *J. Genet. Psychol., 39:*284-287, 1931.

43. Snedecor, G. W. *Statistical Methods,* 5th ed. Ames, Iowa State University Press, 1956.

44. Tapp, T. J. Infant handling: effects on avoidance learning, brain weight, and cholinesterase activity. *Science, 140:*486-487, 1963.

45. Tilney, F. Behavior in its relation to the development of the brain: II. Correlation between the development of the brain and behavior in the albino rat from embryonic states to maturity. *Bull. Neurol. Inst. N. Y., 3:*252-358, 1933.
46. Wase, A. W., and Christensen J. Stimulus deprivation and phospholipide metabolism in cerebral tissue. *AMA Arch. Gen. Psychiat., 2:*171-173, 1960.
47. Weiss, P. Nervous system. *In* Willier, B. H.; Weiss, P. A., and Hamburger, V. *Analysis of Development.* Philadelphia, Saunders, 1955, pp. 346-401.
48. Widdowson, E. M., and McCance, R. A. Some effects of accelerating growth: I. General somatic development. *Proc. Roy. Soc., B, 152:*188-206, 1960.
49. Williams, J. R., and Scott, R. B. Growth and development of Negro infants: IV. Motor development and its relationship to child-rearing practices in two groups of Negro infants. *Child Develop., 24:*103-121, 1953.

T HE QUESTION of genetically determined differences in behavior among racial groups arises periodically. This issue provokes a considerable amount of heated discussion and emotion when investigators attempt to support or refute racial differences in intelligence. But, there probably are some aspects of behavior and development in which differences occur in a comparison of homogeneous genetic groups. Science must determine what these differences are and their importance in human development. Interest in differential motor abilities reoccurred when Dr. M. Geber and Dr. R. Dean reported on the precocious development of Ganda infants in Africa. The Ganda newborn was more advanced in motor behavior than his European or American counterpart. Precocity in motor development was maintained at a high level the first year of life, decreased somewhat during the second year and subsequently declined in the next couple of years. The Ganda infant received almost constant, but varied, stimulation from his caretakers during his first year which might partially explain advanced motor behavior. It is, however, the Ganda baby's ability at birth which intrigues many developmentalists. Replication of the study and further investigations should be fruitful.

Chapter 9

Gesell Tests on African Children

MARCELLE GEBER AND R. F. A. DEAN

IT IS OUR PURPOSE to describe the results of the examination by Gesell tests of 183 African children between 1 and 72 months of age, seen in Kampala or in the country districts around. The work has not been continuous, but has been carried out during three separate visits by one of us (M.G.), each from July to September, in 1954, 1955, and 1956. In 1954, a study was made of the psychologic changes accompanying kwashiorkor in children admitted for treatment to the hospital wards of the Infantile Malnutrition Group. The disease is most prevalent in Uganda during the second year of life, probably because the diet given at weaning is inadequate, and a control group of well-nourished children of the same age was examined at the same time as the children in hospital. It was found that most of the healthy children were precocious in their psychomotor development and that the precocity was greater the younger the child, but that towards the end of the second year it tended to diminish. Younger and older children were therefore tested, and it is now possible to present results for 183 children, of all the ages covered by the development schedule of Gesell: that is, of all ages from 1 month to 6 years. The results are supplemented by an account of findings on 113 newborn children, who were examined by the method described by André Thomas.[1]

From *Pediatrics, 20:*1055-1065, 1957. Reprinted by permission.

The expenses of the investigation were paid from grants made by the International Children's Centre, Paris, and the Mental Health Section of the World Health Organization, Geneva, and we wish to express our thanks especially to Dr. Maurice Gaud, in charge of the African affairs of the Centre, and to Dr. Ronald Hargreaves, formerly Chief of the Section.

We wish to thank Mme. J. Aubry for her encouragement in this investigation and for the benefit of her experience of the effects of separation.

CHILDREN STUDIED

The children were obtained in various ways. One group was seen in the building of the Infantile Malnutrition Group at Mulago Hospital, Kampala, the largest general hospital of the Medical Department of the Uganda Government: They numbered 43 and had been brought to hospital for the treatment of some minor and unimportant illness, or merely to accompany other members of their families. Another 15 children were examined at the Group's Child Welfare Clinic, in a country district about 16 miles from Kampala, and 12 more at a Child Welfare Clinic in the labor lines of a large agricultural estate, also in a country district, and about twenty miles from the town. Forty-five were seen in their own homes in villages a few miles outside the town, and 68 in a kindergarten at a Theological College, thirteen miles from Kampala, where their fathers were training for ordination.

The advantages of a longitudinal study were realized, but for various reasons such a study could not be carried out fully, but 51 children were seen twice in successive years, and 5 were seen three times. Nearly all were children of the theological students or were those who had been seen in their village homes.

The amount of contact with Europeans, the educational level, the social status, and the economic circumstances of the families varied considerably, and most classes were represented except the highly educated (none of the parents had been students at Makerere, the University College of East Africa, or at any other University) and the most wealthy. The agricultural laborers, most of whom belonged to the Wakiga tribe of southwestern Uganda, had the least knowledge of Europeans and their ways, and were the poorest. The families whose children came to hospital, those seen at the Group's Welfare Clinic, and those seen in their own village homes, were nearly all of the Ganda tribe, which inhabits the district around Kampala, and were mostly small holders who could afford more than the bare necessities of life, and were in fairly comfortable circumstances. The villagers were selected originally by their local chief to take part in a socioanthropologic investigation to which the Gesell tests were added. They were selected because the chief believed that they would collaborate well, and they were probably above the other Ganda in general intelligence; most of the fathers had well-paid work in Kampala, and some only returned to their homes on weekends. The theological students had probably had the best schooling of all the fathers, although their wives were mostly less well educated; they had little money, but were well housed by the Theological College, had adequate cheap food, lived as a community and were well accustomed to Europeans. Nearly all were of tribes other than the Ganda.

None of the children examined was suffering, so far as could be ascertained, from any illness likely to affect his performance in the test. If a child due for a test was found to be unwell, the test was postponed until he was better.

CONDUCT OF THE TESTS

The Gesell technique as used in Paris[3] was used without any important modification except that the child, his mother, and the examiner all sat on the floor. Forty of the examinations, and those all of children more than 2 years of age, were carried out by an African assistant who had watched many tests, had been carefully instructed, and had an excellent understanding of the principles involved. The forty examinations were, however, done under the observation of one of us (M.G.) who herself carried out all the rest completely. The mothers attended all the tests except those on the kindergarten children, for which the teacher was present.

The conditions for the test were best in the hospital where a room in the Group's building could be kept free from disturbance, and in the village homes, where peaceful rooms could usually be found, although in some of them visitors were likely to appear and to interrupt the proceedings with the interminable greetings that are essential for politeness, and by laughing at the children. They were worst at the agricultural estate, because it was impossible to prevent spectators crowding the windows of the clinic room and making continuous comment. They were fairly good at the Theological College, where a large hall was used, but as the hall had open sides the children were distracted occasionally by passersby.

The test was always preceded by the exchange of a few words with the mother and child, to put them at ease. The child usually sat between the mother and the examiner. The examiner was a little way behind the child, in which position he could make use of her, or not, as he desired. The same order of examination was always followed. For children under 6 months the order was rattle, ring, cubes, cup, bottle and tablets, bell, ball, mirror, and tests of motor activity. For older children it was cubes, cup, bottle and tablets, form board, book, pencil, questions, ball, steps, and mirror. A few minutes were allowed if necessary at the beginning for the child to make himself familiar with the material, and if he did not perform a test spontaneously, he was encouraged verbally, and sometimes by example. The test usually took between 45 and 60 minutes. It was completed by questioning the mother about the previous history of the child, about his present behavior and about his environment, and also about the other children in the family. It was preferable to do the questioning after the test, and not before, because the child was not then kept waiting, and the mother was to some extent prepared. Nearly always, the questioning had to be done through an interpreter.

Over a hundred of the tests were photographed with a high-speed flashlight which never caused any discernible upset to the child. For many of the tests, the number of photographs was large enough to record the whole sequence. The photographs could sometimes be used to confirm the written description of the tests, and at all times made a permanent and unequivocal record.

RESULTS

The analysis of the results was qualitative as much as quantitative; the behavior of the child, the way he set about the tests, and his ability to make contact with the examiner were all considered as carefully as the failures or successes in performance.

From the first, the precocity of psycho-motor development was obvious and striking. It was found in all the group of children, and whatever the conditions of the examination. Most of the children accepted the test situation immediately, were interested in the material, and passed easily from one performance to another, but did not object when the material was changed or when it was finally put away. Their attitude was all the more remarkable because most of them could never have previously handled anything like the material. A few of the older children, especially some about 4 years of age, turned to the examiner as though asking for approval before taking the first objects. A word of assurance was all that was needed for the child to start the test, and after that the sequence was uninterrupted. The results have been set out by age, in divisions corresponding more or less to the ordinarily accepted "milestones" of development; for instance, the first ending at 6 months when standing began, and the next at 12 months to correspond with walking. For each age, motor activity (bodily movement, locomotion, and prehension), intellectual development (with special reference to *adaptivity,* the term used for a combination of motor and sensory development, ability to concentrate, to observe, to imitate, to remember, and to make a synthesis of experience), and affective development (the relation of the child to his parents, to other people and to his surrounding) have been described.

Children 1 to 6 Months of Age

There was remarkable precocity of motor development. From the first month, when the child was put on his back, he held his head in the midline. When he was drawn up by his hands into a sitting position, there was no "head-lag," and when he was held sitting, his back was straight and his head was stable. At 3 months in some children, but in more at 4 months, sitting unsupported for a few seconds was possible. At 5 months the sitting position was fully achieved; the children could remain sitting for half an hour or more, could lean forwards at will, and sit up again. The children liked to be stood up, and very early, sometimes in the first month when they were drawn into the sitting position they went further and became erect and could remain momentarily standing, raising and putting down one foot. From 2 months they could support, when standing, the greater part of their weight; at

4 months they could stand if they were held by their two hands, and a few of them if they were held by only one hand. At 6 months they could stand by themselves against a support. Standing was tested in this way: They were shown the ball, and it was put into the Gesell box; they would then try to raise themselves, sometimes looking for help, sometimes alone, and would finally reach a standing position holding on to the box. Sometimes they held on by only one hand whilst they used the other to point at the ball.

Prehension could be tested even in the first month, because the hands were already half-open and the eyes followed movements closely. The various stages of prehension—cubito-palmary, palmary, and radio-palmary—which could be very well studied with the cubes, were passed through rapidly. The children were very interested in the test material and always tried to pick it up.

At 5 to 6 months they could pick up an object between the thumb and the other fingers held together, and with the thumb opposed to the fingers and not beside them, and they could let go at will. From the age of 3 months, they took a lively interest in everything around and this, and their motor ability, and their pleasure in making contact with the examiner, allowed the usual performance of many tests that European children of the same age could not accomplish.

Thirty-three children were examined, and the Gesell quotients were as follows: (For those unfamiliar with the Gesell scores, it may be helpful to add that 100 represents the average performance of an American or European child at the age in question.)

Motor activity: usual score about 140, none under 100, the range 106-345

Manual ability: usual score about 130, one under 100, the rest 109-360

Adaptivity: usual score about 120, one under 100, the rest 104-275

Language: usual score about 120, one under 100, the rest 100-300

Personal-social behavior: usual score about 120, three under 100, the rest 100-250

Quotient for general development: usual score about 130, none under 100, the rest 110-260

The younger children—those up to 16 weeks of age—had high quotients for motor development and somewhat lower quotients for adaptivity. The older children—those who were 17 to 26 weeks of age—had quotients for motor development that were slightly lower, but were still high, and their quotients for adaptivity were raised to be equally high. The equality gave the test homogeneity. In the group as a whole, interest was especially great in the examiner and in the mirror, and after them in the bell.

Children 7 to 12 Months of Age

At 7 months the children could stand without support, at 8 months they began to walk, holding on to the wall, and at 9 months they took their first steps alone. At 10 months they could walk well, but with a certain stiffness, and at 1 year they could run. Manual dexterity continued to develop and at 10 months they could take a tablet between the thumb and index finger. At 12 months they could take objects perfectly between the pulps of these digits, whilst the others were held separate and stepwise. The economy of movement was especially notable, as well as this extreme precision. The harmonious development that was first recognized between 3 and 6 months lent homogeneity to the test, and the motor development was paralleled by adaptivity, language, and personal-social behaviour. In 34 children who were examined the quotients were consistently high.

Motor activity: usual score about 135, one under 100, the rest 100-150

Manual ability: usual score about 125, two under 100, the rest 106-165

Adaptivity: usual score about 125, two under 100, the rest 100-160

Language: usual score about 120, five under 100, the rest 100-150

Personal-social behaviour: usual score about 120, one under 100, the rest 100-148

Quotient for general development: usual score about 130,
two under 100, the rest 102-145

It was particularly the cubes that pleased the children and they
liked to exchange them with the examiner.

Children 1 to 2 Years of Age

At this age the precocity tended to be lost and a certain stag-
nation began to appear. The rate of development slowed down, so
that only about 9 months' progress, by European standards, was
made in the year. The slight progress made in language was
especially notable. On the other hand, the average child was starting to eat alone, was dry and clean, and was already beginning
to imitate his mother. He was however very dependent on her,
and it was obvious during the test that his need of her was greater
than the need of a younger child would have been. He established
contact with the examiner less rapidly and tended to give objects
more to his mother than to the examiner. He was particularly
interested in the tablet and the bottle and liked to go on repeatedly putting the tablets in and out. Another great attraction
was the book, and he liked to caress the pictures. The quotients,
although falling, were still mostly above the average for European
children. Fifty children were tested.

Motor activity: usual score about 110, 9 under 100, the rest
100-150

Manual ability; usual score about 110, 5 under 100, the
rest 100-150

Adaptivity: usual score about 105, 7 under 100, the rest
100-148

Language: usual score about 100, 24 under 100, the rest
100-125

Personal-social behaviour: usual score about 110, 9 under
100, the rest 100-138

Quotient for general development: usual score about 110,
10 under 100, the rest 100-132

Children 2 to 3 Years of Age

In this age group, it was necessary to consider separately, for many purposes, the kindergarten children and the rest.

Motor ability was fully developed. At 2 years, not only could the child run well, but he could go up and down the steps alone and with one foot on each step and could jump from the last. He could also stand momentarily on one foot. Manual dexterity was surprising and prehension was rapid and sure, so that all the ten tablets could be put into the bottle in less than 20 seconds—an accomplishment of the European child at 4 years. Even in these motor tests, however, there was a difference between the kindergarten children and the others. The kindergarten children quickly grasped what was wanted of them, but the others were much less understanding. For instance, before they would stand on one foot, a number of demonstrations was usually necessary. They found the tablets and the bottle very attractive, however, and when asked to put the tablets into the bottle as quickly as possible, they did so eagerly. There was little noticeable difference in the use of right and left hands. Some of the children took 15, 17 and 20 seconds to put in all the tablets with the right hand, and 17, 20 and 24 seconds when they used the left. About one third of the children were left-handed.

The children who were not in the kindergarten were very dependent on their mothers and turned to them during the tests for encouragement or approval. Their interest in the material was less, and less well-sustained, than that of the kindergarten children, who succeeded better in the tests that showed adaptivity, and whose tests as a whole were more dynamic and more quickly finished.

In one respect, there was no difference between the two groups: There was general acceleration in the development of language, more in comprehension than in expression.

As at the previous age, performances of the various components of the test were very even.

There were 36 children of this age.

Motor activity: usual score about 120, 9 under 100, the rest 100-137

Manual ability: usual score about 110, 9 under 100, the rest 100-131

Adaptivity: usual score about 100, 15 under 100, the rest 100-125

Language: usual score about 90, 28 under 100, the rest 100-130

Personal-social behavior: usual score about 110, 9 under 100, the rest 103-159

Quotient for general development: usual score about 105, 9 under 100, the rest 101-135

Children Over 3 Years of Age

The difference between the kindergarten children and the others was more accentuated after 3 years of age. Of the 13 village children, only 3 seemed really to be interested in the test and eager for it, and all 3 were the children of teachers. The seven children seen at the hospital or the clinic all had development below normal for their age, except for the motor tests, and only in expression did they continue the progress that was first shown at about age $2\frac{1}{2}$ years. On the whole these 20 children did not adapt themselves to the turning of the form board, as if their appreciation of shape was defective. They placed the round block time after time in its former position, and tried by various means to force it into place. They were also unable to make steps or a bridge with the cubes. The kindergarten children not only made the steps and the bridge, but had a much greater interest in all the objects, carried out their performances more rapidly, showed better comprehension and were more varied in their expression.

The kindergarten children gave names to the things they drew, and most often spontaneously drew a motor car, which they always began with the wheels. The others did not name their drawings; they scribbled spontaneously and roughly imitated, or copied more or less, what they were shown. In front of the mirror, the kindergarten children recognized themselves at once and at once began to describe what they could see, but the others remained fixed, and usually silent, although some finally managed to name something. The kindergarten children had a more extensive vocabulary and could name nearly all the animals in the book that was being used *(Père Castor's Farm)* although most of those animals were different from anything they could have seen. They not only named the goat, which is common in Uganda, but also named animals such as the horse and pig that they could have known only from pictures. They could distinguish between horse and donkey, and between several kinds of bird, and one child even recognized a peacock. The other children had only two names for everything—*goat* for all the four-footed beasts and *chicken* for all the birds.

Thirty-one children were tested.

Motor activity: usual score about 108, 12 under 100, the rest 100-142

Manual ability: usual score about 108, 11 under 100, the rest 100-156

Adaptivity: usual score about 95, 42 under 100, the rest 100-142

Language: usual score about 95, 26 under 100, the rest 100-136

Personal-social behaviour: usual score about 100, 23 under 100, the rest 100-142

Quotient for general development: usual score about 100, 34 under 100, the rest 100-142

Children Who Were Tested More Than Once

Figure 9-1 shows the general quotients for development of those children who were tested in 1955 and 1956, and who were under $4\frac{1}{2}$ years of age on the second occasion. It is clear that the repetitions gave results identical with those of the transverse study, and that the rate of falling-off was rapid in the first year and slower afterwards.

The figure, because it expresses averages of all the components of the tests, does not show the fall in the language quotients already described that was first noticed between 1 and 2 years and the subsequent partial recovery of those quotients.

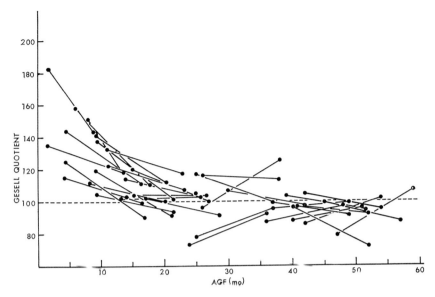

Figure 9-1 The Gesell quotients for general development of children who were tested in successive years. The quotients usually fell as age increased.

Newborn Children

A series of 113 newborn African children were examined during 1956 at Kampala by the method of André Thomas and Saint-Anne Dargassies.[1] Although the method is largely concerned with the determination of the degree of muscular tone and the eliciting of "primitive" reflexes, many of the details are carried over into the Gesell tests for children 4 to 8 weeks of age, or even older. For instance, in both examinations attention is paid to the attitude adopted by the child when he is placed on his back, to the carriage of the head and the straightness of the back when he is drawn into the sitting position, and to the way in which the fingers are held, or resist extension.

The findings on the African children have been described elsewhere.[6] They can best be summarized by saying that they showed development that is, to say the least, highly unusual in European children at birth or in the first weeks of life, and the

African children in fact behaved much like European children 3 to 4 weeks of age. They were not only less hypertonic in their flexion, but had a remarkable control of the head, and many of them could even raise the chin completely free of the table when they were lying on their fronts. Few showed the primitive reflexes after the first day or so of life, even the near-convulsive Moro reflex—usually a very consistent finding in European children—being found in only 6 of the 79 children more than 24 hours of age. The well-known grasp reflex, which enables the European child to suspend himself from a stick in a somewhat simian manner, was feeble and poorly sustained, and automatic walking was rare. Children only 2 days old were able to follow movement with their eyes, and some appeared to be able to focus.

A study of the African child at birth, more detailed and exact than was possible for this series, would probably show a large number of other points of difference from European children. No explanation was offered for the precocity, but it was fairly clear that it had a genetic basis. There was, unfortunately, no way in which the length of gestation period could be determined. The dates of the last menstruation were not accurately known.

DISCUSSION

The results of the examination of the newborn children were consistent with the results of the Gesell tests. From birth, the muscular tone of the African infant is different from that of the European, and the head is held better. The lesser degree of flexion may explain why there is in the African earlier standing, prehension, and manipulation.

At every stage of development it was necessary to take into account the manner in which the children were reared. Four infants, one aged 3 weeks, twins aged 20 weeks, and one aged 27 weeks, were treated in the European manner—that is to say, were fed "by the clock" during the day and not fed at night, were allowed to lie in their cradles almost the whole of the 24 hours and were lifted only for feeding and for toilet purposes. The infant 3 weeks of age, when drawn into the sitting position, could not hold his head up, had a marked kyphosis, and when held horizontally on the examiner's hand, face downwards, could not raise his head. His hands were half-open, this being the only precocity he had in common with the other children of the same age. The twins were girls who had weighed 3.64 and 4.10 kg at birth; their physical appearance was excellent, they had a bright look, and their smile showed the liveliness of their interest, but their development, according to the Gesell standard, was that of infants of only 23 to 24 weeks, giving a general quotient of 118. An infant 19 weeks of age, chosen from the records merely because he was nearest in age, and in no way exceptional among African children, had development corresponding to 36 to 38 weeks, which gave a general quotient of 188. The two infants next in age (21 weeks) had quotients of 171 and 178.

The continual carrying on the back by the mother may strengthen the child's innate ability to hold his head firmly, by forcing him to compensate for her various movements. In the same way, his sitting position on her back, with his back straight and his legs pressing against her waist, may help him to sit alone earlier than the European child. He is always with his mother when she goes to the fields, or to visit her neighbors, and his life in the changing scene is more stimulating than that of the child who remains in his cradle. The greater stimulation and the constant meetings with other people may account in part for the precocity of his interest in his environment and his good contact with the examiner. Another asset that may help to make him so lively and interested, and so much at ease with a stranger—nearly all the children smiled at the examiner and caressed her face— is the perpetual comfort in which he lives. He is fed on demand, given the breast at the slightest cry, is always with his mother who is always ready to satisfy his every want, is in intimate contact with her, often with his skin touching hers, and sleeps with her. She introduces him very early to toilet habits, but at first only by holding him out, and she shows no sign of being upset if he fails. There is no forbidding, no refusal, no punishment for the African infant, and when we went into the homes the first thing the mothers did, after the usual formal greetings had ended, was to offer us their babies. It was their usual gesture to all visitors; it was noticed during the examinations that if a visitor were to arrive a baby would always be offered in the same way. The child would remain on the knees of the person to whom he was given, tranquil, at ease and cheerful; from the age of 3 months he would smile at that person and show his pleasure by gurgling and by his lively movements. If finally he began to whimper, the mother took him back immediately and put him to the breast.

The mother begins to offer food besides her breast milk at about the age of 6 months, but continues to give the breast on demand and to sleep with the child. The date for complete weaning is decided arbitrarily. The decision made, not only does she stop breast feeding, but she no longer[8] carries him on her back, or sleeps with him, no longer consoles him, but laughs at him if he cries or merely tells him to stop crying. She teaches him to stay quiet, and especially to sit without fidgeting or speaking when a visitor comes. This method of education may explain the remarkably silent behavior of the older children who happened to be present when the younger ones were being tested. They took part in the test completely passively, watching but making no movement towards the test material and without interfering in any way. When they were tested in their turn, they always sought the approval and permission of the mother.

After the age of 2 years, it is exceptional for the African child to have an adult treat him as though he was of any importance, or play with him. He has lived in a warm friendly world, but now finds himself in the cold. The only thing that his mother asks of him is that he should help her, without thanks if he does what he is told to do, and very often he must fetch and carry for the younger infant who now has the comfort that once was his. Thus, although it is the custom that in the first year the child should be satisfied completely, should be made the center of importance, and should be offered to every visitor, it is exactly the opposite in the second year, in which very little attention is given him, in which answers to his questions will be refused and he will even be forbidden to speak.

Even more, weaning is often reinforced by geographical separation. It is another custom to send the child to a grandmother or an aunt, to honor her, or to get him out of the way. Very often the substitute for the mother does not know the child at all and lives so far off that the mother cannot come easily or often to visit. The custom has already been described in an account of the psychologic changes accompanying kwashiorkor[5] and has been related to the separation of European children.[2] This year, two of the children examined last year, when they were both about 15 months old and who had since been separated from their mothers, were examined again. One was living alone with a grandmother and the other with an aunt who had other young children who were already as much as she could manage. The grandmother and the aunt both told us that all was well, but both had noticed something unusual: The grandmother said that her child had been difficult to feed in the first 3 to 4 months and had slept a great deal in that time, and the aunt said that the other child still very often refused to eat altogether. One of the children, a boy, had been separated for 6 months, and the other, a girl, for 8 months. The boy had slight edema of the dorsum of the feet, and hair that was almost red, but his test showed no difference from that of the year before (the quotients were 104 and 102). The girl was thin, her hair pale, and her look vague; her test was extremely slow, and the quantitative result gave the very low quotient of 72. The year before, when she had been with her mother, the quotient was 109. The result for the boy, showing no fall in the quotient despite the separation, was at first surprising. There was, however, another child left with the mother who had been tested in 1955 and found to have a quotient of 96. He was tested again and his quotient had fallen to 72; he was very inhibited, and was continually being bothered by the mother during the test. It seemed, then, likely that the boy who had been separated had in fact benefited by the separation, and had found, with his grandmother, a more satisfactory relationship than he could achieve with his mother.

Two African women, one a nurse in the maternity department of the hospital and the other a deaconess in training who had been a school teacher, told us without being asked that they had noticed how children changed when they were separated. They thought that the custom was applied to 90 percent of the Ganda children, but to a smaller percentage of children of other tribes. The fact that the theological students were mostly non-Ganda may have been one of the reasons why there was less falling-off in the quotients of the kindergarten children.

It was obvious to us that in the children over 3 years there was a great difference between those who were given the opportunity to learn and those who were left to pick up what learning they could. The three children of teachers seen in their homes have already been mentioned. They were considerably in advance of other children of their age, and of the rest of the children it was only those of the theological students who were really at their ease in the tests, were keenly interested in the material, and had a direct contact with the examiner. If the test objects were unfamiliar, they were accustomed to the other material offered in the kindergarten, and were also accustomed to communicating with adults. Some of these children, but none of the rest, when we asked questions to which they did not know how to reply, asked us what we meant.

The kindergarten children had many advantages, but it is doubtful if their parents were of a higher social standing or were more intelligent than the parents of the village children. It seemed that it was not the parents that made the difference, but the way in which the children were reared. There is nothing surprising in the fact that a child asked constantly to exercise his capacities of observation, of imitation, or reasoning and of memory, and who is allowed to ask questions, will have better success in a test of intelligence than a child who has constantly been told to keep quiet. The memories of some of the children of 5 years, who were 4 years of age when they were seen last year, were surprising. They had been asked to make the steps with the cubes— a performance expected at 5 years—and could not do it. This year they made the steps spontaneously, as soon as the cubes were offered. Although most of them gave no explanation, two said they were doing it because we had asked them last year.

For the children from 4 to 6 years the Gesell tests were used although they are less satisfactory for children of that age than for younger ones. We have collected drawings from these older children on which we hope to report at a later date. We have already emphasised the importance of the ears in the drawings of a man and speculated on the relation of the importance to the African way of life, which is founded so largely on oral tradition and communication.[7]

The Applicability of the Gesell Test to the African Infants and Children

The material of the Gesell test was very attractive to the African infant. The tablets and cubes were excellent for the study of manual ability, and the possibility of construction with the cubes, and the form board, were very apt for the exploration of ideas of shape and form. The material also helped in appreciation of the affective structure of the infant, an inhibited one choosing the things that were less brightly coloured and shiny, and a happy one preferring the red cubes and the ball. The mirror, which was used extensively, was of course especially important for children who were unaccustomed to it. Personal-social behavior could not be adequately explored by the Gesell schedule in its present form. Eating with a spoon, lacing shoes, and recognizing coins are not the best of tests of a child in Uganda, and some adaptation is called for. The extremely advanced development of motor activity suggested that other modifications might be necessary, for the first year of life, and especially for the first 6 months. A level of development of 12 weeks found for an infant of 4 weeks indicates that the test is not altogether appropriate.

We regard our work as being no more than a preliminary to a complete study, and believe that it should be reported on a much larger number of children, of different tribes in Uganda and of different countries in Africa. The basic finding of precocity, especially in the younger children, will probably be constant —similar precocity has been observed in Dakar by Faladé[8]—but there will undoubtedly be local variations, some determined genetically and some by environment. The mode of production of the variations will be worth special investigation which will probably require the cooperation of physiologists and social anthropologists, amongst others.

An experimental study of the possibility of preventing the loss of precocity might be the most fascinating of the many lines for future work suggested by these results. Because of its potential value to the African, such a study might also be by far the most important. If it could be undertaken immediately, it might help to ease some of the difficulties that are becoming acute in the present period of rapid transition from illiteracy to higher education. At the moment, in East Africa and in most other parts of the continent, it is only the very exceptional student who is ready for university education at 18 or 19 years, the usual age for entrance to a European university, and anything which could accelerate the earlier training is greatly to be encouraged.

SUMMARY

The results of a series of Gesell tests on African infants and children are presented.

The most remarkable finding was the precocity of the younger infants. The motor development was greatly in advance of that of European infants of the same age, but was not an isolated phenomenon; it was paralleled by advanced adaptivity, language, and personal-social behavior.

The precocity was usually lost in the third year, but was retained by some children who had the advantages of a kindergarten.

The results of the Gesell tests were confirmed by a study of newborn African infants, whose state of development was also precocious by European standards.

The findings are discussed in relation to some details of the African environment, and especially to some local customs which may affect early development. Emphasis is placed on the potential value of finding means by which the early precocity could be maintained.

REFERENCES

1. Thomas, A., and Saint-Anne Dargassies, C.: *Études neurologiques sur le nouveau-né et le nourrisson.* Paris, Masson, 1952.

2. Aubry, J.: *La carence de soins Maternels.* Paris, Presses Universitaires de France, 1955.

3. Roudinesco, J., and Guiton, M.: *Le développement de l'enfant.* Paris, Presses Universitaires de France, 1950.

4. Roudinesco, J., and Geber, M.: De l'utilisation du test de Gesell pour l'étude du comportement des jeunes enfants. *Enfance, 4:*309, 1951.

5. Geber, M., and Dean, R. F. A.: The psychological changes accompanying kwashiorkor. *Courrier, 6:*3, 1956.

6. Geber, M., and Dean, R. F. A.: The state of development of new-born African children. *Lancet, 1:*1216, 1957.

7. Geber, M.: Développement psycho-moteur de l'enfant africain. *Courrier, 6:*17, 1956.

8. Faladé, S.: *Le développement psychomoteur du jeune africain originaire du Sénégal au cours de sa première année.* Paris, Imprimerie R. Foulon, 1955.

PART IV
PERCEPTUAL DEVELOPMENT

A BROAD DEFINITION of perception is the meaning we ascribe to sensory stimuli in our environment. The process includes awareness, discrimination, and selectivity of response to events. Even the most casual observer can infer that the infant, unlike the adult, cannot extract information from impinging stimuli. This ability comes from the accumulation of experience. Then, does the infant have any perception of the environment? Research by Dr. Robert Fantz indicates the infant shows some primitive pattern selectivity. Babies as young as 48 hours old fixated longer on a patterned stimulus than on an unpatterned stimulus. It has been argued that these preferences are not true visual perceptions because they are not active, directed responses. Dr. Fantz, however, suggests that the unlearned primitive selections are the beginnings of perceptual development, a process that started at brith. The preferences presumably have an adaptive value as they provide a basis for the infant's visual, and later active, exploration of his surroundings.

Chapter 10

Visual Perception from Birth as Shown by Pattern Selectivity

ROBERT L. FANTZ

CASUAL OBSERVATION of the infant in the early months of life suggests two outstanding behavioral characteristics: First, the young infant is helpless; he is uncoordinated in his movements and able to make few active responses to objects or places. Second, the young infant is receptive to sensory stimulation; he often appears to be responsive to sound, touch, taste, and kinesthesis, and in particular he appears to look at his surroundings through most of his waking hours.

Of these two points of contact of an individual with the environment (i.e. sensory input and motor output), sensory input would seem to precede motor output as an influence in the development of behavior. In other words, it would seem reasonable that the early months during which the infant passively experiences his surroundings, without acting upon them directly, are of some value in preparing for later attempts to explore, manipulate, and control the environment. However, uncontrolled observations and reasonable interpretations of events are not trustworthy sources of knowledge, especially when these are opposed to the prevailing theories of infant development. For example, for Gesell,[12] the maturation and use of various action systems must precede visual development, and the appearance of coordinated movements is used to measure psychological development; for Piaget,[20] action is transformed to perception and cognition

Previously unpublished research was supported by Public Health Service Research Grant HD-00314 from the National Institute of Child Health and Human Development.

through a series of stages requiring repeated responses and learning; while behaviorists and learning theorists usually assume reinforcement and feedback from past responses to be crucial for behavior development.

Solid empirical support is needed for the characteristics of the young infant suggested by casual observation. Their motor incoordination is easily verified since overt responses to objects are observable events. Tracing the development of visual pursuit, reaching, or walking requires only the use of standardized, objective criteria to determine the degree of coordination of the response.

On the other hand, the reception of sensory stimulation cannot be observed directly and must be inferred from subsequent overt reactions. This creates a dilemma for the study of early perceptual development. Perception can be shown only by coordinated responses to objects, but most such responses are absent in the early months. The usual practice has been to trace the subsequent perfection of sensory-motor coordination and the appearance of learned responses to objects for evidence of perceptual development, and to assume that visual perception is absent until this evidence can be obtained. But an object be seen and discriminated from other objects before it can be grasped and before the significance of the object has been learned.

A better way of resolving the dilemma is to take advantage of the limited response capabilities which are present in young infants to test their sensory capacities. This approach has been used often relative to certain stimulus features. Gross sensitivity to light intensity has been shown soon after birth by eyeblink, pupillary, and tonic-neck reflexes, and by change in activity level, heart rate, and respiration; a degree of spatial localization has been shown by fixation of a light source; responsiveness to movement has been shown by visual pursuit; sensitivity to color has been shown by pursuit of a spot of light differing from the background only in wave length; and a primitive type of pattern vision has been shown by optokinetic nystagmus to a moving striped field.[21] But these results give no information on pattern discrimination, form perception and depth perception, which are necessary for the adaptive use of vision. This information can be obtained, however, from the *visual preference* method, as the results summarized in this paper will indicate.

The method is amazingly simple in principle. The young infant appears to see things because he explores his surroundings with his eyes, gazing in the direction of various objects or parts of the room and on occasion looking for a longer period in a particular direction, as if something of particular interest had caught his attention. By recording this behavior in a well-controlled situation, it is possible to make certain not only of what is being looked at but also what visual aspects are seen and discriminated. By reducing the stimulus field to one or two figures against a relatively homogeneous background, the fixation of one of the figures is clearly observable. By presenting the targets repeatedly for short exposures with position controlled, it can be determined whether the fixations are random or related to position rather than to what is seen; thus, a consistent choice of a particular target indicates that it can be distinguished from the other targets. By using targets differing in pattern but equated in aspects such as color, brightness, and size, pattern discrimination can be shown.

The procedure is to place the infant face up in a comfortable hammock-type crib inside a stimulus chamber. The stimulus targets are then exposed on the ceiling of the chamber while the experimenter observes the infant's reactions through a peephole in the chamber ceiling. The lighting and the contrast of the targets with the background are adjusted so that tiny images of the targets are clearly visible to the observer, mirrored in the infant's eyes. The location of these images relative to the pupil provides a quick and objective criterion of fixation. When the left reflection, for example, is over the center of the pupil, the infant is looking at the target on the left. A response is recorded by pressing the appropriate finger switch, operating a timer, for the duration of the fixation.

This general method was originally developed using chimpanzee infants.[4] Many studies of human infants, involving several thousand tests and hundreds of subjects, have subsequently been made with various modifications of the method. More recently, it has been adapted for the study of the effects of altered rearing conditions on the perceptual development of monkey infants.[9]

The first experiment with human infants,[5] as with many of the subsequent experiments, used a paired-comparison technique. A pair of targets was affixed to the chamber ceiling one foot apart and one foot above the infant. They were hidden from the infants between exposures by shields across the chamber. They were exposed for two 30-second periods with reversed right and left positions. Fixation times for the two periods were combined to cancel position preferences.

Four pairs of targets were presented in random order during a test session. Figure 10-1 gives the overall results for 22 infants,

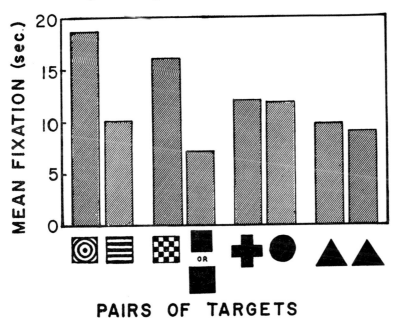

PAIRS OF TARGETS

Figure 10-1. Visual preference among eight stimulus targets presented in pairs, showing the fixation time during one minute for each pair, averaged for repeated tests of 22 infants ranging from one week to 6 months of age. Black areas of drawings were bright red; white areas were gray to match the inside of the stimulus chamber. The checked pattern was paired on two successive exposures with squares of same area of red and of same overall size; other pairs were equated in area of red. The large squares measured five inches; others are to scale. (Adapted from Fantz[6])

each given 10 weekly tests during the first six months of life. The control pair of identical triangles received least attention, the pair of relatively complex patterns the most, and the pairs of intermediate complexity received intermediate fixation times. The differential among the pairs was consistent among the subjects for all ages combined and also for tests given under 2 months of age.

Within pairs, consistent preferences were shown only for bull's-eye over stripes and checks over plain square. The average results, given in Figure 10-1, obscure a striking developmental change for the first pair. These patterns were discriminated at all ages tested; however, the striped pattern was significantly preferred by infants under two months of age, while the bull's-eye pattern was strongly preferred after this age. This change was not due to repeated testing since it was also evident from the first tests of infants of varying ages as shown in Figure 10-2. It may have been due either to maturation or to everyday visual experience during the first two months of life. In any case the differential fix-

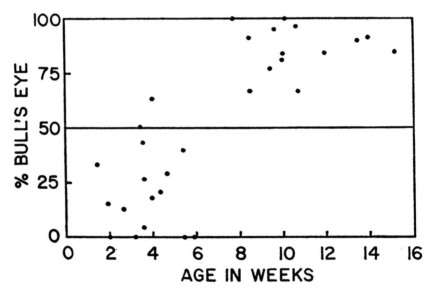

Figure 10-2. A scatterplot between age and degree of visual preference for a bull's-eye relative to total fixation of bull's-eye and stripes during two 30-second exposures, each point representing one infant. (From Fantz[5]).

ation suggests discrimination of the form of contours from the early months of life.

These patterns were fairly large, $\frac{1}{2}$-inch stripes and 1-inch checks. To determine the limits of pattern vision, finer striped patterns were paired with plain gray targets of the same overall brightness. Since a square with vertical black-and-white stripes was preferred to a gray square at all ages, the finest width of stripes which continued to elicit this differential response gave an estimate of visual acuity.

A number of acuity studies[7,10] have brought out three main facts. First, vision becomes progressively more acute during the first six months of life, as would be expected from the maturation of the visual system during this period and from improvement in oculomotor coordination. Second, pattern vision is surprisingly good throughout this time, much better than had been suggested in the few earlier studies using other techniques.[3] Third, acuity level varies with stimulus.

Results from a recent study using a modified procedure for studying the development of pattern discrimination will be given in detail. The subjects were 119 infants ranging from birth to six months. The newborn infants and most of those up to two weeks of age were tested at a newborn ward of a hospital. The rest of the subjects were from a foundling home; 16 of these were tested twice at different age levels (according to the groupings in Figure 10-3). Thus a total of 135 tests was made.

The stimulus targets are pictured at the top of Figure 10-3. They were exposed at a distance of 9 inches for newborns and 12 inches for older infants. The five patterns were each constructed of the same number $\frac{3}{4}$-inch squares of black paper glued to white poster board in varying arrangements, while the square of gray paper was matched with the patterns in total reflected light. All six were $\frac{1}{2}$-inch squares bordered with blue felt (Western Felt Works, No. 2263). which covered the remainder of the stimulus card and also lined the stimulus chamber. This background, contrasting with the lighter, achromatic targets, made the targets more visible to the infants and made the corneal reflections of the targets more visible to the observer; a blue background also had

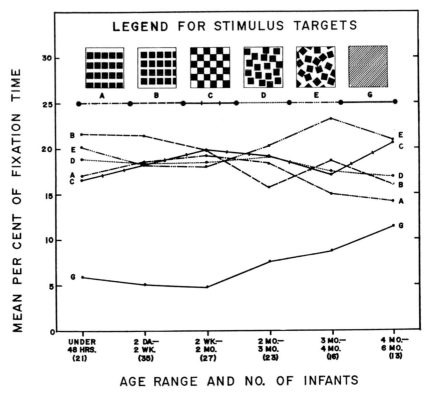

Figure 10-3. Relative visual response to five different arrangements of black squares and to plain gray, exposed successively, randomly, and repeatedly, by groups of infants of increasing age range (unpublished data)

appeared to quiet the infants in preliminary work, in agreement with Smith's study of newborn infants.[24]

Tests were first made using a constant 30-second exposure period for each target. They were presented in a random sequence which was repeated until the infant started crying or fell asleep. Each infant had a minimum of two complete sequences. Fixations were cumulated during the exposure. Infants from about one to three months of age tended to fixate each of the patterned targets steadily throughout the exposure, thus decreasing the chance of differential response. Therefore, further tests were made without a fixed exposure time. Each target was exposed for the duration of

the initial fixation (that is until the infant closed its eyes or looked away), and the length of this fixation was recorded, up to a
maximum of 90 seconds. Random sequences of the targets were
repeated as before. As expected, differential response to the patterns was, in general, higher with this procedure. There was no
reliable difference in direction of preference so infants tested with
one or the other procedure were combined at each age level, after
first converting the scores for each infant to percentages of total
response time. To compensate partly for the unequal numbers of
subjects available at various ages, they were divided into groups
with unequal age ranges for a rough analysis of changes occurring
during the first six months of life.

Figure 10-3 shows the average response to each stimulus target by successive age groups. The most consistent differential at
all ages was the low fixation of the plain (unpatterned) gray
square. In the 135 tests, gray was fixated longer than any of the
five patterns only once; but it was fixated less than each of the five
in 116 tests. The relative response to gray increased for the older
infants; this change among the groups was significant at the 0.001
probability level (Kruskal-Wallis analysis of variance of ranked
percentages). This may have been related to the general decrease
in attention to the targets and the more rapid shifts in gaze by the
older infants. Regardless of what the change might mean, the low
initial response to gray gives no support for the idea that the ability to see patterns and the tendency to look at patterns develop
only through postnatal maturation or experience.

The differentiation among the five patterns was less marked.
However, a consistent differential was shown by the two groups
under 2 weeks of age, taken together, and by the two groups over
3 months, together (0.01 level, Friedman analysis of variance of
ranks of the five patterns alone), whereas responses to the five patterns were about equal at the intermediate ages. The direction of
preference was different at the two ends of the age curves. Response to pattern "B" (see Fig. 10-3) was highest for newborn
infants; but for the older infants response to "E" was highest,
whereas both "A" and "B" were low. This change in preference
was also suggested from another analysis of the data: the longest

fixation times were for pattern "A" by 12, for "B" by 16, and for "E" by 8 of the 56 infants under two weeks; whereas the longest fixations were for "A" by 1, for "B" by 5, and for "E" by 13 of the 25 infants over 3 months (omitting repeated tests for four of these infants).

These results give partial support for an hypothesis which was made before the experiment, based partly on recent neurological findings of Hubel and Wiesel.[16] Electrical recordings from single neural cells in the visual areas of the brain of cats and monkeys revealed highly selective responsiveness of particular cells to particular stationary or moving patterns falling on the retina, typically to an illuminated slit, to a dark bar, or to an edge placed in a particular spatial orientation; whereas other patterns or diffuse light often elicited no response. A subsequent study showed a similar selective neural response to patterns in newborn kittens.[17] These results seem to indicate an unlearned, neural mechanism for pattern discrimination and pattern selectivity in support of the behavioral findings given in this chapter, as for example, the high visual interest in the five patterns of Figure 10-3.

In addition to these general implications, the findings of Hubel and Wiesel suggest that *linear* patterns stimulate certain levels of the visual system more than other patterns. If so it would be plausible that linear patterns are also more stimulating behaviorally and would elicit longer visual fixations. This would most likely be evident at a very early age, before higher-level neural organizations and the effects of learning had come to influence motor output so as to obscure the initial neural-sensory organization.

From this reasoning, it would be expected that young infants would prefer the patterns toward the left of Figure 10-3. The five patterns are arranged from what appeared to be the highest degree of linear organization to the least organized pattern (the intermediate checked pattern, although linear in organization, has reversals of black and white along each line). There is some support for this hypothesis in the preference for pattern "B" under 2 weeks of age, even though the low response to "A," with accentuated horizontal linearity, is not in agreement. The later preference for the random organization (pattern "E") might then indicate that stimulus variables other than linearity have become prepotent after three months due to learning or further complexity of brain processes. These interpretations are only speculative, but it is interesting to note the possible relevance of the shift from preference for a linear to a nonlinear organization which was evident in Figure 10-2. The changes in the present results are much less marked, perhaps due to the high similarity of all the patterns in many stimulus features.

Up to this point, pattern preferences have been used to assess the pattern vision capacities of young infants. But visual perception means more than the ability to resolve and discriminate pattern; it implies the use of these abilities in behavior. In the early months of life, they cannot be used to direct manual or locomotor responses, but they might be used in visual exploration and familiarization with the environment. To determine whether this might actually occur, the visual preference results will be approached from a different viewpoint: *which* targets or objects are selected for special visual attention; and are the choices related in any way to the later adaptive use of vision?

One answer is suggested by the simple fact that patterns large enough to be resolved by the infants were strongly preferred over plain, unpatterned surfaces. This preference was shown further in the comparison of six discs, three of them patterned and three plain but bright or colored.[8] They were presented one at a time, in repeated random sequences, for the length of the first fixation. The average responses shown in Figure 10-4 indicate a strong preference for patterned over plain discs for both newborn and older infants. More than half of each group looked longest at the schematic face pattern, while none looked longest at white, fluorescent yellow, or red. No consistent differences in response were evident for the three discus differing in color and brightness.

The high attention value of pattern relative to other stimulus variables, as shown in these various results, is in opposition to the traditional belief that color, brightness, and size are primary sense qualities, whereas form perception is secondary and acquired. However, the results make good sense if we consider how vision is

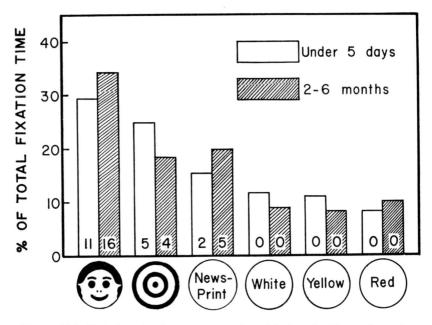

Figure 10-4. Relative visual response to three black-and-white and to three plain 6-inch discs by 18 newborn and by 25 older infants. Number of infants looking longest at a particular target is given at bottom of each bar. (From Fantz[10])

actually used to explore and respond to the environment. An infant who looked only at unpatterned surfaces or open space, however bright or colored, could learn little about the environment, since visual information is conveyed almost entirely by patterns or configurations falling on the central retina. Thus, the individual is able to walk or crawl without bumping into things or falling off edges largely because he notices variations in surface patterning or contouring which indicate an obstacle or a dropoff in the path ahead;[13] while the individual is able to recognize objects largely by noticing the general configuration produced by fine details, edges, curved surfaces, texture, and shading.[10] In contrast, the color, brightness, size, and outline of objects often vary with the conditions under which the objects are seen (e.g. illumination, distance, orientation). These aspects also vary widely among the objects of a class, so that food objects, trees, automobiles, books, dogs, or people, for example, are known by their general pattern or configuration, but not by their color, brightness, size, or outline alone. In particular, the configuration of the face and head is the best means of distinguishing a human being for the infant or adult; finer perception of facial pattern allows recognition of a particular person; while still finer details of facial configuration can indicate emotional state.

Thus, to use vision effectively in spatial orientation, object recognition, and social perception, the individual must come to attend selectively to patterns in general and to the specific types of pattern which provide the most constant cues for behavior. The unlearned selection of patterns by the young infant may be the necessary starting place for this developmental process; this selectivity certainly facilitates the process. Whether the beginning stage of the process, that is, the visual preferences of the newborn infant, is to be considered visual perception is a matter of definition. Perception is sometimes taken to begin only after effects of experience and learning have occurred, but this begs the question of the origin of perception and obscures the interrelation between innate and experiential factors. Perception is sometimes operationally defined so as to require active, directed responses to what is perceived, but this avoids the question of whether visual exploration and incidental visual experience are important in behavior development. These difficulties do not arise if we consider perceptual development to be a continuous process which begins at birth, even though the initial perceptions are primitive in nature and without immediate value in directing behavior.

The remaining studies will illustrate in more detail how familiarization with the environment and responsiveness to important parts of it can be facilitated by the pattern selectivity of the young infant. The object of prime importance to the helpless infant is the human being. Observations of the attention value of the human face for the young infant have been frequent.[12,20,22] This interest is usually attributed to movement and to brightness or shininess. But the many configurational attributes may be of equal or greater attention value, just as they are critical for eliciting the smiling response to the face when this appears at several months of age.[1,26] We have studied three of these attributes of the face and head: pattern complexity, arrangement of features, and solidity.[10]

The complexity of the facial configuration was varied by using oval targets with decreasing numbers of schematic features as shown in Figure 10-5. The left pair of patterns is presumably most like a real face in complexity, and the plain white and gray ovals least similar. The figures given here are for 15 infants under one week of age, exposed to the targets for 30-second periods in repeated random sequence. The more complex patterns were strongly preferred throughout the first six months. This would have been expected from the preference for complexity shown with abstract patterns. The similar results in this case simply illustrates how a general interest in patterns may have the adaptive consequence of attracting attention to objects of importance to the infant.

No differential was shown relative to the arrangement of features by these newborn infants. At later ages a differential did appear but was never pronounced. The preference for the correct facial arrangement over the scrambled face was most consistent from two to three months of age in the totals for several studies

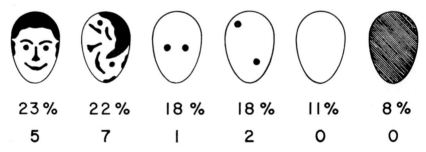

| 23% | 22% | 18% | 18% | 11% | 8% |
| 5 | 7 | 1 | 2 | 0 | 0 |

Figure 10-5. Response to stimulus targets of varying numbers and arrangements of schematic facial features, exposed successively for 30-second periods, by infants less than one week of age: mean percentage of fixation time (top figures) and number of infants showing highest preference for that pattern (bottom figures). The ovals were all 6 by 9 inches and exposed 12 inches from the infant. The gray (on right) reflected about the same amount of light as the complex patterns. (Data from Fantz[10])

using different groups of infants and different procedures. The "eye spots" pattern was also consistently preferred to the off-center spots by infants between 2 and 3 months.

Selective attention to facelike configurations, even when shown by newborn infants, does not imply instinctive recognition of people, since "looking" is a general *exploratory* activity rather than a specifically *social* response. Neither does the later appearance of preference for additional aspects of the face or head necessarily imply learned recognition of people since the change may represent increased attention to a broad category of targets, such as solid, contoured objects or circular, symmetrical patterns, the increase having resulted from general visual experience, from oculomotor practice, or even from maturation. Selective attention to the complexity of pattern, arrangement of features, and solidity of social objects *does* indicate that young infants have more visual contact and more opportunity to become familiar with people than they have with parts of the environment lacking these characteristics. In this light the adaptive but yet nonspecific and non-teleological visual interest in those configurations which accompany social objects, or in those which will later aid in object recognition and spatial orientation, is seen as a type of primitive knowledge of the environment which "provides a foundation for the vast accumulation of knowledge through experience." (Fantz,[6] p. 72; see also Gibson[13]) .

In addtion to configurational aspects, other stimulus characteristics such as movement, figure-ground contrast, and voice, add to the attraction of the face and increase the visual experience with people. Furthermore, Haynes[15] has recently shown that during the first few weeks the infant can accommodate only for a certain close distance, averaging about eight or nine inches. Since the mother's face is often at this optimal distance for clear focus in the course of feeding and fondling the baby, the face will tend to be favored in the baby's visual explorations over more distance objects which are seen somewhat less clearly.[10] The poor visual acuity of the young infant would also favor the near objects.

These various stimulus and optical factors assure the young infant, under normal rearing conditions, multiplied opportunities to experience people. It has been suggested by Rheingold[22] that this early perceptual contact (rather than either physical contact or need reduction) may be the primary basis for the development of sociability in humans.

Increased responsiveness to people, developing from the unlearned attraction to their intrinsic stimulus characteristics, and from the resulting selective experience, illustrates one use of early visual perception and one effect of early experiences. A different effect, decrease in responsiveness to familiar objects or patterns, is illustrated in the final experiment.

Eleven photographs were cut from magazines, each complex and interesting but quite different from the others. For a given infant, one of these, the "constant pattern," was exposed repeatedly, for ten periods of one minute each, with position varied. It was paired in turn with each of the other ten "novel" patterns in random order.

Figure 10-6 shows changes in attention to the constant pattern relative to the fixation time for both patterns. The trend is clear and significant in spite of wide fluctuations in response among the infants and among successive exposures. Infants under two months showed no change, whereas the three older groups showed a decrease in response to the repeatedly exposed pattern. In terms of absolute fixation time, the novel patterns came to receive more attention as the constant pattern received less, so that the total fixation time remained high throughout the test.[10] Thus, the change cannot be attributed to sensory adaptation, fatigue, decreased arousal, or any general response decrement. It indicates instead the perception, recognition, and satiation of visual interest in a specific complex stimulus. High response to novelty is seen in this context as the unlearned visual interest in a pattern which has *not* been satiated by repeated exposure.

This effect of experience as well as other demonstrated changes in preference very likely aid in visual exploration of the environment. In the beginning the unlearned visual attention to patterns serves to concentrate attention on the patterned parts of the environment, which will include adaptively important objects and surfaces. Fixations among these will not be very discriminat-

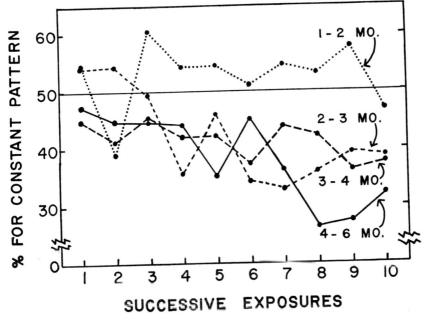

SUCCESSIVE EXPOSURES

Figure 10-6. Change in amount of visual fixation of a repeatedly exposed (constant) pattern relative to a noval pattern on successive paired exposures with positions reversed midway in each 1-minute exposure. The entire test covered a period of 15 minutes. Each curve is the mean for six to eight infants. Decrease from first five to last five exposures was significant for 2-3 and for 4-6 month groups and for older three groups combined; also for those infants given an achromatic constant pattern as well as for those given a color photograph. (From Fantz[11])

ing at first, but developmental changes may make them more so. For example, the appearance of a visual preference for solidity will give increased attention to objects over flat surfaces;[10] while the apparent shift of interest from linear to circular or random patterns (see above) might allow concentration of attention on more complex configurations which require longer examination for familiarization. Finally, decreased interest in those patterns which have recently been visually explored facilitates familiarization with the environment by giving more exposure to the less familiar objects, or to familiar ones seen from different angles.

It may be concluded from these various findings, and from

similar findings of other investigators,[23,25,27] that infants can see and discriminate patterns from birth, that they selectively attend to the patterning of objects and surfaces from birth and that the selectivity can be altered by visual experience at least by 2 months of age. This provides the necessary basis for visual perception, visual exploration, and visual learning in young infants. The adaptive value of some of the early visual preferences, both in visual exploration and in preparing for more active exploration and response to objects later on, gives further support for the importance of early visual experiences and for the priority of perception over action in behavior development.

Thus, it would seem that the casual observer of the infant and the mother, who thinks her baby does see in spite of what she has been told to the contrary, are right after all. But why have the experts thought for so long that the young infant has little or no pattern vision and that perception as a developmental influence must await motor development and the consequences of action? There are probably a number of contributing causes.

First, tests of infant perception in the past were restricted almost entirely to spatial localization of objects as shown by the degree of sensorimotor coordination.[12,18] The coordination of the infant in maintaining fixation, showing visual pursuit, or reaching for an object is initially poor and gradually is perfected. But such tests tell nothing about object discrimination and recognition. Thus, in spite of the poor oculomotor coordination, the newborn infant is able to tell the difference between a patterned and plain surface and to turn his eyes in the approximate direction of the pattern. Earlier procedures operationally defined perception as accurate localization of objects; the present procedures defined it as discrimination or recognition of objects, which is more comparable to the procedures used for the study of perception in the child and adult.

Second, the immaturity of the eye and brain of the young infant had seemed to preclude all but gross visual sensitvity so that testing pattern vision had seemed useless.[2,21] But this made the unwarranted assumption that one could predict the degree of visual function by examining visual structures in a microscope or by recording gross electrical activity from visual centers. Furthermore, recent results with more refined techniques have refuted some of the early evidence against retinal and cortical function in the newborn infant.[3]

Third, *a priori* beliefs have caused opposing data to be discarded or misinterpreted. Several early studies of color preferences incidentally found a pattern to be preferred to any of the colors, even in newborn infants,[19,28] but this evidence has been largely ignored. Reports of what the young infant likes to look at are highly colored by preconceptions. For example, windows are supposedly favored because of brightness, inspite of the striking and complex pattern formed by the design and folds of drapes, the outline and panes of the window against the light sky, and perhaps trees and houses seen through the window.

Finally, a true picture of visual perception and its development has been hindered by the conception, persisting from early English philosophers, that form perception is the product of combinations and associations between elementary sensory qualities of color, brightness, and extent. But it is known that no quality can be directly taken in through the sense organs; colors as well as patterns are schematically reproduced from incoming patterns of neural impulses in relation to ongoing patterns of neural activity.[14] Furthermore, the visual system is set up primarily for reception of patterned stimulation: retinal receptors are activated more readily by complex contours than by plain surfaces, while cells in the visual brain are often stimulated only by specific types of pattern falling on the retina (see above).

There is now little basis in fact or theory for rejecting the visual preference data indicating that perception of patterns is possible from birth and that visual experience with important parts of the environment begins in the early months of life. The world of the infant is patterned and organized. This world is selectively explored in the only way possible for the helpless but visually active infant. When and under what conditions this visual experience begins to provide useful knowledge of the environment remains to be determined.

REFERENCES

1. Ahrens, R. Beitrag zur Entwicklund des Physiogonmie und Mimikerk-ennes. *Z. Exp. Angew. Psychol., 2:*413-454; 599-633, 1954.

2. Dewey, Evelyn. *Behavior Development in Infants.* New York, Columbia Univ. Press, 1935.

3. Eichorn, Dorothy H. Biological correlates of behavior. In H. W. Stevenson (Ed.), *Child Psychology.* Chicago, The National Society for the Study of Education, 1968.

4. Fantz, R. L. A method for studying early visual development. *Percept. Motor Skills, 6:*13-16, 1956.

5. Fantz, R. L. Pattern vision in young infants. *Psychol. Rec., 8:*43-48, 1958.

6. Fantz, R. L. The origin of form perception. *Sci. Am. 204*(5):66-72, 1961.

7. Fantz, R. L.; Ordy, J. M., and Udelf, M. S. Maturation of pattern vision in infants during the first six months. *J. Comp. Physiol. Psychol., 55:* 907-917, 1962.

8. Fantz, R. L. Pattern vision in newborn infants. *Science, 140:*296-297, 1963.

9. Fantz, R. L. Ontogeny of perception. In Alan S. Schrier, H. F. Harlow, and F. Stollnitz (Eds.), *Behavior of Nonhuman Primates: Modern Research Trends.* New York, Academic Press, 1965.

10. Fantz, R. L. Pattern discrimination and selective attention as determinants of perceptual development from birth. In Aline H. Kidd and Jeanne L. Rivoire (Eds.), *Perceptual Development in Children.* New York, Interna. Univ. Press, 1965.

11. Fantz, R. L. Visual experience in infants: decreased attention to familiar patterns relative to novel ones. *Science, 146:*668-670, 1964.

12. Gesell, A.; Ilg, F. L., and Bullis, G. E. *Vision: Its Development in Infant and Child.* New York, Harper & Bros., 1949.

13. Gibson, J. J. *The Perception of the Visual World.* Boston, Houghton Mifflin, 1950.

14. Hayak, F. A. 1952. *The Sensory Order.* Chicago, Univ. Chicago Press, 1952.

15. Haynes, H. M. Development of Accommodative Behavior in Infants. Paper read at Conference on Theoretical Optometry and Visual Training at St. Louis, Mo., 1963.

16. Hubel, D. H. and Wiesel, T. N. Receptive fields, binocular interaction and functional architecture in the cat's visual cortex. *J. Physiol., 160:* 106-154, 1962.

17. Hubel, D. H., and Wiesel, T. N. Receptive fields of cells in striate cortex of very young, visually inexperienced kittens. *J. Neurophysiol., 26:* 994-1002, 1963.

18. McGraw, M. B. *The Neuromuscular Maturation of Human Infants.* New York, Columbia Univ. Press, 1943.

19. Marsden, R. E. 1903. A study of the early color sense. *Psychol. Rev., 10:* 37-47.
20. Piaget, J. *The Origins of Intelligence in Children.* New York, Internat. Univ. Press, 1952.
21. Pratt, K. C. The neonate. In L. Carmichael (Ed.), *Child Psychology.* New York, John Wiley, 1954, pp. 251-271.
22. Rheingold, Harriet. The effect of environmental stimulation upon social and exploratory behavior in the human infant. In B. M. Foss, (Ed.), *Determinants of Infant Behavior.* London, Methuen, 1961, pp. 171-178.
23. Saayman, G.; Ames, Elinor W., and Moffett, Adrienne. Response to novelty as an indicator of visual discrimination in the human infant. *J. Exp. Child Psychol., 1:*189-198, 1965.
24. Smith, J. M. The relative brightness values of three hues for newborn infants. *Univ. Iowa Stud. Child Welfare, 12*(1):91-140, 1936.
25. Spears, W. C. The Assessment of Visual Discrimination and Preference in the Human Infant. Doctoral Dissertation. Providence, R. I., Brown Univ., 1962.
26. Spitz, R. A. The smiling response: a contribution to the ontogenesis of social relations. *Genet. Psych. Monogr., 34:*57-125, 1946.
27. Stechler, G. The effect of medication during labor on newborn attention. *Science, 144:*315-317, 1964.
28. Stirnimann, F. Ueber das Farbenempfinden Neugeborener. *Ann. Paediat., 163:*1-25, 1944.

T HE WORLD as perceived by the young child is diffuse, homogeneous, unstable; people, objects, and events are not clear and definitive. Impressions that are the most salient for the child are what captures his attention. With learning and experience perception undergoes transitions: from awareness of an amorphous whole to a reaction to discrete parts of the whole; from gross discrimination to increasing capacity to differentiate stimuli in terms of similarities and differences; from perceptual inconstancies to an awareness of the invariance of form. The ability to use a language to label stimuli and call attention to component features aids the process of perceptual awareness and integration. Perception takes time to develop as Dr. M. D. Vernon discusses in the following article. Dr. Vernon's theoretical perspective is maturational in viewpoint, but she also emphasizes the active exploration of the child as he seeks to bring the world to himself. This also influences perceptual development.

Chapter 11

The Development of Perception in Children

M. D. Vernon

INTRODUCTION

IT IS OFTEN difficult for adults to realize that children, even when they have learnt to run about and to speak, do not perceive the world around them in the same way as do adults. Children are so surprisingly quick to notice and comment on everything that goes on; yet at the same time the things they perceive, and the manner in which they perceive them, may differ quite considerably from the things we notice. It is perhaps particularly important for teachers of young children to recognize these facts clearly, and to allow for them in their teaching, since misunderstandings may occur when children seem wilfully to overlook or to make mistakes in perceiving what is shown them. Nor should it be forgotten that the ability to perceive in an adult manner develops probably more through maturation than through learning. True, the child requires certain experiences to expand and refine his perceptual capacities; but no amount of experience, nor even of direct teaching, can force him to proceed beyond the stage which he has reached through natural maturation.

It is often not at all easy to determine the stage of maturation. It does not depend solely on chronological age, but neither is it entirely a function of intelligence, particularly of intelligence as measured by an intelligence test. Emotional maturity is also of importance; and so is the experience which the child has gained from his physical and social environment. When in the subsequent discussion it is stated that children of a certain age in years can perform such-and-such a task, it must be understood that this age is merely an average. Many children will be either older or younger when they can first perform it.

From *Educational Research*, 3:2-11, 1960. Reprinted by permission.

PERCEPTUAL DEVELOPMENT IN EARLY CHILDHOOD

Before we examine the gradually developing perceptual abilities of the child when he first goes to school, it is important to consider the outlook of the preschool child in perceiving the world around him. His main concern is with the objects and events he encounters in his ordinary everyday life, particularly those which are useful and interesting to him. He needs to know what things are; what they do; what he can do with them. Though in early infancy he has no understanding of the nature of his environment, nor what objects are like, he can discover a good deal, as Piaget[26] has shown, by examining closely everything that comes within his reach, putting it in his mouth, manipulating it and exploring it with his fingers. In this way during his first year he comes to realize that objects are stable, solid, resistant to touch; and that they have a shape which remains the same although its visual appearance varies as he turns the object round in his hands. He knows also that objects retain their identity although their apparent size varies as they approach and recede from him; and that they continue to exist while they are out of sight. Before he realizes this, he tends to think that a hidden object has altogether disappeared, and seems quite surprised when it reappears. The realization of the continued existence of objects out of sight is very important to the development of understanding, since it enables the child not only to ask for things not perceived at the moment, but later to think and talk about them. Thus, Lewis's son at about $1\frac{1}{2}$ years of age began to ask for chocolate hidden in a drawer;[18] but it was not until he was about 2 years old that he began to talk about past and future events unrelated to his immediate needs.

During his first year the child also begins to learn something about cause and effect.[26] He is extremely interested in pushing and pulling things and making them move about or rattle. But for some while he does not realize that it is necessary to touch them in order to do this, and sometimes he tries to "magic" them into moving by waving his hands at them from a distance. During his second year he also comes to understand that a moving object must touch another object to make it move in turn. Thus, even at this period he is extremely interested in finding out, as far as he is able, how and why things happen.

In his second year the child begins to use language to help him to understand and come to terms with his surroundings. Earlier, during his first year, vocalization is used primarily as a means of getting what he wants, crying when he is hungry or needs attention. Even his first words, "Mama," "go," "up," are really "word sentences,"[21] expressing his desires and needs. Listening to, smiling at, and babbling in response to human voices seems to be carried on in order to establish social contact with the people around him. Soon he finds that he can get what he wants more easily by asking people for it than by crying or grabbing. Also he often seems to enjoy babbling and repeating his early words as a form of vocal play, just as he enjoys waving his arms and legs and playing with his fingers and toes.[17]

The child's first words are most often names of objects, sometimes spoken in order to obtain these objects, but sometimes as a means of identifying an object and knowing what it is. It seems that the child establishes this identity in his mind by giving the object a name. At first the names are used for certain particular objects, but after a time for classes of objects. Thus, Lewis's son at about 9 months would look and reach for a small white ball when someone asked him, "Where's ballie?"[17] But it was not until he was over a year old that he responded in the same way to a large coloured ball. However, as the child begins to encounter more and more objects, he comes to perceive that certain of them are alike. He hears adults calling these similar objects by the same name, and so he begins also to class them together and give them a common name. Thus, balls may be big or small, hard or soft, white or coloured; but they all have the same name. This classificatory procedure is extremely useful to the child, since instead of remembering the nature and identity of each separate object, he can, once he has classified them, perceive, and recognize them as a group of things of similar behavior and use.[35] Thus, balls are things which can be thrown and caught, and which bounce. When the child encounters a new object, he immediately tries to classify it and to know what sort of a thing it is. If he cannot do this, he asks, "What's that?" Thus, we find that "What" questions begin towards the end of the second year, and are exceedingly frequent for the next two years.[30]

Of course, at first the child makes many mistakes in classification and naming. A single name may be used for a number of objects roughly similar in appearance to which we give quite different names. Thus, one child learnt the name "moo-i" for the moon, and subsequently used it for various round objects and even for circles drawn on paper.[38] Lewis's son used the word "tee" (kitty) for the cat, and also for dogs, cows, sheep and horses.[19] Later, he called his toy dog "goggie," but for some time retained the word "tee" for the live dog. About the same time he learnt the name "hosh" for a horse, and then applied it to a large St. Bernard dog. Thus, the child develops his own schemes of classification before he learns to name and use them in the way that we do.

As the child begins to know what things are, he becomes increasingly interested in what they do and what he can do with them and use them for. Thus, Valentine[33] noted that his 2-year-old daughter was constantly asking, "What this for?" A rather older child of 5, when asked what various things were, described them in terms of use and function: "What is a hen?" "Something that lays eggs for you." The child also needs to acquire an understanding of how and why things happen, what people and things do and why. This is reflected in his questions as to how and why, which become increasingly frequent in the fourth and fifth years.[30] Indeed, it has been calculated that at this period questions form 10 to 15 percent of everything the child says.[6] Even what appear to be statements of fact are often made with the intention of inviting confirmation or contradiction.

But in the process of classifiying objects according to their appearance and use, there is naturally a tendency to overlook details which are not important for identification. The child obtains a broad general impression of the object as a whole, but pays little attention to the specific qualities of particular objects. Neither does he notice these qualities, shape, colour, size, weight, in themselves, as apart from the objects to which they belong. The purpose of Montessori teaching was to encourage children to abstract such qualities and scale them in order. With specially prepared material, in which only one quality varies at a time, this is easier for the child than it is with ordinary objects which, as we have noted, the child regards mainly from the point of view of general appearance and use. We shall see later that these processes of abstraction and generalization constitute a real difficulty for the child when he begins to be taught formal school subjects.

When he first comes to school, the child needs to discover the nature and identity of the features of his new environment. He wants to know what things are, how and why events happen. Thus, he requires explanation rather than instruction. Still more, perhaps, he needs the opportunity, as he did in infancy, to work things out for himself by exploration, experimentation, manipulation, and construction. Susan Isaacs,[14] in her book *Intellectual Growth in Young Children,* gives numerous descriptions of the experimental play carried out by the children at the Malting House School at Cambridge, with sand, water, building blocks, water pipes, gas burners, etc., and how they weighed, measured, melted things, dissolved them in water, and so on. These experiments, the discussions of them and the explanations given by the teachers, enabled the children to learn and understand much about the nature of materials and the causes of physical phenomena. Their natural intense interest in how and why was furthered; and their powers of reasoning developed and were reinforced.

DEVELOPMENT OF VISUAL PERCEPTION

We see, then, that the primary need of children is to learn to understand and deal with "real" things and events. There is considerable evidence to show that it is some while before they have any desire or capacity to perceive things which may be educationally important, such as details of shape, pattern, arrangement, and number. It is true that children can learn at the age of 2 years or even younger to pick out a simple shape, such as a square, a circle, and a triangle, from among others if their choice is re-

warded by a piece of chocolate.[8] And by 4 years a child of average
intelligence can match eight out of the ten outline shapes used in
one of the Terman-Merrill test items.[31] But it is more doubtful
if they can remember these shapes. Piaget and Inhelder[28] showed
that a circle and a square could not be copied correctly before
about 4 years of age, a triangle before about 5 and a diamond
before 6. With complicated shapes made up of several parts of
containing interior details, accurate perception is slower to develop. This is perhaps best illustrated by Gesell and Ames[9] in the
reproductions made by children of various ages of a figure like a
Union Jack (see Fig. 11-1). Similar mistakes in the reproduction
of complex forms have been noted by Meili,[22] Bender,[1] and Piaget
and Inhelder.[28] They all indicate that children under 6 or 7 years
do not grasp the relationship between the parts of a complex
figure. They may perceive the outline, or some of the parts separately, but not the manner in which these are fitted together. The
ability to do this may depend as much upon the understanding
of relationships as upon immediate perception of shape. Thus,
when children begin to learn to read, they may notice the length
of a word, and certain letters in it. But they may not perceive or
remember correctly the exact shapes of any letter, nor all the
letters in the word, nor the relationship or order in which the
letters occur.

There is another difficulty frequently encountered in teaching
children to perceive accurately, namely, that they tend to see
things as part of a total situation from which they cannot be isolated. An instance of this is given by Piaget[26] of a child of $1\frac{1}{2}$

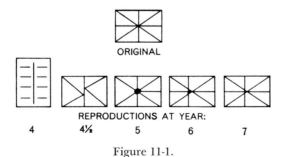

ORIGINAL

REPRODUCTIONS AT YEAR:

4   4½   5   6   7

Figure 11-1.

years who used the name "papa" only for her father sitting in his study; when she saw him elsewhere she did not associate this name with him. In older children this phenomenon appears in an inability to differentiate shapes from their background, and to perceive shape as such independently of its surroundings. Thus, children are particularly susceptible to visual illusions such as that shown in Figure 11-2, in which the capacity to perceive that the two horizontal lines are of equal length depends upon isolating them from the attached arrowheads.[36] Piaget[27] has also made a large number of studies of children's perceptions of visual illusions and concluded that they do not know how to direct attention towards the significant features of the figures and ignore the less relevant. If the children's eye movements are recorded, it is found that the eyes of the younger children wander about all over the figures; whereas those of older children concentrate on particular points of importance.

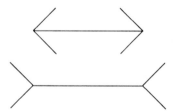

Figure 11-2.

That children find difficulty in analyzing complex shapes and picking out certain parts of them is also shown by their reactions to figures of the type designed by Gottschaldt.[12] He presented a number of simple figures until they were thoroughly familiar. Afterwards he showed complex figures each of which contained one of the simpler ones embedded in it and found that adults had great difficulty in perceiving the simple figures embedded in the complex ones. Ghent[10] presented a simple and a complex figure together (such as those shown in Fig. 11-3) and asked children to trace out the simple figure in the complex one. No children could do this before 6 years, and many not even at 8 years. But Witkin[39] has recently brought evidence to show that the ability to restructure what is presented by analyzing it and extracting particular parts is a function not only of age and intelligence, but also of certain qualities of personality. He considers that children who are in themselves self-reliant and able to act on their own initiative are more capable of such tasks than are children who tend to relay passively on external circumstances or depend on others.

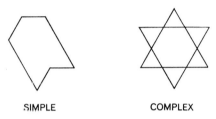

SIMPLE   COMPLEX

Figure 11-3.

There is evidence to show that the ability to perceive shape in general more accurately is not greatly improved by giving practice in perceiving particular shapes. Nor is the ability to perceive letters and words in reading much affected. Thus, Goins[11] gave 6-year-old children extensive training in perceiving figures and numbers exposed for a short period of time only. They became more skillful in perceiving this particular material; but their achievement in reading improved no more than did that of similar children who were given no such training. Again, as Gates[7] and Kendall[16] have shown, there appears to be little or no relationship between ability to perceive shapes correctly and to learn to read. This at first sight seems surprising. We can only suppose that by the time children are sufficiently mature to learn to read, they have developed an ability to perceive shapes visually which is adequate for the purpose of reading; whereas less mature children do not improve sufficiently in perception as the result of special training for there to be any effect on their reading capacities.

There is another form of perceptual ability which may be of

considerable indirect importance in learning to read, namely, the perception and understanding of pictures. These also seem to depend to a considerable extent on maturation, though naturally they do not develop unless the children are given some experience with pictures. Binet[3] pointed out that this understanding developed only gradually; and his observations have been confirmed by later experiments.[34] Up to the age of 4 to 5 years, children, though they can identify familiar objects in pictures, will enumerate them one after the other but will not relate them together in any way. At about 6 to 7 years they will begin to give simple descriptions of the pictures; but it is not until they are 10 to 11 years that they can "interpret" what is happening, what the people are doing, and so on. Thus, children of 11 years are supposed to be able to interpret the picture in the Terman-Merrill test[31] of the telegraph boy whose bicycle has broken down and who is signalling to a car to stop and give him a lift. Naturally, the age of interpretation varies somewhat with the obviousness and familiarity of the incidents depicted. But before they are able to interpret, children may not even pick out the salient features of the picture or the principal actors in the scene depicted, but may notice instead comparatively irrelevant features. Thus, in a picture used by the author[34] of a man stopping a runaway horse and cart, the man himself was sometimes omitted from their descriptions, but people looking on were included. This behavior of course parallels that which appears in children's perceptions of complex forms. The inability to extract the significant features of pictures may be of some importance if children are taught to read words describing the actions of people shown in pictures.

LANGUAGE DEVELOPMENT

We have already noted that in their early language development children learn first to express their wishes and then to name objects and ask questions about them. At first, the phonetic pattern of children's speech is so unlike that of adults that few except their mothers are able to understand them. But Morley and Court[24] stated that among a sample of over 100 children they tested, about 70 percent were intelligible to strangers by the age of 2 years, though they tended to relapse into unintelligibility when they were excited or upset. Sheridan[29] however, found that the phonetic pattern of speech of 5-year-old children was frequently defective and sometimes so much so as to make their speech unintelligible outside their families. Therefore, when they first come to school such children must have considerable difficulty in making themselves understood.

Children's speech also differs grammatically and syntactically from that of adults. Towards the end of the second year they speak in short two to three word sentences consisting mainly of nouns and verbs, prepositions and conjunctions being omitted.[21] Sentences increase in length from about four words each at 3 years to $7\frac{1}{2}$ words at 8 years, according to Templin.[32] Grammatical errors, at first frequent, decrease in number; sentences become more complex in structure and subordinate clauses begin to appear.

It is generally agreed that children understand speech before they speak themselves. Even in early infancy children can often understand and respond to the emotions of adults speaking to them; they comprehend the intonational pattern of adult speech which reflects the emotions of the speaker, before the phonetic pattern. Then also the adult helps the child to understand words by gesturing, pointing to objects named, and so on. It is difficult to judge how soon and to what extent children hear the phonetic patterns of single words and understand their meanings. Watts[37] estimated that about 2,000 words were understood at 5 years, and 4,000 to 5,000 at 7 years. Templin,[32] however, estimated 8,500 at 6 years. These estimates vary with the manner in which they are calculated. They also presuppose that the children hear the words sufficiently clearly to understand them. Yet Midgeley[23] found that a fair number of 6-year-old children failed to hear correctly single words spoken by the teacher, such as "mouse," "rose," "spoon," etc.

The speech and understanding of children clearly varies greatly according to the manner in which they have been brought up. Those whose parents themselves speak well, and frequently talk to their children, will learn much faster than those brought up by parents with phonetically and grammatically incorrect speech and limited vocabulary Several studies have shown that in middle-class children both articulation and language structure are more advanced than in working-class children;[4,21] and, indeed, the differences may increase as the children's ages increase. Bernstein[2] has put forward the thesis that children in working-class homes grow up to speak and understand mainly what may be called "public language": short, crude and obvious statements about immediate feelings, wishes, and actions. Middle-class children, especially those from educated homes, become accustomed to hearing "formal language": more complex and more logical language conveying the finer shades of meaning and expressing feelings and wishes more subtly and indirectly. So also objects are not taken simply at their face value, but become a point of departure for inquiry and for interpretation of more recondite meaning and significance. These constitute the language and outlook of the school. Not surprisingly, therefore, the middle-class child is more ready than the working-class child to accept and profit by his school education. In fact, the latter may resent and react against school teaching. In support of this thesis Bernstein found that working-class boys aged 15 to 18 of normal intelligence often gave subnormal performances on a vocabulary test; and, indeed, the higher the nonverbal I.Q., the greater the difference between it and the vocabulary test score. Although these were older children, the same type of difficulty and the same discrepancy may well appear in younger children.

But also close personal contact with adults is immensely important in speech development. Kellmer Pringle[15] found that children brought up in institutions, without close personal contacts with adults, were particularly backward in their ability to understand and to express themselves in speech. Their linguistic development was slower than their intellectual development. Speech develops slowly in children who are mainly in contact with other children. McCarthy[21] found that children who associated mainly with adults were more advanced than those who associated chiefly with other children; and Davis[4] showed that in only children speech was more advanced than in others. Retardation may be particularly marked in twins.[4] The Russian psychologists, Luria and Yudovich,[20] described a pair of identical twins, aged 5 years, whose mother was retarded in speech, and who, when they first came to school, were so inarticulate as to be incapable of playing with the other children. But they could communicate with each other by noises and gestures. It is often alleged that the children of overindulgent parents are liable to be backward in speech, because the parents give them everything they want without requiring them to ask for it intelligibly. We do not know if such children are equally backward in understanding speech; but since speaking and understanding speech are closely related to each other in childhood, it seems possible that they are.

Thus, we see that unless in early childhood they have been helped and encouraged by adults to speak and understand clearly, children have little capacity for, or interest in, listening to what the teacher says. Neither can they express their ideas or talk conversationally.

But in order to learn to read children must not only be able to hear and understand words spoken to them, the meaning of which can be understood from the context of the sentence in which they occur; the child must also hear the exact phonetic pattern of the word, and, indeed, be able to analyze this into its constituent sounds, the sounds of the letters or letter groups. Such a process of analysis is probably even more difficult than the analysis of the printed word shape into its constituent letter shapes. Many years ago a German psychologist, von Ehrenfels,[5] pointed out that a sound pattern such as a tune possessed "Gestaltqualität" (form quality). It was heard as a whole; and the listener was hardly aware of the individual notes apart from their relationship to one another in the tune. Speech also possesses "Gestaltqualität." The child hears sentences as wholes conveying instructions or statements. He is not clearly aware of the words as isolated and independent entities. Still less is he aware of the particular letter sounds within the word. Yet before he can read properly he must be able first to isolate the letter sounds from the word sound, and then associate the independent letter sounds with their shapes in the printed word. Unfortunately, in the English language the vowels have many different sounds, and the child may be unable to tell which is the correct one until he has sounded the whole word. Furthermore, the child may be accustomed to hear and speak vowel sounds with a local accent which distorts them until they are quite unlike those of the teacher.

DEVELOPMENT OF NUMBER CONCEPTS

It appears, therefore, that in many of the school tasks which confront the child he cannot go far as long as he is limited to the use of his spontaneous perceptions. He must use his intelligence to refine these and improve their accuracy. And he must learn to break up what is immediately perceived, to analyze it into its constituent parts and use these independently of the whole pattern of sight or sound in which they are presented.

The ability to analyze and abstract particular features from what is perceived is particularly important in beginning number work. Piaget[25] has made a number of studies which demonstrate the inability of children below the age of five or six to understand the abstract notions of number, quantity and volume. Thus, if they are shown a number of blocks scattered over a wide area, they say that there are more of these than when the blocks are placed close together. Again, if they are shown water in a wide-necked vessel which is then poured into a narrow-necked vessel, they say that there is now more water than before, because it rises higher in the neck of the vessel. They cannot conceive of the number or volume remaining constant, whatever the manner in which objects or substances are distributed; and do not realize that these are qualities which are independent of the objects or substances quantified and the setting in which they are placed.

In a recent pamphlet Nathan Isaacs[13] has described some of Piaget's observations of children's concepts of number and quantity and has pointed out how impossible it is for children to do number work satisfactorily until they really understand that number is an abstract quality, independent of the particular objects numbered. If the children are taught number work before they are quite clear about this, names of numbers and computation processes become a kind of verbal ritual which they learn by heart without understanding in the least what it means. Fortunately, many children seem to acquire this understanding spontaneously as their powers of reasoning mature. But others may require prolonged exercises in estimating numbers of objects in different settings.

CONCLUSIONS

We may conclude that both in vision and in hearing perceptual development is active rather than passive. The child does not rest content with a passive reception of the information from the outside world which impinges on his senses. Rather, because of his need to find out, to understand, to get what pleases him, he sets out to explore and to investigate for himself; and to induce adults to give him the objects and the information which he requires. All the time he uses his powers of reasoning to seek knowledge about how, why, and wherefore. At first he can reason only by action—by doing things and discovering what happens. But verbal reasoning develops as an accompaniment to such activities. Perceptual and reasoning abilities improve through natural maturation: but they also require the opportunity for exercise, and they require encouragement and help from adults. Children are able to profit from formal teaching in school only when they have reached the necessary stage of maturation, and if and when this teaching appeals to their natural interests.

REFERENCES

1. Bender, L. *A Visual Motor Gestalt Test and its Clinical Use.* New York, American Orthopsychiatric Association, 1938.
2. Bernstein, B. Some sociological determinants of perception. *Brit. J. Sociol., 9:*159, 1958.
3. Binet, A., and Simon, T. Le development de l'intelligence chez les enfants. *Ann. Psychol., 14:*1, 1908.
4. Davis, E. A. *The Development of Linguistic Skill in Twins, Singletons with Siblings and Only Children from Age 5 to 10 Years.* Minneapolis, University of Minnesota Press, 1937.
5. Ehrenfels, C. von. Uber Gestaltqualitäten. *Vierteljahrsch. wiss. Philos., 14:*249, 1890.

6. Fisher, M. S. Language patterns of pre-school children. *Child Devel. Monogr.,* No. 15, 1934.
7. Gates, A. I. The psychology of reading and spelling. *Teachers' Coll. Contrib. Educ.,* No. 129, 1922.
8. Gellerman, L. W. Form discrimination in chimpanzees and two-year-old children. *J. Genet. Psychol., 42:*3, 1933.
9. Gesell, A., and Ames, L. B. The development of directionality in drawing. *J. Genet. Psychol., 68:*45, 1946.
10. Ghent, L. Perception of overlapping and embedded figures by children of different ages. *Amer. J. Psychol., 69:*575, 1956.
11. Goins, J. T. Visual perceptual abilities and early reading progress. *Suppl. Educ. Monogr.,* No. 87, 1958.
12. Gottschaldt, K. Uber den Einfluss der Ehrfahrung auf die Wahrnehmung von Figuren *Psychol. Forsch., 8:*261, 1926.
13. Isaacs, N. *New Light on Children's Ideas of Number.* London, Educational Supply Association, 1960.
14. Isaacs, S. *Intellectual Growth in Young Children.* London, Routledge, 1930.
15. Kellmer Pringle, M. L. Learning difficulties of deprived children. *Proc. XVth Internat. Congr. Psychol.,* 1930.
16. Kendall, B. A note on the relation of retardation in reading to performance on a memory for designs test. *J. Educ. Psychol., 39:*370, 1948.
17. Lewis, M. M. *Infant Speech.* London, Kegan Paul, 1936.
18. Lewis, M. M. The beginning of references to past and future in the child's speech. *Brit. J. Educ. Psychol., 7:*39, 1937.
19. Lewis, M. M. *How Children Learn to Speak.* London, Harrap, 1957.
20. Luria, A. R., and Yudovich, F. I. *Speech and the Development of Mental Processes in the Child.* London, Staples Press, 1959.
21. McCarthy, D. *The Language Development of the Pre-school Child.* Minneapolis, University of Minnesota Press, 1930.
22. Meili, R. Les perceptions des enfants. *Arch. de Psychol., 23:*25, 1931.
23. Midgeley, J. D. *Report to the Medical Research Council on the Educational Treatment of Deafness* 1952 (unpublished) .
24. Morley, M. E., and Court, D. *The Development and Disorders of Speech in Childhood.* Edinburgh, Livingstone, 1957.
25. Piaget, J. *The Child's Conception of Number.* London, Routledge & Kegan Paul, 1952.
26. Piaget, J. *The Child's Construction of Reality.* London, Routledge & Kegan Paul, 1955.
27. Piaget, J. *Proc. XVIth Internat. Congr. Psychol.* 1960.
28. Piaget, J., and Inhelder, B. *The Child's Conception of Space.* London, Routledge & Kegan Paul, 1956.
29. Sheridan, M. D. *The Child's Hearing for Speech.* London, Methuen, 1948.

30. Smith, M. E. The influence of age, sex and situation on the frequency, form and function of questions asked by pre-school children. *Child Devel., 4:*201, 1938.

31. Terman, L. M., and Merrill, M. A. *Measuring Intelligence.* London, Harrap, 1937.

32. Templin, M. C. *Certain Language Skills in Children.* Minneapolis, University of Minnesota Press, 1957.

33. Valentine, C. W. *The Psychology of Early Childhood.* London, Methuen, 1942.

34. Vernon, M. D. The relation of cognition and phantasy in children. *Brit. J. Psychol., 30:*273, 1940.

35. Vernon, M. D. *A Further Study of Visual Perception.* Cambridge University Press, 1952, Ch. II.

36. Walters, A. A genetic study of geometrical-optical illusions. *Genet. Psychol. Monogr., 25:*101, 1912.

37. Watts, A. F. *The Language and Mental Development of Children.* London, Harrap, 1944.

38. Werner, H. *Comparative Study of Mental Development,* 2nd ed. New York, Internat. Univ. Press, 1948.

39. Witkin, H. A. *Proc. XVIth Internat Congr. Psychol.* 1960.

W HEN WE attempt to define "normal" children we tend to think of behavior that does not deviate markedly from the average or norm. This definition lacks precision and specificity as is apparent when factors such as range of behavior, individual variation in responses, and cultural emphases are considered. Nonetheless, behavior is frequently reviewed and then labeled, formally or informally, normal and abnormal. The label though is not as crucial as is the identification of the child with a problem and the subsequent determination of how to help him. In order to do this we must know the range and components of behavior of the child who does not seem to have problems which interfere with his development, i.e. the "normal" child. Dr. A. J. Ayres has studied perceptual motor functioning in groups of children, some with learning problems, others without. The study reported here deals with factor analysis of perceptual-motor behavior as manifested by children without learning difficulties. The results suggest that not only are there quantitative differences (test scores) between children considered normal and those with perceptual-motor problems but qualitiative differences in functioning may also be present.

Chapter 12

Interrelations Among Perceptual-Motor Abilities in a Group of Normal Children

A. Jean Ayres

T HE STATE of abnormality is defined by the accepted parameters of normality. Deviation from the norm may be a function of quantity or may be expressive of a specific qualitative variation. Both conditions could, or course, prevail simultaneously in any given aberrant state. In fact, such a dichotomy may be artificial and pursuit of its exploration may have its greatest value in heuristic purposes only. In any event, the focusing of interest and therapeutic practice on atypical perceptual-motor function in children requires guidance from concomitant study of the nature of this function in the normal child.

Data are presented here to contribute toward a clearer understanding as to whether irregularities in the perceptual-motor maturational pattern represent generalized quantitative developmental failure or a qualitative difference, if indeed, the two different conditions do exist. The objective in providing material of this type lies not only in increasing knowledge of human development but also in providing guidance in treatment planning based on possible qualitative versus quantitative deviations.

METHOD

A battery of perceptual-motor tests was administered to 64 adopted children ages 4 through 8 years who had been administered the Gesell Developmental Schedules at 7 through 10 months of age. All but three children were assigned Gesell quoti-

At the time of this study the author was a National Institute of Mental Health postdoctoral trainee, University of California, Los Angeles. The UCLA Health Sciences Computing Facility was utilized for statistical analysis of the data.

From *The American Journal of Occupational Therapy,* 20:288-292, 1966. Reprinted by permission.

ents of 100 or above, the remaining scores falling at 93, 95 and 97. Placement in the adoptive home was made within the first three months of the child's life. The families of the Ss appeared to be from the middle socioeconomic class, with further similarity of sample characteristics resulting from conditions prevailing as part of the adoptive process. Willingness to participate in the study may have operated as an additional selective factor. Considering these variables of selection, the sample was assumed to be a highly homogeneous group of normal children. Support of this assumption was found in the group mean perceptual-motor test score, which was only slightly above the average for the normative scores on the standardized tests. The variance on perceptual-motor tests was smaller than would be expected from a sample chosen at random.

The perceptual-motor tests, all designed to detect dysfunction, included the following standardized tests: the four visual perception subjects of the Marianne Frostig Developmental Test of Visual Perception,[8] the Southern California Kinesthesia and Tactile Perception Tests[5] (tests 7 through 12 in Table 12-I), the Southern California Figure-ground Visual Perception Test,[4] the Southern California Motor Accuracy Test,[6] and the Ayres Space Test.[1] In addition, three nonstandardized tests were included with scores based on normative data from a limited sample. These tests included one of motor planning involving imitating postures assumed by the examiner (Imitation of Postures), the ability to coordinate bilateral rhythmical movement of arms and hands (Bilateral Motor Coordination) and a simplified version of Head's[9] test of crossing the midline of the body. The subjects of the study were rated on the degree of freedom from hyperactivity and distractibility and on freedom from tactile defensiveness.

The scores of all tests were intercorrelated using computer program BMD O2D[7] and then subjected to R-technique orthogonal rotation factor analysis with computer program BMD O3M.[7] The correlation matrix was modified by insertion in the diagonal of the multiple correlation coefficients. Extracted factors were rotated by the Kaiser varimax criterion,[10] the number of factors rotated being equal to the number of eigenvalues greater

TABLE 12-I

Correlation and Factor Matrices Correlations Between Tests

Test	1	2	3	4	5	6	7
1. Southern California Figure-ground Visual Perception	40						
2. Frostig Figure-ground	38	60					
3. Frostig Form Constancy	34	44	59				
4. Frostig Position in Space	18	24	48	45			
5. Frostig Spatial Relations	07	09	27	39	33		
6. Ayres Space	32	41	50	25	30	51	
7. Kinesthesia	—03	01	19	—03	—17	20	32
8. Manual form perception	—01	19	21	17	17	33	02
9. Finger identification	19	15	22	02	—02	13	39
10. Graphesthesia	—09	49	14	14	09	21	14
11. Localization of tactile stimuli	06	01	10	19	—07	07	13
12. Perception of double tactile stimuli	—08	14	12	—14	—10	10	05
13. Imitation of postures	12	08	03	00	—05	02	09
14. Crossing midline of body	15	24	13	05	—02	10	07
15. Southern California motor accuracy	29	37	31	14	14	48	07
16. Bilateral motor coordination	22	24	41	14	06	22	07
17. Freedom from hyperactivity/distractibility	—01	22	21	26	03	10	—05
18. Freedom from tactile defensiveness	01	08	10	—03	—13	16	—05
19. Mean perceptual-motor score	44	62	67	46	29	63	28

Note: Decimals have been omitted. Squared multiple correlations have been inserted in diagonal of correlation matrix. An r of .25 is required for significance at at .05 level and an r. 32 for significance at the .0 level.

than zero. The procedure was analagous to that used in similar earlier studies.[2,3]

RESULTS AND DISCUSSION

The rotated factors and the coefficients of correlation between each pair of scores, including a mean of scores on tests 1 thorugh 16 are shown in Table 12-I. The correlations as well as the commonalities in the right-hand column are quite low for this type of statistical procedure, probably reflecting the fact that in a highly homogeneous group of normal children there is little systematic variation within the perceptual-motor functions under study. Each commonality expresses the degree to which a given test is measuring the same variance that all of the rest of the tests are

8	9	10	11	12	13	14	15	16	17	18	Rotated Factors			Communalities
											A	B	C	
											50	05	—10	.27
											54	38	11	.45
											71	21	11	.56
											55	—06	20	.35
											44	—17	04	.23
											66	22	03	.48
											07	32	—27	.18
37											22	36	15	.20
—05	35										20	33	—31	.24
29	11	51									14	59	12	.38
04	31	26	33								08	32	06	.11
25	04	30	12	33							—10	52	—02	.28
14	04	12	20	20	14						—01	27	—11	.08
33	19	29	11	33	14	42					09	57	15	.35
22	15	13	16	01	01	22	42				50	19	—03	.28
16	07	29	14	10	18	35	00	44			24	37	35	.32
17	—04	14	21	—03	—11	09	—01	35	48		14	11	68	.49
—04	—11	01	06	—03	—08	18	22	18	45	42	03	07	54	.30
48	37	54	36	32	29	50	51	50	21	07				

measuring. If children do not vary in performance in a systematic manner, there is less opportunity for the intercorrelations of scores upon which the emergence of factors is dependent. Consequently, those tests which measured functions on which individual variation did not follow similar variation in most of the other tests carried low commonalities. Low commonalities do not indicate either degree of reliability or validity of an individual test, but that the test did not have much chance of correlating with the other tests. The fact that all of the tests were designed primarily to discriminate between normal and dysfunction rather than among normal functions may contribute to the low degree of interassociation. The data indicate that the greatest amount of consistent variation in test performance was on the tests of visual perception, especially form perception, and the least amount on the measures of somatosensory perception and motor planning.

Most of the variance under measurement in this study is accounted for by factor A, which appears to fit into the conventional concept of visual-motor ability, with emphasis on the visual component, especially form perception. Factor B is less easily categorized. Two tests of tactile function and crossing the midline of the body share the major portion of the variance and indicate a definite alliance between these two dimensions of perceptual-motor function in this sample. The factor seems to reflect an interaction of function of the two sides of the body with special emphasis in the tactile domain. The third factor (C) is considered to be a reflection of the mechanism previously identified as tactile defensiveness. The relationship between this behavioral response and hyperactivity and distractibility is demonstrated.

Comparison of the factor structure of the scores from this normal group with the factor structure derived from study[3] of children with dysfunction may help to clarify possible differences between developmental deviation and developmental lag. It is postulated that a defined constellation of test scores which appears among children with dysfunction and fails to appear among children without dysfunction is more likely to be expressive of a syndrome of dysfunction than delayed perceptual development. It is not implied that delayed development is normal.

The clearest difference between the factorial structure of the scores from the normal children of this study and that previously reported[3] on a group with dysfunction is the failure for the dimensions of praxis and form and space perception to appear as separate factors in the normal group. The tactile-motor planning alliance appearing so clearly in subjects with deficits in these domains is essentially unreflected in the intercorrelation of scores from the normal children. A pattern of low scores on tests of motor planning and tactile perception, then, suggests a developmental deviation best identified as dyspraxia. Similarly, if deficits in tests involving form and space appear without comparable

deficits in other perceptual-motor parameters, a qualitative difference in perceptual development might be considered.

Comparable hypotheses cannot be formulated about the previously proposed syndrome of integration of function of the two
sides of the body or of tactile defensiveness. The ability to coordinate motor actions bilaterally and to cross the midline of the
body maintained an association in the normal group that was also
seen in the dysfunction group. The difference in the pattern of
scores for the two groups could be attributed to methodological
matters as well as to true sample differences. Freedom from hyperactive and distracted behavior as well as from tactile defensiveness
showed an affiliation similar to that observed in the earlier dysfunction group, although the low association with tactile functions
did not appear. The presence of this type of behavior reflected in
this factor may be associated with maturational factors in young
children.

Rigid interpretation of pattern of test scores in terms of dysfunction or maturational delay are certainly not in order. There
is insufficient evidence to warrant the practice, and furthermore,
to do so may be contrary to the actual ontogenesis of perceptual
motor ability. Perceptual-motor dysfunction, if present, tends to
be pervasive although clusters of scores do occur. Identification
of constellations of dysfunction may best serve the purpose of
directing therapeutic emphasis. Consistently low scores on all
tests may be considered lag but they may also mean generalized
poor perceptual-motor integration.

Comparison of the factor structure in Table 12-I with a comparable analysis of scores[3] from a random sample of children
chosen without reference to perceptual ability reveals some
similarities that may be helpful in understanding normal development. In both instances, motor accuracy affiliated with visual perception in a manner suggesting a general relation of visual and
motor development not especially influenced by somatosensory
perception falling within or above average.

Both analyses indicate an association in normal children between tactile perception and crossing the midline of the body. In

both instances, perception of double tactile stimuli showed the most definite affiliation, suggesting as a common denominator to both tasks an integration for interpretation of the sensory flow from both sides of the body.

The value of a test in detecting perceptual disorders cannot be inferred from this study. Size of factor loading in no way indicates the ability of a test to discriminate between children with and without dysfunction. It does indicate the purity of a test relative to the behavioral dimension reflected in the factor. In therapeutic practice there is a certain advantage to the use of tests which tap areas of function which show little variation in normal children but considerable variation in children with disorders.

SUMMARY

A battery of perceptual-motor tests was given to 64 normal adopted children and the correlations between scores subjected to factor analysis. The three emerging factors identified as (1) visual-motor ability, (2) an interaction of function of the two sides of the body with emphasis on tactile perception and (3) tactile defensiveness. A factor similar to factor A previously has been identified in a presumably normal group but not in children with dysfunction, where praxis and visual form and space abilities clearly separated. Factors B and C were identified previously in modified forms in normal and dysfunction groups.

REFERENCES

1. Ayres, A. J. *Ayres Space Test.* Los Angeles, Western Psychological Services, 1962.
2. Ayres, A. J. Interrelationships among perceptual-motor functions in children." *AJOT, 20*:68-71, 1966.
3. Ayres, A. J. Patterns of perceptual-motor dysfunction in children: a factor analytic study. *Perceptual and Motor Skills, 20*:335-368, 1965.
4. Ayres, A. J. *Southern California Figure-ground Visual Perception Test.* Los Angeles, Western Psychological Services, 1966.
5. Ayres, A. J. *Southern California Kinesthesia and Tactile Perception Tests.* Los Angeles, Western Psychological Services, 1966.
6. Ayres, A. J. *Southern California Motor Accuracy Test.* Los Angeles: Western Psychological Services, 1964.

7. Dixon, W. J. (Ed.) *BMD Biomedical Computer Program.* University of California, 1964.

8. Frostig, M., Lefever, D. W., and Whittlesey, J. R. B. *Marianne Frostig Developmental Test of Visual Perception,* 3rd ed., Palo Alto, California: Consulting Psychologists Press, 1961.

9. Head, H. *Aphasia and Kindred Disorders of Speech.* Cambridge University Press, 1926, Vol. I.

10. Kaiser, H. F. The Varimax criterion for analytic rotation in factor analysis. *Psychometrika, 23:*187-200, 1958.

PART V
COGNITIVE DEVELOPMENT

ONE OF THE MOST IMPORTANT contributions to the understanding of intellectual development has been made by the Swiss psychologist, Jean Piaget. Proceeding from his earlier interest in biology and then to psychology, his work has been characterized by profound thinking, keen observations, and marked productivity. Although Professor Piaget's early writings met with enthusiasm in the 1920's it was not until the 1950's that large-scale attempts were made to comprehend and verify many of his ideas. At present, there is considerable research on cognitive development derived from the Piaget model. Recently Professor Piaget has been concerned with expanding his psychological theories to a study of knowledge in general. In the following article Dr. D. E. Berlyne summarizes some of the basic Piaget theory of cognitive development. Note that inherent in this theory is the concept of stages of development; that is, there are certain patterns of behavior associated with an age-related period. The stages occur in an orderly sequence which implies a process of organization of behavior within each stage. This must occur before the next stage can be attained. Professor Piaget does not merely describe the behavior expected in each stage, he also proposes a theory which accounts for the behavior.

Chapter 13

Developments in Piaget's Work

D. E. BERLYNE

INTRODUCTION

PIAGET IS KNOWN to English-speaking psychologists mainly for his early writings, with their thought-provoking but, according to some critics, disputable accounts of the quaint notions of young children. Doubts have been expressed about the validity of the method of interrogation used for these studies and about the generality of the findings. Repetitions with other populations have not always produced the results that Piaget's works would lead one to expect. At least one writer was moved to dismiss his "subjective approaches to the analysis of child behavior" as "little removed from ordinary literary speculation."[19]

Since the 1930's, however, Piaget's researches have been undergoing some gradual but profound changes. He has been turning to more exact and behavioristic methods of collecting data: close observation of infants, setting older children practical tasks or putting precise questions to them about events enacted in front of them, and psychophysical experiments with both child and adult subjects. His theory has become more detailed and more ambitious in scope, drawing on his knowledge of biology, logic, and history of science, all of them fields to which he has contributed. These developments can be summed up by saying that he has changed from one of the most celebrated *developmental* psychologists into one of the most important of contemporary *general* psychologists. But this does not mean that his work has lost any of its importance for those faced with the practical problems of childhood in their everyday work.

Like most contemporary psychologists, Piaget starts from the

From *British Journal of Educational Psychology, 27*:1-12, 1957. Reprinted by permission of the author and publisher.

biological concept of "adaptation." He sees adaptation as an interplay of two complementary processes, which he calls "assimilation" and "accommodation." Assimilation occurs when an organism uses something in its environment for some activity which is already part of its repertoire. At the physiological level, it is exemplified by the ingestion of food, and, at the psychological level, it embraces a variety of phenomena. Piaget sees assimilation at work, for example, whenever a situation evokes a particular pattern of behavior because it resembles situations that have evoked it in the past, whenever something new is perceived or conceived in terms of something familiar, whenever anything is invested with value or emotional importance. Accommodation, on the other hand, means the addition of new activities to an organism's repertoire or the modification of old activities in response to the impact of environmental events.

Psychologists accustomed to other conceptual schemes may wonder whether it really helps to group together such multifarious processes under the same rubrics. Is the role played by a cow appearing as roast beef on a horse really analogous to that played by a cow appearing as roast beef on the child's dinner plate? Although Piaget discusses assimilation and accommodation at great length, some readers may feel that the concepts need to be analyzed more minutely before they can yield unequivocal predictions rather than describe facts already discovered. At all events, assimilation seems to include what learning theorists call "generalization" and "discrimination," processes determining which response a particular stimulus will elicit, while accommodation covers "differentiation of responses" and the learning of new responses.

As the child's development proceeds, a more and more complete balance and synthesis between assimilation and accommodation is achieved. The child is able to take account of stimuli more and more remote from him in space and time and to resort to more and more composite and indirect methods of solving problems.

Piaget agrees with many other theorists in distinguishing "affective" and "cognitive" factors. The former release energy, while the latter determine how the energy will be applied. Piaget's writings have concentrated on the "cognitive" aspect of behavior rather than on motivation and emotion, but he insists that neither aspect must be overlooked. The child does not undergo separate intellectual and emotional developments. The most dispassionate pursuit of knowledge must be driven by some motive, and the directions in which drives and emotions impel behavior must depend on the structures made available by the growth of intelligence.

THE PERIOD OF SENSORIMOTOR INTELLIGENCE (BIRTH TO 2 YEARS)

During his first two years, the child gradually advances towards the highest degree of intelligence that is possible without language and other symbolic functions. He begins life with innate reflexes, but these are, from the start, modified and made more effective by learning. New responses are soon acquired, and then complex solutions to problems are achieved by piecing together familiar responses in novel combinations. By the end of the second year, the first signs of the human capacity for symbolization appear: he invents new patterns of behavior which show him to be representing the results of his actions to himself before they occur. In short, the sensorimotor period sees attainments comparable to the highest found in subhuman animals.

This growing ingenuity in the face of practical problems goes hand in hand with the formation of a less "egocentric" and more "objective" conception of the world. For some weeks after birth, the world must consist of a succession of visual patterns, sounds, and other sensations. The infant comes naturally to pay attention to those external events which are associated with satisfactions or which are brought about by his own actions. Gradually, he builds up a view of the world as a collection of objects continuing to exist even when they are out of his sight and generally preserving the same sizes and shapes, despite the changes in their appearance that come with changes in position. Whereas no distinction between himself and what is outside him can have any meaning for him at first, he comes to conceive of himself as one object among the many that people the world, most of them unaffected by his activities.

The concept of an *object* is bound up with objective notions of *space, time,* and *causality,* which the child does not possess as part of his native endowment but has to build up gradually through interaction with the world. After learning to select appropriate spatial directions and temporal successions for his actions, he comes to respond to the positions and times of occurrence of events outside himself, using his own body and his own actions as reference points. Finally, he conceives of a space and a time in which both he himself and external objects are located. He learns, for example, to distinguish occasions when objects are moving independently of him from occasions when they merely appear to be changing positions because he is moving among them. Similarly, he progresses from an understanding of the relationship between his responses and their consequences to an understanding of the causal influence inanimate objects can exert on one another and even on him.

THE ORIGIN OF SYMBOLIC PROCESSES

Anything the child has achieved during the sensorimotor period is dwarfed by the prospects introduced by signs and symbols, particularly words and images. They expose him to a world of real and imaginary entities extending far beyond his momentary range of vision or even his life span. It is a stable and consistent world, whereas the objects he perceives come and go.

Piaget deprecates the long-established belief that images are mere reactivations of traces of past experiences, passively registered by the nervous system. He insists that imagery is an extremely complex and active process, as can be seen from the time it takes to appear after birth. It grows out of the child's imitative capacities and is, in fact, "internalized imitation." The gradual extension of imitation during the sensorimotor period proceeds from a tendency to reproduce sounds and visual effects which have just been produced by the infant himself or by somebody else to an ability to copy an increasing range of new responses from an increasing range of models. It reaches its climax and the point at which it can perform symbolic functions with "deferred imitation," the imitation of the behavior of an absent person of whom the child is "reminded."

Inanimate objects also can evoke imitation, as, for example, when a child opens his mouth on finding it difficult to open a match box. Imagery consists of just such symbolic imitation "internalized," that is, so reduced in scale that only the subject himself is aware of it. It consists, in other words, of what behaviorists call "implicit" or "fractional" responses. When the first indications of imagery emerge about the middle of the second year, the child is beginning, significantly enough, to turn from "practice" games, in which pleasure is derived from exercising simple activities, to "symbolic games," which involve make-believe or role playing. The child understands, however, the nature of the relation between a symbol and what it signifies; he knows that the doll is not really a baby or that he is not really a cowboy.

Having learned to use actions and images as symbols and having by now acquired a sufficient vocabulary, he finds himself using words in a similar way. But words, more than images, are responsible for the progressive socialization of thought. Words and the concepts corresponding to them are taken over from the social group. They are, therefore, bound to edge the child's thoughts into line with those of other persons. He can influence and be influenced by, benefit from or suffer from, the beliefs and values of other members of his group and so arrive at an equilibrium and harmony with his social as well as his physical environment.

RELATIONS BETWEEN PERCEPTION AND THOUGHT

In recent years, Piaget has been spending a great deal of time, together with Lambercier and other collaborators, on the painstaking investigation of visual illusions and related phenomena. This area of research, a time-honored preserve of the more prosaic type of experimental psychology, may seem remote from the work for which he is best known. It has, nevertheless, given rise to some of his most original and comprehensive ideas, forming the kernel of his whole theory of intellectual functions. Whereas writers influenced by Gestalt psychology or by certain trends in American social psychology have tended to lump all "cognitive" processes together, Piaget finds the differences between perceptual and conceptual processes illuminating.

There are two obvious ways in which perception contrasts with thought. One arises from the fact, emphasized by the Gestalt school, that the perceived properties of a stimulus vary according to the pattern of which it is a component. The concepts participating in thought do not share this instability. The essential nature of a number does not change, no matter what the structure into which a mathematician fits it. A journey between two towns may seem longer or shorter in different circumstances, but the distance separating the towns according to our knowledge or our calculations does not fluctuate.

Secondly, perceptions are notoriously variable from person to person and from moment to moment. If we take 1,000 subjects, show them a line three inches long and another two inches long, and ask them to select a third line equal in length to the two combined, we shall expect a distribution of results with a high variance. We shall even expect each subject's response to vary from trial to trial, especially if the two lines are shown in different arrangements. On the other hand, if we take the same 1,000 subjects, show them the figure 2 and the figure 3, and ask them to select a third figure, equal to the sum of the two, the uniformity of the responses will be remarkable.

These differences can be traced back to two related factors which inevitably distort all perception. First, perception is always "centered" *(centré)*. Senseorgans have to be oriented in one direction at once, and the optical apparatus in particular is so constructed that the center of the visual field is seen more clearly and in more detail than other parts. As some of Piaget's psychophysical experiments show, the size of a fixated object is overestimated in comparison with the sizes of peripheral objects. The various parts of the visual field expand and shrink in turn as the gaze wanders from one point to another. The second source of error is the fact that larger portions of a figure are likely to catch the eye more often than others, with the result that the distortions that arise when they are the center of attention play a disproportionately large part in the net impression of the figure. What we have is, in fact, a biased sample of all possible fixations. From these assumptions, Piaget has derived a formula predicting the direction and extent of "primary" visual illusions, that is, those which are found in infants and lower animals as much as, if not more than, in adult human beings and which can be ascribed to the inherently "probabilistic" nature of perception.

Perception is analogous to certain processes in physics, notably in statistical mechanics, which are likewise governed by probability. These processes are irreversible, since they always lead from a less probable to a more probable state. For example, when a hot body is brought into contact with a cool body, heat is transmitted from the former to the latter and not vice versa. A spoonful of sugar diffuses evenly through a cupful of tea, but particles of sugar in a mixture do not forgather at one spot. Similarly, the distortions to which perceived figures are subject work predominantly in one direction. They cannot be relied on to balance out.

Thinking can escape from these limitations, because it is comparable with physical systems of a different type, namely those possessing *reversibility*. An example is a balance with equal weights in the two pans. The depression of one pan is followed by an upward swing which restores the original situation. Such systems are in stable equilibrium precisely because a change can be cancelled by an equal change in the opposite direction. A balance, however, is inflexible in the sense that there is one state to which it invariably reverts. Thought processes require structures which permit of more mobility without threatening disequilibrium. They must be free to flit rapidly from one idea to another and to arrange ideas in new combinations. But systems of concepts must preserve their organization, despite this mobility, if thoughts are to be consistent and if they are to produce a stable conception of the world. The "dynamic equilibrium" which Piaget attributes to thought can perhaps best be compared with that of a lift and its counterweight. The lift can move freely up and down, and the system remains intact and in equilibrium, no matter what floor is reached. This is because of its reversibility: any movement of the lift is compensated by an equal and opposite movement of the counterweight, and it can also be nullified by an equal and opposite movement of the lift.

The reversibility of logical thought is acclaimed by Piaget as the acme in which the growth of intelligence culminates. The spoken word and the performed action can never be recalled. The influence of something which has been perceived and then disappears from view lingers to infect subsequent perceptions. But a thought can be entertained and then unthought, and everything is as if it had never occurred. We are consequently able to conceive possible solutions for problems which it would be costly, dangerous, or impossible to test by action. And no matter how extravagant an idea is considered and then rejected, the coherence of conceptual systems is not threatened. The world represented by thought, unlike that presented by perception, is relatively free from "centering" *(centration)*. It does not change with the location of the thinker or the direction of his attention.

These contrary characteristics are found in a pure form only in the naive perception of the infant on the one hand and in the rigorous thought of the scientist, mathematician, or logician on the other. The principal merit of this part of Piaget's work, as far as child psychology is concerned, is the light it sheds on certain processes forming compromises between perception and thought. As we shall see when we return to the chronological sequence, the first attempts at thinking are still contaminated with the shortcomings of perception. And perception, after the first months of life, is usually accompanied by "perceptual activities" which mitigate its imperfections. There is no way of removing distortion completely from perception, but one distortion can be set against another. The focus of attention can be systematically varied, so that information from a succession of fixations is compared and collated to yield something approaching an objective impression. What appears from one point of view can be related to the perseveration or anticipation of what has been or will be seen from a different angle. "Perceptual activities" thus contribute to the "decentering" *(decentration)* of perception and the achievement of "semireversibility," so called because errors are not corrected exactly but merely tend to cancel out in the long run. Although these activities generally enhance accuracy of perception, they can on occasion lead to "secondary illusions," which are less pronounced in younger than in older children. An example is the "size-weight illusion," which makes a small object seem heavier than a larger one of equal weight.

THE PERIOD OF PRECONCEPTUAL THOUGHT
(2 TO 4 YEARS)

Before his use of symbolic processes can reach fruition, the child has to relearn on a conceptual level some of the lessons he has already mastered on the sensorimotor level. For instance, he may have learned to recognize transient stimulus patterns as shifting appearances assumed by enduring objects. But this does not immediately make him at home with the *concept* of an object. Adults are familiar with the concept of a particular *object* ("this table," "Socrates"), with the concept of a *class* ("all four-legged tables," "all men"), and with the relation of *class-membership* which joins them ("This is a four-legged table," "Socrates is a man."). These underlie our deductive reasoning, since having, for example, placed Socrates in the class of men, we can infer that Socrates has all the properties characteristic of this class.

The 3-year-old child still lacks this equipment and has to use something midway between the concept of an object and that of a class, which Piaget calls the "preconcept." On a walk through the woods, for example, he does not know whether he sees a succession of different snails or whether the same snail keeps reappearing. The distinction, in fact, means nothing to him; to him they are all "snail." Similar phenomena are, in some hazy way, identified, so that a shadow under a lamp in a room has something to do with the shadows under the trees in the garden. Contrariwise, a person in new clothes may be thought to require a new name.

Unlike adults, who reason either *de*ductively from the general to the particular or *in*ductively from the particular to the general, the child at the preconceptual stage reasons *trans*ductively from the particular to the particular. It is a form of argument by analogy: "A is like B in one respect, therefore A must be like B in other respects." Transduction may often lead to valid conclusions, that is, that if Daddy is getting hot water he must be going to shave, since he shaved after getting hot water yesterday. But it will at other times lead the child into errors of a sort said to be common in psychotics but certainly not unknown in intellectual circles.

THE PERIOD OF INTUITIVE THOUGHT
(4 TO 7 YEARS)

When the child's reasoning has overcome these deficiencies, other limitations remain, mainly because thought has not yet freed itself from perception and become "decentered." Intuitive thought can best be understood from an experiment Piaget is fond of quoting. The child sees some beads being poured out of one glass into a taller and thinner glass. It is made clear to him that all the beads that were in the first glass are now in the second; none has been added or removed. He is asked whether there are now more or fewer beads in the second glass than there were in the first. The usual answer at this stage is either that there are more (because the level has risen) or that there are fewer (because the second glass is narrower).

To explain such errors, it may be worth asking why we, as adults, are able to avoid them. The first reason is that we are told by our thought processes that the number of objects in a set, if nothing is added or subtracted, must necessarily remain the same. We usually regard our thought processes as more trustworthy than our perceptions whenever the two conflict. At a conjurer's performance, for example, we do not really believe that the rabbit has been created *ex nihilo* or the lady has been sawn in half. The child at the intuitive stage is, on the other hand, still dominated by his perceptions. His conclusions are still at the mercy of the changes resulting from successive "centerings." The second reason is that we take into account several aspects of the situation at once or in turn. We can see that the height of the column of beads has increased and that the width has decreased just enough to compensate for the increase in height. But the child focusses on one aspect and overlooks others. In his reasoning as in his perception, "centering" causes one element to be overemphasized and others to be relatively ignored. The instructiveness of such examples for adults, who might smile at the child's mistakes in the bead experiment but be liable to precisely the same sort of misjudgment in relation to, say, political or social problems, need hardly be labored.

THE PERIOD OF CONCRETE OPERATIONS
(7 TO 11 YEARS)

We come at last to the first reasoning processes that would satisfy logicians. Logical (or, as Piaget calls it, "operational") thought emerges when a certain basic stock of concepts has been acquired and when these concepts have been organized into coherent systems. The concepts which figure in operational thought are called "operations" because they are *internalized responses*. They grow out of certain overt actions in exactly the same way as images grow out of imitation. Three sorts in particular are of importance:

1. *Classes.* The concept of a "class" or operation of "classification" is an internalized version of the action of grouping together objects recognized as similar. Having learned to pick out all the yellow counters in a heap and *place* them together in one spot, the child acquired the ability to *think of* all yellow objects together and thus form the concept of the "class of all yellow objects." This means that some part of what happens in the nervous system and musculature when yellow objects are manually gathered together occurs whenever yellow objects are grouped together in thought. Once formed, classes can be joined to form more inclusive classes, so that elaborate systems of classification are built up, the one used by biologists being the clearest illustration.

2. *Relations.* Asymmetrical relations, such as "a is longer than b" or "x is the father of y," derive by internalization from *ordering* activities, for example, from placing objects in a row in order of increasing size. The best example of the complex systems which ordering relations can form is the family tree.

3. *Numbers.* The number system is the joint product of classification and ordering. The number 17, for instance, depends on the operation of grouping 17 objects together to form a class and that of placing 17 between 16 and 18 in the sequence of natural numbers.

Systems of operations are called "grouping" *(groupments)*, and their stability depends on their having five properties. Unless these properties are present, the relations between the elements of a grouping will change as attention is directed to different parts of them, as happens with perceptual patterns, and thought will not be immune from inconsistency. The five properties are as follows:

1. *Closure.* Any two operations can be combined to form a third operation (e.g. $2 + 3 = 5$; all men and all women $=$ all human adults; A is 2 miles north of B and B is 1 mile north of $C = A$ is 3 miles north of C).

2. *Reversibility.* For any operation there is an opposite operation which cancels it (e.g. $2 + 3 = 5$ but $5 - 3 = 2$; all men and all women $=$ all human adults, but all human adults except women $=$ all men; A is 2 miles north of B and B is 1 mile north of $C = A$ is 3 miles north of C, but A is 3 miles north of C and C is 1 mile south of $B = A$ is 2 miles north of B).

3. *Associativity.* When three operations are to be combined, it does not matter which two are combined first. This is equivalent to the possibility of arriving at the same point by different routes (e.g. $(2 + 3) + 4 = 2 + (3 + 4)$; all vertebrates and all invertebrates $=$ all human beings and all subhuman animals; a is the uncle of b and b is the father of $c = a$ is the brother of d and d is the grandfather of c).

4. *Identity.* There is a "null operation" formed when any operation is combined with its opposite (e.g. $2 - 2 = 0$; all men except those who are men $=$ nobody; I travel 100 miles to the north and I travel 100 miles to the south $=$ I find myself back where I started).

5. The fifth property has two versions, one for classes and relations and the other for numbers:

(a) *Tautology.* A classification or relation which is repeated is not changed. This represents the fact, recognized by logicians but not always by conversationalists, that saying something over and over again does not convey any more information than saying it once (e.g. all men and all men $=$ all men; a is longer than b and a is longer than $b = a$ is longer than b).

(b) *Iteration.* A number combined with itself produces a new number (e.g. $3 + 3 = 6$; $3 \times 3 = 9$).*

THE PERIOD OF FORMAL OPERATIONS
(11 TO 15 YEARS)

The 11-year-old can apply "operational" thinking to practical problems and concrete situations. The adolescent takes the final steps towards complete "decentering" and "reversibility" by acquiring a capacity for abstract thought. He can be guided by the *form* of an argument or a situation and ignore its *content*. He need no longer confine his attention to what is real. He can consider hypotheses which may or may not be true and work out what would follow if they were true. Not only are the hypotheticodeductive procedures of science, mathematics, and logic open to him in consequence but also the role of would-be social reformer. The adolescent's taste for theorizing and criticizing arises from his ability to see the way the world is run as only one out of many possible ways it could be run and to conceive of alternative ways that might be better.

Quite a variety of new intellectual techniques become available at the same time. The most important new equipment of all is the *calculus of propositions.* At the concrete-operations stage, he was able to use the branches of logic, known as the *algebra of classes* and the *algebra of relations.* Now he can supplement these with forms of reasoning bearing on the relations between propositions or sentences. Propositional calculus uses "second-order operations" or operations on operations. An example would be "either sentence p is true or sentence q is true." Another would be "if sentence r is true, then sentence s must be true" or, in the parlance favored by logicians, "r implies s."

A large part of Piaget's information on this period comes from Inhelder's ingenious experiments, in which children were invited to discover elementary laws of physics for themselves with the

---

*Readers with mathematical interests will notice that, insofar as these properties refer to numbers, they are equivalent to the defining characteristics of a *group.* Groupings of classes and relations, on the other hand, are almost, but not quite, *groups* and almost, but not quite, *lattices.*

help of simple apparatus. Children at the intuitive-thought stage vary conditions haphazardly and observe what happens in particular cases without deriving any general principles. At the concrete-operations stage, one factor at a time is varied, and its effects are duly noted. Not before the formal-operations stage does the child plan truly scientific investigations, varying the factors in all possible combinations and in a systematic order. The pedagogical implications of Inhelder's work are unmistakable. Children with no previous instruction appear to be capable of learning scientific laws in this way, with, presumably, more motivation and more understanding than are produced by traditional teaching methods. But, according to Piaget and Inhelder, they are not capable of the sort of thinking that makes use of such laws before the advances of the formal-operations stage have been completed.

Piaget asks why so many new ways of thinking become available about the same time, despite their superficial dissimilarity. It is, he concludes, because they all require systems of operations with similar structures, and the child is not able to organize his thinking in accordance with such structures before adolescence. He has recently been much impressed with the possibilities of modern symbolic logic and certain nonnumerical branches of mathematics as means of describing the structures common to apparently different intellectual processes. This is not one of the ways in which logic has usually been used by psychologists in the past; Piaget is interested in using "logical models" for much the same purpose as other psychologists have begun to use "mathematical models."

One new acquisition is the ability to use systems of operations in which each operation has two distinct opposites. A class (for example, "all vertebrate animals") has the sort of opposite called an *inverse* ("all invertebrate animals"). A relation (for example, "a is twice as heavy as b") has a *reciprocal* ("b is twice as heavy as a"). But "p implies q" has both an inverse ("p does not imply q") and a reciprocal ("q implies p"). Likewise, when the adolescent experiments with a balance, he discovers that the effects of one operation (for example, increasing the weight in the right-hand pan) can be cancelled either by the inverse operation (reducing the weight in the right-hand pan to its original value) or by the reciprocal operation (increasing the weight in the left-hand pan by the same amount.) Such systems with two opposites have a structure known to mathematicians as the "four group."

The four group can be shown to provide the operations necessary for dealing with *proportionality*. It is no accident that the laws governing equilibrium between weights in the pans of a balance are understood at about the same age as the laws governing the sizes of shadows. In one of Inhelder's experiments, the subject is given two vertical rings of different diameters and has to place the rings between a candle and a screen in such a way that their shadows will coincide. Adolescents discover that the problem is solved when the ratio between the distances of the two rings from the candle is the same as the ratio between their diameters. Understanding proportionality opens the way to understanding *probability*, since, when we speak of the probability of a six in a game of dice, we mean the proportion of throws that will produce sixes in the long run.

Combinatorial analysis, depending on the structures mathematicians call "lattices," is another equally fruitful new attainment. Suppose that we have two ways of dividing up animals—into "vertebrates (V) " and "invertebrates (v) " and into flying (F) " and "nonflying (f) ." A child at the concrete-operations stage is capable of allotting a particular animal to one of the four possible classes, (V.F.) , (V.f.) , (v.F.) , and (v.f.) . An adolescent at the formal-operations stage is capable of going further and considering all the sorts of animals that there are in the world or the sorts there conceivably could be. There are now sixteen possibilities: there might be no animals at all, there might be animals of all four classes, there might be (v.F.) only, there might be (V.F.), (V.f.) and (v.f.) animals but no (v.F.) , and so on. Now each of these sixteen combinations corresponds to one of the sixteen relations between two propositions recognized by modern logic. For example, "if an animal can fly, it must be a vertebrate" would correspond to (V.F.) or (V.f.) or (v.f.) , that is, the (v.F.) possibly is excluded. We can understand, therefore, why permutations and combinations and complex logical relations are mastered more or less simultaneously.

The mastery of logical relations between propositions is well illustrated in Inhelder's experiments. All attempts to study the relations between the phenomena of nature, whether in the laboratory or in practical life, must use them: "If I put the kettle on the stove and light the gas, the water will boil"; "It will rain or snow tomorrow unless the forecast was wrong or unless I read a description of today's weather and thought it was the forecast for tomorrow," and so on. The ability to think in terms of all possible combinations, which appears together with the ability to use complex statements like these, is clearly revealed when adolescents are set one of Inhelder's most instructive problems. Five vessels, all containing colorless liquids, are provided; A, B, and C, when mixed, will turn pink, D will remove the color, and E will have no effect. The properties of the liquids can be discovered only by systematically examining mixtures of every possible pair, every possible trio, etc., in turn.

AFFECTIVE DEVELOPMENT

The child's physiological constitution makes him liable, right from birth, to emotional and drive states. These pleasant and unpleasant states come to be aroused, through some sort of conditioning, by the external stimulus patterns which regularly accompany them, and, when he had learned to perceive in terms of objects, he comes to like or dislike these. Human beings are naturally more important sources of satisfaction and distress than other objects, and so their actions and they themselves will have especially strong positive and negative values attached to them.

The social influences to which the appearance of language and other symbols makes the child amenable are manifested particularly clearly in the formation of "interindividual feelings." The ability to picture how the world looks from another person's point of view includes the power to represent to oneself the feelings aroused in him by one's own actions. The child takes over other people's evaluations of his own behavior and builds up an attitude to himself derived from his estimates of their attitudes to him. The stage is then set, during the preconceptual and intuitive periods, for the first moral feelings. These take the form of a belief in absolute prohibitions and prescriptions, derived from parental orders but somehow enjoying an existence and validity in their own right. Acts are felt to deserve punishment according to how far they depart from what is permitted, without reference to intentions or other mitigating circumstances.

When he reaches the period of concrete operations, the child can form groupings of values, as of other classifications and orderings. He can systematize his values according to their relative priorities and their mutual affinities, so that his evaluations and his motives may be consistent with one another. He can subordinate his actions to future needs, thereby achieving that "decentering" from the present which we call *will*. His addiction to "games with rules," which replace "symbolic games" about this time, shows him to have arrived at a less primitive conception of moral rules. He now sees them as conventions, accepted by a social group for the benefit of all, capable of being changed by common consent, and arising out of mutual respect between equals.

By the end of the formal-operations stage, feelings become "decentered" still further, as they are released from the domination of what is known to be actually true. Motivation and evaluation now depend on *ideals,* and everything tends to be judged by how far it approximates to or falls short of the theoretical states of affairs that would fulfill these ideals. The adolescent views his own activities and plans as part of the total activity of the social group. He begins to think of himself as a fully fledged member of society, free to imitate or criticize adults. With the "decentering" which implants the individual in the community and subordinates his activities to collective goals, the formation of the personality is complete.

CONCLUSIONS

It is evident that Piaget's latest work will not silence his critics altogether. He still does not pay much attention to questions of sampling. Some projects, for example, Inhelder's on adolescents, seem to have used a large part of the school population of Geneva. The data on the sensorimotor period, on the other hand, come mainly from observation of Piaget's own three children, hardly the children of the Average Man. But Piaget might well retort, like Kinsey, that such bodies of data, however imperfect, are all we have of comparable density.

Except for some means and mean deviations in his reports of perceptual experiments, he provides few statistics. There are generally no measures of variance, which one suspects must be considerable, no tests of significance, just a categorical statement that at such and such an age children do such and such, with a few specific illustrations. He is not much affected by the growing vogue for rigorous theories, with precise statement of assumptions, derivation of predictions and operational definition of concepts.

Be that as it may, Piaget is, without any doubt, one of the outstanding figures in contemporary psychology, and his contributions will eventually have to be reckoned with much more than they are both in the management of children and in many areas which may not seem directly connected with child psychology. His ideas are closely tied to observation of behavior, and this makes them the sort of psychology which moves science forward because it is testable by reference to the facts of behavior. At the same time, it goes beyond the facts just sufficiently to open up new lines of research and to attempt the sort of synthesis which is one of the chief aims of science.

Not the least reason for paying attention to Piaget's work is the relation it bears to trends followed by English-speaking psychologists. At times, his conclusions parallel those reached independently by other investigators; at other times, they serve to correct or supplement what psychologists with other approaches have to say. Like those influenced by Gestalt psychology, Piaget affirms that perceptions and thoughts cannot be understood without reference to the wholes in which they are organized. He disagrees with them in denying that wholes are unanalyzable into component relations and in insisting that the wholes figuring in thought are radically different from those figuring in perception.

There are, throughout his writings, many reminders of psycho-analytic concepts—the "omnipotence" and "oceanic feeling" of infancy, "functional pleasure," the formation of the ego and the superego, the advance from the pleasure principle to the reality principle. But he makes many detailed criticisms of psychoanalytic theories, and the child as described by him certainly seems tranquil and studious by comparison with the passion-torn "polymorphous pervert" that emerges from Freudian writings.

But Piaget's closest affinities are undoubtedly with the neo-behaviorists. He does not hold with early attempts to explain everything by "conditioned reflexes" or "association." But many of his observations and many aspects of his theory harmonize extremely well with conceptions of learning based on studies of what has come to be called "instrumental" or "operant conditioning." The sequence of more and more complex behavior patterns which he depicts as outgrowths of simple reflexes and habits parallels Hull's list of progressively more intricate "adaptive behavior mechanisms," found in animals.[20] And Piaget's view of images and thought operations as "internalized" overt responses approximates very closely the view prevalent among stimulus-response learning theorists.

One body of work which has grown up in Great Britain and the U.S.A. and which Piaget is eagerly endeavoring to bring into relation with his own findings is that centering on cybernetics, information theory, and game theory.[17] But it is to be hoped that other common ground between his psychology and others with different starting points will be explored. It is certainly high time that the national self-sufficiencies which disfigure psychology in contradistinction to other branches of science were left behind.

REFERENCES

1. Mays, W. "How We Form Concepts," *Science News, 35*(1955) , 11-23.

2. Mays, W. "Professor Piaget's Epistemologie Genetique." Proceedings of the Second International Congress of Philosophical Science (1954) , pp. 94-99.

3. Piaget, J. *The Origin of Intelligence in the Child.* London: Routledge and Kegan Paul, Ltd., 1953.

4. Piaget, J. *The Child's Construction of Reality.* London: Routledge and Kegan Paul, Ltd., 1955.
5. Piaget, J. *Play Dreams and Imitation in Childhood.* London, William Heinemann, Limited, 1951.
6. Piaget, J. *The Psychology of Intelligence.* London, Routledge and Kegan Paul, Ltd., 1950.
7. Piaget, J. *Logic and Psychology.* Manchester, England, University Press, 1953.
8. Piaget, J. Genetic psychology and epistemology. *Diogenes, 1:*49-63, 1952.
9. Inhelder, B., Les attitudes expérimentales de l'enfant et de l'adolescent *Bull. Psychol., 7:*272-282, 1954.
10. Inhelder, B., and Piaget, J. *De la logique de l'enfant à la logique de l'adolescent.* Paris, Presses Universitaries de France, 1955.
11. Piaget, J. *Traité de logique.* Paris, Colin, 1949.
12. Piaget, J. *Introduction à l'épistémologie génétique.* Tome I: *La pensée mathématique,* Tome II: *La pensée physique,* Tome III: *La pensée biologique, La pensée psychologique, La pensée sociologique.* Paris, Presses Universitaries de France, 1950.
13. Piaget, J. Les relations entre l'intelligence et l'affectivité dans le développement de l'enfant. *Bull. Psychol., 7:* passim, 1953-54.
14. Piaget, J. Le développement de la perception de l'enfant à l'adulte. *Bull. Psychol., 8:* passim, 1954-55.
15. Piaget, J. La période des opérations formelles et le passages de la logique de l'enfant à celle de l'adolescent. *Bull. Psychol., 7:*247-253- 1954.
16. Piaget, J. Le probléme neurologique de l'intériorisation des actions en opérations réversibles. *Arch. Psychol., 32:*241-258, 1949.
17. Piaget, J. Structures opérationelles et cybernétique. *Année Psychol., 53:* 379-388, 1953.
18. ————, "Les lignes générales de l'épistémologie génétique," *Proc. II. Int. Cong. Phil. Sci., 1*(1954) , 26-45.
19. Pratt, K. C. The neonate. In C. Murchison (Ed.) , *A Handbook of Child Psychology,* Worcester, Mass., Clark University Press, 1933.
20. Hull, C. L.: *A Behavior System.* New Haven, Yale University Press, 1952, pp. 347-350.

MAN HAS the need and the ability to modify his behavior to meet the challenges of his milieu. Learning, which implies adaptability, is defined as the process by which behavior is changed as a result of experience, practice, or training. Humans probably learn more in their first few years of life than in any other period of the life cycle. However, there are different kinds of learning with marked variation in levels of complexity. Dr. Marion Blank, in the following article, traces the progression of learning from basic conditioned responses to abstract reasoning. She also uses the Piagetian model to explain part of the learning process. Note that Dr. Blank's analysis of learning is inferred on the basis of what has been observed in the child's behavior. Until we have physiological or biochemical evidence which can inform us when learning has occurred, observation is the only way we can study learning.

Chapter 14

How Children Learn

MARION BLANK

Many of us, I'm sure, have looked at a newborn infant and reflected on how dependent it is. Perhaps we've even marveled at the wonderful transformation between birth and childhood, not only in physical appearance, but in mental aptitude: It's been said that the human being learns more in the first five or six years of life than in all its remaining years.

How does it some about? How is it that the tiny infant with a near vacuous mind develops into the rational thinking, idea-making adult?

In physics, many phenomena can be studied either classically or quantum mechanically; in mathematics, calculus problems may often be solved with the existing variables or parametrically. In a like vein, learning can be studied from different vantage points. Since the seat of learning resides in the brain, a compelling approach is to concentrate on the cerebral process, noting how it evolves. Brain research of itself is not restricted to a single mode since the researcher has the option of including or excluding the effects of information received from the body's sensory apparatus. The researcher also has the option of exploring via chemically, physically, and biologically oriented endeavors.

Another, completely opposite approach to learning is to ignore the fact that there is a brain at all, noting only that for a given set of inputs there will be a corresponding set of outputs.

Yet another approach is to study the outward developments in learning capability and somehow infer what is happening to the learning center. Let's review these approaches.

From *Science and Technology*, No. 85, 62-70, 1969. Reprinted by permission from Science and Technology. Copyright 1969 by International Communications, Inc.

SEEKING A SUITABLE TACK

Since World War II, and more particularly within the last decade, quite a bit of progress has been made in probing the brain for clues as to how it functions. But when you get down to brass tacks, researchers know noting about how functions of, or changes within, the brain relate to learning.

For example, we now know about some of the brain's gross manifestations: the brain is bilateral but its halves are not equal; certain portions of the brain are reserved for certain functions. Nevertheless, we don't know how the parts work.

We also know that chemistry plays a vital part in the functioning of the brain: certain chemicals induce impulses between neurons; other stop them. We don't however, know how these chemicals are generated.

Again, we suspect that biologically active DNA is involved with the learning process inasmuch as the form of DNA changes with "information" received by the cell; also intelligence varies proportionately with the brain's DNA content. What we don't know is the DNA code and precisely how it relates to assimilating and retrieving information.

In fact, all of the literature dealing with the learning process of the brain is studded with such qualifiers and modifiers as "perhaps," "may," and "probably." It's clear then, that if we're to study learning, there's not much that we can relate about the brain's involvement.

Which brings us to the second approach—that is, that the brain is a black box between input and output. Advocates of this approach are commonly called behavioral psychologists. Although behaviorists come in a variety of shadings of belief, as a group they generally tend to evade qualitative differences between man and lower animals. (There are behaviorists, however, who have recently shown not only differences between man and animal, but qualitative differences between progressively higher orders of animals: so, the rat thinks differently from the pigeon.)

Behaviorists are exponents of controlled laboratory studies, inferring concept formation from overt subject behavior to a given problem. Many of their theories on children are merely extrapolations from work on animals.

The behaviorists' assault on learning may have deficiencies, but it also has considerable merit. After all, if certain inputs produce predictable responses, it may not be too important what the black box is doing. In line with this, much of their work is being put to practical use in modern teaching programs. Among these practical applications is programmed learning, where the student takes tests, corrects the tests, and then refers to specific exercises in areas of weakness. The teaching-machine programs are also founded on models formulated by behaviorists. But, while behaviorists can in some measure control and predict learning, they can't—nor do they want to—explain how what they are doing works. If we're to study evolution of the learning process, we find the behaviorists' approach is also insufficient to our purpose.

And this brings us to the methodology of inferring the growth of intelligence by observing the outward symptoms of internal development. This, like the black box method, is a psychological approach—adherents of this philosophy being called cognitivists. Unlike the behaviorists, the cognitivists are concerned only with man and his introspective thought processes. As such, they are not interested in restricting behavior to controlled, limited laboratory conditions, relying instead on observing children in actual or simulated conditions of the "normal" environment. In other words, the cognitivists become freely involved with thought processes—something that can't be measured and so is dismissed by the behaviorists.

The cognitivists' approach is not without its weaknesses. For the greater part, they have simply observed; there has been little, if any, attempt to influence and manipulate and then study effects. Another fault with their approach is that there is no precise theory for the way experience is assimilated.

Nevertheless, I believe that the cognitivist approach represents the only real attempt to understand the mind of the developing child.

There are several reasons for justifying this approach. The learning pattern sequences in a child, whether genius or moron,

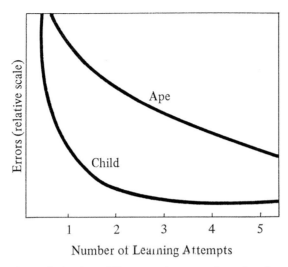

Figure 14-1. One of the big differences between learning in a child and an animal is the child's quicker "uptake." Graph shows typical learning curves of ape and man.

are invariant—though of course, quite differently paced. The implication here is that there is a specific mental (internal) progression which depends on information perceived and assimilated. Then too, there has been a gradual trend, implicit perhaps in behaviorist theory, toward recognizing the virtues of at least some of the cognitivists' theories. The behaviorists' biggest concession has been (again implicitly) to concede the value of language which is an abstract (mentalistic) tool; and as we shall see toward the end of this paper, language plays a vital role in learning development.

THE BABY AT BIRTH

All the learning schools also agree on just how intelligent the newborn is. So before becoming steeped in the modes and intricacies of learning I'd like to review briefly what attributes the baby is born with and how deficiencies in these qualities can affect the learning process. After all, the baby must make a start on some foundation.

As helpless as the newborn baby may appear, it does possess some very important built-in attributes. Contrary to earlier beliefs, a recently born child can see, at least to the extent that it discriminates patterns. It can also distinguish sounds, and interestingly, is particularly "tuned" to human voice frequencies. The infant can also taste, suck, is temperature-sensitive, has full body movement (motor) facility, including fair control of eye movements, and even has a primitive sense of direction. And those early smiles may not just be gas-induced grimaces. In sum, the normal baby is prepared to receive stimuli and give primitive responses.

We know that all of the child's senses are important to natural development. However, their importance is relative, and varies with the period of early life. At birth, visual perception is probably the principal sense for gathering information. Without it, motor coordination is seriously impaired. Hearing, on the other hand, is not important to learning in the first six months.

Tactual (touch) and motor deprivation can also affect proper hand-eye coordination. While a cat is far removed from the human, experiments with cats have provided a clear understanding about the importance of touch and motion. Consider this experiment: A cat was supported in a harness, with its paws unable to touch the floor, and moved about the cage from birth. It was given every opportunity to familiarize itself with every portion of the cage. Yet when finally released from its harness, it showed complete disorientation, hitting obstacles and the limits of its confines. This was in complete contrast to the behavior of a "control" which was allowed the opportunity to traverse its confines at will.

Even though a child has full sensory faculties, learning prowess of all children in the first few months is attenuated by a limited ability to assimilate information from their senses. Information, so to speak, is "band-limited." Up to the three-month mark, unless the stimulus is particularly startling, the child will undergo little discernible intellectual progress. Even when there is some effect, only style of response, and not the level of intelligent response, will be affected by the particularly strong stimulus.

By three months this band-limited deficiency is outgrown, and the normal child makes rapid progress.

LEARNING THE HARD WAY

As I've already stated, the schism between the two main camps of learning—the behaviorists and the cognitivists—is being

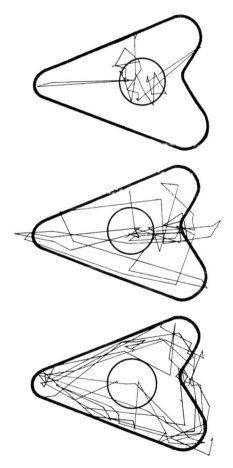

Figure 14-2. The very young child can't study an isolated object and then pick it out from a group. Tests show why. The 2-year-old centers its eyes on the object (top); the 4-year-old's eyes make excursions outwards, picking up enough information (middle) to select the object from a group. The 6-year-old actually bottom traces the periphery with its eyes.

bridged. In addition to some common understanding on the use-fulness of language, they also agree that children build to and through several learning modes. That is, they agree to a point.

Although the newborn requires several months for its senses to fully mature it is receptive at a very early stage to learning at a primitive level. Within the first five weeks therefore, the child —like Pavlov's dog—develops *conditioned responses* or rote be-havior. Consequently, if it is presented with a white, familiarly shaped bottle, it will anticipate placement of the nipple into its mouth.

The next small increment in the learning evolution comes in the form of *external trial and error*. It is such small increment over rote learning that some psychologists prefer to dispense with the distinction. The modifier "external" denotes the traditional form of trial and error in which the child keeps physically trying different approaches until one of them works.

Rote and/or external trial-and-error learning seem to be the precursor of what we as psychologists term *vicarious learning* or learning while watching others. Rote learning develops the child's "memory bank." And, while the child's sensory receptors at three months are equal to the task, vicarious learning requires a sus-tained concentration from the child. So, it's not until the child is about 8 months old that it enters this learning stage.

Don't confuse vicarious learning with simple emulation. It's more: The child reviews in its mind the chain of events physically caused by others. If the child is then required to duplicate the solution to the problem it does so without having to repeat all the trials of its exemplar.

The progression from rote to vicarious learning prepares the way for the other half of the trial-and-error process—*internal trial-and-error*. Here, the child confronted with a problem will, through imagery, project the consequences of tentative actions as they relate to the problem's solution. An elementary example of this learning mode is the child who's given variously sized and shaped blocks to fit through corresponding holes in a box. The older child does not attempt overt trials but predetermines the correspondences between the holes and the objects by mentally transferring them.

A BIG STEP UP

The next learning stage, what we call *insight learning,* represents more of a jump than mere transition. The solutions adopted through trial-and-error learning may admit a certain amount of transfer; thereby, analogous problems may be solved. Trial-and-error learning may even aid resolution of reversed situations: For example, after learning that selection of the white ball from among white and black balls is the solution sought, the subject can quickly adapt to picking the black ball, should the problem be reversed. But, trial-and-error learning weakens in its ability to solve other problems as other problems become more remote in concept. Insight learning enables such gaps to be spanned.

There is a classic experiment with a chimpanzee—a particularly bright one—which is often cited to illustrate insight learning. The ape was put in a cage. Placed outside of the cage beyond its reach, even beyond its reach when using one of two tapered hollow sticks put in the cage with it, were some bananas. After trying its luck at reaching its prize with one stick, the chimp seemed to reflect on the other stick, and then pieced the sticks together end to end. It was as if the proverbial light flashed in its head and the chimpanzee was able to take a step, not previously learned, but logically deduced.

SEPARATING THE CHILD FROM CHIMP

The next step up from insight learning and one which separates the human from other animals is called *cross-modal transfer,* or the ability to interpret a registered image obtained by one mode of sensory perception into another. Cross-modal transfer is important because it enables the child to depict an object by totally different sensory perceptions. The chimpanzee is incapable of such transfer. Cross-modal transfer is a gradual development and not automatically a two-way street: the young child may be able to select by touch an object it has seen but the opposite won't hold true—it won't be able to select by sight an object discriminated by touch.

Cross-modal transfer either lays the ground work, or is in fact a peripheral form of the next important learning step.

It's best called, for our purposes—because it describes the information-transfer process that occurs—by one of its pseudonyms: mediational. Like vicarious learning, *mediational learning* is apparently a transitional learning step. The difference between the two is this: Insight learning involves a singular extrapolation (as in the case of the chimpanzee and the sticks) ; mediational learning involves the generalization of a particular so that, from the generalization, other particular problems, seemingly totally dissimilar to the original, can be solved. Numbers, therefore, are a mediational tool. In mediational learning a long sound and a long stick will be associated.

A better way of illustrating mediational learning is to show the result of its not being available: the chimpanzee who learns to choose the louder sound from the softer sound at a specific pitch will fail completely to distinguish loud from soft if the sound's pitch is altered.

Mediational learning is not a one-level process. It evolves subtly through to higher and higher levels of abstraction, reaching its peak with the young adult. To illustrate, it's only necessary to give the same simple test to the child, the preadolescent, and the young adult.

If the picture has both colors and numbers to be matched, the child will match colors since it's at a perceptual level; the preadolescent, who is at the functional level, will match numbers; the young adult will not only group both color and number but will understand that all of the elements are related by virtue of their being in the picture. There will also be a conscious understanding of the intent of the test stemming from the adult's tendency to group into broader categories.

The last mode of learning involves learning through verbal communication. Communication learning evolves only after mediational learning is established since it involves transfer of abstract quantities. In some ways, communication learning is analogous to vicarious learning. In the former, the mind uses symbolic imagery; in the latter the mind can only function with tangible illustrations.

GROWING UP

To this point in this article I've begged some vital questions about the learning process. For example, the infant is completely egocentric. How does it evolve to a child that partakes of its surroundings? At what ages do various transitions occur?

Possibly no one has done more to develop a common theoretical groundwork of conceptual development for most cognitivists than Jean Piaget, the Swiss psychologist. For Piaget, learning is a slow, purposeful, continuous, internal, adaptive process, where progression can only be made after the proper foundation has been assimilated and properly organized into the previous learning structure. For example, Piaget would say that our ability to read a map harkens back to all our experiences from birth related to the task. The newborn can sense up and down motion; it then learns to evaluate its own position within its confines, then learns about the permanence of objects, proceeds to accept mental substitutes for the real objects and eventually begins to reason abstractly so that words and lines can be transposed, in thought, back into the world as it actually is.

Strangely, while learning grows imperceptibly as an internal process, its outward manifestations appear to take place as discrete, well-separated stages. A child may, therefore, suddenly seem to blossom from disjunctive word use to use of full sentence structure.

According to Piaget there are two "great eras" in the development of intelligence: (1) sensorimotor (sensing and motor skills) up to the age of about two years and (2) conceptual intelligence extending onward through various stages to maturity.

(I must add that the "two-year" time period just mentioned, as well as other specific time periods I'll be mentioning later, are normative times intended only for reference. Some children naturally advance more rapidly or more slowly.)

The child in its first month appears little more than a bundle of reflexes. Give it a nipple and it sucks; if it's cold, it cries. In the one- to three-month period, behavior patterns develop and the infant begins to coordinate them. So it is that the eye guides the hand and the infant feebly accommodates to its surrounding via chance gropings. For the one- to three-month old, all the world is not a stage; in fact, for the infant, the world is just the child itself. It has no understanding of space, time, or causality. It follows an object with its eyes only so long as it is in view, beyond which the object ceases to exist. There is no causal connection in what it hears, sees, or feels; it's therefore not uncommon for an infant to bite its foot and then cry in pain.

PIAGET'S SCHEME OF LEARNING

Up to this point in the life of an infant there is neither means nor end, let alone a means to an end. These deficiencies begin to be overcome from the fourth through the sixth month. A good illustration of the advancement in this period is the child's relation to a rattle. The 4- to 6-month old stumbles across its rattle, grabs it, and notes the noise that accompanies movement. Still there's no cause and effect here; rather it's some magical phenomenon in which noise accompanies movement, or some vague comprehension of sequential events in terms of the child's own actions. (The child, for example, may shake its hand if the rattle is sounded by someone else.) This example is not only indicative of causality development, but also shows that information from different senses is now being integrated.

At this four- to six-month stage the child will also have an incipient sense of object permanence: Now its eyes continue past the point that an object disappears from view. The child also tends to fix its eyes around the point of the object's departure, as if to anticipate a reappearance. Nevertheless, the object still exists only in the "eye's mind."

In the next sensorimotor stage, the child accomplishes, according to Piaget, its first truly intelligent acts, which on the surface appear to involve elementary reasoning. For example, the child who has previously learned to grasp and lift might push an object under its pillow and then lift its pillow to see the object reappear.

It will even seek the object if placed under the pillow by someone else. What we may adduce as an introspective act has, however, been shown to be strictly behavioral—not embracing any real understanding of events.

But this example does show that the child of four to six months has developed a true cause-and-effect concept and that the child now conceives of objects as having permanence in their own right. Moreover, there is at this point an understanding of sequential events. In sum, its memory is expanding, allowing it to fix on and relate different events.

With the succeeding sensorimotor stage, the child comes to recognize that there's more to its existence than its egocentric self. Position of objects in the space about the child are now recognized as independent of the child's perception or action: Thus the sofa will always appear in the same place each time the child is in the living room. It masters cause and effect and even alters the means to see what happens to the ends. For example, after noting that a ball, when released, drops, the child may throw the ball downwards and note that it still lands on the floor.

The child also now realizes that it can induce causal action by others: it may therefore assume a position indicating that it wants to be picked up. Meanwhile the concept of time has evolved to a point where the child can retain memory of events—at least for short periods—in their proper order.

In the final sensorimotor stage the child becomes fully integrated with its surroundings and events. Space, time, and causality

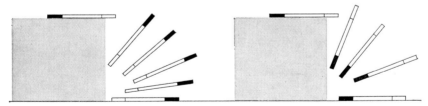

Figure 14-3. The young child can't visualize abstract concepts and hence can't envision the effects of forces, so he fails to predict the way in which the marked stick will fall when flipped from its platform. Invariably the child gives the way the stick will fall as depicted by the drawing on the right—not the left.

can be modeled via internal trial and error. So, given a cause—a ball rolls under the table—the child will draw from its memory bank and note "internally" that the ball will continue to the other side. The child unhesitatingly goes to the far side of the table to pick up the ball. The child's time-storage capability has also grown to a point where it can retain orders of events for days at a time.

TOWARD INTELLIGENT THOUGHT

By its second birthday the "average" child has embarked into the area of human intelligence—that of conceptual development. This is the ability to reason in abstract terms.

Piaget breaks down conceptual learning into four sub-eras which he labels: (1) preconceptual, 2-4 years; (2) intuitive thought, 4-7 years; (3) concrete operations, 7-11 years; and (4) formal thought, 11 years and beyond.

The way to this new era has been prepaved with a developed memory which allows the child to conjure absent objects, and a learned ability to associate itself with other objects. The child continues to learn by assimilating what is new and then working (adapting) the new concepts into its learning base structure. Interestingly, the same patterns of progression that marked the child's sensorimotor era repeat at the conceptual level. Thus, early conceptual thought is self-centered and not very abstract—in the same way that early sensorimotor thought was egocentric and not inducive to ideas about object permanence.

In the preconceptual stage, the transitory stage between sensorimotor and conceptual development, the child reasons from particular event to particular event. The child cannot yet handle cause-and-effect relationships which are not concretely obvious. A child promised to be given a large bicycle a few years hence, "when you are bigger," may reply "No, a little one . . . I'm not big." The child has found it impossible to project from the concrete present.

Another symptom of this stage is the child's inability to focus on more than one feature at a time. A good example of this behavior is how the child views an object: it will do little more than focus on its center. No wonder, then, that it fails subsequently to discriminate it from other objects.

THE TRANSITIVE YEAR

Before it can advance to true conceptual thought, the 4- to 7-year-old child transits through a sub-era of intuitive thinking. Now that the child is 4, concrete or tangible operations are translated into internal images. Nevertheless, the child's thinking is still centered on individual characteristics or aspects, and while the child may reason from one set of conditions to another, it can't reverse the process. If you've a child in this age group, you can convince yourself of this particular limitation: Fill two equal glasses with water to the same height. After your child agrees that the water in each is equal, pour the water from one of the glasses into a wider glass while the child watches. Don't be surprised when your boy or girl now says that the wider glass has less water. This simple experiment gives us an insight and some examples of a child's conceptual scheme of things: (1) Although it has long since learned that individual articles or objects are "conserved" —to use the common scientific word—it cannot conceive of the conservation of a collection of objects; (2) it can only concentrate on one dimension at a time (there's less water in the wider glass because the water level is shallower) ; (3) it cannot mentally reverse the pouring process and thereby compare the two original objects.

From experiments such as the one just described, Piaget concludes that the child can consider simultaneously in thought only that which has simultaneity in action. Yet simultaneity in action, even when observed, will not equate with simultaneity in time. The "transitive" child will contest that two objects traveling different distances but at correspondingly compensatory velocities could arrive at their destinations simultaneously.

I mentioned earlier how outward changes in the child's reasoning prowess may appear to progress in surges. The 8-year-old child might be puzzled that you should even question him about the water in the glasses. For the 8-year-old it's obvious that water in both glasses is equal no matter what container they're poured into. The level difference between 7-11 years (concrete operations period) and the earlier period is seemingly large because the child has been able to bring together concepts which previously could only be considered individually. The child is therefore able to look at a problem from many points of view. Transposition of events may now be seen as producing the same end, analogous to the way the year-old child at the sensorimotor level discovers that the thrown ball or the dropped ball both ultimately reach the floor.

Yet, the concrete-operations group still gropes rather than copes with problems not founded on tangible entities or with problems that apparently refute previous impressions. The 7- to 8-year-old child given a glob of clay will say matter is conserved even if the clay is deformed, but weight and volume are thought to change. At age 9-10, weight is seen as conserved. It's not until 11-12 that volume conservation is recognized.

The formal operations level represents as much a departure from the concrete operations level as the conceptual era from the sensorimotor. Formal operations implies logical thought divorced from reality. Formal thought is said to be, in a sense, the application of operations to operations in ever-developing complexity.

LIKE LOVE AND MARRIAGE

While much of what I've set down so far explains the way in which the learning process expands, no mention has been made of the factors which promote learning.

No one would disagree that practice makes perfect. But, from what experiences does the child draw its building blocks of knowledge? The very young baby literally discovers itself. It finds its foot, bites it, and eventually gains an understanding that the foot is part of itself. Later on the child draws from its environment. If the environment is rich, the child's concepts grow rapidly. The deprived child, whether it lacks sense deprivation or external stimulus, will learn more slowly. I believe that of all the factors contributing to advanced learning, that is, learning beyond the sensorimotor stage, language is crucial. Because it is an abstract tool, it aids the synthesis of abstract ideas. When I talk about language I'm not referring to use of singular words. Sentences are meaningless to the year-old child, although it responds to individual words or cues from which language (or communication) evolves.

Verbal language, in its extent and complexity, is unique to human beings. The "language" of bees for example is much more restricted, confined to set routines which convey only a limited amount of information.

A recent finding of considerable interest, dispelling previous notions, is that nonhuman primates may be capable of "speaking" at the level of the 2- to 3-year-old child. Some psychologists recently decided to train primates by using gestures or sign language such as the deaf use. Preliminary work indicates that they have trained a chimpanzee to both produce and interpret over seventy signs such as give, please, drink, etc. There are even some indications that the animal may be able to use two or three signs together so as to form simple sentences.

Interestingly, new findings indicate that an ape's failure to speak may not only be due to vocal deficiences but also, as mentioned earlier, to limited cross-modal skills, as well as auditory-vocal modal deficiencies. Thus, labeling a visual object with an oral word requires cross-modal associations, including sound and sight transfers.

By contrast, a human being's language can be extended and revised. Language plays such a role in our lives (in reading, discussion, inner contemplation, to name just a few elements) that its importance seems obvious. Yet because it plays such an extensive role, it has been difficult to gain a precise understanding of the role of language for human beings.

One of the key issues in this area concerns the way language develops in the young child. Just as the child must learn to deal with perceptions, the child must learn to organize language. This task is amazingly complex, for language involves not simply the learning of words, but also the rules by which these words are organized. The particular labels (words) are not too difficult; but the ability to structure these discrete labels into sentences takes effort. Yet the child gains great proficiency in this aspect of his native language by 4 or 5 years of age.

How he achieves this is still not fully determined, but the child's errors have told us a great deal.

Among the common errors we hear in children are such things as "runned," "broked," "feets," "some milks," and so on. These are not terms that the child has heard in its environment. Rather, they are word forms which it has invented to follow the general format or rules which are applicable to other words in its environment. This is not to say that the child is consciously aware of these rules, but merely that it is, in some ways, implicitly using these rules both to organize its own language (expressive language) and to interpret heard (receptive) language.

Of course, the child does not begin with such rules. He starts at about 18 months with single words to describe clearly discernible people, objects, effects, and actions ("daddy," "car," "bottle," "bye-by," "pretty"). These words soon become joined into two- or three-word constructions, such as "nice mommy," "no bye-bye," etc. Of interest here is that the child seems to abstract the meaning of several of these words and then uses these words almost as pivots around which he forms several sentences. Thus, "pretty" can be paired with "pretty car," "pretty dolly," and "no" with "no bye-bye," "no milk," "no daddy," etc.

By about $2\frac{1}{2}$ to 3 years, the child rapidly passes the two- or three-word sentence phase and begins to produce long and complex sentences involving ideas such as negation, interrogation, time (as expressed, for example, in the verb tenses of past and future) and conditionality. These developments are receiving increasing attention with the result that our understanding of the structure of the child's language is becoming much clearer.

Unfortunately, the role that language plays in the child's learning is less clear than its development. Language certainly seems to be important to a child's conceptional development— evinced by the acceleration in a child's "learning curve" once language is effectively employed. For example, once an object is labeled, the ability to recognize that object on a subsequent occasion is greatly enhanced. Also language helps the child form categories, since with a single label he can group other disparate objects; for instance, animals, houses, and tools. Whether it's the power that language gives the child, or the child's inability to see things in a larger perspective, the child gets so bound up with words that he does not see them as arbitrary labels that simply aid communication. It believes they are magically linked with the identity of objects. Thus it is common for a child of 3 or 4 when told that a table is not a table, but a mesa, to argue adamantly this contention as if a basic tenet of truth had been violated.

There is, however, no one-to-one correspondence between language and thinking. Many nonverbal types of thought are available to the child, such as imagery. The child may often possess the necessary labels, but he may not fully understand their meaning. This becomes evident when the tasks involve not simple labeling or description but rather more complex problem solving such as causal reasoning. In these cases, the child will use causal words, but the underlying reasoning is limited. Thus, a child may say that "the leaves of the tree blow because they want to." It commonly attributes its own motives to inanimate objects.

The use of language describes the child's view of the world and this is basically one that is limited to his perceptions and experiences. While this is true to some degree even at the adult level, adults can grasp many ideas which have no place in their own past (e.g. "imagine for a moment that you are riding in a rocket to the moon") and we can even grasp abstract ideas which have no direct representation in reality (e.g. gravity, infinity). This type of abstraction is highly, if not totally, dependent on a symbolic system (whether a natural language such as speech or an artificial language such as mathematics). Thus language ultimately comes to play an essential role in the achievement of the highest levels of abstraction. And language deficiencies lead to serious limitation in higher cognitive skills—evidenced by children born deaf or who grow up deprived of language.

The deaf may make excellent adaptations to life in terms of social relationships, occupations, and general situations. Their verbal language development, however, is usually restricted and this seems related to the serious limitations that they frequently have in academic achievement, particularly in areas requiring reading and mathematics. Of course, many develop complex gestural language. However, the structure of sign language has not been worked out and we do not fully know the relative merits and disadvantages of this type of communication.

It's also known that the memory capability of the language-deprived child often consists of sporadic, random details. (And, by memory I'm not referring to remembering names and numbers but an ability to organize and store information into meaningful concepts.) For the language-deprived child, language and abstract thought may quite literally have no meaning and the child is tied to tangibles and events of the moment.

Twelve Is Not An Age To Be Scoffed At

Looking back at all that's been stated, it appears that by early adolescence (e.g. about 12 years) most of the highest level thinking processes are already established. Most of the changes in intellectual growth have already taken place; there will still be changes in amount of information to be learned, acquisition of increasing skill, greater understanding of people and situations— namely, all the things we like to think of as maturity. But in essence, there will be little change in the intellectual processes available to the individual. These twelve years may seem short for all the amount of growth that has taken place it is far longer than the time required for adulthood in any other primate. For the average child, the time is well spent in gathering the necessary skills and concepts which it needs to cope with an increasingly complex world.

T HE ORIENTING reflex, also called the orienting reaction or response, is an investigating response to a novel stimulus. Both animals and humans demonstrate the behavioral and physiological changes associated with the response: cessation of ongoing activities, increased sensitivity of sense organs, electroencephalographic changes, heart-rate changes, etc. The OR is incompletely developed in the newborn; however, components such as respiration changes and cessation of ongoing activity are present. These changes are an indication that the newborn is sensitive to stimuli, and this is the forerunner of attention. In the following article, Dr. W. E. Jeffrey discusses the OR and attention in relation to salient cues in the environment and their eventual role in problem-solving behavior. He suggests that when the organism ceases to respond, physiologically and/or behaviorally (habituation of an OR), to a particular cue an OR may occur to another, previously less salient, cue. In this way attention may be directed to several cues of a stimulus complex. Dr. Jeffrey then analyzes how this may lead to the formation of schema and to problem solving.

Chapter 15

The Orienting Reflex and Attention in Cognitive Development

W. E. JEFFREY

T HE READILY demonstrable differences between the selective learning and problem-solving abilities of children and adults have been the subject of much interest over the past decade. The approaches taken to study these differences have varied, and the range of problems studied is immense. As a consequence, there has been considerable conflict over how these differences in ability might be explained. Although it is not necessary to examine in detail the various arguments, a brief example of the type of problem with which we are concerned may serve to illustrate some of the issues as well as to indicate the approach to be taken in this paper.

If an adult subject is told that a coin can be found under one of two boxes, one black and the other white, he should make no more than one error when given a series of choices. He is likely to make two or three errors on the average, however, and the reasons for them are not trivial. An adult, or even a college sophomore, being more or less rational and curious, may wonder, after a correct choice, whether there might be coins under both boxes. He may also have misunderstood the instructions, or he might even be so unsophisticated as to think that no one, not even a psychologist, is likely to pay him for solving such as simple problem. Or he may develop a complex strategy that dictates a pattern

From *Psychological Review, 75:*323-334, 1968. Copyright 1968 by the American Psychological Association. Reproduced by permission.

Part of the contents of this paper was presented at a meeting of the Society for Research in Child Development, New York, 1967.

The author is grateful to Kent Dallet, Tom Trabasso, Leslie Cohen, Kathryn Nelson, and Tamar Zelniker for their numerous helpful comments on various versions of this paper.

of shifts, in which case we might say that he is attending to cues other than (or in addition to) those of interest to the experimenter. The behavior of a 4- or 5-year-old child might be essentially the same as that described for the adult. However, if boxes of two properly selected shades of gray were substituted, although the performance of the adult would remain essentially the same, a child might not learn to solve the problem, at least within any reasonable time period.[23]

How do we account for this latter difference? It is probably not the result of inadequate sensory ability, inasmuch as human infants have been shown by Fantz,[15] Bower[3] and Doris and Cooper,[13] among others, to be capable of making very fine discriminations on a variety of dimensions. To propose that the child has difficulty because he does not or cannot label the cues is hardly tenable inasmuch as nonspeaking deaf children have been shown to be able to make similar discriminations.[31] Labels, of course, have been demonstrated to be helpful to the hearing child of $4\frac{1}{2}$ to 5 years of age,[7] but as Tighe and Tighe[10] have recently pointed out, whether labels make stimuli more distinctive through the addition of cues, or whether they function to call attention to the distinctive aspects of the stimuli is unclear. The correlation of language usage with differences in problem-solving behavior in the human being, along with our intuitive conception of language as a mediator of many adult behaviors, may lead us to attribute to language a more crucial role in the performance of problem solving than it deserves, particularly in children.

It is proposed that a more satisfactory explanation of human problem-solving behavior will be found with a more adequate understanding of the development of attention.[28] The research of Zeaman and House[43] was the first in recent years to be specifically concerned with attending responses in selective learning in children and there is now a growing body of support for the influence of attentional factors. For example, Murphy and Miller[30] and Jeffrey and Cohen[23] have demonstrated that young children have difficulty utilizing cues that are not integrated with responses in such a way as to ensure receptor orientation. It has also been demonstrated that in the absence of obvious cues, children show a strong tendency to respond on the basis of positional cues.[24] Although the naive adult may also respond to position cues following the first reinforcement, he shifts quickly among cues after a nonreinforced response. Such flexibility in adult problem-solving behavior probably reflects hierarchies of both cue-utilization strategies and cue salience. It is proposed here that the latter, a hierarchy of cue salience, is more fundamental, and that in order to understand the development of problem-solving ability it is necessary to learn more about the variables controlling the development of cue salience.

Only a little is known about those stimulus attributes that are most salient for the infant, and much less about how the hierarchy of cue salience changes with maturation and experience. It is with changes in cue salience that attention theories must specifically be concerned. Inasmuch as it is the reaction of the child and not the stimulus that changes, it would appear to be useful, if not necessary, to postulate a mediating mechanism to account for this change. Although verbal mediators have had special appeal because of their potential observability, the lack of directly observable evidence for perceptual mediators, be they called images, concepts, cognitive structures, or schemata, is hardly sufficient reason to deny either their existence or their potential functional relationship with overt behaviors. Furthermore, the search for verbal mediators may be far less parsimonious than the postulation of nonverbal ones. Good scientific method does not require that we see or hear the mechanism, but only that we specify the conditions under which it develops or occurs.

THE ORIENTING REFLEX AND THE DEVELOPMENT OF SCHEMATA

The behavior to which the word attention is commonly applied has an alerting or arousal component, a receptor orienting component, and an internal cue selection component. In order to reduce confusion, the arousal component of attention will be identified with the "orienting reflex" (OR), which Sokolov[37] defines as a pattern of physiological responses that occurs to novel stimulation. Attention will continue to include both the overt receptor orienting activities and the more central cue selection events unless one or the other is specifically excluded.

A variety of explanations has been proposed for the stimulus-seeking behavior of organisms,[2,16,19] but the precise mechanism is unimportant to the present development. It is sufficient if one accepts the following propositions: first, that cues can be ordered in terms of their salience, for example, the magnitude of the OR, or the likelihood that a cue will elicit an OR; second, that when a cue elicits an OR, attentional responses follow that tend to optimize the perception of that cue; and third, that as the OR habituates, attention also declines. If the OR is a reinforcing state of affairs, as Maltzman and Raskin[29] suggest, then one could propose that attending behaviors are shaped by the occurrence of the OR. Although this notion is convenient for those who are accustomed to analyzing behavior in such terms, the simple fact of habituation of attention is sufficient to account for an orderly progression of attending responses.

The Serial Habituation Hypothesis

In the newborn infant the OR habituates slowly if at all, and therefore the attention of the infant is dominated by those few stimuli that are most salient. With continued exposure, with development, or with both, the OR does habituate to those cues that were initially most salient, finally allowing less salient cues to elicit appropriate attending responses. As the OR habituates to each cue the infant may either attend to a new cue or to a previously attended cue whose OR has recovered from habituation. With repeated experience the OR will habituate more and more quickly to each separate cue of a stimulus complex and under certain conditions an orderly set of rapidly shifting attending responses should occur. For example, if a cube is suspended above an infant's crib it is quite likely that his first response will be to the color or brightness of its surface. As the OR to this aspect of the cube habituates, other parts of the cube may now elicit ORs. The infant may attend to a corner, then an edge, and at some point, with movement of his head, he will attend to changes in the relationship of the cube to its back-

ground. With repeated exposure and increasingly rapid habituation of the OR to each of these cues, this set of attending responses
will become a continuous, integrated, response sequence. Furthermore, this response sequence will at some point become clearly
discontinuous with those response sequences that precede and
follow the sequence elicited by the cube. That is, attention to the
most salient cue of the cube will not consistently follow attention
to any other specific cue, nor will the cue to which the infant turns
after attending to the cube always be the same. It is both the integration of a pattern of attending responses and the discontinuity
of that pattern with other attending responses or patterns that
define an object percept or what we shall call more generally a
schema.

The abstractness of a schema will be a function of the consistency with which less abstract cues are present. For example,
as long as the infant is exposed to cubes of the same color, color
will be part of the cube schema. However, as he experiences cubes
of differing sizes in various orientations an even more abstract
schema will result because responses to nondefining aspects of the
cube would be expected to drop out of the sequence if the cues
for these responses are not present consistently.

It is noteworthy that this analysis predicts that an object
schema can develop only in a relatively variable context; yet, if
the environment was so variable as to include a large number of
high-salience cues, attention to the less salient features of the cube
or any other object would be unlikely. Thus, under such circumstances object schemata would quite probably be delayed in their
development because of continued attention to high-salience cues.

A common cue of all objects is the movement parallax that
accompanies movement of the head. Inasmuch as movement has
high salience for infants,[17] it is not unlikely that the observation
of movement parallax during the formation of object schemata
would provide a schema for depth.[3,41] This schema, although an
early and probably important part of object schemata, may also
exist independently of these schemata inasmuch as it represents
a sequence of responses that can and does occur independently of
the various object schemata incidental to it. Although there

should be little doubt that appropriate effector responses such as reaching and touching would markedly enhance the infant's perception of depth, the serial habituation hypothesis provides a plausible basis for asserting that the infant already has developed a concept or schema of depth long before he has had more specific motor experience with his environment.

One may question the degree to which schema formation must depend on eye movements. Photographic techniques used by Salapatek and Kessen[36] as well as measures of observing responses and the OR as used by Kagan and Lewis[25] would provide relevant information for the serial habituation hypothesis, but it should be emphasized that although the potential verifiability of this hypothesis when applied to object schemata is appealing, one would expect well-developed object schemata to involve relatively little of the scanning involved in the initial formation of a schema. It is more likely that object schemata will take the final form of attending responses to one or two of the more salient cues plus a cluster of associations to these cues. The original and longer sequence of attending responses will reoccur only when some discrepancy in stimulus input signals that something has changed. For example, although a point with three edges radiating from it is likely to be a cube, this is not necessarily the case and given that one line appeared disproportionate, additional responses might occur to verify the existence of other critical features of "cubeness," such as eight corners and six surfaces.

Of course overt scanning responses are almost entirely missing in auditory or color perception; nevertheless one can conceptualize central attentional events that might follow similar serial habituation patterns, and therefore the scanning model as applied to visual stimuli may be propaedeutic. Careful attention to the kinds of conditions that are most likely to facilitate perceptual development within these dimensions may help determine a more appropriate form for the model to take.

Color is a highly salient cue for the infant and it is probable that in his early perceptual experience as he habituates to one color he may, given proper circumstances, transfer his attention to a second color nearby. As he now habituates to the second color he may move on to a third or return to the first. The order of scanning, although possibly constant when the different colors are part of a single object, will not be constant in the infant's more general experience and as habituation occurs more rapidly to each color, color will be more likely to be isolated from the object of which it is a part. It must also be noted, however, that color is an inherent part of some objects and that color and brightness differences frequently provide the boundaries around and within objects. Therefore, in spite of the salience of color it is not very clear that color schemata necessarily develop early, and indeed, the somewhat ambiguous role of color in the environment of the child, as well as the gross differences that may exist in the early color experience of children, may account for the somewhat capricious role of color as a cue in discrimination learning tasks of 3-, 4-, and 5-year-old children and the difficulty some children have in learning to name colors.

Although auditory perception also lacks observable receptor adjustments that might provide a basis for a schema, timbre presents a stimulus complex not unlike an object as far as the serial habituation hypothesis is concerned. When one is stimulated by a complex tone one must habituate to the dominant frequency and then come to attend to the overtones. If this is true, discrimination between tones differing in timbre, given that the child has had appropriate experiences with such tones, should be easier for the child than discriminating between tones differing in pitch. The former would be comparable to discriminating objects, whereas the latter is more similar to discriminating colors. It is of interest that although infants can be shown to be capable of differentiating tonal frequency by an habituation technique[4] they also can be shown to have considerable difficulty with pitch discriminations at older ages.[21] Is this because children are seldom presented with the opportunities to form an appropriate pitch schema under normal circumstances? Or is it because responses to frequency are not made critical for most children until much later, when the ORs are so thoroughly habituated to those cues that subsequent training is very difficult, particularly when the cues are impossible to point at?

It is probably not fruitful to engage in additional speculation about details of the basic mechanism without more empirical data. It is important to point out, however, that even at this level of development the model not only suggests how a stimulus-rich environment could have positive effects on an infant's cognitive development but in addition indicates that certain types of environmental stimulation might be more facilitative of cognitive development than others.

IMPLICATIONS FOR DEVELOPMENT AND TRAINING

An environment of too little or too much complexity will exercise little control over attention. The inverted U-shaped function that so typically describes the relationship between preference and stimulus complexity[2] may be derived by assuming that cue salience is an inverse function of complexity and that OR habituation is an inverse negatively accelerated function of stimulus complexity, or, more specifically, of number of cues in the stimulus complex that will independently elicit an OR. As can be seen in Figure 15-1, the difference between these two curves is an inverted U. In other words, when there are very few cues in a stimulus complex, habituation to the complex will occur quickly, but with greater numbers of cues, successive habituation of the OR to each cue in the complex will take sufficient time to permit the OR to the most salient cue in the complex to recover, thus causing the attending sequence to be repeated. Although more complex stimuli would also permit iterative attending responses, these stimuli would not compete because of their lesser salience. Of course when experience with the more salient stimuli results in either a schema or such rapid attending that there is no longer sufficient time for the OR to any specific cues to recover, the subject's attention will shift to a more complex stimulus.[8] Specific predictions could be made from information about habituation times for the stimulus components and the relative saliences of various component stimuli.

The serial habituation model also has obvious practical implications for the manipulation of attention in certain problem-solving situations. For example, if as the OR habituates to the

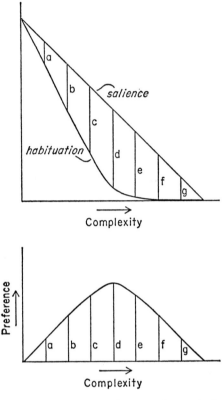

Figure 15-1. The differences between the two theoretical curves in the top figure produce the inverted U curve below.

more salient cue the infant shifts his attention to previous less salient cues, then in order to obtain a response to a cue of low salience one may add to that cue a cue that is minimally sufficient to assure an attending response. Given a generally impoverished environment this more salient cue should elicit appropriate attention, but as the OR and attention wane to the more salient cue, the subject should now attend to the next most salient cue. If only the critical cue remains, and if reinforcement occurs while the subject attends to this cue, then the low salience cue becomes a CS for those internal events consequent to the delivery of a reinforcer, or at least a discriminative stimulus for the delivery of a reinforcer. Such a mechanism is particularly appropriate for explaining how a so-called color-dominant child may come to use form as a cue in a simple selective learning experiment.[9]

If the above procedure fails, a variety of other steps may be taken to increase the salience of the relevant stimuli. For example, the salience of form can be increased by using stereometric rather than planometric drawing,[14] or even better, by using true stereometric forms.[38] Also, if the subject handles the forms, he may do better than if he only sees them. Although handling would appear to ensure differential sensory input, it is not likely that the differential proprioceptive stimulation is as important as the fact that the subject attends to a stimulus visually in order to make the appropriate motor adjustment in picking it up.[32]

Cues of spatial orientation have been shown to be particularly difficult for young children to utilize,[11,35] yet Jeffrey[21,22] has shown that if the child's responses increase the likelihood of attention to the directional cues, young subjects can respond appropriately. In a more recent experiment in our laboratory, marbles rolling down an oblique line were used to elicit attention to the directional cue. Learning proceeded readily whether or not the reinforced motor response was related to the direction the ball was rolling. Furthermore, there was considerable transfer to a more difficult labeling task involving the oblique lines as discriminanda. These results lend some support to the assertion that once a subject's attention to a critical cue is elicited, the salience of that cue will be increased if reinforcement follows.

LANGUAGE DEVELOPMENT AS THE ENCODING OF SCHEMATA

Having indicated a lesser role for language in problem solving than is frequently presumed, it is important to indicate just what role early verbal behavior does play. The term "behavior" is used advisedly because it may be helpful to reserve the word "language" for something more comprehensive than labeling or the use of one- and two-word sentences. Even with the latter, the level of communication between child and adult is hardly better than that between dog and master, and it is with this level of verbal behavior that verbal mediation research has in theory been concerned; when words have no meaning beyond what they acquire in the experiment it is hard to imagine how they can facilitate problem solving however distinctive they may be. Brown[5] proposed some time ago that the application of labels to schemata is "the original word game." We would go on to suggest that nouns are acquired first because object schemata develop first. Names for abserct concepts will be learned only after the more abstract schemata are formed. Contrary to acquired distinctiveness notions,[7] the serial habituation hypothesis suggests that abstract schemata cannot develop until schemata for irrelevant aspects of an instance of an abstract schema are formed and their ORs habituated. Thus, the richer the early cognitive experience, the earlier the child should be able to form abstract concepts, but also, it is quite likely that if labels are to be useful, it would be in their application to irrelevant component schemata. The application of words to the component schemata would aid in the delineation of the boundary conditions for more abstract schemata and thus facilitate the formation of the more abstract schema. This would be particularly true in instructional situations and also at older age levels when one actively talks to oneself while solving a problem. Indeed, very abstract concepts may absolutely require an active rather than passive process of cue elimination. Nevertheless, it is emphasized that the "insight" that appears to be contiguous with the application of a label is not inherent in the label but in the final formation of an integrated set of attending responses to which the label, as well as any other responses, can be reliably attached. These attending responses may be guided by language but are typically not inherent in the label.

HIGHER LEVEL COGNITIVE ABILITIES

Certain selective learning problems allow more than one basis for problem solution, and therefore may reveal different levels of cognitive development. The transposition problem, for example, permits a test of a child's ability to respond to a relational as opposed to an absolute quality of stimuli. Kuenne[26] and Alberts and Ehrenfreund[1] have each found that ability to respond to relationships correlates positively with age and the ability to verbalize the relationships. On the other hand, Rudel[34] has demonstrated that under certain circumstances transposition may be obtained in young children without implicating a verbal mediator, and Lawrence and deRivera[27] have obtained relational responding in rats. Within the framework presented in this paper it should be obvious that transposition behavior requires a schema of comparison, a schema that involves attention to some aspect of the size difference. This schema is relatively late to develop because it does not occur to as precise a set of cues as do most object schemata, nor does its stimulus have the salience of movement or disappearance which aid in the early formation of the depth schema. Indeed, it depends on sufficiently fast visual oscillation between object schemata that the size difference itself becomes a schema. Given the comparison of size difference schema, looking from smaller to larger becomes a *larger than* schema, and from larger to smaller becomes a *smaller than* schema. After the occurrence of either schema has been reinforced a few times it is not unreasonable to propose that it could become a more likely response than the object schema first elicited, and thus would occur regardless of the absolute size of the test stimuli.

Obviously children will bring varying amounts of experience with such a schema to the learning task. And the older they are, the more likely they are to have such a schema or to develop it quickly, for the simple reason that the schemata that are elicited by the more salient cues are so well differentiated that they will not continue to be utilized as relevant problem-solving cues in the absence of consistent reinforcement. It should be noted that reversal shifts would be similarly facilitated by such a comparison schema. That is, as the child scans two cues, a comparison schema will be developed and he will then be reinforced for responding to one or the other ends of the comparison schema. A subsequent reversal of reinforcement contingencies would not necessarily cause a shift in schema but only a shift within the schema, for example, if not larger, then smaller, or if not black, then white. The development of such a schema would clearly be facilitated when there is some associative strength between two cues, such as black and white, but then that may only be a way of measuring the extent to which a schema already exists.[39]

The middle-size problem is only a slight modification of the transposition problem described above, and a study by Reese[33] provides some support for the explanation presented. A group of children who were told that reinforcement was "not under the big or little one" did slightly but not significantly better than a group who were told it was the "medium one," and both groups did better than a nonlabeling control group. Presumably instructions invoking the responses "not large, not small" would be much more likely to develop the appropriate schema than those asking the child to label the "medium one." This would be true, however, only for those children who were in the process of developing the middle-size concept as opposed to those who have a fairly well-developed concept and would thus do equally well with either instruction. The much smaller variance for the "not big, not little" group would tend to support this latter assertion. That is, "the medium one" response was effective for only part of the group whereas the other instruction was more broadly effective. It is additionally interesting to note that the middle-size problem requires the same schema as the seriation problem in that each involves attention to two differences or relationships, as opposed to only one in the simpler transposition test. Thus, ability to seriate might provide a reasonable test for ability to solve the middle-size problem and vice versa.

Any application of the serial habituation model to problem-solving behavior involving relatively abstract concepts or schemata must be concerned not only with attention and approach responses but also with inhibition of approach tendencies.[12] Responding to abstract properties of the environment typically requires that one inhibit response to the most salient cue, and this cannot always be achieved by habituation. However, given a sizeable repertoire of schemata that exist in some hierarchy, some understanding of the game situation, expectation of 100% reinforcement, and a learning set that has long ago excluded position and alternation, then the child will come to actively dissociate overt responses from the more salient schema and utilize less salient schemata or even form new schemata. Thus, inhibition not only goes hand-in-hand with learning set formation, but also becomes a part of being able to understand and accept the experimenter's rules for the game. Children show decided improvement in these attributes over the years from 4 to 6. Cross and Vaughter[10] have even found that whereas 3-year-old children, like monkeys, show better Trial 2 performance following nonreinforcement rather than reinforcement on Trial 1, 4-year-old children show the opposite effect. This finding may not reflect the specific effects of reinforcement and nonreinforcement on learning, but the inability of the 3-year-old child to inhibit his response to the alternate (negative) cue on Trial 2 following a response to the positive cue on Trial 1. The problem-solving facility that becomes evident at 6 and 7, which White[42] has discussed in terms of the temporal stacking of responses, and which has been indicated here as involving hierarchies of cue salience, may actually be evidence of the first important use of language in the control of behavior. The child of 6 is becoming able to understand instructions to a greater extent; he begins to ask questions about instructions, he begins to instruct himself, question his own actions, and so forth. It is at this time that we begin to speak of education rather than training. It is then that the child arrives at the stage Piaget identifies as "concrete operations," and where Bruner sees the child shifting from the use of "iconic" to "symbolic" representation. Possibly it is then that we might also speak of hierarchies of strategies as well as hierarchies of cue salience.

Interestingly enough, only Piaget (cf. Hunt[18]) has developed any very specific measures of cognitive development of children in the age range from 6 to 12. Those tests that have proved most popular have involved the development of concepts of conservation. A simple example is a common test for the conservation of mass. After a child has acknowledged that a pair of Plasticine balls are identical "in amount," one ball is deformed, preferably by rolling it into an oblong shape. The child is then asked if the two are still the same in amount. Before a certain age, he is likely to report that they are not. The evidence from a variety of replications indicates that nonconservation is not entirely attributable to lack of understanding of the synonyms and circumlocutions used to communicate the notion of amount. There is some evidence[6] that part of the problem lies in the inability of the child to respond to changes in two dimensions. According to the notions expressed in this paper it is reasonable that he would respond only to the most salient cue and whether he responds to length, height, or breadth, the judgment of sameness would be rejected. Furthermore, it is not easy to arrange a training situation that encourages the compensatory judgments that are required. And it should be noted that to attempt to make the judgment on the basis of form it actually inappropriate. Indeed, the correct judgment can be made entirely independently of any specific demonstration. The only important or relevant information is whether anything has been added or taken away. If there is a point to the typical demonstration it can only be to obfuscate the solution. To an adult, the demonstration would be considered at the least ridiculous, and at the best the beginning of a trick.

For the young child the experimental situation is a far more potent determiner of his choice behavior than any verbal instructions he may be given. Thus, he is more likely to attend to apparent differences than to the more abstract dimension alluded to in the instructions. Therefore, in conservation experiments, as in the other testing situations that have been discussed, we must be careful to recognize that although such tests may provide perfectly adequate measures of problem-solving maturity, they measure considerably more than pure cognitive development, and any theory that is to prove adequate must take this fact into account.

SUMMARY AND CONCLUSIONS

Three main points were made. First and foremost it was asserted that the control of selective learning and problem-solving behavior is primarily a matter of controlling attention. Second, a mechanism for the control of attention and the formation of schemata was postulated. It was proposed that a consequence of the orienting reflex (OR) is attending responses, which optimize the reception of stimuli. With repeated stimulation the OR habituates to a specific cue and the subject will shift his attention. As the result of such serial habituation, chains of attending responses (schemata) will be formed to cue sets in which the habituation of the OR to two or more cues takes place in constant order.

The third point was that if stimuli producing rapidly habituating ORs are paired with stimuli that produce ORs that habituate more slowly, the habituation of the OR to the first stimulus will be retarded. This notion is primarily a restatement of the secondary reinforcement paradigm with emphasis on the OR rather than the reinforcing stimulus. It was noted that a virtue of what is typically called reinforcement is the strength of the OR associated with it.

Finally, these notions were applied to a variety of problem-solving situations with particular emphasis on what must occur before the child may perform adequately. Whether or not the more precise formulation of the development of schemata proves correct, we would emphasize the importance of a better understanding of the variables controlling attention for a better understanding of cognitive development in general.

REFERENCES

1. Alberts, E. and Ehrenfreund, D. Transposition in children as a function of age. *J. Exp. Psychol., 41*:30-38, 1951.
2. Berlyne, D. E. Conflict, Arousal, and Curiosity. New York, McGraw-Hill, 1960.
3. Bower, T. G. R. The visual world of infants. *Scientific Amer., December,* 1966, pp. 80-92.
4. Bridger, W. H. Sensory habituation and discrimination in the human neonate. *Amer. J. Psychiat. 117*:991-996, 1961.
5. Brown, R. *Words and Things.* Glencoe, Illinois, The Free Press, 1958.
6. Bruner, J.; Oliver, R., and Greenfield, P. *Studies in Cognitive Development.* New York, Wiley, 1966.
7. Cantor, J. H. Transfer of stimulus pretraining to motor paired-associate and discrimination learning tasks. In L. P. Lipsitt and C. C. Spiker (Eds.), *Advances in Child Development and Behavior.* Vol. 2. New York, Academic Press, 1965.
8. Cohen, L. B. Observing Responses, Visual Preferences and Habituation to Visual Stimuli in Infants. Unpublished doctoral dissertation. University of California, Los Angeles, 1966.
9. Corah, N. L. The influence of some stimulus characteristics on color and form perception in nursery-school children. *Child Develop. 37*:205-212, 1966.

10. Cross, H. A., and Vaughter, R. M. The Moss-Harlow effect in preschool children as a function of age. *J. Exp. Child Psychol. 4:*280-285, 1966.

11. Davidson, H. P. A study of the confusing letters d, b, p, and q. *J. Genetic Psychol. 47:*458-468, 1935.

12. Diamond, S.; Balvin, R. S., and Diamond, F. R. *Inhibition and Choice.* New York, Harper & Row, 1963.

13. Doris, J., and Cooper, L. Brightness discrimination in infancy. *J. Exp. Child Psychol. 3:*31-39, 1966.

14. Dornbush, R. L., and Winnick, W. A. The relative effectiveness of stereo-metric and pattern stimuli in discrimination learning in children. *Psychonomic Sci., 5:*301-302, 1966.

15. Fantz, R. L. The origin of form perception. *Scientific Amer.* May, 1961, pp. 1-8.

16. Fowler, H. *Curiosity and Exploratory Behavior.* New York, Macmillan, 1965.

17. Haith, M. M. Response of the human newborn to movement. *J. Exp. Child Psychol. 3:*225-234, 1966.

18. Hunt, J. McV. *Intelligence and Experience.* New York, Ronald Press, 1961.

19. Hunt, J. McV. Motivation inherent in information processing and action. In O. J. Harvey (Ed.), *Motivation and Social Interaction.* New York, Ronald Press, 1963.

20. Jeffrey, W. E. Variables in early discrimination learning: I. Motor responses in the training of a left-right discrimination. *Child Develop. 29:*269-275, 1958.

21. Jeffrey, W. E. Variables in early discrimination learning: II. Mode of response and stimulus difference in the discrimination of tonal frequencies. *Child Develop. 29:*531-538, 1958.

22. Jeffrey, W. E. Discrimination of oblique lines by children. *J. Comp. Physiol. Psychol. 62:*154-156, 1966.

23. Jeffrey, W. E., and Cohen, L. B. Effect of spatial separation of stimulus, response, and reinforcement on selective learning in children. *J. Exp. Psychol. 67:*577-580, 1964.

24. Jeffrey, W. E., and Cohen, L. B. Response tendencies of children in a two-choice situation. *J. Exp. Child Psychol. 2:*248-254, 1965.

25. Kagan, J., and Lewis, M. Studies of attention in the human infant. *Merrill-Palmer Quart. 11:*95-127, 1965.

26. Kuenne, M. R. Experimental investigation of the relation of language to transposition behavior in young children. *J. Exp. Psychol., 36:*271-290, 1946.

27. Lawrence, D. H., and deRivera, J. Evidence for relational transposition. *J. Comp. Physiol. Psychol., 47:*465-471, 1954.

28. Mackintosh, N. J. Selective attention in animal discrimination learning. *Psychol. Bull., 64:*124-150, 1965.

29. Maltzman, I., and Raskin, D. C. Effects of individual differences in the orienting reflex on conditioning and complex processes. *J. Exp. Res. Personal. 1:*1-16, 1965.

30. Murphy, J. V., and Miller, R. E. The effect of the spatial relationship between the cue, reward, and response in simple discrimination learning. *J. Exp. Psychol. 56:*26-31, 1958.

31. Oléron, P. Le développement des réponses à la relation identité-dissemblance. Ses rapports avec le langage. *Psychologie Française, 7:*4-16, 1962.

32. Otteson, M. I.; Sheridan, C. L., and Meyer, D. R. Effects of stimulus-response isolation on primate pattern discrimination learning. *J. Comp. Physiol. Psychol. 55:*935-938, 1962.

33. Reese, H. W. Verbal effects in the intermediate-size transposition problem. *J. Exp. Child Psychol. 3:*123-130, 1966.

34. Rudel, R. G. Transposition to size in children. *J. Comp. Physiol. Psychol. 51:*386-390, 1958.

35. Rudel, R. G., and Teuber, H. L. Discrimination of direction of line in children. *J. Comp. Physiol. Psychol. 56:*892-898, 1963.

36. Salapatek, P., and Kessen, W. Visual scanning of triangles by the human newborn. *J. Exp. Child Psychol., 3:*155-167, 1966.

37. Sokolov, E. N. *Perception and the Conditioned Reflex.* New York, Macmillan, 1963.

38. Stevenson, H. W., and McBee, G. The learning of object and pattern discriminations by children. *J. Comp. Physiol. Psychol. 51:*752-754, 1958.

39. Strommen, E. A. Associations As Dimensions in Discrimination Shift. Unpublished doctoral dissertation, University of California, Los Angeles, 1967.

40. Tighe, L. S., and Tighe, T. J. Discrimination learning: Two views in historical perspective. *Psychol. Bull. 66:*353-370, 1966.

41. Walk, R. D., and Gibson, E. A comparative and analytical study of visual depth perception. *Psychol. Monogr. 75*(15, Whole No. 519), 1961.

42. White, S. Evidence for a hierarchical arrangement of learning processes. in L. P. Lipsitt and C. C. Spiker (Eds.), *Advances in Child Development and Behavior.* Vol. 2. New York, Academic Press, 1965.

43. Zeaman, D., and House, B. J. The role of attention in retardate discrimination learning. In N. R. Ellis (Ed.), *Handbook of Mental Deficiency* New York, McGraw-Hill, 1963.

PART VI
THE DEVELOPMENT OF LANGUAGE

CONSIDER Anthony Hope's statement, "Unless one is a genius, it is best to aim at being intelligible." What animal could have communicated the concepts, humor, and admonition contained within? None save man, for no subhuman society has a language. Dance, sounds, and gestures constitute the means of animal communication. The study of language, once again stimulating great interest, will hopefully provide clues as to why man is capable of language, how it develops, what the role of experience is in language acquisition, and how language affects thinking. The following article demonstrates that we are accummulating understanding. Dr. Eric Lenneberg proposes that we look at the development of language in children in the context of developmental biology. He emphasizes maturation of certain structures for language acquisition, but also suggests how experiences interact with and modify the organism's responses. Language is thought to be a reflection of human thought processes and not its cause or effect.

Chapter 16

On Explaining Language

ERIC H. LENNEBERG

MANY explanations have been offered for many aspects of language; there is little agreement, however, on how to explain various problems or even on what there is to be explained. Of course, explanations differ with the personal inclinations and interests of the investigator. My interests are in man as a biological species, and I believe that the study of language is relevant to these interests because language has the following six character-istics: (1) It is a form of behavior present in all cultures of the world. (2) In all cultures its onset is age correlated. (3) There is only one acquisition strategy—it is the same for all babies every-where in the world. (4) It is based intrinsically upon the same formal operating characteristics whatever its outward form.[1] (5) Throughout man's recorded history these operating characteristics have been constant. (6) It is a form of behavior that may be im-paired specifically by circumscribed brain lesions which may leave other mental and motor skills relatively unaffected.

Any form of human behavior that has all of these six character-istics may likewise be assumed to have a rather specific biological foundation. This, of course, does not mean that language cannot be studied from different points of view; it can, for example, be investigated for its cultural or social variations, its capacity to reflect individual differences, or its applications. The purpose of this article, however, is to discuss the aspects of language to which biological concepts are applied most appropriately.* Further, my

From *Science, 164*:635-643, (9 May), 1969. Copyright 1969 by the American Association for the Advancement of Science. Reproduced by permission of the author and publisher.

I thank H. Levin and M. Seligman for comments and criticisms.

*For complete treatment, see Lenneberg.[2]

concern is with the development of language in children—not with its origin in the species.

PREDICTABILITY OF LANGUAGE DEVELOPMENT

A little boy starts washing his hands before dinner no sooner than when his parents decide that training in cleanliness should begin. However, children begin to speak no sooner and no later than when they reach a given stage of physical maturation (Table 16-I). There are individual variations in development, particularly with respect to age correlation. It is interesting that language development correlates better with motor development than it does with chronological age. If we take these two variables (motor and language development) and make ordinal scales out of the stages shown in Table 16-I and then use them for a correlation matrix, the result is a remarkably small degree of scatter. Since

TABLE 16-I

Correlation of motor and language development*

Age (years)	Motor Milestones	Language Milestones
0.5	Sits using hands for support; unilateral reaching	Cooing sounds change to babbling by introduction of consonantal sounds
1	Stands; walks when held by one hand	Syllabic reduplication; signs of understanding some words; applies some sounds regularly to signify persons or objects, that is, the first words
1.5	Prehension and release fully developed; gait propulsive; creeps downstairs backward	Repertoire of 3 to 50 words not joined in phrases; trains of sounds and intonation patterns resembling discourse; good progress in understanding
2	Runs (with falls); walks stairs with one foot forward only	More than 50 words; two-word phrases most common; more interest in verbal communication; no more babbling
2.5	Jumps with both feet; stands on one foot for 1 second; builds tower of six cubes	Every day new words; utterances of three and more words; seems to understand almost everything said to him; still many grammatical deviations
3	Tiptoes 3 yards (2.7 meters); walks stairs with alternating feet; jumps 0.9 meter	Vocabulary of some 1000 words; about 80 percent intelligibility; grammar of utterances close approximation to colloquial adult; syntactic mistakes fewer in variety, systematic, predictable
4.5	Jumps over rope; hops on one foot; walks on line	Language well established; grammatical anomalies restricted either to unusual constructions or to the more literate aspects of discourse

*Ref. 3, pp. 128-130.

motor development is one of the most important indices of maturation, it is not unreasonable to propose that language development, too, is related to physical growth and development. This
impression is further corroborated by examination of retarded
children. Here the age correlation is very poor, whereas the correlation between motor and language development continues to be
high.[3] Nevertheless, there is evidence that the statistical relation
between motor and language development is not due to any immediate, causal relation; peripheral motor disabilities can occur
that do not delay language acquisition.

Just as it is possible to correlate the variable language development with the variables chronological age or motor development,
it is possible to relate it to the physical indications of brain maturation, such as the gross weight of the brain, neurodensity in the
cerebral cortex, or the changing weight proportions of given substances in either gray or white matter. On almost all counts,
language begins when such maturational indices have attained at
least 65 percent of their mature values. (Inversely, language acquisition becomes more difficult when the physical maturation of
the brain is complete.) These correlations do not prove causal
connections, although they suggest some interesting questions for
further research.

EFFECT OF CERTAIN VARIATIONS IN
SOCIAL ENVIRONMENT

In most of the studies on this topic the language development
of children in orphanages or socially deprived households has been
compared with that of children in so-called normal, middle-class
environments. Statistically significant differences are usually reported, which is sometimes taken as a demonstration that language
development is contingent on specific language training. That
certain aspects of the environment are absolutely essential for language development is undeniable, but it is important to, distinguish between what the children actually do, and what they can
do.

There is nothing particularly surprising or revealing in the
demonstration that language deficits occur in children who hear

no language, very little language, or only the discourse of unedu-
cated persons. But what interests us is the underlying capacity for
language. This is not a spurious question; for instance, some
children have the capacity for language but do not use it, either
because of peripheral handicaps such as congenital deafness or
because of psychiatric disturbances such as childhood schizophrenia; other children may not speak because they do not have
a sufficient capacity for language, on account of certain severely
retarding diseases.

There is a simple technique for ascertaining the degree of
development of the capacity for speech and language. Instead of
assessing it by means of an inventory of the vocabulary, the grammatical complexity of the utterances, the clarity of pronunciation,
and the like, and computing a score derived from several subtests
of this kind, it is preferable to describe the children's ability in
terms of a few broad and general developmental stages, such as
those shown in Table 16-1. Tests which are essentially inventories
of vocabulary and syntactic constructions are likely to reflect
simply the deficiencies of the environment; they obscure the
child's potentialities and capabilities.

I have used the schema described to compare the speech development of children in many different societies, some of them
much more primitive than our own. In none of these studies could
I find evidence of variation in developmental rate, despite the
enormous differences in social environment.

I have also had an opportunity to study the effect of a dramatically different speech environment upon the development of
vocalizations during the first three months of life.[4] It is very common in our culture for congenitally deaf individuals to marry one
another, creating households in which all vocal sounds are de-
cidedly different from those normally heard and in which the
sounds of babies cannot be attended to directly. Six deaf mothers
and ten hearing mothers were asked, during their last month of
pregnancy, to participate in our study. The babies were visited
at home when they were no more than 10 days old and were seen
biweekly thereafter for at least three months. Each visit consisted
of three hours of observation and twenty-four hours of mechanical

recording of all sounds made and heard by the baby. Data were analyzed quantitatively and qualitatively. Figure 16-1 shows that although the environment was quantitatively quite different in the experimental and the control groups, the frequency distributions of various baby noises did not differ significantly; as seen in Figure 16-2, the developmental histories of cooing noises are also

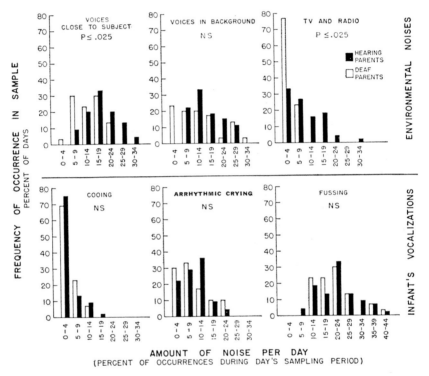

Figure 16-1. Frequency distributions of various noises. The basic counting unit is individual recording days.

remarkably alike in the two groups. Figure 16-3 demonstrates that the babies of deaf parents tend to fuss an equal amount, even though the hearing parents are much more likely to come to the child when it fusses. Thus the earlier development of human sounds appears to be relatively independent of the amount, nature, or timing of the sounds made by parents.

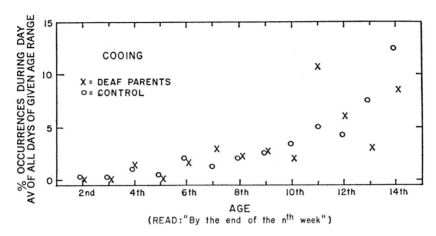

Figure 16-2. Each baby's day was divided into 6-minute periods; the presence or absence of cooing was noted for each period; this yielded a percentage for each baby's day; days of all babies were ordered by their ages, and the average was taken for all days of identical age. Nonaveraged data were published in Lenneberg et al.[4]

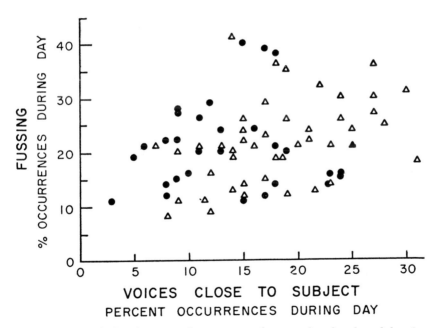

Figure 16-3. Relation between the amount of parents' noises heard by the baby and the amount of fussing noises made by the baby. Each symbol is one baby's day; (solid circles) deaf parents; (triangles) hearing parents.

I have observed this type of child-rearing through later stages as well. The hearing children of deaf parents eventually learn two languages and sound systems: those of their deaf parents and those of the rest of the community. In some instances, communication between children and parents is predominantly by gestures. In no case have I found any adverse effects upon the language development of standard English in these children. Although the mothers made sounds different from the children's, and although the children's vocalizations had no significant effect upon attaining what they wanted during early infancy, language in these children invariably began at the usual time and went through the same stages as is normally encountered.

Also of interest may be the following observations on fairly retarded children growing up in state institutions that are badly understaffed. During the day the children play in large, bare rooms, attended by only one person, often an older retardate who herself lacks a perfect command of language. The children's only entertainment is provided by a large television set, playing all day at full strength. Although most of these retarded children have only primitive beginnings of language, there are always some among them who manage, even under these extremely deprived circumstances, to pick up an amazing degree of language skill. Apparently they learn language partly through the television programs, whose level is often quite adequate for them!

From these instances we see that language capacity follows its own natural history. The child can avail himself of this capacity if the environment provides a minimum of stimulation and opportunity. His engagement in language activity can be limited by his environmental circumstances, but the underlying capacity is not easily arrested. Impoverished environments are not conducive to good language development, but good language development is not contingent on specific training measures;[5] a wide variety of rather haphazard factors seems to be sufficient.

EFFECT OF VARIATIONS IN GENETIC BACKGROUND

Man is an unsatisfactory subject for the study of genetic influences; we cannot do breeding experiments on him and can use only statistical controls. Practically any evidence adduced is susceptible to a variety of interpretations. Nevertheless, there are indications that inheritance is at least partially responsible for deviations in verbal skills, as in the familial occurrence of a deficit termed congenital language disability.[2] Studies, with complete pedigrees, have been published on the occurrence and distribution of stuttering, of hyperfluencies, of voice qualities, and of many other traits, which constitute supporting though not conclusive evidence that inheritance plays a role in language acquisition. In addition to such family studies, much research has been carried out on twins. Particularly notable are the studies of Luchsinger, who reported on the concordance of developmental histories and of many aspects of speech and language. Zygosity was established in these cases by serology (Fig. 16-4). Developmental data of this kind are, in my opinion, of greater relevance to our speculations on genetic background than are pedigrees.

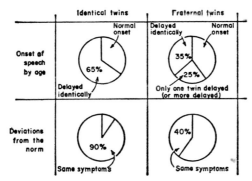

Figure 16-4. The onset of speech and its subsequent development tend to be more uniform among identical twins than fraternal twins.

The nonbiologist frequently and mistakenly thinks of genes as being directly responsible for one property or another; this leads him to the fallacy, especially when behavior is concerned, of dichotomizing everything as being dependent on either genes or environment. Genes act merely on intracellular biochemical processes, although these processes have indirect effects on events in the individual's developmental history. Many alterations in structure and function indirectly attributable to genes are more immediately the consequence of alterations in the schedule of developmental events. Therefore, the studies on twins are important in that they show that homozygotes reach milestones in language development at the same age, in contrast to heterozygotes, in whom divergences are relatively common. It is also interesting that the nature of the deviations—the symptoms, if you wish—are, in the vast majority, identical in homozygotes but not in heterozygotes.

Such evidence indicates that man's biological heritage endows him with sensitivities and propensities that lead to language development in children, who are spoken to (in contrast to chimpanzee infants, who do not automatically develop language—either receptive or productive—under identical treatment). The endowment has a genetic foundation, but this is not to say that there are "genes for language," or that the environment is of no importance.

ATTEMPTS TO MODIFY LANGUAGE DEVELOPMENT

Let us now consider children who have the capacity for language acquisition but fail to develop it for lack of exposure. This is the case with the congenitally deaf, who are allowed to grow up without either language or speech until school age, when suddenly language is brought to them in very unnatural ways. Before this time they may have half a dozen words they can utter, read, write, or finger-spell, but I have known of no profoundly deaf child (in New England, where my investigations were conducted) with whom one could communicate by use of the English language before school age.

When deaf children enter an oralist school, lipreading and speech become the major preoccupation of training. However, in most children these activities remain poor for many more years, and in some, throughout life. Their knowledge of language comes through learning to read and write. However, teachers in the oral tradition restrict expression in the graphic medium on the hypothesis that it interferes with lipreading and speech skills. Thus, exposure to language (1) comes much later in these children's lives than is normal, (2) is dramatically reduced in quantity, (3) is presented through a different medium and sensory modality, and (4) is taught to the children rather as a second language is taught, instead of through the simple immersion into a sea of language that most children experience. The deaf children are immediately required to use grammatically correct sentences, and every mistake is discussed and explained to them.

The results of this procedure are interesting but not very encouraging from the educational point of view. During the early years of schooling, the children's spontaneous writings have a very unusual pattern; there is little evidence that the teachers' instruction in "how to compose correct sentences" is of any avail. Yet, careful analysis of their compositions shows that some subtleties of English syntax that are usually not part of the grammar taught in the school do make their appearance, sometimes quite early. There can be no question that the children do not simply imitate what they see; some of the teachings fall by the wayside, whereas a number of aspects of language are automatically absorbed from the written material given to the children.

There are other instances in which efforts are made to change a child's language skills by special training, as in the mildly retarded, for example. Many parents believe that their retarded child would function quite normally if somebody could just teach him to speak. At Children's Hospital in Boston I undertook a pilot study in which a speech therapist saw a small number of children with Down's syndrome (mongolism) for several hours each week, in an effort to speed up language development. Later, two graduate students in linguistics investigated the children's phonetic skills and tried to assess the capacities of each child for clearer enunciation. Throughout these attempts, it was found that if a child had a small repertoire of single words, it was always possible to teach him yet another word, but if he was not joining these words spontaneously into phrases, there was nothing that could be done to induce him to do so. The articulatory skills were somewhat different. It was often possible to make a child who had always had slurred speech say a specific word more clearly. However, the moment the child returned to spontaneous utterances, he would fall back to the style that was usual for him. The most interesting results were obtained when the retarded children were required simply to repeat well-formed sentences. A child who had not developed to a stage in which he used certain grammatical rules spontaneously, who was still missing the syntactic foundations and prerequisites, could not be taught to repeat a sentence that was formed by such higher rules. This was true even in sentences of very few words. Similar observations have since been made on normal children,[6] with uniformly similar results; normal children, too, can repeat correctly only that which is formed by rules they have already mastered. This is the best indication that language does not come about by simple imitation, but that the child abstracts regularities or relations from the language he hears, which he then applies to building up language for himself as an apparatus of principles.

WHAT SETS THE PACE OF LANGUAGE DEVELOPMENT?

There is a widespread belief that the development of language is dependent on the motor skills of the articulating organs. Some psychologists believe that species other than man fail to develop language only because of anatomical differences in their oral structures. However, we have evidence that this is not so.

It is important that we are clear about the essential nature of language. Since my interests are in language capacities, I am concerned with the development of the child's knowledge of how language works. This is not the same as the acquisition of "the first word." The best test for the presence and development of this knowledge is the manner in which discourse is understood. In most instances, it is true that there is a relation between speech and understanding, but this relation is not a necessary one.[7]

By understanding, I mean something quite specific. In the realm of phonology, understanding involves a process that roughly corresponds to the linguists' phonematization (in contrast, for example, to a "pictographic" understanding: phonematization results in seeing similarities between speech sounds, whereas pictographic understanding would treat a word as an indivisible sound pattern). In the realm of semantics, understanding involves see-

ing the basis on which objects are categorized, thus enabling a
child to name an object correctly that he has never seen before.
(The child does not start out with a hypothesis that "table" is the
proper name of a unique object or that it refers to all things that
have four appendages.) In the realm of grammar, understanding
involves the extraction of relations between word classes; an example is the understanding of predication. By application of these
tests, it can be shown empirically that Aunt Pauline's favorite
lapdog does not have a little language knowledge, but, in fact,
fails the test of understanding on all counts.

A survey of children with a variety of handicaps shows that
their grasp of how language works is intimately related to their
general cognitive growth, which, in turn, is partly dependent on
physical maturation and partly on opportunities to interact with
a stimulus-rich environment. In many retarding diseases, for example, language development is predicted best by the rate of advancement in mental age (using tests of nonverbal intelligence).
In an investigation of congenitally blind children,[8] we are again
finding that major milestones for language development are highly correlated with physical development. A naive conception of
language development as an accumulation of associations between
visual and auditory patterns would be hard put to explain this.

BRAIN CORRELATES

In adults, language functions take place predominantly in the
left hemisphere. A number of cortical fields have been related to
specific aspects of language. The details are still somewhat con-
troversial and need not concern us here. It is certain, however,
that precentral areas of the frontal lobe are principally involved
in the production of language, whereas the postcentral parietal
and superior temporal fields are involved in sensory functions.
These cortical specializations are not present at birth, but become
only gradually established during childhood, in a process very
similar to that of embryological history; there is evidence of differentiation and regulation of function. In the adult, traumata causing large left-sided central cortical lesions carry a highly predictable prognosis; in 70 percent of all cases, aphasia occurs, and in

about half of these, the condition is irreversible (I am basing these figures on our experience with penetrating head injuries incurred in war).

Comparable traumatic lesions in childhood have quite different consequences, the prognosis being directly related to the age at which the insult is incurred. Lesions of the left hemisphere in children under age 2 are no more injurious to future language development than are lesions of the right hemisphere. Children whose brain is traumatized after the onset of language but before the age of 4 usually have transient aphasias; language is quickly reestablished, however, if the right hemisphere remains intact. Often these children regain language by going through stages of language development similar to those of the 2-year-old, but they traverse each stage at greater speed. Lesions incurred before the very early teens also carry an excellent prognosis, permanent residues of symptoms being extremely rare.

The prognosis becomes rapidly worse for lesions that occur after this period; the young men who become casualties of war have symptoms virtually identical with those of stroke patients of advanced age. Experience with the surgical removal of an entire cerebral hemisphere closely parallels this picture. The basis for prognosticating operative success is, again, the age at which the disease has been contracted for which the operation is performed.

If a disturbance in the left hemisphere occurs early enough in life, the right hemisphere remains competent for language throughout life. Apparently this process is comparable to regulation, as we know it from morphogenesis. If the disease occurs after a certain critical period of life, namely, the early teens, this regulative capacity is lost and language is interfered with permanently. Thus the time at which the hemispherectomy is performed is less important than the time of the lesion.

CRITICAL AGE FOR LANGUAGE ACQUISITION

The most reasonable interpretation of this picture of recovery from aphasia in childhood is not that there is vicarious functioning, or taking over, by the right hemisphere because of need, but rather that language functions are not yet confined to the left hemisphere during early life. Apparently both hemispheres are involved at the beginning, and a specialization takes place later (which is the characteristic of differentiation), resulting in a kind of left-right polarization of functions. Therefore, the recovery from aphasia during preteen years may partly be regarded as a reinstatement of activities that had never been lost. There is evidence that children at this age are capable of developing language in the same natural way as do very young children. Not only do symptoms subside, but active language development continues to occur. Similarly, we see that healthy children have a quite different propensity for acquiring foreign languages before the early teens than after the late teens, the period in between being transitional. For the young adult, second-language learning is an academic exercise, and there is a vast variety in degree of proficiency. It rapidly becomes more and more difficult to overcome the accent and interfering influences of the mother tongue.

Neurological material strongly suggests that something happens in the brain during the early teens that changes the propensity for language acquisition. We do not know the factors involved, but it is interesting that the critical period coincides with the time at which the human brain attains its final state of maturity in terms of structure, function, and biochemistry (electroencephalographic patterns slightly lag behind, but become stabilized by about 16 years). Apparently the maturation of the brain marks the end of regulation and locks certain functions into place.

There is further evidence that corroborates the notion of a critical period for primary language acquisition, most importantly, the developmental histories of retarded children. It is dangerous to make sweeping generalizations about all retarded children, because so much depends on the specific disease that causes the retardation. But if we concentrate on diseases in which the pathological condition is essentially stationary, such as microcephaly vera or mongolism, it is possible to make fairly general predictions about language development. If the child's mental developmental age is 2 when he is 4 years old (that is, his I.Q. is 50), one may safely predict that some small progress will be made in language development. He will slowly move through the usual stages of infant language, although the rate of development will gradually slow down. In virtually all of these cases, language development comes to a complete standstill in the early teens, so that these individuals are arrested in primitive stages of language development that are perpetuated for the rest of their lives. Training and motivation are of little help.

Development in the congenitally deaf is also revealing. When they first enter school, their language acquisition is usually quite spectacular, considering the enormous odds against them. However, children who by their early teens have still not mastered all of the principles that underlie the production of sentences appear to encounter almost unsurmountable difficulties in perfecting verbal skills.

There is also evidence of the converse. Children who suddenly lose their hearing (usually a consequence of meningitis) show very different degrees of language skill, depending on whether the disease strikes before the onset of language or after. If it occurs before they are 18 months old, such children encounter difficulties with language development that are very much the same as those encountered by the congenitally deaf. Children who lose their hearing after they have acquired language, however, at age 3 to 4, have a different prospect. Their speech deteriorates rapidly; usually within weeks they stop using language, and so far it has proved impossible to maintain the skill by educational procedures (although new techniques developed in England and described by Fry[9] give promise of great improvement). Many such children then live without language for a relatively long time, often two to three years, and when they enter the schools for the deaf, must be trained in the same way that other deaf children are trained. However, training is much more successful, and their language habits stand out dramatically against those of their less fortunate colleagues. There appears to be a direct relation between the length of time during which a child has been exposed to language and the proficiency seen at the time of retraining.

BIOLOGICAL APPROACH:
DEFINING LANGUAGE FURTHER

Some investigators propose that language is an artifact—a tool that man has shaped for himself to serve a purpose. This assumption induces the view that language consists of many individual traits, each independent of the other. However, the panorama of observations presented above suggests a biological predisposition for the development of language that is anchored in the operating characteristics of the human brain.* Man's cognitive apparatus apparently becomes a language receiver and transmitter, provided the growing organism is exposed to minimum and haphazard environmental events.

However, this assumption leads to a view different from that suggested by the artifact assumption. Instead of thinking of language as a collection of separate and mutually independent traits, one comes to see it as a profoundly integrated activity. Language is to be understood as an operation rather than a static product of the mind. Its modus operandi reflects that of human cognition, because language is an intimate part of cognition. Thus the biological view denies that language is the cause of cognition, or even its effect, since language is not an object (like a tool) that exists apart from a living human brain.

As biologists, we are interested in the operating principles of language because we hope that this will give us some clues about the operating principles of the human brain. We know there is just one species *Homo sapiens,* and it is therefore reasonable to assume that individuals who speak Turkish, English, or Basque (or who spoke Sanskrit some millennia ago) all have (or had) the same kind of brain, that is, a computer with the same operating principles and the same sensorium. Therefore, in a biological investigation one must try to disregard the differences between the languages of the world and to discover the general principles of operation that are common to all of them. This is not an easy matter; in fact, there are social scientists who doubt the existence of language universals. As students of language we cannot fail to

---

*For details, see Lenneberg.[10]

be impressed with the enormous differences among languages. Yet every normal child learns the language to which he is exposed. Perhaps we are simply claiming that common denominators must exist; can we prove their existence? If we discovered a totally isolated tribe with a language unknown to any outsider, how could we find out whether this language is generated by a computer that has the same biological characteristics as do our brains, and how could we prove that it shares the universal features of all languages?

As a start, we could exchange children between our two cultures to discover whether the same language developmental history would occur in those exchanged. Our data would be gross developmental stages, correlated with the emergence of motor milestones. A bioassay of this kind (already performed many times, always with positive results) gives only part of the answer.

In theory, one may also adduce more rigorous proof of similarity among languages. The conception of language universals is difficult to grasp intuitively, because we find it so hard to translate from one language to another and because the grammars appear, on the surface, to be so different. But it is entirely possible that underneath the structural difference that makes it so difficult for the adult speaker to learn a second language (particularly one that is not a cognate of his own) there are significant formal identities.

Virtually every aspect of language is the expression of relations. This is true of phonology (as stressed by Roman Jakobson and his school), semantics, and syntax. For instance, in all languages of the world words label a set of relational principles instead of being labels of specific objects. Knowing a word is never a simple association between an object and an acoustic pattern, but the successful operation of those principles, or application of those rules, that lead to using the word "table" or "house" for objects never before encountered. The language universal in this instance is not the type of object that comes to have a word, nor the particular relations involved; the universal is the generality that words stand for relations instead of being unique names for one object.

Further, no language has ever been described that does not have a second order of relational principles, namely, principles in which relations are being related, that is, syntax in which relations between words are being specified. Once again, the universal is not a particular relation that occurs in all languages (though there are several such relations) but that all languages have relations of relations.

Mathematics may be used as a highly abstract form of description, not of scattered facts but of the dynamic interrelations—the operating principles—found in nature. Chomsky and his students have done this. Their aim has been to develop algorithms for specific languages, primarily English, that make explicit the series of computations that may account for the structure of sentences. The fact that these attempts have only been partially successful is irrelevant to the argument here. (Since every native speaker of English *can* tell a well-formed sentence from an ill-formed one, it is evident that some principles must exist; the question is merely whether the Chomskyites have discovered the correct ones.) The development of algorithms is only one province of mathematics, and in the eyes of many mathematicians a relatively limited one. There is a more exciting prospect; once we know something about the basic relational operating principles underlying a few languages, it should be possible to characterize formally the abstract system *language* as a whole. If our assumption of the existence of basic, structural language universals is correct, one ought to be able to adduce rigorous proof for the existence of homeomorphisms between any natural languages, that is, any of the systems characterized formally. If a category calculus were developed for this sort of thing, there would be one level of generality on which a common denominator could be found; this may be done trivially (for instance by using the product of all systems). However, our present knowledge of the relations, and the relations of relations, found in the languages so far investigated in depth encourages us to expect a significant solution.

ENVIRONMENT AND MATURATION

Everything in life, including behavior and language, is interaction of the individual with its milieu. But the milieu is not constant. The organism itself helps to shape it (this is true of cells and organs as much as of animals and man). Thus, the organism and its environment is a dynamic system and, phylogenetically, developed as such.

The development of language in the child may be elucidated by applying to it the conceptual framework of developmental biology. Maturation may be characterized as a sequence of states. At each state, the growing organism is capable of accepting some specific input; this it breaks down and resynthesizes in such a way that it makes itself develop into a new state. This new state makes the organism sensitive to new and different types of input, whose acceptance transforms it to yet a further state, which opens the way to still different input, and so on. This is called epigenesis. It is the story of embryological development observable in the formation of the body, as well as in certain aspects of behavior.

At various epigenetic states, the organism may be susceptible to more than one sort of input—it may be susceptible to two or more distinct kinds or even to an infinite variety of inputs, as long as they are within determined limits—and the developmental history varies with the nature of the input accepted. In other words, the organism, during development, comes to crossroads; if condition A is present, it goes one way; if condition B is present, it goes another. We speak of states here, but this is, of course, an abstraction. Every stage of maturation is unstable. It is prone to change into specific directions, but requires a trigger from the environment.

When language acquisition in the child is studied from the point of view of developmental biology, one makes an effort to describe developmental stages together with their tendencies for change and the conditions that bring about that change. I believe that the schema of physical maturation is applicable to the study of language development because children appear to be sensitive to successively different aspects of the language environment. The child first reacts only to intonation patterns. With continued exposure to these patterns as they occur in a given language, mechanisms develop that allow him to process the patterns, and in most instances to reproduce them (although the latter is not a necessary condition for further development). This changes him so that he reaches a new state, a new potential for language development. Now he becomes aware of certain articulatory aspects, can process them, and possibly also reproduce them, and so on. A similar sequence of acceptance, synthesis, and state of new acceptance can be demonstrated on the level of semantics and syntax.

That the embryological concepts of differentiation, as well as of determination and regulation, are applicable to the brain processes associated with language development is best illustrated by the material discussed above under the heading "brain correlates" and "critical age for language acquisition." Furthermore, the correlation between language development and other maturational indices suggests that there are anatomical and physiological processes whose maturation sets the pace for both cognitive and language development; it is to these maturational processes that the concept differentiation refers. We often transfer the meaning of the word to the verbal behavior itself, which is not unreasonable, although, strictly speaking, it is the physical correlates only that differentiate.

PSEUDO-HOMOLOGIES AND NAIVE "EVOLUTIONIZING"

The relation between species is established on the basis of structural, physiological, biochemical, and often behavioral correspondences, called homologies. The identification of homologies frequently poses heuristic problems. Common sense may be very misleading in this matter. Unless there is cogent evidence that the correspondences noted are due to a common phylogenetic origin, one must entertain the possibility that resemblances are spurious (though perhaps due to convergence). In other words, not all criteria are equally reliable for the discovery of true homologies. The criteria must pass the following two tests if they are to reveal common biological origins: (1) They must be applicable to traits that have a demonstrable (or at least conceivable) genetic basis; and (2) the traits to which they apply must not have a sporadic and seemingly random distribution over the taxa of the entire animal kingdom. Homologies cannot be established by relying on similarity that rests on superficial inspection (a whale is not a fish) ; on logical rather than biological aspects (animals that move at 14 miles per hour are not necessarily related to one another); and on anthropocentric imputation of motives (a squirrel's hoarding of nuts may have nothing in common with man's provisions for his future) .

Comparisons of language with animal communication that purport to throw light on the problem of its phylogenetic origins infringe on every one of these guidelines. Attempts to write generative grammars for the language of the bees in order to discover in what respect that language is similar to and different from man's language fail to pass test 1. Syntax does not have a genetic basis any more than do arithmetic or algebra; these are calculi used to describe relations. It may be that the activities or circumstances to which the calculi are applied are in some way related to genetically determined capacities. However, merely the fact that the calculus may or may not be applied obviously does not settle that issue.

The common practice of searching the entire animal kingdom for communication behavior that resembles man's in one aspect or another fails test 2. The fact that some bird species and perhaps two or three cetaceans can make noises that sound like words, that some insects use discrete signals when they communicate, or that recombination of signals has been observed to occur in communication systems of a dozen totally unrelated species are not signs of a common phylogeny or genetically based relationship to language. Furthermore, the similarities noted between human language and animal communication all rest on superficial intuition. The resemblances that exist between human language and the language of the bees and the birds are spurious. The comparative criteria are usually logical* instead of biological; and the very idea that there must be a common denominator underlying all communication systems of animals and man is based on an anthropocentric imputation.

Everything in biology has a history, and so every communication system is the result of evolution. But traits or skills do not

---

*See, for instance, Hockett.[12]

have an evolutionary history of their own, that is, a history that is independent of the history of the species. Contemporary species are discontinuous groups (except for those in the process of branching) with discontinuous communication behavior. Therefore, historical continuity need not lead to continuity between contemporary communication systems, many of which (including man's) constitute unique developments.

Another recent practice is to give speculative accounts of just how, why, and when human language developed. This is a somewhat futile undertaking. The knowledge that we have gained about the mechanisms of evolution does not enable us to give specific accounts of every event of the past. Paleontological evidence points to the nature of its fauna, flora, and climate. The precursors of modern man have left for us their bones, teeth, and primitive tools. None of these bears any necessary or assured relation to any type of communication system. Most speculations on the nature of the most primitive sounds, on the first discovery of their usefulness, on the reasons for the hypertrophy of the brain, or the consequences of a narrow pelvis are in vain. We can on longer reconstruct what the selection pressures were or in what order they came, because we know too little that is securely established by hard evidence about the ecological and social conditions of fossil man. Moreover, we do not even know what the targets of actual selection were. This is particularly troublesome because every genetic alteration brings about several changes at once, some of which must be quite incidental to the selective process.

SPECIES SPECIFICITIES AND COGNITIVE SPECIALIZATION

In the nineteenth century it was demonstrated that man is not in a category apart from that of animals. Today it seems to be necessary to defend the view (before many psychologists) that man is not identical with all other animals—in fact, that every animal species is unique, and that most of the commonalities that exist are, at best, homologies. It is frequently claimed that the principles of behavioral function are identical—in all vertebrates, for example—and that the differences between species are differences of magnitude, rather than quality. At other times, it is assumed that cognitive functions are alike in two species except that one of the two may have additionally acquired a capacity for a specific activity. I find fault with both views.

Since behavioral capacities (I prefer the term cognition) are the product of brain function, my point can well be illustrated by considering some aspects of brain evolution. Every mammalian species has an anatomically distinct brain. Homologies are common, but innovations can also be demonstrated. When man's brain is compared with the brain of other primates, extensive correspondences can be found, but there are major problems when it comes to the identification of homologies. Dramatic differences exist not only in size but also in details of the developmental histories; together with differences in cerebrocortical histology, topography, and extent, there are differences in subcortical fiber-connections, as pointed out by Geschwind[13] most recently and by others before him. The problem is, what do we make of the innovations? Is is possible that each innovation (usually an innovation is not a clear-cut anatomical entity) is like an independent component that is simply added to the components common to all the more old-fashioned brains? And if so, is it likely that the new component is simply adding a routine to the computational facilities already available? Both presumptions are naive. A brain is an integrated organ, and cognition results from the integrated operation of all its tissues and suborgans. Man's brain is not a chimpanzee's brain plus added "association facilities." Its functions have undergone reintegration at the same pace as its evolutionary developments.

The identical argument applies to cognitive functions. Cognition is not made up of isolated processes such as perception, storing, and retrieval. Animals do not all have an identical memory mechanism except that some have a larger storage capacity. As the structure of most proteins, the morphology of most cells, and the gross anatomy of most animals show certain species specificities (as do details of behavioral repertoires), so we may expect that cognition, too, in all of its aspects, has its species specificities. My assumption, therefore, is that man's cognition is not essentially that of every other primate with merely the addition of the capacity for language; instead, I propose that his entire cognitive function, of which his capacity for language is an integral part, is species-specific. I repeat once more that I make this assumption not because I think man is in a category all of his own, but because every animal species must be assumed to have cognitive specificities.

CONCLUSION

The human brain is a biochemical machine; it computes the relations expressed in sentences and their components. It has a print-out consisting of acoustic patterns that are capable of similar relational computation by machines of the same constitution using the same program. Linguists, biologists, and psychologists have all discussed certain aspects of the machine.

Linguists, particularly those developing generative grammar, aim at a formal description of the machine's behavior; they search mathematics for a calculus to describe it adequately. Different calculations are matched against the behavior to test their descriptive adequacy. This is an empirical procedure. The raw data are the way a speaker of a language understands collections of words or the relationships he sees. A totally adequate calculus has not yet been discovered. Once available, it will merely describe, in formal terms, the process of relational interpretation in the realm of verbal behavior. It will describe a set of operations; however, it will not make any claims of isomorphism between the formal operations and the biological operations they describe.

Biologists try to understand the nature, growth, and function of the machine (the human brain) itself. They make little inroads here and there, and generally play catch-as-catch-can; everything about the machine interests them (including the descriptions furnished by linguists).

Traditionally, learning theory has been involved neither in a specific description of this particular machine's behavior nor in its physical constitution. Its concern has been with the use of the machine: What makes it go? Can one make it operate more or less often? What purposes does it serve?

Answers provided by each of these inquiries into language are not intrinsically anatagonistic, as has often been claimed. It is only certain overgeneralizations that come into conflict. This is especially so when claims are made that any one of these approaches provides answers to all the questions that matter.

REFERENCES

1. Lenneberg, E. H. In J. A. Fodor and J. J. Katz (Eds.), *The Structure of Language, Readings in the Philosophy of Language.* Englewood Cliffs, N. J., Prentice-Hall, 1964.
2. Lenneberg, E. H. *Biological Foundations of Language.* New York, Wiley, 1967.
3. Lenneberg, E. H.; Nichols, I. A., and Rosenberger, E. F. In D. Rioch (Ed.), *Disorders of Communication.* Research Publications of Association for Research in Nervous and Mental Disorders, New York, 1964, vol. 42.
4. Lenneberg, E. H.; Rebelsky, F. G., and Nichols, I. A. *Hum. Develop., 8:* 23, 1965.
5. Brown, R.; Cazden, C., and Bellugi, U. In J. P. Hill (Ed.), *The 1967 Minnesota Symposium on Child Psychology.* Minneapolis, Univ. of Minnesota Press, 1969.
6. Slobin, D. Personal communication.
7. Lenneberg, E. H. *J. Abnorm. Soc. Psychol., 65:*419, 1962.
8. Lenneberg, E. H.; Fraiberg, S., and Stein, N. Research in progress.
9. Fry, D. B. In F. Smith and G. A. Miller (Eds.), *The Genesis of Language: A Psycholinguistic Approach.* Cambridge, MIT Press, 1966.
10. Lenneberg, E. H. *Perception in Language.* In preparation.
11. Chomsky, N. The formal nature of language. In Lenneberg,[2] Appendix A.
12. Hockett, C. F. In W. E. Lanyon and W. N. Tavolga (Eds.), *Animal Communication.* American Institute of Biological Sciences, Washington, D.C., 1960; and *Sci. Amer. 203:*89, 1960.
13. Geschwind, N. *Brain, 88:*237, 585, 1965.

How does a child learn syntax, the grammatical structure of our language? Learning theorists suggest reinforcement, imitation, and practice are central to modification of the child's vocal responses. Opponents of this point of view argue that the child generates vast numbers of original utterances that could not have been practiced, imitated, or reinforced by his parents. To the psycholinguist, who studies the acquisition and use of language, the child has a set of rules for specifying a sequence of words. The child may not be able to formulate the rules but he is aware of them and knows when syntax is correct. The basis of this ability, some linguists suggest, is a built-in information processing capability in the brain which the child uses when he is exposed to a language system. Dr. Roger Brown and his associates, proponents of the latter point of view, have carefully observed language development in longitudinal studies. In this particular analysis, the authors focus on three processes which young children use in expanding their language system, processes that seem to be indicative of a general rule structure.

Chapter 17

Three Processes in the Child's Acquisition of Syntax

ROGER BROWN AND URSULA BELLUGI

SOME TIME in the second six months of life most children say a first intelligible word. A few months later most children are saying many words and some children go about the house all day long naming things *(table, doggie, ball,* etc.) and actions *(play, see, drop,* etc.) and an occasional quality *(blue, broke, bad,* etc.). At about 18 months children are likely to begin constructing two-word utterances; such a one, for instance, as *Push car.*

A construction such as *Push car* is not just two single-word utterances spoken in a certain order. As single word utterances (they are sometimes called holophrases) both *push* and *car* would have primary stresses and terminal intonation contours. When they are two words programmed as a single utterance the primary stress would fall on *car* and so would the highest level of pitch. *Push* would be subordinated to *car* by a lesser stress and a lower pitch; the unity of the whole would appear in the absence of a terminal contour between words and the presence of such a contour at the end of the full sequence.

By the age of 36 months some children are so advanced in the construction process as to produce all of the major varieties of English simple sentences up to a length of ten or eleven words. For several years we have been studying the development of English syntax, of the sentence-constructing process, in children between 18 and 36 months of age. Most recently we have made a longitudinal study of a boy and girl whom we shall call Adam and

From *Harvard Educational Review 34:*133-151 (Spring), 1964. Copyright 1964 by President and Fellows of Harvard College.

This investigation was supported in whole by Public Health Service Research Grant MH7088 from the National Institute of Mental Health.

Eve. We began work with Adam and Eve in October of 1962 when Adam was 27 months old and Eve 18 months old. The two children were selected from some thirty whom we considered. They were selected primarily because their speech was exceptionally intelligible and because they talked a lot. We wanted to make it as easy as possible to transcribe accurately large quantities of child speech. Adam and Eve are the children of highly educated parents; the fathers were graduate students at Harvard and the mothers are both college graduates. Both Adam and Eve were single children when we began the study. These facts must be remembered in generalizing the outcomes of the research.

While Adam is nine months older than Eve, his speech was only a little more advanced in October of 1962. The best single index of the level of speech development is the average length of utterance and in October, 1962, Adam's average was 1.84 morphemes and Eve's was 1.40 morphemes. The two children stayed fairly close together in the year that followed; in the records for the thirty-eighth week Adam's average was 3.55 and Eve's, 3.27. The processes we shall describe appeared in both children.

Every second week we visited each child for at least two hours and made a tape recording of everything said by the child as well as of everything said to the child. The mother was always present and most of the speech to the child is hers. Both mother and child became very accustomed to our presence and learned to continue their usual routine with us as the observers.

One of us always made a written transcription, on the scene, of the speech of mother and child with notes about important actions and objects of attention. From this transcription and the tape a final transcription was made and these transcriptions constitute the primary data of the study. For many purposes we require a "distributional analysis" of the speech of the child. To this end the child's utterances in a given transcription were cross classified and relisted under such heading as: "A + noun"; "Noun + verb"; "Verbs in the past"; "Utterances containing the pronoun *it*," etc. The categorized utterances expose the syntactic regularities of the child's speech.

Each week we met as a research seminar, with students of the psychology of language,* to discuss the state of the construction process in one of the two children as of that date. In these discussions small experiments were often suggested, experiments that had to be done within a few days if they were to be informative. At one time, for instance, we were uncertain whether Adam understood the semantic difference between putting a noun in subject position and putting it in object position. Consequently one of us paid an extra visit to Adam equipped with some toys. "Adam," we said, "show us the duck pushing the boat." And, when he had done so: "Now show us the boat pushing the duck."

Another week we noticed that Adam would sometimes pluralize nouns when they should have been pluralized and sometimes would not. We wondered if he could make grammatical judgments about the plural, if he could distinguish a correct form from an incorrect form. "Adam," we asked, "which is right, 'two shoes' or 'two shoe'?" His answer on that occasion, produced with explosive enthusiasm, was "Pop goes the weasel!" The 2-year-old child does not make a perfectly docile experimental subject.

The dialogue between mother and child does not read like a transcribed diaglogue between two adults. Table 17-I offers a sam-

TABLE 17-I

A Section from Adam's First Record

Adam	*Mother*
See truck, Mommy.	
See truck.	
	Did you see the truck?
No I see truck.	
	No, you didn't see it?
	There goes one.
There go one.	
	Yes, there goes one.
See a truck.	
See truck, Mommy.	
See truck.	
Truck.	
Put truck, Mommy.	
	Put the truck where?
Put truck window.	
	I think that one's too large to go in the window.

*We are grateful for intellectual stimulation and lighthearted companionship to Dr. Jean Berko Gleason, Mr. Samuel Anderson, Mr. Colin Fraser, Dr. David McNeill, and Dr. Daniel Slobin.

ple section from an early transcribed record. It has some interesting properties. The conversation is, in the first place, very much in the here and now. From the child there is no speech of the sort that Bloomfield called "displaced," speech about other times and other places. Adam's utterances in the early months were largely a coding of contemporaneous events and impulses. The mother's speech differs from the speech that adults use to one another in many ways. Her sentences are short and simple; for the most part they are the kinds of sentences that Adam will produce a year later.

Perhaps because they are short, the sentences of the mother are perfectly grammatical. The sentences adults use to one another, perhaps because they are longer and more complex, are very often not grammatical, not well formed. Here for instance is a rather representative example produced at a conference of psychologists and linguists: "As far as I know, no one yet has done the in a way obvious now and interesting problem of doing a in a sense a structural frequency study of the alternative syntactical in a given language, say, like English, the alternative possible structures, and how what their hierarchical probability of occurrence structure is."[3] It seems unlikely that a child could learn the patterns of English syntax from such speech. His introduction to English ordinarily comes in the form of a simplified, repetitive, and idealized dialect. It may be that such an introduction is necessary for the acquisition of syntax to be possible but we do not know that.

In the course of the brief interchange of Table 17-I Adam imitates his mother in saying: "There go one" immediately after she says "There goes one." The imitation is not perfect; Adam omits the inflection on the verb. His imitation is a reduction in that it omits something from the original. This kind of imitation with reduction is extremely common in the records of Adam and Eve and it is the first process we shall discuss.

IMITATION AND REDUCTION

Table 17-II presents some model sentences spoken by the mothers and the imitations produced by Adam and Eve. These were selected from hundreds in the records in order to illustrate

TABLE 17-II

Some Imitations Produced by Adam and Eve

Model Utterance	Child's Imitation
Tank car	Tank car
Wait a minute	Wait a minute
Daddy's brief case	Daddy brief case
Fraser will be unhappy	Fraser unhappy
He's going out	He go out
That's an old time train	Old time train
It's not the same dog as Pepper	Dog Pepper
No, you can't write on Mr. Cromer's shoe	Write Cromer shoe

some general propositions. The first thing to notice is that the imitations preserve the word order of the model sentences. To be sure, words in the model are often missing from the imitation but the words preserved are in the order of the original. This is a fact that is so familiar and somehow reasonable that we did not at once recognize it as an empirical outcome rather than as a natural necessity. But of course it is not a necessity, the outcome could have been otherwise. For example, words could have been said back in the reverse of their original order, the most recent first. The preservation of order suggests that the model sentence is processed by the child as a total construction rather than as a list of words.

In English the order of words in a sentence is an important grammatical signal. Order is used to distinguish among subject, direct object, and indirect object and it is one of the marks of imperative and interrogative constructions. The fact that the child's first sentences preserve the word order of their models partially accounts for the ability of an adult to "understand" these sentences and so to feel that he is in communication with the child. It is conceivable that the child "intends" the meanings coded by his word orders and that when he preserves the order of an adult sentence, he does so because he wants to say what the order says. It is also possible that he preserves word order just because his brain works that way and that he has no comprehension of the semantic contrasts involved. In some languages word order is not an important grammatical signal. In Latin, for instance, "Agricola amat puellam" has the same meaning as "Puellam amat agricola" and subject-object relations are signalled by case endings. We would be interested to know whether children who are exposed to languages that do not utilize word order as a major syntactic signal preserve order as reliably as do children exposed to English.

The second thing to notice in Table 17-II is the fact that when the models increase in length there is not a corresponding increase in the imitation. The imitations stay in the range of two to four morphemes which was the range characteristic of the children at this time. The children were operating under some constraint of length or span. This is not a limitation of vocabulary; the children knew hundreds of words. Neither is it a constraint of immediate memory. We infer this from the fact that the average length of utterances produced spontaneously, where immediate memory is not involved, is about the same as the average length of utterances produced as immediate imitations. The constraint is a limitation on the length of utterance the children are able to program or plan.* This kind of narrow span limitation in children is characteristic of most or all of their intellectual operations. The limitation grows less restrictive with age as a consequence, probably, of both neurological growth and of practice, but of course it is never lifted altogether.

A constraint on length compels the imitating child to omit some words or morphemes from the mother's longer sentences. Which forms are retained and which omitted? The selection is not random but highly systematic. Forms retained in the examples of Table 17-II include: *Daddy, Fraser, Pepper,* and *Cromer; tank car, minute, briefcase, train, dog,* and *shoe; wait, go,* and *write; unhappy* and *old time.* For the most part they are nouns, verbs, and adjectives, though there are exceptions, as witness the initial pronoun He and the preposition out and the indefinite article a. Forms omitted in the samples of Table 17-II include: the possessive inflection –s, the modal auxiliary *will,* the contraction of the auxiliary verb *is,* the progressive inflection –ing, the preposition *on,* the article *the* and *an,* and the modal auxiliary *can.* It is possible to make a general characterization of the forms

*Additional evidence of the constraint on sentence length may be found in R. Brown and C. Fraser.[2]

likely to be retained that distinguishes them as a total class from the forms likely to be omitted.

Forms likely to be retained are nouns and verbs and, less often, adjectives, and these are the three large and "open" parts of speech in English. The number of forms in any one of these parts of speech is extremely large and always growing. Words belonging to these classes are sometimes called "contentives" because they have semantic content. Forms likely to be omitted are inflections, auxiliary verbs, articles, prepositions, and conjunctions. These forms belong to syntactic classes that are small and closed. Any one class has few members and new members are not readily added. The omitted forms are the ones that linguists sometimes call "functors," their grammatical *functions* being more obvious than their semantic content.

Why should young children omit functors and retain contentives? There is more than one plausible answer. Nouns, verbs, and adjectives are words that make reference. One can conceive of teaching the meanings of these words by speaking them, one at a time, and pointing at things or actions or qualities. And of course parents do exactly that. These are the kinds of words that children have been encouraged to practice speaking one at a time. The child arrives at the age of sentence construction with a stock of well-practiced nouns, verbs, and adjectives. Is it not likely then that this prior practice causes him to retain the contentives from model sentences too long to be reproduced in full, that the child imitates those forms in the speech he hears which are already well developed in him as individual habits? There is probably some truth in this explanation but it is not the only determinant since children will often select for retention contentives that are relatively unfamiliar to them.

We adults sometimes operate under a constraint on length and the curious fact is that the English we produce in these circumstances bears a formal resemblance to the English produced by 2-year-old children. When words cost money there is a premium on brevity or to put it otherwise, a constraint on length. The result is "telegraphic" English and telegraphic English is an English of nouns, verbs, and adjectives. One does not send a cable reading:

"My car has broken down and I have lost my wallet; send money to me at the American Express in Paris" but rather "Car broken down; wallet lost; send money American Express Paris." The telegram omits: *my, has, and I, have, my, to, me, at, the, in*. All of these are functors. We make the same kind of telegraphic reduction when time or fatigue constrain us to be brief, as witness any set of notes taken at a fast-moving lecture.

A telegraphic transformation of English generally communicates very well. It does so because it retains the high-information words and drops the low-information words. We are here using "information" in the sense of the mathematical theory of communication. The information carried by a word is inversely related to the chances of guessing it from context. From a given string of content words, missing functors can often be guessed but the message "my has and I have my to me at the in" will not serve to get money to Paris. Perhaps children are able to make a communication analysis of adult speech and so adapt in an optimal way to their limitation of span. There is, however, another way in which the adaptive outcome might be achieved.

If you say aloud the model sentences of Table 17-II you will find that you place the heavier stresses, the primary and secondary stresses in the sentences, on contentives rather than on functors. In fact the heavier stresses fall, for the most part, on the words the child retains. We first realized that this was the case when we found that in transcribing tapes, the words of the mother that we could hear most clearly were usually the words that the child reproduced. We had trouble hearing the weakly stressed functors and, of course, the child usually failed to reproduce them. Differential stress may then be the cause of the child's differential retention. The outcome is a maximally informative reduction but the cause of this outcome need not be the making of an information analysis. The outcome may be an incidental consequence of the fact that English is a well-designed language that places its heavier stresses where they are needed, on contentives that cannot easily be guessed from context.

We are fairly sure that differential stress is one of the determinants of the child's telegraphic productions. For one thing, stress will also account for the way in which children reproduce poly-syllabic words when the total is too much for them. Adam, for in-stance, gave us *'pression* for *expression* and Eve gave us *'raff* for *giraffe;* the more heavily stressed syllables were the ones retained. In addition we have tried the effect of placing heavy stresses on functors which do not ordinarily receive such stresses. To Adam we said: "You say what I say" and then, speaking in a normal way at first: "The doggie will bite." Adam gave back: "Doggie bite." Then we stressed the auxiliary: "The doggie *will* bite" and, after a few trials. Adam made attempts at reproducing that auxiliary. A science fiction experiment comes to mind. If there were parents who stressed functors rather than contentives would they have children whose speech was a kind of "reciprocal telegraphic" made up of articles, prepositions, conjunctions, auxiliaries, and the like? Such children would be out of touch with the commun-ity as real children are not.

It may be that all the factors we have mentioned play some part in determining the child's selective imitations; the reference-making function of contentives, the fact that they are practiced as single words, the fact that they cannot be guessed from context, and the heavy stresses they receive. There are also other possible factors: for example, the left-to-right, earlier-to-later position of words in a sentence, but these make too long a story to tell here.* Whatever the causes, the first utterances produced as imitations of adult sentences are highly systematic reductions of their models. Furthermore, the telegraphic properties of these imitations ap-pear also in the child's spontaneously produced utterances. When his speech is not modeled on an immediately prior adult sentence, it observes the same limitation on length and the same predilec-tion for contentives as when it is modeled on an immediately prior sentence.

IMITATION WITH EXPANSION

In the course of the brief conversation set down in Table 17-I, Adam's mother at one point imitates Adam. The boy says, "There go one," and mother responds, "Yes, there goes one." She does not

---

*See Brown and Fraser.[2]

exactly reproduce the model sentence of the child but instead adds something to it or expands it. What she adds is a functor, the inflection for third-person on the verb, the very form that Adam had omitted when he imitated his mother.

One of the first things we noticed when we began to study child speech several years ago was the frequency with which adults imitated children. Indeed they seemed to imitate more often than did the children themselves. We later came to realize that adult imitations are seldom exact reproductions; they are usually expansions. The mothers of Adam and Eve responded to the speech of their children with expansions about 30 percent of the time. We did it ourselves when we talked with the children. Indeed we found it very difficult to withhold expansions. A reduced or incomplete English sentence seems to constrain the English-speaking adult to expand it into the nearest properly formed complete sentence. Table 17 III lists a few sample expansions from the hundreds in the records.

TABLE 17-III
Expansions of Child Speech Produced by Mothers

Child	Mother
Baby highchair	Baby is in the highchair
Mommy eggnog	Mommy had her eggnog
Eve lunch	Eve is having lunch
Mommy sandwich	Mommy'll have a sandwich
Sat wall	He sat on the wall
Throw Daddy	Throw it to Daddy
Pick glove	Pick the glove up

The first thing worthy of attention in the expansions of Table 17-III is the fact that the words spoken by the mother preserve the order of the words in the child's sentences. To be sure, words, and inflections are added but they are fitted in, before, and after and between the words the child used; they are not generally permitted to disturb the order of the child's words. It is as if these latter were taken as constants by the mother, constants to which some sentence had to be fitted. She acts as if she were assuming that the child means everything he says, all the words and also their order, but as if he might also mean more than he says. From the mother's point of view an expansion is a kind of communication check; it says in effect "Is this what you mean?"

The second thing to notice about Table 17-III is the character of the forms added to the child's utterances. They include the auxiliaries *is* and *will;* the prepositions *in, on, to,* and *up;* the verb forms *is, have, had,* and *having;* the articles *a* and *the;* the pronouns *her, he,* and *it.* For the most part, the words added are functors and functors are of course the words that the child omits in his reductions.

The interaction between mother and child is, much of the time, a cycle of reductions and expansions. There are two transformations involved. The reduction transformation has an almost completely specifiable and so mechanical character. One could program a machine to do it with the following instructions: "Retain contentives (or stressed forms) in the order given up to some limit of length." The expansion accomplished by Adam's mother when she added the third-person inflection to the verb and said "There goes one" is also a completely specifiable transformation. The instructions would read: "Retain the forms given in in the order given and supply obligatory grammatical forms. To be sure this mother-machine would have to be supplied with the obligatory rules of English grammar but that could be done. However, the sentence "There goes one" is atypical in that it only adds a compulsory and redundant inflection. The expansions of Table 17-III all add forms that are not grammatically compulsory or redundant and these expansions cannot be mechanically generated by grammatical rules alone.

In Table 17-III the topmost four utterances produced by the child are all of the same grammatical type; all four consist of a proper noun followed by a common noun. However, the four are expanded in quite different ways. In particular the form of the verb changes: it is in the first case in the simple present tense; in the second case the simple past; in the third case the present progressive; in the last case the simple future. All of these are perfectly grammatical but they are different. The second set of child utterances is formally uniform in that each one consists of a verb followed by a noun. The expansions are again all grammatical but quite unlike, especially with regard to the preposition supplied. In general, then, there are radical changes in the mother's expansions when there are no changes in the formal character of the utterances expanded. It follows that the expansions cannot be produced simply by making grammatically compulsory additions to the child's utterances.

How does a mother decide on the correct expansion of one of her child's utterances? Consider the utterance "Eve lunch." So far as grammar is concerned this utterance could be appropriately expanded in any of a number of ways: "Eve is having lunch"; "Eve had lunch"; "Eve will have lunch"; Eve's lunch," etc. On the occasion when Eve produced the utterance, however, one expansion seemed more appropriate than any other. It was the noon hour, Eve was sitting at the table with a plate of food before her, and her spoon and fingers were busy. In these circumstances "Eve lunch" had to mean "Eve is having lunch." A little later when the plate had been stacked in the sink and Eve was getting down from her chair the utterance "Eve lunch" would have suggested the expansion "Eve has had her lunch." Most expansions are not only responsive to the child's words but also to the circumstances attending their utterance.

What kind of instructions will generate the mother's expansions? The following are approximately correct: "Retain the words given in the order given and add those functors that will result in a well-formed simple sentence that is appropriate to the circumstances." These are not instructions that any machine could follow. A machine could act in the instrutcions only if it were provided with detailed specifications for judging appropriateness and no such specifications can, at present, be written. They exist, however, in implicit form in the brains of mothers and in the brains of all English-speaking adults and so judgments of appropriateness can be made by such adults.

The expansion encodes aspects of reality that are not coded by the child's telegraphic utterance. Functors have meaning but it is meaning that accrues to them in context rather than in isolation. The meanings that are added by functors seem to be nothing less than the basic terms in which we construe reality: the time of an action, whether it is ongoing or completed, whether it is presently relevant or not; the concept of possession and such relational concepts as are coded by *in, on, up, down,* and the like; the difference between a particular instance of a class ("Has anybody seen *the* paper?") and any instance of a class ("Has anybody seen *a* paper?") ; the difference between extended substances given shape and size by an "accidental" container *(sand, water, syrup,* etc.) and countable "things" having a characteristic fixed shape and size *(a cup, a man, a tree,* etc.) . It seems to us that a mother in expanding speech may be teaching more than grammar; she may be teaching something like a worldview.

As yet it has not been demonstrated that expansions are *necessary* for learning either grammar or a construction of reality. It has not even been demonstrated that expansions contribute to such learning. All we know is that some parents do expand and their children do learn. It is perfectly possible, however, that children can and do learn simply from hearing their parents or others make well-formed sentences in connection with various nonverbal circumstances. It may not be necessary or even helpful for these sentences to be expansions of utterances of the child. Only experiments contrasting expansion training with simple exposure to English will settle the matter. We hope to do such experiments.

There are, of course, reasons for expecting the expansion transformation to be an effective tutorial technique. By adding something to the words the child has just produced one confirms his response insofar as it is appropriate. In addition one takes him somewhat beyond that response but not greatly beyond it. One encodes additional meanings at a moment when he is most likely to be attending to the cues that can teach that meaning.

INDUCTION OF THE LATENT STRUCTURE

Adam, in the course of the conversation with his mother set down in Table 17-I, produced one utterance for which no adult is likely ever to have provided an exact model: "No I see truck." His mother elects to expand it as "No, you didn't see it," and this expansion suggests that the child might have created the utterance by reducing an adult model containing the form *didn't*. However, the mother's expansion in this case does some violence to Adam's original version. He did not say *no* as his mother said it, with primary stress and final contour; Adam's *no* had secondary stress and no final contour. It is not easy to imagine an adult model for this utterance. It seems more likely that the utterance was created by Adam as part of a continuing effort to discover the general rules for constructing English negatives.

In Table 17-IV we have listed some utterances produced by Adam or Eve for which it is difficult to imagine any adult model. It is unlikely that any adult said any of these to Adam or Eve since they are very simple utterances and yet definitely ungrammatical. In addition it is difficult, by adding functors alone, to build any of them up to simple grammatical sentences. Consequently it does not seem likely that these utterances are reductions of adult originals. It is more likely that they are mistakes which externalize the child's search for the regularities of English syntax.

TABLE 17-IV
Utterances Not Likely to be Imitations

My Cromer suitcase	You naughty are
Two foot	Why it can't turn off?
A bags	Put on it
A scissor	Cowboy did fighting me
A this truck	Put a gas in

We have long realized that the occurrence of certain kinds of errors on the level of morphology (or word construction) reveals the child's effort to induce regularities from speech. So long as a child speaks correctly, or at any rate so long as he speaks as correctly as the adults he hears, there is no way to tell whether he is simply repeating what he has heard or whether he is actually constructing. However, when he says something like "I digged a hole" we can often be sure that he is constructing. We can be sure because it is unlikely that he would have heard *digged* from anyone and because we can see how, in processing words he has heard, he might have come by *digged*. It looks like an overgeneralization of the regular past inflection. The inductive operations of the child's mind are externalized in such a creation. Overgeneralizations on the level of syntax (or sentence construction) are more difficult to identify because there are so many ways of adding functors so as to build up conceivable models. But this is difficult to do for the examples of Table 17-IV and for several hundred other utterances in our records.

The processes of imitation and expansion are not sufficient to account for the degree of linguistic competence that children regularly acquire. These processes alone cannot teach more than the sum total of sentences that speakers of English have either modeled for a child to imitate or built up from a child's reductions. However, a child's linguistic competence extends far beyond this sum total of sentences. All children are able to understand and construct sentences they have never heard but which are nevertheless well-formed, well-formed in terms of general rules that are implicit in the sentences the child has heard. Somehow, then, every child processes the speech to which he is exposed so as to induce from it a latent structure. This latent rule structure is so general that a child can spin out its implications all his life long. It is both semantic and syntactic. The discovery of latent structure is the greatest of the processes involved in language acquisition and the most difficult to understand. We will provide an example of how the analysis can proceed by discussing the evolution in child speech of noun phrases.

A noun phrase in adult English includes a noun but also more than a noun. One variety consists of a noun with assorted modifiers: *The girl; The pretty girl; That pretty girl; My girl,* etc. All of these are constructions which have the same syntactic privileges as do nouns alone. One can use a noun phrase in isolation to name or request something; one can use it in sentences, in subject position or in object position or in predicate nominative position. All of these are slots that nouns alone can also fill. A larger construction having the same syntactic privileges as its "head" word is called in linguistics an "endocentric" construction and noun phrases are endocentric constructions.

For both Adam and Eve, in the early records, noun phrases usually occur as total independent utterances rather than as components of sentences. Table 17-V presents an assortment of such utterances at Time 1. They consist in each case of some sort of modifier, just one, preceding a noun. The modifiers, or as they are sometimes called the "pivot" words, are a much smaller class than the noun class. Three students of child speech have independently discovered that this kind of construction is extremely common when children first begin to combine words.[1,2,4]

TABLE 17-V

Noun Phrases in Isolation
and Rule for Generating Noun Phrases at Time 1

A coat	More coffee
A celery*	More nut*
A Becky*	Two sock*
A hands*	Two shoes
The top	two tinker-toy*
My Mommy	Big boot
That Adam	Poor man
My stool	Little top
That knee	Dirty knee

$$NP \rightarrow M + N$$

$M \rightarrow$ a, big, dirty, little, more, my, poor, that, the, two.
$N \rightarrow$ Adam, Becky, boot, coat, coffee, knee, man, Mommy, nut, sock, stool, tinker-toy, top (and very many others).

*Ungrammatical for an adult.

It is possible to generalize the cases of Table 17-V into a simple implicit rule. The rule symbolized in Table 17-V reads: "In order to form a noun phrase of this type, select first one word from the small class of modifiers and select, second, one word from the large class of nouns." This is a "generative" rule by which we mean it is a program that would actually serve to build constructions of the type in question. It is offered as a model of the mental mechanism by which Adam and Eve generated such utterances. Furthermore, judging from our work with other children and from the reports of Braine and of Miller and Ervin, the model describes a mechanism present in many children when their average utterance is approximately two morphemes long.

We have found that even in our earliest records the M + N construction is sometimes used as a component of larger constructions. For instance, Eve said: "Fix a Lassie" and "Turn the page" and "A horsie stuck," and Adam even said: "Adam wear a shirt." There are, at first, only a handful of these larger constructions but there are very many constructions in which single nouns occur in subject or in object position.

Let us look again at the utterances of Table 17-V and the rule generalizing them. The class M does not correspond with any syntactic class of adult English. In the class M are articles, a possessive pronoun, a cardinal number, a demonstrative adjective or pronoun, a quantifier, and some descriptive adjectives—a mixed bag indeed. For adult English these words cannot belong to the same syntactic class because they have very different privileges of occurrence in sentences. For the children the words do seem to function as one class having the common privilege of occurrence before nouns.

If the initial words of the utterances in Table 17-V are treated as one class M then many utterances are generated which an adult speaker would judge to be ungrammatical. Consider the indefinite article *a.* Adults use it only to modify common count nouns in the singular such as *coat, dog, cup,* etc. We would not say *a celery,* or *a cereal,* or *a dirt; celery, cereal,* and *dirt* are mass nouns. We would not say *a Becky* or *a Jimmy; Becky* and *Jimmy* are proper nouns. We would not say *a hands* or *a shoes; hands* and *shoes* are plural nouns. Adam and Eve, at first, did form ungrammatical combinations such as these.

The numeral *two* we use only with count nouns in the plural. We would not say *two sock* since *sock* is singular, nor *two water* since *water* is a mass noun. The word *more* we use before count nouns in the plural *(more nuts)* or mass nouns in the singular *(more coffee).* Adam and Eve made a number of combinations involving *two* or *more* that we would not make.

Given the initial very undiscriminating use of words in the class M it follows that one dimension of development must be a progressive differentiation of privileges, which means the division of M into smaller classes. There must also be subdivision of the noun class (N) for the reason that the privileges of occurrence of various kinds of modifiers must be described in terms of such subvarieties of N as the common noun and proper noun, the count noun and mass noun. There must eventually emerge a distinction between nouns singular and nouns plural since this distinction figures in the privileges of occurrence of the several sorts of modifiers.

Sixteen weeks after our first records from Adam and Eve (Time 2), the differentiation process had begun. By this time there were distributional reasons for separating out articles *(a, the)* from demonstrative pronouns *(this, that)* and both of these from the residual class of modifiers. Some of the evidence of this conclusion appears in Table 17-VI. In general one syntactic class is distinguished from another when the members of one class have combinational privileges not enjoyed by the members of the other. Consider, for example, the reasons for distinguishing articles (Art) from modifiers in general (M). Both articles and modifiers appeared in front of nouns in two-word utterances. However, in three-word utterances that were made up from the total pool of words and that had a noun in final position, the privileges of *a* and *the* were different from the privileges of all other modifiers. The articles occurred in initial position followed by a member of class M other than an article. No other modifier occurred in this first position; notice the "Not obtained" examples of Part A. If the children had produced utterances like those (for example, *blue a flower, your a car*) there would have been no difference in the privileges of occurrence of articles and modifiers and therefore no reason to separate out articles.

TABLE 17-VI
Subdivision of the Modifier Class

A) Privileges Peculiar to Articles	
Obtained	*Not Obtained*
A blue flower	Blue a flower
A nice nap	Nice a nap
A your car	Your a car
A my pencil	My a pencil
B) Privileges Peculiar to Demonstrative Pronouns	
Obtained	*Not Obtained*
That my cup	My that cup
That a horse	A that horse
That a blue flower	A that blue flower
	Blue a that flower

The record of Adam is especially instructive. He created such notably ungrammatical combinations as "a your car" and "a my pencil." It is very unlikely that adults provided models for these.

They argue strongly that Adam regarded all the words in the residual M class as syntactic equivalents and so generated these very odd utterances in which possessive pronouns appear where descriptive adjectives would be more acceptable.

Table 17-VI also presents some of the evidence for distinguishing demonstrative pronouns (Dem) from articles and modifiers (Part B). The pronouns occurred first and ahead of articles in three-and-four-word utterances—a position that neither articles nor modifiers ever filled. The sentences with demonstrative pronouns are recognizable as reductions which omit the copular verb *is*. Such sentences are not noun phrases in adult English and ultimately they will not function as noun phrases in the speech of the children, but for the present they are not distinguishable distributionally from noun phrases.

Recall now the generative formula of Table 17-V which constructs noun phrases by simply placing a modifier (M) before a noun (N). The differentiation of privileges illustrated in Table 17-VI, and the syntactic classes this evidence motivates us to create, complicate the formula for generating noun phrases. In Table 17-VII we have written a single general formula for producing all noun phrases at Time 2 [NP → (Dem) + Art) + (M) + N] and also the numerous more specific rules which are summarized by the general formula.

By the time of the thirteenth transcription, twenty-six weeks after we began our study, privileges of occurrence were much more finely differentiated and syntactic classes were consequently more numerous. From the distributional evidence we judged that Adam had made five classes of his original class M: articles, descriptive adjectives, possessive pronouns, demonstrative pronouns, and a residual class of modifiers. The generative rules of Table 17-VII had become inadequate; there were no longer, for instance, any combinations like "A your car." Eve had the same set except that she used two residual classes of modifiers. In addition nouns had begun to subdivide for both children. The usage of proper nouns had become clearly distinct from the usage of count nouns. For Eve the evidence justified separating count nouns from mass nouns, but for Adam it still did not. Both children by this time

TABLE 17-VII
Rules for Generating Noun Phrases at Time 2

$NP_1 \to Dem + Art + M + N$	$NP \to (Dem) + (Art) + (M) + N$
$NP_2 \to Art + M + N$	
$NP_3 \to Dem + M + N$	
$NP_4 \to Art + N$	( ) means class within
$NP_5 \to M + N$	parentheses is optional
$NP_6 \to Dem + N$	
$NP_7 \to Dem + Art + N$	

were frequently pluralizing nouns but as yet their syntactic control of the singular-plural distinction was imperfect.

In summary, one major aspect of the development of general structure in child speech is a progressive differentiation in the usage of words and therefore a progressive differentiation of syntactic classes. At the same time, however, there is an integrative process at work. From the first, an occasional noun phrase occurred as a component of some larger construction. At first these noun phrases were just two words long and the range of positions in which they could occur was small. With time the noun phrases grew longer, were more frequently used, and were in a greater range of positions. The noun phrase structure as a whole, in all the permissible combinations of modifiers and nouns, was assuming the combinational privileges enjoyed by nouns in isolation.

In Table 17-VIII we have set down some of the sentence positions in which both nouns and noun phrases occurred in the speech of Adam and Eve. It is the close match between the positions of nouns alone and of nouns with modifiers in the speech of Adam and Eve that justifies us in calling the longer constructions noun phrases. These longer constructions are, as they should be, endocentric; the head word alone has the same syntactic privileges as the head word with its modifiers. The continuing failure

TABLE 17-VIII
Some Privileges of the Noun Phrase

Noun Phrase Positions	*Noun Positions*
That (a blue flower)	That (flower)
Where (the puzzle) go?	Where (ball) go?
Doggie eat (the breakfast)	Adam write (penguin)
(A horsie) crying	(Horsie) stop
Put (the red hat) on	Put (hat) on

to find in noun phrase positions whole constructions of the type "That a blue flower" signals the fact that these constructions are telegraphic versions of predicate nominative sentences omitting the verb form *is*. Examples of the kind of construction not obtained are: "That (that a blue flower)"; "Where (that a blue flower)?"

For adults the noun phrase is a subwhole of the sentence, what linguists call an "immediate constituent." The noun phrase has a kind of psychological unity. There are signs that the noun phrase was also an immediate constituent for Adam and Eve. Consider the sentence using the separable very *put on*. The noun phrase in "Put the red hat on" is, as a whole, fitted in between the verb and the particle even as in the noun alone in "Put hat on." What is more, however, the location of pauses in the longer sentence, on several occasions, suggested the psychological organization: "Put . . . the red hat . . . on" rather than "Put the red . . . hat on" or "Put the . . . red hat on." In addition to this evidence the use of pronouns suggests that the noun phrase is a psychological unit.

The unity of noun phrases in adult English is evidenced, in the first place, by the syntactic equivalence between such phrases and nouns alone. It is evidenced, in the second place, by the fact that pronouns are able to substitute for total noun phrases. In our immediately preceding sentence the pronoun "It" stands for the rather involved construction from the first sentence of this paragraph: "The unity of noun phrases in adult English." The words called "pronouns" in English would more aptly be called "pronoun-phrases" since it is the phrase rather than the noun which they usually replace. One does not replace 'unity" with "it" and say "The *it* of noun phrases in adult English." In the speech of Adam and Eve, too, the pronoun came to function as a replacement for the noun phrase. Some of the clearer cases appear in Table 17-IX.

Adam characteristically externalizes more of his learning than does Eve and his record is especially instructive in connection with the learning of pronouns. In his first eight records, the first sixteen weeks of the study, Adam quite often produced sentences containing both the pronoun and the noun or noun phrase that

TABLE 17-IX

Pronouns Replacing Nouns or Noun Phrases and Pronouns Produced
Together with Nouns or Noun Phrases

Noun Phrases Replaced by Pronouns	Pronouns and Noun Phrases in Same Utterances
Hit ball	Mommy get it ladder
Get it	Mommy get it my ladder
Ball go?	Saw it ball
Go get it	Miss it garage
Made it	I miss it cowboy boot
Made a ship	I Adam drive that
Fix a tricycle	I Adam drive
Fix it	I Adam don't

the pronoun should have replaced. One can here see the equivalence in the process of establishment. First the substitute is produced and then, as if in explication, the form or forms that will eventually be replaced by the substitute. Adam spoke out his pronoun antecedents as chronological consequents. This is additional evidence of the unity of the noun phrase since the noun phrases *my ladder* and *cowboy boot* are linked with *it* in Adam's speech in just the same way as the nouns *ladder* and *ball*.

We have described three processes involved in the child's acquisition of syntax. It is clear that the last of these, the induction of latent structure, is by far the most complex. It looks as if this last process will put a serious strain on any learning theory thus far conceived by psychology. The very intricate simultaneous differentiation and integration that constitutes the evolution of the noun phrase is more reminiscent of the biological development of an embryo than it is of the acquisition of a conditional reflex.

REFERENCES

1. Braine, M. D. S. The ontogeny of English phrase structure: the first phrase. *Language, 39:*1-13, 1963.
2. Brown, R., and Fraser, C. The acquisition of syntax. In C. N. Cofer and Barbara Musgrave (Eds.), *Verbal Behavior and Learning.* New York, McGraw-Hill, 1963.
3. Maclay, H., and Osgood, C. E. Hesitation phenomena in spontaneous English speech. *Word, 15:*19-44, 1959.
4. Miller, W., and Ervin, S. The development of grammar in child language. In Ursula Bellugi and Roger Brown (Eds.) *The Acquisition of Language.* Child Development Monograph, 1964.

PART VII

THE DEVELOPMENT OF BODY IMAGE
AND LATERALITY

MOST INDIVIDUALS have feelings about their bodies, derived in part, from physical characteristics, perceptions of other's evaluations of these characteristics, psychological experiences, and the physical attributes prized by a culture. These feelings are subsumed under the label of body image. The development of the body image is conjectured to occur as the infant slowly differentiates himself from his environment, as he is both active and reactive in his surroundings. Careful observations form the basis of most of the inferences about early body image development, many of which are detailed in the sensitive article by Dr. James Anthony. With the older child and adult, clinical impressions and "draw a picture of yourself" are frequently used tools to assess body image, although these techniques do have limitations.

Chapter 18

The Child's Discovery of His Body

E. James Anthony

I WAS TALKING to a child the other day, and he said to me, in the pontifical manner characteristic of children of a certain age, something that set up a train of thought and led me to a general conception of the subject presented here. What he said was: "The body is a house. It's got an outside and an inside. It's got windows up here (pointing to his eyes) and a door (pointing to his mouth). It's also got a garbage disposer which we haven't even got at home."

To illustrate his statement, he drew me a house, a typical 6-year-old's boxlike structure, but where the windows were he put eyes, and where the door should be, a rounded mouth. I remarked that his house seemed to be all head, and this left him at first a little nonplussed until he recollected that human houses were not sedentary and required legs to get around. Otherwise, it was just the same. His insistence on the analogy reminded me of Freud's remark that "The only typical, regularly occurring representation of the human form as a whole is a house and is symbolized thus in dreams."

I thought I would pursue the matter further with him. "Do you," I asked him, "like living inside your house?" He deliberated this for a moment or two, and then remarked like the oldest inhabitant of a village, "Well, I get a little tired of always being in the same old place with the same old furniture. You know what, I'd like to get out sometime and see what it's like inside other houses. I'd like to try fat houses and thin houses and tall houses and short houses. It must feel funny to live inside the fattest man in the world."

He went on to explain the circumstances further. "It's only when you die that you can come out, and then you don't go into

Reprinted by permission of *Physical Therapy*, *48*:1103-1114 (October) , 1968.

another body, you go to heaven where you don't need bodies." He warmed to his theme. "It's like being locked up for life in prison."

I must confess to having experienced a small spasm of claustrophobia at this point. Having recently been on a diet of somewhat tasteless biscuits, I was immediately reminded of Cyril Connoly's well-known observation that in every fat man there is a thin man struggling to get out. As if conscious of my reaction, he said that he expected that some people liked their body houses and some people didn't, and added that probably a lot of people were living in the wrong houses.

I am always surprised by what I learn from children. Their prehension of facts is often so direct and devastating that one becomes conscious of how much one loses in developing the typical circumlocutional thought of the average adult. One has forgotten how to get to the heart of the matter. Here, in a few sentences, this 6-year-old has summarized some of the theoretical headaches and preoccupations of centuries: the mind-body relationship, the growth of the body image, and the conflict between the actual and the idealized images. He had hinted at the Sheldenian classification of body types into ectomorphic or cerebral, mesomorphic or muscular, and endomorphic or glisceral by his reference to fat, square, and thin houses.

With a final interpretive blast to end the session, he remarked, with apparent sympathy and also some sadism, "Boy, I bet you'd like to change houses!" How could he have known that for years I have been suffering from what one author has referred to succinctly as "body discontentment" and that indeed I was a most conflicted tenant: an endomorph with an ectomorphic personality and mesomorphic aspirations.

What this interview did for me was send me back to some of the sources of our knowledge regarding the body and its mental representation, particularly with reference to the manner in which the individual gets to know them both.

UNITY OF THE BODY

Let me start off with the average adult with an intact brain and body, which would roughly describe me. The relationship which unites me to my body is a curious one, for when I do not think about it, I seem to live as if the union of the somatic and psychological experience was a coherent center from which all my activity radiated. This is a general and undiscriminated experience, but when I stop to consider it, I immediately become aware of its dual character in the two senses that I *am* my body and I *have* my body: on the one side, I feel united to my body, but on the other, I feel almost as if I have a separate existence and that my body is simply something close at hand which I see objectively as part of the external world. The unity of experience has been referred to as senesthesia which is simply the sense of conscious existence. In its dissociated form, the experience comprises the existence of a psychological "me" and the existence of a body "me." This body "me" is not an invariant, the passive outcome of a constant inflow of information from the various bodily parts. It is not a fixed "me" like the sun in a human solar system, receiving messages from the periphery and discharging its energy outward from a fixed point. In fact, it depends very much on the activity of the person. If I tried to construct an image of my body introspectively as I stand before you and I then proceed to sit down, my body "me" becomes differently located. The activity contains my experience and is mine.

It would, therefore, be true to say that my body has me as much as I have my body, which means that the body limits the possibilities of meaning that I can give to my life. And when my body becomes ill, finding a meaning in that illness is like finding a meaning in life and is a process of illuminaton which cannot be absolutely extended. It has its limits, its inaccessibility. As far as the body is concerned, illness has a dark, mysterious aspect to it which cannot be totally illuminated. What the body experiences in illness is sometimes an alteration in the morbid area of function. Parts and organs and functions that are normally silent are brought to our conscious attention. A sort of schism takes place within the body and a part separates out from the complex of our perception of the body, so that the unified feeling of health becomes disrupted. It is this fissure in the unity of the self, this disruption of the "me" feeling that is, in fact, the essence of the sickness. The adult seems to revert to a stage when the body, the body image, and the self are not too well integrated, and, if one adds to this the general pain and malaise, it is not surprising that being ill is really a very peculiar state of affairs.

If this is so far the adult, it is even more so for the child since he seems less able to hold the various pieces together and integrate them into a total experience, so that even more than the adult he may develop alarming feelings of falling apart.

To summarize, body image is not merely an awareness of the physical body; it is not based on perceptions alone, nor is it necessarily an accurate mental representation of the individual's actual body structure. It involves knowledge and awareness of the inside as well as the outside of the body. The picture that we create, flexible, dynamic, is gradually organized by means of all the influences affecting an individual which include constitutional factors, sensory impressions, inner psychic experiences, environmental attitudes, together with the person's interpretation of these influences and their integration into his total personality. The presence of disease or deformity in some part of the body can alter this body image or influence its subsequent organization, as can excessive attention by persons in the individual's environment to the body or some specific part of it. It follows an orderly, maturational process and is constantly changing, undergoing reorganization and elaboration, depending on the individual's present and total life experiences. Some of Alice's experiences in Wonderland can be seen as vivid examples of the fluidity of the child's body image and the pleasure that can be derived from experimentation with it. Simply by eating, Alice can make herself bigger or smaller. I am reminded here of De La Mare's poem about the little child's wonder about his governess, Miss P., and why everything that Miss P. eats, whether it is jam or bread or meat or cake, eventually turns into Miss P. Once again we have the child's fascination with the problem of the body and the self and the way in which the two transact. When asked to consider the self that is Miss P. and its localization, he would be prepared to say that this is scattered diffusely throughout the body, whereas when the question is referred back to himself, he may locate the essential "me" in his arms, his legs, his abdomen, his chest, and, as he grew older, in his head, somewhere between his eyes.

There is no doubt that for most people after a certain age, the self appears to reside somewhere in the head. If you touch the body successively starting from the head and going toward the toes, it will feel almost as if you were going away from some central point. Even when you have reached the toes, however, you are still, as the little boy would say, in your own house, and you know it, and a touch of gout would soon convince you if the feeling was at all ambiguous. This is the human predicament. We have developed an extraordinary self-awareness, unknown to animals, but it is locked up within our bodies, and although we have learned to communicate freely with one another, we are still profoundly separated. It was William James who once said to a friend: "The biggest problem that we have in life is that I cannot feel your toothache." No matter how much communicative spirit there is, our bodies are islands. They are the most "me" things in life, and I am now going to discuss how this human house becomes so much part and parcel of the resident-owner.

THE INFANT CARTOGRAPHER

I have entitled this section "The Infant Cartographer" since it has to do with how the baby gradually maps out the geography of its body in terms of its inlets and protuberances and flatlands and hairy forests. It is a fascinating piece of geography, and, at the beginning, a *terra incognita* that apparently does not seem to belong to the individual who sets about exploring it.

The infant is simultaneously engaged in two important parallel differentiations during the first year of life. At first he has no knowledge of the object world and of his own separateness. He and the world are one, undifferentiated mass of impressions and experiences. His psychological task is to differentiate his "me" from everything that is "not-me." The most important part of the "not-me" is his mother with whom he is in the closest symbiotic tie. His physical task is to differentiate his body from every other solid thing in the world, and, once again, the most important solid object which he must distinguish from his own is his mother's breast and body. In carrying out these two tasks successfully, he establishes boundaries at the edge of his own being between external and internal reality. The mouth is the great organ of primitive reality, and it seems likely that the first feelings of separateness are experienced during the ingestion of food. The mouth is the most mature organ at birth and the most sensitive. It provides the child with his first experience of bodily pleasure in sucking, and it serves two opposing functions, namely the admission of suitable foodstuffs and the exclusion of unwanted matter. Therefore, it constitutes the basis for an early discrimination between external reality which can be taken in or denied admission and internal reality which is always present and constant, the structure of the mouth and the manipulation of the tongue. While the mouth appears to be the first center of perception, the eyes, ears, and hands develop as the child's next perceptual foci. In the beginning, each of these functions independently of all the others; coordination and integration into combined perceptual patterns are lacking. The visual system matures slowly and develops later than the oral system. What the infant sees is not manipulated or brought to the mouth at first. He stares at his legs, feet, arms, and hands in surprise, as if they were strange objects emerging out of a void and disappearing from his view again. Any part of his body that moves out of his perceptual field is regarded as nonexisting, and the child loses interest in it. While eye-ear coordination develops fairly soon, eye-hand coordination takes time, and it is a little later that the eyes learn to converge upon parts of the body that are brought up by the hand. By the third month, the eyes can focus and converge upon bodily movements and follow their course by enlisting head movements to accompany them. Thus, the child's realm of experience expands.

With the attainment of the ability to utilize the combined aid of all the senses in an increasingly well-coordinated manner, the child begins to explore the various parts of his body through touching, scratching, fingering, and various other types of manipulation of his legs, feet, arms, head, and so forth. His awareness of their interrelated functions sharpens. He learns to distinguish not only the parts of his own body, but also the body parts of his mother and other persons in his environment. His prolonged exploration of his body leads to the realization of a distinct "body feeling," and he becomes increasingly conscious of the fact that his own body is different from the bodies of other people and of the inanimate objects in his environment.

Differentiation of the Body

There are several mechanisms at work that help in the differentiation of his body and the establishment of his "body feeling." Pain is one of these factors, and repeated experiences begin to convince him that this is his pain and only he can feel it.

A second mechanism is the strange difference in sensation when he touches his own body in contrast to touching the bodies of others.

In the former situation, two different sets of stimuli are relayed from within his own body boundaries, whereas in the latter instance, only one set of messages is transmitted. Sucking his thumb, therefore, is radically a different experience from sucking his mother's nipple.

A third mechanism that helps him in the process of differentiation is the perception of his image in the mirror which allows him to acquire a more realistic body concept. For the first time in his life, he is confronted with the appearance of his own body as it is seen by other people. His reaction to his image undergoes the same sort of development as his reaction to people. At first, he smiles at it indiscriminately as he smiles at any human face.

Next, he greets it with a wild spasm of distress. He discriminates it as someone who is not his mother or a familiar person, and he treats it like a stranger. A little later still, he takes a huge, evolutionary step forward by recognizing his image in the mirror which animals are unable to do, and he greets his reflected appearance, as the French say, with jubilation. This is an important point in his ego development. The external image is incorporated into the body image and ultimately into the self-concept, and with the ability to form a self-concept, man becomes the only animal that can make himself the object of his own thoughts, perceptions, reflections, and imaginations. The self-concept is also freed from the body concept, and with this dissociation in thought of his self from his body-bound present existence, he is able to engage in long-range planning to gain a more efficient control and mastery over the external environment and to explore his own internal world. Man is the only animal that has an internal world into which he can retreat and reflect. The remainder of the animal world can be either active or asleep. They have nowhere else to go.

The Plastic Body

The development of the plastic body schema is a complex process. The primitive organism experiences proprioceptive and vestibular sensations contributing to the development of what has been termed the postural model of the body. These later become integrated with other sensory impressions such as visual, the auditory, and the olfactory. As the infant becomes increasingly motile, he develops new tactile sensations and begins to acquire an awareness of the relationships of various parts and to distinguish between his own body and those of others. The neurological integration of the body image occurs in the cortex, in the parietal of parieto-occipital regions. Every sensation contributes to the building up of the body image, and there is no fundamental difference between the various sensations in this respect, although some authors have stressed the significance of inner sensations. The important fact is that this internal representation of the body has to be built up. It is an act of creation, not a given. The perceptual process feeds in raw data to the central system which in turn interprets and feeds back to the periphery.

One of the more important discoveries made by Freud related to the fact that certain parts of the body acquired greater significance than others during particular stages of development. These body openings or body protrusions acquired particular emotional importances and, therefore, contributed to the individual's unique body image formation. What Freud described as the psychosexual development of the infant related to this shifting, erotic interest from one part to another, and, based on this, Freud constructed a whole new psychology.

Social factors contribute to the process of body image development, both through the child's reaction to the bodies of others and through the attitudes of others to his body. The child perceives, compares, and identifies his own body with the bodies of those in his environment, and these impressions are interpreted and integrated into his personality according to his own unique psychological mechanisms. Bodily contact with his mother and other significant persons begins the process of incorporation of social factors into the body image. The infant recognizes and reacts to attitudes conveyed to him about his body by physical handling and contacts, whether of approval or disapproval, excessive concern or attention, unrealistic evaluation or dissappointment. These then become part of his self-image, whether accurate or distorted. He identifies also with parts of the bodies of others and in some way incorporates them into his own image and develops certain attitudes toward them. Thus, the parents' body concepts in addition to their attitudes about the child and his body influence his composite body image.

The differentiation between the infant and his mother and between the infant's body and the mother's body proceeds slowly and involves a gradual integration of sensations, perceptions, and responses. Only through the painful experience of losing his mother periodically, says Anna Freud, does the child learn very gradually that the big pleasure-self he has constructed in his mind is not all his own. Parts of it walk away from him and become the environment while other parts remain with him forever. The observer can watch the infant giving increasing evidence that he is learning to recognize the true extent and limits of his own body. Actually, the first insight picture which the human individual has of himself is an image of his body. While adults think in terms of "self," infants think or rather feel in terms of a body. As the infant develops the capacity to give relief or pleasure to himself by rubbing or rocking, this represents his growing independence from his mother and from his identification with her. His perception that his own body contour is separated from that of his mother is necessary before he can develop a true love relationship with her.

The timetable for these different developments is difficult to pinpoint, but, according to Spitz, the separation of I from not-I occurs round about 3 months, the recognition of I at 8 months, and the development of an observable self at 15 months. The development of the body as an object concept, in Piaget's terms, passes through the stages in which the body is simply a fleeting picture that has no substance or permanence or spatial organization. As a result of certain movements, such as grasping, a beginning of permanence is conferred on the body, but there is still no systematic search for it when it is covered. A little later parts of the body will be searched for but without regard for their displacements, and still later the child will take account of changes brought about outside his field of direct perception. In the final stage, he carries an internal image of the various parts of his body, and predominantly searching behavior gives way gradually to predominantly reaching behavior. His body becomes familiar to him, and he can reach for his toes, his nose, his fingers, or his penis at will.

Spatial Image

The spatial image of the body is a little more complex. At first, body space consists of many separate spaces predicated by the various activities of the infant. Thus we have a mouth space, a visual space, an auditory space, a tactile space, postural and kinesthetic spaces, and so forth. These spaces can be more or less interconnected according to the degree of coordination of the different activities which engender them, but they remain primarily heterogeneous in that they are far from constituting a single space in which each one would be situated. Later these different spaces coordinate and become unified, and gradually a single objective space in which the whole body is localized as an object just like other objects in space.

Here are a few illustrations of Piaget's three famous children discovering their bodies gradually during the period of infancy.

1. On the first day of life, Laurent searches for his thumb

which brushed his mouth, and the mouth, as it were, went in pursuit of it.

2. At 4 months, Jacqueline looks at her own hand, then opens and closes it alternately, meanwhile examining it most attentively.

3. At 5 months, Lucienne tries to grasp a rattle about 1 yard away, but ends by grasping her own hands.

4. At 11 months Lucienne hides her feet under a coverlet, then raises the coverlet, looks at them, hides them again, and so on.

5. At 11 months Jacqueline is in her baby swing and perceives her foot through one of the two openings for the use of the legs. She looks at it with great interest and visible astonishment, then stops looking to lean over the edge and discover her foot from the outside. Afterwards, she returns to the opening and looks at the same foot from this perspective. She alternates thus five or six times between the two points of view.

6. At 11 months Piaget holds Jacqueline's feet with his hand, and both are hidden under a coverlet so that she sees neither her feet nor his hand. First she tries to disengage herself, but not succeeding, she leans over and pushes back the part of his arm that is visible, so that his arm is clearly conceived of as the cause of the retention of her foot.

7. At 11 months Lucienne is seated, and Piaget tickles her belly. He then places his hand on the edge of the bassinet. She laughs, waves her hand while watching his, then touches his hand, and tries to push it, and ends by grasping it and bringing it to her belly. It would seem that during this stage the child ceases to consider his own action as the sole source of causality and attributes to someone else's body and aggregate of particular powers.

8. At 1 year and three months, after having with great pleasure heard her mother sing, Lucienne tries to make her continue. She begins by touching her mother's lips with her index finger and pressing lightly. Then, this being inadequate, she stares at her mother's mouth while slowly opening and closing her own.

These illustrate fairly well the development of the body concept and the way in which the infant gradually begins to conceive of his own body as an object in time and space and subject to the laws of causality and different from all other bodies.

The Toddler's Achievement of Body Autonomy

We now pass from the more or less passive infant to the active toddler who begins to achieve a certain amount of body autonomy on the basis of identification with his active mother. He takes over her role toward him in a series of identifications, and with every successful identification he makes his mother less necessary to him, and consequently he begins to resent her restrictions and demands. He is now beginning to see himself as a separate person and shows a sensitivity toward his mother's ambivalence and a vulnerability toward her disappointment. The growth of language now becomes an important tool in the further differentiation of body and not-body and of different parts of the body. The body parts are gradually named and may undergo an elementary classification of nameable and unnameable parts which are mentionable and nonmentionable. The body surface, apart from its original mapping out into various pleasurable and not so pleasurable areas, now develops public and private zones, the latter becoming subjected to systematic concealment from the outside world. In addition, the child may be genuinely puzzled by certain anatomical arrangements, especially in the genital area, and may use single labels to cover different geographical barriers. Depending on the general prudishness of his environment, the child may show differing degrees of curiosity and interest in the unmentionable or untouchable or unnameable parts of his own anatomy as well as in those of others.

Getting control over his bodily function is another big step in his ego development and in the elaboration of his self-concept. The more competent he becomes at bowel or bladder control, the more independent he generally seems to be. At this time, he is particularly sensitive to strangers who manage or manipulate any of his bodily parts, or with any alterations imposed on his body routines, such as times for eating or elimination. If separated from his mother at this stage, he either shows a marked regression in his bodily habits or else in almost a precocious way he begins to look after himself almost like an elderly hypochondriac. He fusses over his body, over his food, over his bowels, all of which substitutes for his missing mother's concern.

The differentiation of self from nonself is accomplished a second time at a new level (what Piaget has referred to as decalage). The toddler is able to observe the separation of his excreta from his body, of something that was body becoming not-body, and of something that was self becoming not-self. Having control over this fact of differentiation creates an enhanced sense of autonomy as if he were in full command over the boundaries of his ego. In this context, I recall Bruno Bettelheim mentioning his arrival in a concentration camp as a young person and an old inhabitant taking him aside and telling him, "If you want to remain psychologically alive, if you want to be your own master, if you want to remain yourself, be sure that every morning you have a good bowel motion. This will be your own doing, and no one can take that away from you." This is the feeling of autonomy that the toddler achieves.

The Preschooler's Realization of Body Differences

If the toddler is interested in body processes, it may be said that the preschooler is interested in body surfaces, and his most important discovery at this stage is that human beings can be classified into two main groups: those who have and those who haven't. The little boy treats this novel piece of knowledge in ways different from that of the little girl. Both respond to what Freud referred to as the castration complex, but both in their different ways. The knowledge may be denied or rationalized. It is a great stimulus to theory building. The little boy hypothesizes that everyone has a penis, including women, and, therefore, he has nothing to worry about. The little girl, for her part, may conclude that her penis is still inside, waiting to come out, or that it may grow, or that penises tend to grow at different rates, some faster and some slower, and that this accounts for the apparent differences to be observed. The dynamic epistemology built up around these questions posed by his body may reach different levels of accuracy depending on the household from which the child comes, the freedom with which he can ask questions, and the readiness with which he receives answers.

Many observations do support the fact that the boy, round about 4 or 5 years, does seem to develop intense pride in his clearly visible genital and has an intermittent urge to use it aggressively and to exhibit it. It seems to become the center of his body feeling, and he soon begins to form a complex of feelings, some associated with intense anxiety that he may lose what he values so highly. His realization that girls lack a penis may lead him to interpret this fact as her having lost or been robbed of it, and he is then apprehensive that a similar fate may befall him. His counterpart, the girl, has a more complex and difficult situation to cope with, as she has nothing visible to show and at first believes that all people are constructed like herself until she finds out that little boys are made differently. Then she may feel overtly cheated and deprived and may resort to blaming her mother for the lack. She may then turn toward her father to receive what she has been denied. In her fantasy, she imagines herself growing such an appendix or robbing her little brother of his. At the same time, she may develop vague fears that her body may be penetrated and injured because of her feminine desires. Her successful identification with her mother may prevent her from any extreme forms of reaction, but during the period of discovery, she may deny the anatomical facts in many different, devious ways. I can well remember two small girls who were being brought up by their divorced mother in a remote part of the country, the mother deliberately rejecting any male contacts. I had brought with me a small baby boy. On that first evening, the two girls watched with inordinate interest whilst the little boy was given his bath, and later the mother overheard the following dialogue from their bedroom. The younger girl to the older: "Did you see *it!*" The older to the younger: "Yes." Significant pause, and then she added: "He's very lucky it doesn't grow on his forehead!"

At puberty, several important bodily changes take place with the development of the secondary sexual characters. For many children, this is a period of great ambivalence; they both want to grow up and take their place among their peers, and at the same time they may resent the dramatic physical changes that are occurring. Nevertheless, the early maturers often find themselves envied by the rest of their group and may exploit the new status granted them by nature. Some recent investigations, however, have shown that early maturers may be social stars to start off with in the nature of their constitution and not become so by reason of their early maturing. Late maturers may have a rough time in a peer group and be filled with a mixture of feelings made up of shame, diffidence, inferiority, and inadequacy. It does them no good to tell them about the developmental spurt or that their bodies will eventually catch up; the trauma lies in the discrepancy around their present predicament. For many young years, the failure to develop adequate breasts reactivates the earlier hurt from their failure to develop adequate penises. The onset of menstruation is received with equally mixed feelings. The mature child, closely identified with her mother's femininity and fully appreciative of her sexual role and reproductive hopes, seems quickly to come to terms with this "little piece of regular suffering." The girl who still has strong, unconscious hopes of developing a penis will look upon the latest innovation with horror and shock and regard it as a confirmation of a castration theory. Physicians and surgeons are often aware that young girls are more difficult to treat or more resistant to treatment at the time of their periods. Several investigations have shown that girls at this time are peculiarly sensitive, difficult, uncooperative, clumsy, and accident-prone.

THE CHILD'S CONCEPTION OF HIS BODY

I have already spoken of the natural epistemology that grows up around the child's understanding of his body and his bodily processes. Even when he is relatively ignorant of parts and functions, he may weave elaborate theories and even construct a conceptual model of his body. We have already seen to what extent the anatomical differences between the sexes act as a stimulus to theory making. Any illness or defect in the child may have a similar result. I once treated a little boy, aged 5, who was referred to me for severe, intractible constipation, headaches, sinus trouble, and a dry, unproductive cough. I found that the little fellow was very aware of his symptoms and that he had elaborated a complex, back-pressure theory to explain them all in a coherent, interrelated framework. The "plops" that didn't come out were turned back and wandered instead into his chest (to give bronchitis), into his face (to produce sinus trouble), and into his head (to produce headaches). In my further investigation of him and other similar cases, I found to my surprise that many of these infantile theories of bodily function were based on primitive notions of animism, magical participation, and phenomenism. The feces, for example, were regarded as being dead, and the child had complete control over them and could regulate their emergence. Once they chose to stay inside him, he regarded them as having a peculiar life of their own, and once they came out on their own as in encopresis or diarrhea, they were also very much alive and capable of all sorts of punitive and treacherous intentions and motivations. This sometimes led to a toilet phobia, the child refusing to go to the bathroom by himself without a great deal of help and encouragement from his mother or her actual presence.

The child's attitude toward its body is closely related to the parents' attitudes toward bodies in general and to the child's body in particular. He will experience guilt or modesty depending on how his basic curiosity and inquisitiveness is handled; he will experience disgust if the parents handle certain parts of his body or his bodily products with disgust, and he will feel shame very much in keeping with the parents' degree of prudishness. Certain parts of his body may be psychologically cordoned off as forbidden, highly dangerous areas, and the child may actually come to believe that the touching of certain structures in the forbidden parts may lead to insanity, neurological degeneration, or some vaguely inferred calamity.

Some interesting techniques for studying the child's conception of the body have been created, and most of these have to do with his external representation or drawing of the body, which is usually understood to mean his body. His physical body, his body image, and his drawn body are felt to be in isomorphic relation to one another.

When the child is immature, dependent, and "undifferenti-ated," his projected body tends to be equally undifferentiated, lacking distinctive sexual characteristics and altogether display-ing what has been referred to as "low body confidence." This poorly put-together picture seems to reflect fairly accurately the poorly put-together body image and self-concept. In general, the head is the first to emerge out of the primordial scribble, the earliest human representations tending to be "cephalopods." With increasing age, the earlier confused concept of parts illogically put together becomes integrated into a recognizable and well-repre-sented human figure. The excellence of the drawing may have to do with a drawing talent, but if the children are blindfolded and then asked to draw a figure, this variable is somewhat better con-trolled. It has been shown, for example, that a blindfolded group of asthmatic children can be differentiated from a blindfolded group of normal children, or a blindfolded group of children with polio of the lower extremities purely on the basis of the figure-drawing differences. There is no doubt that children react to defects or malfunctioning in their body by projecting these into the drawings of themselves. The pathological part is sometimes reduced in size or sometimes amplified. In fact, any preoccupation with a part of a body can lead to its distortion in the drawn per-son. These unconscious reactions to components of one's own body can also be demonstrated by asking individuals to rate a series of photographed hands, for example, in which a photograph of his own hand would be included. Invariably he tends to over-praise or underpraise his own bodily part, although apparently not conscious of doing so. Girls, as compared with boys, tend consistently to pick out smaller bodily parts to indicate their own size, as compared with boys, even when they are not actually small themselves.

Early in this paper, I referred to the projection of the body into set symbolic structures as houses. Erikson has explored the body structure of boys and girls by asking them to construct architectural models out of bricks. Once again, the boys exhibit quite a different form of construction than the girls, and the same fact can be demonstrated when the children are asked to complete incomplete line structures.

Lately, attempts have been made to get children to draw not the body surface, but the inside of the body, and in this test it seems that children make very little reference to internal organs, hardly any at all to the reproductive system, and tend to focus on the skeletal or muscular structure.

Other investigators have made use of a word association approach in which body parts are introduced at random intervals. For example, the child is asked to respond to the word *colon,* and he may answer either with *comma,* or *intestine,* the latter response indicating a greater body preoccupation. It was discovered that the high scorers who made a lot of body references were of two types: a narcissistic type, very much concerned with personal appearance, and the anxious type, very much concerned with pain and damage to the body.

In still another approach, boys and girls were made to wear a distorting lens for a while and then asked about parts of the human figure. It was found that children in general could tolerate more distortion in bodily parts regarding which they feel relatively secure, and that boys, on the whole, distorted more than the girls.

Almost all openings and protuberances in the body tend to attract special interest and to become invested with special feelings. Even when an artificial opening is made into the body, such as a gastrostomy, the same interest builds up around the aperture. At times it may be regarded with embarrassment, humiliation, and even disgust, while at other times it evokes pleasure in its uniqueness, in the attention it seems to get, and in the most voluptuous feelings which it generates when handled. It is gradually incorporated into the body image and may then exert an important influence on the perception of the body as a whole.

Among the many factors that affect the internal representation of the body, an important one is the social and cultural one. From earliest times, the body image is extremely susceptible, as we have already indicated, to the handling given it by the mother, and severe disturbances of the body image may result from deficient physical contact between mother and child, especially when there is inadequate tactile and kinesthetic experience. Many distortions in body size and sexual identity may occur, and a system of somatic delusions may eventually emerge. From a sematic investigation of body language in different cultures, it would seem that there is an idealized body image for a particular culture and that there are shared group norms regarding different body dimensions. In many primitive languages the body dimensions are used to indicate spatial relationships, so that, instead of using such grammatical forms as prepositions, the more primitive languages fall back on references to different parts of the body.

A major cultural factor that operates in the colder climates is clothing, and the body image seems eventually to incorporate the various layers of clothes into the general scholastic schema. The clothes have been seen to operate as an external boundary of the body and set up a complex system of defense in relation to many cultural taboos. It has been noted, for instance, that it is easier to talk to children and with a surprising directness when their clothes are removed. Most parents would substantiate this, having experienced the unabashed observations and confessions in the bathtub.

THE CHILD'S REACTION TO ITS BODILY ILLNESS

Reference has already been made to Adler's theory of organ inferiority in which an individual reacts to a malfunctioning or deficient organ with feelings of inferiority and later compensates for this by an intensified use of the inferior organ. The theory, in fact, generalizes from the inferior organ to the inferior total body image and from that to the inferior self-concept. In the early 1930s, there was a more systematic study of body interest in children and the close relationship between the child's body and the bodies of others who come into contact with him. In one particular investigation, all the children examined presented evidence of physical disease, although these might only be such things as knock-knees, flat feet, and squint. There were many responses indicating special interest in or sensitivity to a part of the body which the children considered inferior. In addition, many of the children complained about the skull—its funny shape, its being big, long, and narrow. Particular interest was also focused on length and strength, for example, of fingers or arms. Of all parts of the body, the visible area was most productive of sensitivity, and a number of the boys, in the stage of prepuberty, objected to the idea of body hair although some accepted it on the face and others had less objection if the hair was light in color. The sensitivity to a discovery on one's own body seemed to draw special attention to the corresponding part in the bodies of others. For instance, a boy with inverted nipples was especially observant of women's breasts. In this particular investigation, it was found that children discover facts about their own body by the talk and observation of others and that family conversations about health, appearance, or illness in the family may also increase the child's interest in his own body. It was fairly easy to correlate special body attitudes and special life problems confronting the children.

The extent to which illness in the family enhances the child's body feelings can be gauged from my own studies in which certain families appear to be vulnerable to pathology in certain parts of their bodies, and it is in these parts that the child tends to develop psychosomatic disorders. This results in large part from what Schilder calls "appersonization" in which an individual identifies with another's emotions, experiences, action, and body image, like an unconscious imitation. The most important processes of identification take place in early childhood, but they never cease throughout our whole life, and as the child gets older, there is a continual "unconscious" wandering of other personalities into his self. There is a continuous blending of body images depending on the closeness and significance of the relationship. In certain overprotective women, the child is very much treated as part of the mother's body schema, so that her own self-absorption or absorption in a certain part of her body directs the child's attention to the corresponding part in his own body. The more symbiotic the relationship, the more this "focal symbiosis," this focal preoccupation with a particular body part chosen in the first place by the mother develops. The physical identification may therefore lead to a focal symbiosis in some cases, a conversion symptom in others, and a *folie à deux* of a hypochondriacal variety in a few. All three contribute to the genesis of hypochondriasis in the child, and ultimately in the adult. The child who does not, developmentally, disconnect his own body from that of his mother's is liable to begin experiencing her pathology. The vulnerability of the child in this respect is very much a function of the efficacy of his ego boundaries. When these boundaries are weak, psychological penetration into the body becomes more possible, and when the barrier is strong, the intrusions are deflected at the surface. Using the Rorschach test, the body vulnerability has been investigated in various conditions. It has been found, for example, that chronic disease produces marked disturbances in the body image which can be studied in the light of somatic symptomatology. It was found that individuals whose body awareness concentrates more on the external parts of the body (the skin and the musculature) can be differentiated from an awareness that focuses on internal features such as visceral sensations.

Occurrence of a disfiguring injury in a child or a recurrent somatic illness focuses attention on the particular affected part and distorts or modifies the child's incorporation of this organ into his total body image. He may deny the presence of the condition, as in the phantom limb, or he may become excessively interested in the affected organ. He may show a compulsive interest in that body part in other persons. Conversely, the presence of an emotional disturbance can also have modifying and distorting effects on the body image or the psychological significance of certain parts. One part of the body may be symbolically substituted for another part, or it may become the site or a somatic expression of an internal conflict.

Some investigators have indicated that children who develop body image disturbances following an injury or other deformity are those whose personality and environment contributed to a distorted or to an unrealistic "ideal" body image prior to the onset of the condition. Denial or minimizing of a disfigurement or deformity either by the child or his parents can result in a body image unrelated to actual body structure. The underlying adequacy of the body image will influence the person's reaction to a disruption of the body structure, just as the individual's underlying personality will influence the degree and manifestation of emotional disturbance in psychological disabilities. Psychotic children often show marked body image distortions, generally more bizarre and unrelated to reality than other types of disturbance. They may express ideas that the body or a certain part is changing, growing smaller or larger. They may experience all sorts of subjective bodily sensations and distortions. The figure drawings by schizophrenic children often mirror this bizarre body image disturbance with distortions in size and shape, displacement of bodily parts, fluidity, and lack of boundaries. In adolescence, body image disturbances are frequently concerned with the hair and the skin, and these are occasionally among the presenting symptoms of adolescent schizophrenia. Children with organic brain damage also show body image distortion and seem unable to integrate their experiences into an adequate body image well oriented in space. They are best approached therapeutically on an understanding of their body image disorganization and their disorientation in a physical environment to which they cannot adequately relate.

Body image disturbances may be profound in severe physical illnesses such as tuberculosis or congenital heart disease, and management of these conditions should include recognition of the body image problems. The same is especially true of children who suffer with obesity.

Although figure drawings by children with physical disabilities reveal varying characteristics depending on the child's adjustment to his disability, the attitude of his environment, the related body image disturbances, the majority may reveal their disability in more indirect ways, such as distortion, amplification, minimization, or some elaboration of the affected part. There are children, however, who show no evidence of physical disability in their drawings which can be understood as a projection of their "ideal" body image.

Children with organic diseases and children with epilepsy tend to draw figures with broad feet firmly planted on the ground, indicating a need for physical support. When the child is anxious or preoccupied with certain specific parts of his body, his enhanced interest may show similar distortions in his figure drawing even when there is a complete absence of actual physical deformity. For this reason, figure drawings cannot be interpreted rigidly and arbitrarily, but only in relation to the total evaluation of the child and his unique body image problem.

CONCLUSION

In this paper, I have ranged over such topics as the child's gradual discovery and recognition of his external and internal body and with his representation of his body both in his mind and as he projects it into the external environment. There seems to be no doubt that the representation of his body undergoes distortion with every illness or abnormality that affects his body and that the understanding of this specific disturbance may be of great importance in his treatment, especially in its prognosis. It is important, as Bender points out, that the physician and therapist be aware of and look for problems in this area in every one of their patients so that they can better guide both child and parent toward a more constructive psychological attitude toward both his body and his actual disability.

Handedness, the preferential use of one hand for certain activities, has been a topic of speculation for many years. Both heredity and experience have been posited as the basis for hand dominance, although the prevalent view at present tends to support the genetic interpretation. It is interesting to note that many cultures, both ancient and current, favored the right-handed individual, and training to force right-handedness in infants still occurs. Recently, attempts have been made to relate left-hand preference or mixed laterality to language and reading difficulties. Opinion varies, with some denying the existence of a relationship, some speaking of a significant relationship, while others suggest that problems in reading and laterality may coexist but not necessarily be correlated. Drs. Belmont and Birch discuss this point tangentially in their paper; however, the main focus of their study is a detailed chronology of lateral preferences in eye, hand, and foot usage, and awareness of right-left relations. Developmental milestones such as these are important as we assess and observe the changes in children's behavior.

Chapter 19

Lateral Dominance and Right-Left Awareness in Normal Children

LILLIAN BELMONT AND HERBERT G. BIRCH

O NE OF THE NORMAL PATTERNS of developmental change consists in the establishment of hand preferences for skilled manual activities. In addition, the development of such consistent preferences in the majority of individuals bears a systematic relation to the establishment of preponderant usage in other bilaterally represented functions such as vision and lower limb utilization. Knowledge of the details of the development of such preferences in normal children is of especial importance because of the emphasis which has been placed upon the significance of this feature of development for normal educational functioning,[8,9] language and reading functions,[11] and personality patterning.[3]

Despite the existence of a large body of normative evidence on lateralization,[9] little information is available as to the ages at which various aspects of lateralization come to be established. A qualitative approach to this problem was made in an early study by Gesell and Ames,[6] and evidence for some specific ages has been reported by Harris for lateral dominance[8] and by Benton[1] for right-left discrimination. However, both these age-specific analyses have covered a restricted age range.

A further complication preventing a clear understanding of the development of laterality is that different methods have been used for determining lateral dominance. Consequently, it is diffi-

From *Child Development, 34*:257-270, 1963. Copyright 1963 by the Society for Research in Child Development, Inc. Reprinted by permission.

This investigation was supported by Grant B-3362 of the National Institutes of Health. National Institute of Neurological Diseases and Blindness, and the Association for the Aid of Crippled Children.

The authors wish to express their gratitude to Juliet Bortner, who participated in the collection of data, and to the West Hempstead School District, which made it possible to conduct this and other studies in their schools.

cult to determine whether reported differences are the result of the differences in the samples of children tested or of the test methods used for determining dominance. In addition, since it has been claimed by many[9] that preferential hand usage in children may be significantly affected by cultural milieu and contemporary styles in the amount of pressure applied to children to cause them to use the right hand, consideration at the present time must necessarily be based on evidence derived from children who have been raised in the current atmosphere of childrearing practices. The problems arising from the above considerations can be resolved by obtaining contemporary data on age specificities in the establishment of lateral dominance.

A second issue with which we have been concerned is the question of right-left awareness. The ability to make reliable right-left discriminations both with reference to the child's own body and to the surrounding environment represents another aspect of lateralized functioning which follows a recognizable developmental course,[12] and disturbance in this area has been related to developmental dysfunctions in a manner very similar to that ascribed to preference in lateral usage.[10,8] Although information is available indicating a small positive relation between discriminative function and handedness,[2] little information is available concerning the relation, if any, between right-left discrimination and a fuller spectrum of preferential usage involved in eyedness and eye-hand preferences. These questions could be answered by obtaining contemporary information on the development of right-left discrimination in the same children in whom the general development of lateral dominance was being studied.

The present study, therefore, is concerned with the analysis of age specificity in preferential lateral usage, the development of right-left awareness, and the relation between the two sets of functions in normal children of school age.

METHOD

Subjects

The subjects studied were 148 children drawn from a suburban elementary school for intellectually normal children. The class placement of children ranged from kindergarten through sixth grade with ages from 5 years, 3 months, to 12 years, 5 months. The number of boys was equal to the number of girls and the two sexes were insignificantly different in IQ, grade placement and age. Selection from the whole school population was made from a master list containing the names of children from kindergarten through sixth grade whose parents had given permission for testing. Within this list, selection at each grade level was on a random basis. Otis Quick-Scoring Tests of Mental Ability were available for all children from the third grade level through the sixth grade. The parents of the children were either in skilled or professional occupations and of middle-class socioeconomic standing. As may be seen from Table 19-I, in which salient characteristics of the sample are presented, the mean IQ was significantly above the general population average, as would be expected on the basis of the socioeconomic groups to which the families of the children belonged.

TABLE 19-I

Age, Sex, and IQ of Subjects

	N	C A Mean	SD	I Q* Mean	SD
Male	74	8-3	2-0	119.8	10.4
Female	74	8-2	2-0	120.2	10.3
Total	148	8-2	2-0	120.0	10.3

*IQ (Otis Quick-Scoring Test of Mental Ability) available for 65 subjects (32 boys; 33 girls) 8 years and older who were routinely tested in school.

Procedure

All children were taken from the classroom by the examiner and tested individually. Lateral dominance was studied first and was followed by the testing of right-left awareness. All testing was conducted in a single session.

HAND PREFERENCE. Lateral preference was tested for hand, eye, and foot. The subjects were required to respond in pantomime to hand preference items. The following four items were used:

a. *Ball throwing.* The experimenter says, "This is how I throw a ball." (demonstrates) "Now let me see you throw a ball."

b. *Turning door knob.* The experimenter says, "I turn a door knob this way." (demonstrates) "Let me see how you turn a door knob."

    c. *Scissor cutting.* The experimenter says, "I cut with scissors this way." (demonstrates) "Let me see how you do it."

    d. *Writing.* The experimenter says, "When I write with a pencil, I move my hand this way." (demonstrates) "Let me see how you move your hand with a pencil when you write."

The hand used by the child for each of these pantomime activities was recorded.

EYE PREFERENCE. In determining eyedness, three tasks were used, a kaleidoscope, a toy rifle, and a square of paper with a $\frac{1}{2}$-inch square hole in the center.

    a. *Kaleidoscope.* The child was handed the kaleidoscope and told, "Look through this."

    b. *Rifle sighting.* The experimenter handed the child the toy rifle and asked, "Do you know how to aim a rifle?" If the child said "Yes," he was asked to do so. If the child said "No," he was told to "close one eye, look through the hole, hold it on your shoulder and make believe you are going to shoot."

    c. *Paper with hole.* E handed the child a 6-inch square of paper with a $\frac{1}{2}$-inch square hole in the center. The child was told, "Look at me through this hole."

The eye which was used was noted for each task.

FOOT PREFERENCE. Foot preference was determined by studying kicking. The experimenter placed a ball 5 inches in diameter on a plastic wedge which was located on the floor. The child was instructed to "kick the ball." After the spontaneous foot usage, the examiner instructed the child to kick the ball with the other foot. Examiner noted the foot first used and which kick was more skillfully executed. When there was no clear-cut difference between the two feet in level of skill, the child was asked, "Which foot do you like to kick with better?"

RATING CRITERIA FOR LATERAL DOMINANCE. Handedness was scored as "right" if all four tasks were mimicked with the right hand; "left" if all four tasks were done with the left hand; "mixed" if in the series of four tasks there was any inconsistency in hand usage.

The subject was judged as right- or left-eyed if he used the given eye consistently on all three of the tasks. The subject was rated "mixed" if on any occasion he was inconsistent in eye usage.

The foot spontaneously chosen for first kick was scored as the preferred foot. If the preferred foot was superior in its performance to the nonpreferred one, preference and dominance were the same. If the nonpreferred foot functioned better, dominance was rated as mixed. Following Harris' standards,[7] footedness was rated as "mixed" if performance on both feet was equally skilled.

AWARENESS OF RIGHT-LEFT RELATIONS. In order to test the child's ability to make right-left discriminations on own body parts, two tests were used. One was a three-item test in which the following questions were asked: (1) Raise your right hand. (2) Touch your left ear. (3) Point to your right eye. The other test had four items: (1) Show me your right hand. (2) Now show me your left hand. (3) Show me your right leg. (4) Now show me your left leg. These last four items form part of the Piaget schedule.

In addition, each subject was asked to respond to a series of other questions derived from Piaget[12] concerning awareness of right-left relations on other than own body. The tasks designed by Piaget include the identification of lateralization on the body of the examiner facing the child, as well as the degree to which awareness of right-left object relations exists. The conditions and questions involved in these tasks are indicated below. All responses were recorded, and any item was scored as correct if all of its component parts were answered appropriately.

RIGHT-LEFT AWARENESS ITEMS (PIAGET)

1. Show me your right hand. ——— Now show me your left hand. ———
   Show me your right leg. ——— Now show me your left leg. ———

2. (*E* sits opposite *S*)   Show me my right hand. ————
   Now my left. ———— Show me my right leg. ————
   Now my left leg. ————

3. (Place coin on table left of a pencil in relation to *S*.)
   Is the pencil to the right or to the left? ————
   And the penny—is it to the right or to the left? ————
   (Have *S* go around to the opposite side of table and repeat questions.)
   Is the pencil to the right or to the left? ————
   And the penny—is it to the right or to the left? ————

4. (*S* is opposite *E*; *E* has a coin in right hand and a bracelet [or watch] on left arm.) You see this penny. Have I got it in my right hand or in my left? ———— And the bracelet. Is it on my right arm or my left? ————

5. (*S* is opposite three objects in a row: a pencil to the left, a key in the middle, and a coin to the right.)
Is the pencil to the left or to the right of the key? ————
Is the pencil to the left or to the right of the penny? ————
Is the key to the left or to the right of the penny? ————
Is the key to the left or to the right of the pencil? ————
Is the penny to the left or to the right of the pencil? ————
Is the penny to the left or to the right of the key? ————

A separate analysis was made of all questions relating to right-left discrimination of the parts of the child's own body.

RESULTS

Lateral Dominance

The overall results on lateralization of hand, eye, and foot functioning, as well as hand-eye interrelations, in our sample of children are presented in Tables 19-II and 19-III. As may be seen

TABLE 19-II

Laterality Preferences for the Group of Normal Children

		*Age-specific Percentages**						
		5-3 to	6-0 to	7-0 to	8-0 to	9-0 to	10-0 to	11-0 to
	Totals	5-11	6-11	7-11	8-11	9-11	10-11	11-11
Category	N = 148	N = 23	N = 25	N = 28	N = 20	N = 17	N = 14	N = 18
Handedness								
Right	113 (76%)	87	60	75	75	82	79	83
Left	14 (10%)	5	12	4	10	12	21	6
Mixed ...	21 (14%)	9	28	21	15	6	0	11
Eyedness								
Right	78 (53%)	44	52	43	60	41	57	78
Left	31 (21%)	31	20	21	15	24	29	6
Mixed ...	39 (26%)	26	28	36	25	35	14	17
Footedness								
Right	125 (85%)	83	88	89	80	88	79	83
Left	17 (12%)	9	8	7	15	12	21	11
Mixed ...	6 (4%)	9	4	4	5	0	0	6
Hand-Eye								
Consistent	17 (48%)	39	36	36	50	41	78	67
Crossed ..	24 (16%)	31	16	14	15	24	8	6
Mixed ...	53 (36%)	31	48	50	35	35	14	28

*Age 12 omitted because of small *N*.

Readings in Early Development

TABLE 19-III

Age Differences in Laterality Preferences

	5-3 to 5-11	6-0 to 6-11	7-0 to 7-11	8-0 to 8-11	9-0 to 9-11	10-0 to 10-11	11-0 to 11-11	12-0 to 12-5	χ^2	df	p†
Handedness											
Right and Left	39		39			49					
Mixed	9		9			3			4.71	2	<.05
Eyedness											
Right and Left	17	18	18	15	11	12	18				
Mixed	6	7	10	5	6	2	3		4.58	6	<.30
Footedness											
Right and Left	45		46		31		20				
Mixed	3		2		0		1		. . .	.	ns
Hand-Eye											
Consistent	9	9	10	10	7	11	12	3			
Crossed and Mixed	14	16	18	10	10	3	6	0	15.45	7	<.02

*Because of the nature of the distributions, it was at times necessary to combine age groups to satisfy the requirements for the use of the chi square test.

†One-tailed test because of directional nature of hypothesis.

from Table 19-II, the children as a whole are predominantly right-handed (76%), 10 percent are left-handed, and 14 percent have handedness which is rated as "mixed." The mixed group is composed of eleven subjects who were preponderantly right-handed in their responses, five subjects who were preponderantly left-handed, and five who exhibited equal right- and left-handed preference. Since the largest number of subjects in the mixed group were in the younger ages, the subjects in the mixed category are a composite of stably mixed individuals and of younger children in whom hand preference has not yet been fully established. If the criterion is lowered and the children who show only single instances of inconsistency in hand preference are included in the dominant group, then the percentages of right-handed and left-handed children increase at the expense of the mixed group. We then find that 13 percent exhibit left preference, 84 percent right preference, and 3 percent remain as truly mixed. The figure of 13 percent left-handed is higher than the percentage usually reported in the general population and may be a reflection of some relaxation in contemporary pressures used in the social induction of hand usage in children.

On the basis of our findings, eye preference does not exhibit the same degree of lateralization as does handedness. More than 25 percent of the children in the age range studied failed to exhibit clear-cut preferential use of one eye and so were rated as mixed. Of the remaining children, 53 percent are consistently right-eyed and 21 percent show left-eye preference. The age specificity of both eye and hand preference will be considered below.

Of all our findings, the one which exhibits the most clear-cut and earliest established preference in usage is footedness. Over 95 percent of the children show clear-cut lateral dominance in foot usage. Only 4 percent showed mixed foot dominance. Within the age range considered no significant difference in degree of foot lateralization is to be found on an age-specific basis (Table 19-III). Thus, by the time the children are in the sixth year of life, preferential foot utilization has already been clearly established. For this reason, an age-specific consideration of footedness is not possible in our sample and would require the study of younger children.

The age specificity of hand and eye preferences may be determined from an inspection of Tables 19-II and 19-III. Table 19-II presents our first order data in terms of age-specific percentages. Table 19-III presents these data in terms of the actual number of cases at various age categories for statistical tests of significance. It will be noted in Table 19-III that right and left preferences are treated as a single variable since we are interested in the developmental course of consistent preferential usage as opposed to mixed usage, rather than in either right or left usage as such. Because of the nature of the distributions, it was at times necessary to combine age groups to satisfy the requirements for the use of the chi-square test.

It is apparent from Table 19-II that mixed handedness is most pronounced in the 6-, 7-, and 8-year-old subjects, but is not evident in the 5-year-old group. It can be seen from the table that mixed handedness characterizes the younger children far more frequently than it does the older ones. These age differences in hand usage are significant at the .05 level of confidence (Table 19-III). As may be seen from Table 19-II, the tenth year of life

appears to be the one at which a high level of consistency in preferential hand usage becomes established. At this age, the developmental curve appears to become asymptotic to the age base.
When the handedness of children below 9 years was contrasted
with the handedness above this age, there was a statistically significant difference ($x^2 = 3.66$; $df = 1$; p $< .03$, one-tailed) between
the two age groups. This suggests that for populations similar to
the one studied age 9 may represent a useful indicator for the existence of reliably established preferential hand usage, when our
criterion of 100 percent consistency in the four-handedness tasks is
employed.

    A similar trend may be found in the establishment of clear-cut
preferences in monocular eye usage (Table 19-II). The level of
mixed eyedness is greater in the younger than in the older age
groups. While the age differences in eyedness do not achieve an
acceptable level of statistical significance (Table 19-III), an examination of the individual cells does appear to show an increase
in right and left eyedness from age 10. When the data were analyzed using age 10 as a cut-off point, statistically significant differences were found between the younger and older children ($x^2 =$
2.67; $df = 1$; $p < .05$, one-tailed). In large part, this results from
the fact that there was a larger proportion of mixed eyedness in
the group below 10 years.

    The relation of preferential hand to preferential eye usage is
also considered in Table 19-II. As may be seen, approximately
one half of the total group exhibits ipsilateral preferences. The
other half of the group shows a pattern of inconsistency in preferential lateral usage. This is expressed either through the contralateral use of hand and eye or as the ill-established dominance in
either one of these functions. In terms of the age specificity of eye-
hand relations, it may be seen that there is a general tendency for
ipsilateral utilization of hand and eye to increase with age. Conversely, as the children grow older a smaller proportion of individuals exhibit mixed or cross hand-eye usage. As may be seen in
Table 19-III, hand-eye relations show highly significant age differences ($x^2 = 15.45$; $p < .02$), which are also reflected in a reliable
difference in functioning in children below and above age 10 (x^2

$= 11.37$; $df = 1$; $p < .001$). Thus, by the age of 10, eye-hand dominance interrelations appear to be reliably stabilized, and children above this age are significantly more ipsilateral.

Since there have been repeated reports[4,9] that left-handedness and confusion in lateralization occur more frequently in boys than in girls, our data were examined for sex differences in preferential hand usage. These findings are summarized in Table 19-IV. In our group of normal children no significant sex differences in handedness were found. On an absolute basis the girls showed somewhat more of a tendency (not statistically significant) to be left- or mixed-handed than did the boys. These findings agree with other current reports[5,8] in which no reliable sex differences in handedness were found.

TABLE 19-IV

Hand Preferences in Boys and Girls

	Right	*Left*	*Mixed*
Boys $(N = 74)$	59 (80%)	6 (8%)	9 (12%)
Girls $(N = 74)$	54 (73%)	8 (11%)	12 (16%)

Right-Left Awareness

The second set of issues with which we have been concerned in the present investigation is the awareness of right-left relations. The study of this awareness involved at least two general features. The first of these was awareness by the child of the lateralization of the parts of his own body. The second concerned awareness of lateral placement of objects in the environment including parts of other individuals located at 180 degrees to the child.

In Tables 19-V and 19-VI our findings on the age-specific awareness of left-right relations on own body are considered. As may be seen from these tables, failures, when they occur, were to be found in the younger age groups. These age differences are statistically significant. In the 5- and 6-year-olds, there was a larger percentage of children who failed one or more of the seven questions (consisting of three of our own items plus four of Piaget's items), which tapped ability to distinguish left from right on own body parts. Rarely were these children characterized by complete

TABLE 19-V

Age-specific Percentages of Accuracy in Right-left
Discrimination of Own Body Parts

				Percentage Failed a Given No. of Questions						
Age	N	Percentage Passed All Questions	1	2	3	4	5	6	7
5-3 to 5-11	23	70	13	9	0	0	4	0	4
6-0 to 6-11	25	68	4	12	4	12	0	0	0
7-0 to 7-11	28	89	4	0	4	4	0	0	0
8-0 to 8-11	20	95	0	0	5	0	0	0	0
9-0 to 9-11	17	94	6	0	0	0	0	0	0
10-0 to 10-11	14	100	0	0	0	0	0	0	0
11-0 to 11-11	18	100	0	0	0	0	0	0	0
12-0 to 12-5	3	100	0	0	0	0	0	0	0

failure to distinguish left from right but rather by an occasional
confusion. However, in the present sample even the youngest children were frequently able to be entirely correct in their ability to
distinguish left and right on their own bodies.

TABLE 19-VI

Age Differences in Accuracy of Right-left Discrimination
of Own Body Parts

	Age Ranges			χ^2	df	p
	5-3 to 6-11	7-0 to 8-11	9-0 to 12-5			
Passed all questions.........	33	44	51			
Failed one or more questions	15	4	1	19.91	2	.001

As may be seen from an inspection of Table 19-V, 95 percent
of the children above 7 years of age make correct responses to all
seven questions concerned with the lateralization of their own
body parts. In contrast, only 69 percent of the children below 7
years of age in our sample correctly answered all questions regarding own body parts. (The significance of the difference in performance between children under 7 and those over this age is at
the .001 level of confidence.) It is of interest to note that the accuracy of right-left awareness of own body parts antedates the
clear-cut establishment of hand preference by two years and of
eyedness and eye-hand consistency by three years.

Table 19-VII presents a comparison of our findings on the ages
at which the subjects passed the various items on the Piaget sched-

TABLE 19-VII

Comparison of Group with Piaget Age Norms on
Left-Right Conceptions

| | *Item No. Passed** | |
	Our Sample	*Piaget Norms*
Age 5	1	1
Age 6	1	1
Age 7	1, 3, 4	1, 3
Age 8	1, 2, 3, 4	1, 2, 3, 4
Age 9	1, 2, 3, 4	1, 2, 3, 4
Age 10	1, 2, 3, 4	1, 2, 3, 4
Age 11	1, 2, 3, 4, 5†	1, 2, 3, 4, 5

*75 percent or more of group passed item.
†72 percent of group passed.

ule of awareness of right and left with those that he has reported.[12] We followed Piaget's procedure and used 75 percent of the
children for any age correct on an item as the criterion for considering an item passed by this age group. Using this criterion, we
found that there was a remarkable agreement in the development
of right-left conceptions in our group and in his. The only apparent discrepancies were that at age 7 our group was able to distinguish the lateral placement of objects on another person's body
(item 4) whereas Piaget's group could not. The findings reported
in Table 19-VII indicate that by age 7 our group is able successfully to distinguish right-left relations on own body parts and on
another person's body placed at 180 degrees to him. However, the
ability to distinguish object lateralization in the environment did
not stabilize until age 11 (item 5). It should be noted that the
criterion for passing is less stringent in this analysis than in the
one presented in Table 19-V.

Right-left awareness was studied in relation to a variety of
other factors. No consistent relation was found between the level
of performance on items of right-left awareness and any other
factor of lateral preference studied (chi-square analysis by age).
There were no significant sex differences in level of performance.
Grade placement was not related in any reliable fashion to right-
left awareness, although there was some tendency for the children
of the same chronological age level who were in higher grades
(e.g. 7-year-olds placed in grade 2 rather than 1) to function some-

what better than did their age mates. There were no reliable differences in performance when right-left awareness was related to IQ within the range represented in our sample.

DISCUSSION

The findings of the present study will be considered in connection with three issues: (1) age specificity in the development of lateralization; (2) the relation between right-left discrimination and lateralization of function; and (3) the implications of age specificity in lateralization and right-left discrimination for the etiology of reading disability.

The question of age specificity in the development of lateralization has received too scant attention. An indication of the age span within which laterality in function becomes stabilized is of especial importance if lateralization is to be used as one of the diagnostic indicators of developmental abnormality in children. An early attempt at age-specific treatment may be found in the report of Gesell and Ames[6] who present some qualitative findings. Although their qualitative findings are suggestive, they do not provide any firm statistical basis for deciding when stable lateral preference is to be expected in the normally developing child. In more recent reports, the studies by Harris[8] and Benton[1] provide some additional data on age-specific functioning.

Although Harris has presented data on the distribution of lateral dominance in hand, eye, and foot usage for two age groups, 7- and 9-year-olds, our findings suggest that these ages do not provide the most significant points for analysis of the developmental course of lateralization. On the basis of our analysis of the ages at which functions become stabilized in the present sample, we would differentiate between ambilaterality in handedness which occurs before age 9 and that which occurs after that time, since we found a critical break at this age in the number of children in the present sample who exhibited mixed handedness. In addition, our findings indicate that the development of preferential handedness is by no means a continuously developing function since the level of consistent preferential usage exhibited by our 5-year-old kindergarten group is not again achieved until the age of 9 years.

This finding is in general agreement with the observation of Gesell and Ames that preferential hand usage is subject to peaks and troughs on an age-specific basis. It would be of considerable interest to explore the reorganizational changes in functioning that underlie these changes in preference.

In considering correspondence between eye and hand usage, we found that a chronological age of 10 was modal for the normal establishment of ipsilaterality. Prior to this age, less than half of the children exhibited consistent ipsilateral hand-eye usage. Since normal children below the age of 9 show evidences of both incomplete lateral preference and hand-eye ambilaterality until the age of 10, the usefulness of such findings for the definition of developmental pathology in younger age groups is of questionable value. If, however, consistent lateral preference and ipsilateral usage of hand and eye do not develop in subsequent years, the findings may be viewed as suggestive of developmental aberration, since it may be indicative of a lag in normal developmental function.

Benton[1] presents data on normative aspects of right-left discrimination in terms of norms for ages 6 through 9. Because of the limitation in the age range he has studied, he has stated that "it is not possible to specify the exact age at which the level of average adult performance is achieved" (p. 27) since his data on the performances of children above 9 are incomplete. However, it is clear from his formulation that age specificity in this function is a problem which he believes to be of major importance. On the basis of our data on bright normal children from a middle-class background, the age of 7 appears to be critical for the development of the ability to distinguish left and right in relation to one's own body parts. Subsequent to this age, up to the age of 12, little significant improvement in this ability takes place, and from age 10 onward all children studied pass all questions asked. When the demand was shifted from own body parts to objects in the external environment, fully accurate right-left awareness was not stabilized in ages below the 11-year-old group.

In our findings no simple relation was found to exist between the establishment of lateral preference in hand usage and the development of the ability to discriminate right from left. Children of a given age in whom preferential hand usage was clearly established did not differ significantly in their ability to distinguish right from left from children of the same age in whom preferential hand usage had not yet come to be firmly established. Conversely, at a given age the ability accurately to discriminate right from left did not permit the prediction of preferential lateralization in hand usage. When considered age specifically, it was found that accurate right-left discrimination, at least of own body parts, preceded the stabilization of lateral hand preference by approximately two years.

Considerable interest attaches to the fact that discrimination of right and left antedates the development of consistent lateral hand usage. It makes it highly improbable that the development of right-left awareness (which develops earlier) is dependent upon consistent lateralization of hand usage (which occurs two years later). A more parsimonious interpretation would view the two functions as independent aspects of development. If this position is taken, the implications that have been drawn between the development of hand preference and reading disability must be reassessed.

Numerous workers[8,11] have reported a relation between reading disability and lag in lateralization in function. At times there has even been the implication, as Benton has noted, that such delay in maturation of lateral dominance may be etiologically related to reading dysfunction because of the frequently expressed assumption that right-left discrimination, necessary in the reading task, requires preferential lateral hand usage for its establishment. An age-specific analysis of both right-left discrimination and lateralization of functions raises questions about the validity of this chain of reasoning. Our own data indicate that the establishment of reliable right-left discrimination antedates by several years the development of consistent lateralized preferences in hand usage. An even greater lag exists between preferential eye dominance and right-left discriminative capacity. It is therefore most unlikely that visual discrimination and awareness of the difference of right from left is dependent upon preferential hand or eye usage. It is far more likely that developmental lag in lateralization and evidence of reading disability are independent manifestations of a more general underlying disturbance in neurological organization and are not etiologically related to one another. A similar line of reasoning can be applied to those studies in which lags in the establishment of lateral dominance have been related to emotional and personality disorders.[3]

SUMMARY

Lateral preferences in hand, eye, and foot usage and awareness of right-left relations were examined in 148 bright normal children from a suburban school system. It was found that clear-cut establishment of hand and eye preferences could be analyzed on an age-specific basis and that ambilaterality more frequently characterized the younger age groups. Discrimination of right-left relations also followed a developmental course with all aspects of discrimination, including own body parts, other person opposite the subject, and object relations in the environment, tending to become stabilized at age 11. Right-left discrimination of own body parts is clearly stabilized at age 7, two years prior to the establishment of consistent handedness and three years prior to the stabilization of eyedness and eye-hand preferences. The presence of deviancy in these two functions in younger children was considered to be of questionable diagnostic value. The appearance of right-left discrimination on own body parts at an earlier age than the clear-cut establishment of handedness suggests that these functions are independent. This was discussed in relation to the question of the etiology of reading disability.

REFERENCES

1. Benton, A. L. *Right-left Discrimination and Finger Localization.* New York, Hoeber-Harper, 1959.
2. Benton, A. L., and Menefee, F. L. Handedness and right-left discrimination. *Child Develop., 28:*237-242, 1957.
3. Blau, A. *The Master Hand: A Study of the Origin and Meaning of Right and Left Sidedness and Its Relation to Personality and Language.* Amer. Orthopsychiat. Ass., 1946.
4. Brain, R. W. Speech and handedness. *Lancet, 2:*837-842, 1945.
5. Falek, A. Handedness: a family study. *Amer. J. Hum. Genet., 11:*52-62, 1959.

6. Gesell, A., and Ames, L. B. The development of handedness. *J. Genet. Psychol., 70:*155-175, 1947.

7. Harris, A. J. *Harris Tests of Lateral Dominance,* 3rd ed. Psychol. Corp., 1947. (Manuel)

8. Harris, A. J. Lateral dominance, directional confusion, and reading disability. *J. Psychol., 44:*283-294, 1957.

9. Hildreth, G. The development and training of hand dominance. *J. Genet. Psychol., 75:*197-275, 1949, *76:*39-144, 1950.

10. Kennard, M. A. Value of equivocal signs in neurologic diagnosis. *Neurology, 10:*753-764, 1960.

11. Orton, S. T. *Reading, Writing and Speech Problems in Children.* New York, Norton, 1937.

12. Piaget, J. *Judgment and Reasoning in the Child.* Kegan Paul, 1928.

T HE FOLLOWING study by Dr. Elizabeth Gellert analyzes how children lateralize front view figures of human beings. Awareness of lateralization involves an orientation to objects in the environment which probably includes a developmental progression of multisensory integration. Many young children do not attend to the spatial orientation of objects. For example, the letters *p*, *q*, *b*, and *d* may all appear to be the same to the young child. This inability to analyze spatial orientation may indicate the child is focusing on the whole stimulus rather than on discrete, salient cues. It is interesting to note that some of the younger children in Dr. Gellert's study devised their own problem-solving technique to lateralize human figure drawings—they turned their bodies to duplicate the pictorial representation and then they were able to transpose spatial elements. The author found age, sex, and intelligence related to the type of lateralization chosen by the child.

Chapter 20

Children's Lateralizations of Human Figures: Analysis of a Developmental Transition

Elizabeth Gellert

INTRODUCTION

THE PRESENT study grew out of attempting to resolve the following question: which side of a frontal, two-dimensional self-likeness do children spontaneously consider to refer to the right and left, respectively, of their real body? That is, do children lateralize such figures as though they were mirror-like *reflections* of themselves (in which case corresponding body parts would be located directly opposite their own), or do they *transpose orientations,* so that they consider the right (or left) side of their real body to correspond to the side that is *diagonally across* (rather than directly opposite) from it in the replica? Unlike situations wherein one is faced by *another person,* a little deliberation will make it apparent that no pervasive perceptual or logical grounds exist for preferring either type of lateralization in relation to a face-on representation of the *self.* It is valid to think of such self-images as being unreversed—as they would appear in a mirror; it is equally cogent to view them as though their sides were reversals of the self—as in a photograph. Both types of self-representation are encountered by children who live in environments where mirrors, photographs, and other kinds of self-images are commonly seen.

From *The Journal of Psychology, 67:*107-126, 1967. Copyright by The Journal Press. Reprinted by permission.

This research has been supported by grants from the United States Public Health Service, National Institutes of Health (MH-11937), and from the Association for the Aid of Crippled Children. Portions[9] of this paper were presented at the 1965 meeting of the Society for Research in Child Development. The author is indebted to Dr. Jacob Cohen for statistical consultation, and to Joan Stern Girgus for her assistance with many aspects of the study.

The writer's interest in the question posed stems from a series of investigations undertaken to explore children's conceptions of their bodily characteristics.[6,7,8,10]

THE SELF-DRAWING TEST

In order to determine whether children lateralize self-replicas from the focus of the person being portrayed or from that of the observer, the following procedure was devised.

Method

S was seated and given an $8\frac{1}{2}$-inch $\times$ 11-inch sheet of paper and a pencil. *E* said, "Draw a picture of yourself . . . . Draw it standing up and facing frontwards."* *E* noted and recorded whether *S* was right- or left-handed. When the drawing was completed, *E* pointed to it and said, "Suppose this is a picture of you—and it really *is* a picture of you—show me which hand you, *in the picture,* would use to make a drawing. Point to the hand that would hold the pencil." (This procedure was used rather than asking *S* to indicate right and left on his body, as well as on the drawing, in order to control for inability to identify right and left, *per se.*) If *S* pointed to the pictured hand that was *directly opposite* the real hand he had used, his response was recorded as "mirror-image designation"; if he indicated the pictured hand that was *diagonally across* from the real hand used, his response was recorded as "diagonal designation."

It was assumed that those who responded with *mirror-image designations* identified corresponding body parts on themselves and on their self-drawings as though these were *reflections* of one another, whereas *diagonal designators* identified them as though the sides of their actual person and of the drawn figure were *reversed* as in a photograph.

The children proved remarkably self-consistent in the type of lateralization made on this test. In evidence, of 25 subjects (be-

---

*The entire instructions were "Draw a picture of yourself wearing a bathing suit. Draw it standing up and facing frontwards. Tell me when you are finished." This procedure was used so that the drawings also might be used for studies exploring aspects of the body percept to be reported elsewhere.

tween ages 5.2 years and 11.7 years) who were retested within a
month, all gave the same designations on both occasions.

Subjects

The foregoing procedure, to be referred to as the Self-Drawing
Test, was administered individually to 388 "normal" boys and
girls ranging in age from 5.2 years to 12.9 years. The children,
who attended a public school in New York City, represented a
broad range of sociocultural backgrounds. Most came from lower-
middle and lower-class families. In ethnic origin, about 38 percent were Jewish, 15 percent Continental Negro, 15 percent
North European Protestant and Catholic, 13 percent Italian, and
10 percent Puerto Rican. Their mean IQ was 108, the range extending from 79 to 168. For the entire sample, no significant sex
differences in mean IQ were found.[†] Fourteen percent were left-
handed.[‡]

Findings

On the Self-Drawing Test, 43 percent gave mirror-image
designations, that is, they lateralized self-images as though these
were *reflections* of themselves; whereas 57 percent responded with
diagonal designations, that is, they pointed to the pictured hand
located *diagonally across* from the real hand used in the drawing.
For all age groups combined, percentage of mirror-image designations was almost identical per sex. Thus, for the sample taken as
a whole, no marked preference for making either mirror-image
or diagonally oriented lateralizations was found.

[†]For most subjects, group IQ scores (Otis Quick-Scoring Mental Abilities Test,
or Pintner-Cunningham Primary Test) were available from the school records. The
group IQs of children with foreign language backgrounds have been deleted. The
group IQs revealed no significant sex differences in mean intelligence. However, on
Goodenough's Drawing Test of Intelligence,[11] the girls' mean IQs were significantly
above those of the boys. This again confirms the frequently reported[13] finding that
the Drawing Test of Intelligence is biased in favor of girls.

[‡]This is the same proportion of left-handed children Belmont and Birch[1] reported in a recent study. The fact that both studies found a somewhat higher
incidence of left-handedness than is generally reported suggests that this characteristic might be on the increase—perhaps as a function of current educational
practices regarding handedness.

Is there any way, then, to predict which type of designation a given child may use?

When the subjects' designations were plotted along an age gradient, it became apparent that there was a positive association between type of designation used and chronological age, Figure 20-1 presents this regression, per sex, in terms of percent diagonal designations. It shows that mirror-image designations predominated in the younger groups. With increasing age, a shift occurred, so that by age 9.8 years, less than one third of the children made mirror-image designations. This percentage dropped further to below 20 percent for the groups whose mean age was 11.9 years. Thus, while 5-year-olds characteristically lateralized self-images as though they were reflections, those beyond age 9 tended to lateralize diagonally. The correlations between age and diagonal designation were .55 among boys and .34 for girls. The significance ($p < .01$) of the sex difference between these coefficients was primarily due to the performance of the 5- to 6-year-olds. Correlations omitting these children were .36 and .30 for boys and girls,

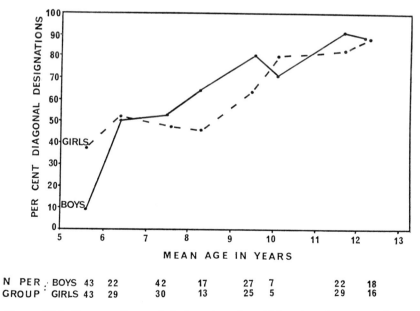

| N PER . | BOYS | 43 | 22 | | 42 | 17 | | 27 | 7 | | 22 | 18 |
| GROUP . | GIRLS | 43 | 29 | | 30 | 13 | | 25 | 5 | | 29 | 16 |

Figure 20-1. Percent diagonal designations in self-drawings by age and sex.

respectively ($p < .01$, two-tailed tests, for all correlations reported above).

What accounts for the observed shift, with age, from mirror image to diagonally oriented lateralization of self-images?

While testing the children, the investigators noticed that some subjects literally or verbally turned themselves around, so that they were facing the same way as their drawing, before they would indicate which hand in the picture corresponded to the one they had used in making the drawing. This implied that at least some children thought of the drawing as though it were oriented comparably to another person facing them, rather than as a reflection. If this conception were predominant, the findings might be explained on the basis of some observations reported by Piaget,[16] Benton,[2] and others. Piaget found that ". . . it is only at the age of 8 that the child is able to place himself (in imagination) at the point of view of others with regard to the left and right . . ." (p. 109). Both he and Benton noted the young child's tendency to use his own "egocentric" locus as a universal reference point. They accounted for their observations in terms of the young child's inability to think of spatial relations in relativistic terms. Thus, if children generally conceived of an *en face* self-image in the same way as of another person facing them, the observed shift with age, on self-drawings, from mirror image to diagonal designations might be explained on the following basis: that an increasing proportion of subjects either have mastered the general principle of transposing orientations or at least have learned a specific rule, such as "the corresponding hand of any figure facing you is diagonally across from your own."

The foregoing line of reasoning can be stated in terms of the following hypotheses:

1. The older the child, the more likely is he to be able to "transpose" spatial relationships, so that he can correctly identify *right* and *left* on other people regardless of their position. Thus, the older the child, the more likely is he to lateralize diagonally figures of others which are facing him.

2. If frontal self-representations are conceived of as though they were oriented like another person facing the subject, the

same kind of lateralization should be made for both kinds of stimuli. That is, a subject either should respond consistently with mirror-image designations when confronted both with self- and with nonself-figures, or he should make diagonally oriented designations in lateralizing both kinds of figures. Moreover, since the ability to transpose points of reference improves with age, per-cent diagonal designations should rise with increasing maturity, both for self-image lateralizations and for frontal-nonself figures. The magnitude of this increase should be the same in response to self-representations as to nonself-figures.

THE RIGHT-LEFT-DESIGNATION TEST

In order to test the preceding hypotheses, it was necessary to find out which subjects were able to lateralize relativistically. The following procedure, named the Right-Left-Designation Test, was devised to ascertain this by determining whether subjects were able to transpose viewpoints or, to put it less inferentially, whether they were able to make diagonal designations when such a response was clearly the correct one.

Method

S was seated, asked to put his hands on a table before him, and to shut his eyes. Then he was instructed to raise his *right* hand. When he had raised *either* hand and then replaced it on the table, he was asked to raise his *left* hand. Both responses were recorded.* This part of the test was carried out with *S's* eyes closed in order to prevent the use of visual cues (such as watches, rings, and so forth) for right-left identification. Next, a $4\frac{1}{2}$-inch by $2\frac{1}{2}$-inch photograph of an adult was stood directly in front of *S*. The figure in the photograph was posed with arms slightly ex-tended, standing up and facing the camera. Pictures of adults whose sex was opposite to that of *S* were used as stimulus figures

---

*None of the subjects raised the *same* hand to refer to his own right, as well as to his left, although some misidentified both sides. Thirteen percent manifested at least some confusion in identifying their own right and left hands. Only one of these children was more than 7.8 years old, and this boy's comprehension of English was below average.

in order to minimize the likelihood that the child might identify the photograph with his own person. *S* was asked to point to the right and left hands, respectively, on the photographed figure. If he pointed to the hand that was directly across from his own correspondingly identified hand, his response was recorded as *mirror image*. Conversely, pointing to the hand located diagonally across from his own, was termed a *diagonal* response. Two trials of this test were given per *S*, and a third was added whenever responses on the first two trials differed from each other. In such cases (13 percent of the total sample), the responses obtained in two out of three trials were considered *S*'s predominant pattern.

Subjects

Two hundred and forty-six subjects, drawn from the entire age range of the previous sample, were given both the Self-Drawing Test and the Right-Left-Designation Test.

Findings

On the Right-Left-Designation Test, that is, in response to the nonself-figure, 40 percent gave diagonal designations.

In Figure 20-2, percent diagonal designations on the nonself-photographs (as well as on the Self-Drawing Test) are graphed according to age and sex. The unbroken line represents boys' and the line interspersed with w's represents girls' lateralizations of nonself-figures. In accord with expectations, percent diagonal designations on this test increased significantly with age. (This developmental regression still obtained when percent diagonal designation was plotted along age and the only subjects used were those who correctly identified their own right and left hands.) As in the Self-Drawing Test, the above relationship was significantly ($p < .01$) more pronounced among boys than among girls ($r_{boys} = .70$, $p < .005$; $r_{girls} = .41$, $p < .005$; two-tailed tests). Figure 20-2 shows that the present data agree fairly well with Piaget's observations[16] (p. 108) regarding the age (8 years) at which 75 percent should be able to lateralize from the point of view of another person facing them. (Belmont and Birch's intellectually high subjects attained this level of proficiency by age 7 years.[1]

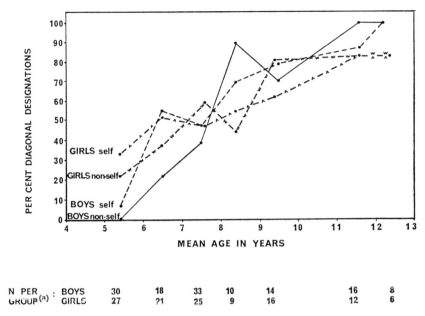

Figure 20-2. Percent diagonal designations on self and nonself-drawings by age and sex. [a]One boy was not included in the graph because he was the only case falling into the age-interval 10-11 years.

However, on the basis of the reported data, an assertion made by Machover[15] (p. 88) that, for most subjects, the right and left of a drawn figure are oriented from the focus of the person being portrayed, must be restricted to individuals beyond age 9. According to Benton[2] (p. 100), even 25 percent of adult subjects occasionally made mirror-image lateralizations when asked to identify right and left body parts on a person who was facing them.

COMPARISON OF LATERALIZATION ON SELF- AND NONSELF-FIGURES

Consistent Treatments

The results of the Right-Left-Designation Test permitted examination of the hypothesis that the observed shift, with age, from mirror-image designation to diagonal designation in lateralizing self-images was a function of an age-associated increase in ability to transpose orientations and to "decenter" one's viewpoint. As suggested, if subjects considered self-drawings to be oriented like other persons, those who made diagonal designations on the Right-Left-Designation Test (i.e. when faced by a figure representing someone other than themselves) also should have lateralized their self-drawings diagonally. Comparing the regressions of diagonal responses on self-replicas with those for nonself-figures (see Fig. 20-2) supports this supposition, and the data presented in Table 20-I clearly confirm it. For the sample taken as a whole, 83 percent of those who made diagonal designations on the nonself-figure also lateralized the self diagonally. Similarly, 76 percent who lateralized the nonself-figure in mirror-image fashion (thereby indicating an inability to transpose orientations in the present context) also gave mirror-image designations in relation to their self-drawings. These results greatly exceed the agreement between designations on the self-drawings and on the nonself-figures that might be expected by chance ($x^2 = 84.87$, $df = 1, p < .001$).

The preceding results confirm the hypothesis that most children conceive of *en face* drawings as though they were oriented like another person facing them. In recapitulation, this conclusion is drawn from the following observations: (1) frontal representations of self and nonself usually were lateralized identically; and (2) when children were able to transpose orientations correctly (i.e. by designating diagonally) on the nonself-figure, most of them also made diagonal designations on the self-drawings.

It is possible that making diagonally oriented lateralizations in response to any figure one is confronted with, regardless of its character or position, does not stem from relativistic thinking or from mastery of the general principle of transposition, but rather from the rigid activation of a specific rule or habit. This hypothesis derives support from the difficulty persons of all ages commonly encounter in matching body sides correctly when looking at reflections of themselves; for example, while attending to their grooming with the help of a mirror. (An elaboration of the present procedure would be required to distinguish clearly be-

TABLE 20-I

Lateralizations on Self-Drawings Which Were Consistent with Designation on Nonself-figures

Group	Consistently Diagonal[a]				Consistently Mirror-image[b]				Total Consistent Designators[c]			
	BOYS		GIRLS		BOYS		GIRLS		BOYS		GIRLS	
	N	%	N	%	N	%	N	%	N	%	N	%
5-6 yrs.	4	100	8	57	36	82	22	65	40	83	30	62
7-8 yrs.	18	82	14	74	16	76	12	80	34	79	26	76
9-10 yrs.	9	90	10	77	3	60	3	100	12	80	13	81
11-12 yrs.	22	92	15	100	0	0	3	100	22	92	18	100
All ages	53	88	47	77	55	79	40	73	108	83	87	75

[a]Diagnoal designators on nonself-figure who also designated diagonally on self-drawing. $N = 100$, $\% = 83$ for all ages and both sexes.

[b]Mirror-image designators on nonself-figure who also made mirror-image designations on self-drawing. $N = 95$, $\% = 76$ for all ages and both sexes.

[c]Consistently diagonal plus consistently mirror-image designators. $N = 195$, $\% = 79$ for all ages and both sexes.

tween subjects whose diagonal designations were based upon a special rule applied to a particular situation and those whose diagonal lateralizations resulted from genuinely relativistic conceptualization. For example, it would be interesting to compare how subjects lateralize figures whose back is facing them, or who are seen from a variety of orientations, with lateralizations made on a front-view figure. Dubanoski's important investigation of children's lateralizations of letters,[4] when these were traced on various parts of their heads, represents another aspect of the issue raised here.) If making diagonal designations on the photograph indeed were the result of relativistic thinking, it should be positively related to IQ—a measure that is partially derived from assessments of ability to conceptualize abstractly. Table 20-II

TABLE 20-II

Mean Intelligence of Mirror-image Responders Compared to Mean Intelligence of Diagonal Responders (Nonself-figures)

Age in years	MIRROR-IMAGE RESPONDERS			DIAGONAL RESPONDERS				p of t (two-tailed tests)	r_{pb}[b]
	N	Mean IQ[a]	SD	N	Mean IQ[a]	SD	t		
5-6	78	98	14.1	18	104	9.3	1.80	<.07	.18
7-8	35	92	11.4	39	102	15.0	3.32	<.01	.37
9-10	8	91	12.3	23	100	13.0	1.62	<.15	.29
11-12	3	83	6.0	39	100	15.5	1.87	<.09	.28
All ages	124	96	13.5	119	101	14.0	3.30	<.005	.20

[a]Combined IQ score based upon mean score for all IQ tests available per S. The number of these tests, per individual, ranged from one to five. Types of tests: Otis Quick-Scoring Mental Abilities Test; Pintner-Cunningham Primary Test; Vocabulary test of the Stanford-Binet Intelligence Scale; Goodenough's Drawing Test of Intelligence. Three children for whom no valid IQ scores were available are omitted from this table.
[b]Correlation of IQ and diagonal designation.

shows the extent to which this was the case. It will be seen that in every group the mean IQ of the diagonal responders exceeded the mean IQ of the mirror-image designators. The differences between the respective means were statistically significant for some groups and approached significance for the remainder. For the total sample, the correlation between IQ* and giving diagonal responses on the Right-Left-Designation Test was .20 ($p < .01$, two-tailed test). Thus, in some degree, intelligence, and by im-

*Pooled IQ scores. For derivation see footnote (a) Table 20-II.

plication, relativistic thinking, were associated with making diagonal designations.

Along with lateralizing nonself-figures diagonally, making diagonal designations on the self-drawings also should have been correlated positively with IQ, since there was a high degree of correspondence in lateralizing self-replicas and nonself-figures. This expectation was confirmed, for the correlation of IQ and diagonal designation on the self-drawing also proved significant ($r = .13$, $p < .05$, two-tailed test). The correlations of IQ with nonself-designations, and of IQ with self-drawing designation did not differ significantly ($t_{\text{diff.bet.nonindep.}rs} = 1.31$, $df = 240$, $p > .05$), though the latter coefficient was the lesser of the two. (It is to be noted that in both total sample correlations cited, unlike the others, age is not controlled; correlations of designation with *mental age* undoubtedly would be substantially higher.) The present findings accord with Hammer's impression[12] that, in children, nonmirror-image lateralization of self-drawings is associated with high intelligence.

It will be recalled that the question that occasioned the present study is "which side of a frontal, two-dimensional self-likeness do children spontaneously consider to refer to the right and left, respectively, of their real body?" It now has been shown that, taken as a group, boys and girls between the ages of 5 years and 13 years are about equally likely to consider *either* side of a self-replica to refer to their own right or left. However, for specific individuals, the mode of such lateralization can be predicted considerably beyond chance expectations by taking the following findings into account: (1) Particularly among boys, the older the child, the more likely is he to lateralize such stimuli diagonally. For both sexes, the majority so lateralize self-images by the age of 9 years. (2) Type of lateralization of self-replicas appears to be largely a function of being able to transpose orientations, in general. Thus, if an individual lateralizes diagonally in response to a figure of another person facing him, he is also very likely to make diagonal designations on self-images presented in corresponding orientation. (3) Finally, especially between ages 7 and 9 years, when most children shift to lateralizing frontal figures diagonally (see Table 20-II), the more intelligent the child, the more likely is he to lateralize self-images diagonally.

Contrary Treatments

Although the correlation between lateralizations of the non-self-figures with those of the self-images was substantial ($r_\phi = .59$, $p < .005$, two-tailed test), 51 children, comprising 21 percent of the sample so compared, did *not* lateralize the two figures *consistently*, but in *contrary* fashion, thereby making different designations in response to the self-replica as compared to the nonself-figure. Thus, for a sizable minority, self-images apparently were not considered to be in the same orientation as were pictures of other people. Since examination of behavior that deviates from predominant or predicted trends often provides clues regarding the processes under investigation, the contrary responders were subjected to further analysis.

Comparison of all consistent with all contrary responders yielded no notable differences between these two groups with respect to handedness, ethnic distribution, or language comprehension. Among children between ages 5 and 9, girls exceeded boys significantly ($\chi^2 = 3.9$, $df = 1$, $p < .05$) in the proportion who lateralized the two figures in contrary fashion. For males, proportion of contrary lateralizations was relatively constant from age to age, whereas the proportion of contrary responses among females decreased chronologically (see Table 20-I). Thus, some sex differences in the consistency of lateralization patterns were encountered. In mean (pooled) IQ, the contrary responders fell between the consistently mirror-image designators and the consistently diagonal designators, but did not differ significantly from either of these groups. With regard to mean age (see Table 20-III), the contrary response group was higher than the consistent mirror-image designators, but significantly below the consistently diagonal lateralizers ($t = 6.97$, $df = 149$, $p < .01$, two-tailed test). As shown in Figure 20-3, contrary responses virtually dropped out by age 11 years, thus suggesting that these were the result of "immature" cognitive functioning. The consistent and contrary response groups also differed from one another with respect to

TABLE 20-III

Age Comparisons of Consistent and Contrary Lateralization Patterns

Lateralization Pattern	Mean Age in Years	N	M-M[a]	D-M[b]	M-D[c]	All Contrary (D-M + M-D)	D-D[d]
M-M[a]	6.7	95	——		$t = 3.02$, df 114		$t = 10.44$, $df = 193$
D-M[b]	6.7	30		——	$t = 2.86$, $df = 49$		$t = 7.02$, $df = 128$
M-D[c]	7.9	21	$t = 3.02$, $df = 114$	$t = 2.86$, $df = 49$	——		$t = 3.20$, $df = 119$
All contrary (D-M + M-D)	7.2	51				——	$t = 6.97$, $df = 149$
D-D[d]	9.5	100	$t = 10.44$, $df = 193$	$t = 7.02$, $df = 128$	$t = 3.20$, $df = 119$	$t = 6.97$, $df = 149$	——

Note: All values significant beyond the 5 percent level of confidence are shown above. In all cases, $p < .01$ (two-tailed tests).

[a] Mirror image on self-drawing, as well as on nonself-figure.
[b] Diagonal on self-drawing, but mirror image on nonself-figure.
[c] Mirror image on self-drawing, but diagonal on nonself-figure.
[d] Diagonal on self-drawing, as well as on nonself-figure.

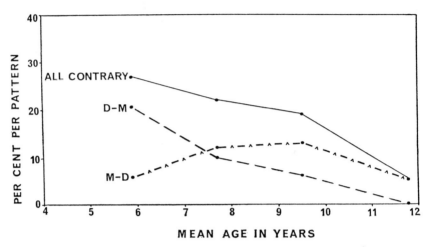

Figure 20-3. Regression of contrary response patterns on age (sexes combined) ; D-M: Diagonal on self-drawing and mirror image on nonself (N = 30) ; M-D: Mirror image of self and diagonal on nonself (N = 21) ; All contrary: Pattern D-M and Pattern M-D (N = 51) .

the percentage who manifested confusion when identifying their own right and left hands. The incidence of such confusion was significantly higher $(x^2 = 11.4, df = 1, p < .001)$ among contrary responders than among the consistent lateralizers.

The most apparent reason for lateralizing self-images in one manner and nonself-figures in another is that self-images are considered tantamount to a reflection, whereas those of others are not. In this case, the self-figure would be correctly lateralized in mirror-image fashion and the photograph, diagonally. This pattern will be referred to as the *M-D Pattern.* Of the 51 contrary designators, 21 followed this pattern. When 16 of these 21 children were retested after about one year, five still responded with "mirror image" to the Self-Drawing Test and with "diagonal" to the nonself-figure (see Table 20-IV) . Thirty cases manifested the converse pattern of making diagonal responses to the self-drawing and mirror-image designations on the nonself-figure. (This pattern will be called the *D-M Pattern.*) Thus, the explanation suggested above cannot account for the majority of contrary responses obtained.

An alternative hypothesis regarding the reason for making contrary lateralizations on the two tests is that the contrary responders were in a transitional phase. In other words, such inconsistency might have been occasioned by the process of shifting from mirror-image to diagonal lateralizing of any frontal figures. If this were the case, (1) the average age of contrary responders should fall between that of consistent mirror-image responders *(Pattern M-M)* and that of consistent diagonal responders *(Pattern D-D)*, and (2) contrary responders, in time, should become consistently diagonal responders. The available evidence pertinent to these expectations follows. In reference to the first criterion, Table 20-III shows that the mean age of the contrary responders did exceed that of the consistent mirror-image responders and that it fell significantly below that of the consistent diagonal lateralizers as well. Thus, ranking designation patterns according to mean age supports the hypothesis that lateralizing self-images differently from nonself figures is a function of being in a transitional phase of development. On the second point, if making contrary lateralizations is due to being in the process of transition, all contrary responders eventually should shift to Pattern D-D (i.e. consistently diagonal responses), since this is the typical mode at maturity. Of 36 contrary responders who were retested after about one year, 16 indeed shifted to making consistently diagonal designations on self-, as well as nonself-, figures. However, as shown in Table 20-IV, this trend was not predominant. In fact, almost as many "reverted" to the presumably less mature pattern of lateralizing all human figures in mirror-image fashion (Pattern M-M). The longitudinal data do suggest that making contrary responses on the two tests usually was not a stable disposition, since the majority changed to a different pattern within a year. But longitudinal scrutiny of the contrary response group does not indicate that most of these subjects were in the process of becoming consistently *diagonal* responders. The small number of subjects retested, the relatively brief span (mean interval $= 11.5$ months) between test administrations per subject, and the lack of a comparable follow-up for consistent responders limit the confidence to be placed in the test-retest data. Nonetheless, the results exemplify the importance of "checking out" apparent developmental trends derived from cross-sectional sampling by following the salient behavior of the same individuals over an extended period.

In addition to the explanations offered thus far, some "spurious" contrary responses might have been due to faulty comprehension of the test instructions or to immature drawing skill.

Among the contrary responders, the following findings suggested that the Pattern M-D group differed in several respects from children presenting the D-M pattern:

1. As shown in Table 20-III and Figure 20-3, the Pattern D-M children were significantly younger than the M-D responders. While mean ages for Pattern D-M and for Pattern M-M were identical, the M-D responders, on the average, were significantly older than both these groups (see Table 10-III).

2. While *none* of the 21 M-D responders misidentified his own right and left hands, 40 percent of the D-M group made such mistakes. Thus, the children presenting the two types of contrary response patterns differed significantly from one another in the number of subjects who manifested confusion regarding their own right and left ($x^2 = 13.81$, $df = 1$, $p < .01$). The D-M responders also significantly exceeded their Pattern M-M agemates in this respect ($x^2 = 9.99$, $df = 1$, $p < .01$). (The incidence of right-left confusion per designation pattern was M-M = 13 percent, D-M = 40 percent, M-D = 0 percent, D-D = 4 percent.) These results suggest that the Pattern D-M contrary responses may have been *indirectly* related to age as a consequence of concomitantly immature conceptions of sidedness, in general. It seems less likely that this factor led to Pattern M-D responses.

3. As shown in Table 20-IV, a further difference between the two contrary response groups was in the proportion who again lateralized self-images and nonself-figures disparately when they were retested about a year later. Whereas a substantial proportion of the M.D group still made contrary designations, *all but one* of the Pattern D-M subjects had shifted to making consistent lateralizations. The difference between these two proportions is significant at the 6 percent level (Fisher Exact Probability Test, two-tailed test). Thus, for some children, the Pattern M-D response

may have been a rather stable disposition, whereas there was little indication of such constancy for the converse pattern group.

On the basis of the limited information available regarding factors that led to making disparate lateralizations on self-drawings as compared to nonself-figures, only very tentative conclusions seem warranted. They are summarized below.

1. No uniform determinant elicited contrary lateralizations. Rather, it seems likely that, for various subgroups, different factors accounted for the contrary response patterns manifested.

2. In some cases (44 percent of Pattern M-D), contrary treatment of the self-images *versus* nonself-figures probably was due to a rather stable tendency to conceive of self-images as though these were reflections, even though the subjects knew how to transpose orientations (see Table 20-IV).

TABLE 20-IV

Retest Lateralization Patterns of Contrary Responders

Type of Change	Pattern M-D[a] N = 16	Pattern D-M[b] N = 20	All Contrary (M-D + D-M) N = 36
Unchanged	5	1	6
Changed to other contrary pattern	2	0	2
Retained contrary pattern (either D-M or M-D)	7	1	8
Changed to M-M[c]	5	7	12
Changed to D-D[d]	4	12	16
Changed to consistent pattern (either M-M or D-D)	9	19	28

[a]Mirror image on self-drawing and diagonal on nonself-figure.
[b]Diagonal on self-drawing and mirror image on nonself-figure.
[c]Mirror image on self-drawing and on nonself-figure.
[d]Diagonal on self-drawing and on nonself-figure.

3. However, for the majority, lateralizing in contrary fashion apparently was a *transitory*—but not necessarily *transitional*—mode which was followed sometimes by consistently making mirror-image designations, but more frequently, by consistently giving diagonal responses.

4. Making contrary responses tended to be associated with

"immature" cognitive levels of development, since it occurred predominantly among the younger children sampled.

5. Children who were confused regarding their own right and left hands were significantly more likely to make disparate lateralizations on the two figures than were subjects who identified their own right and left correctly. This finding suggests that making contrary lateralizations is related to having a fluid or vague notion of sidedness—or perhaps no conception of sidedness at all. In this connection, it would be interesting to compare the performance of hemiplegics, who have lost awareness of one side of their body, with that of normal subjects on the two tests used in the present study. Furthermore, it must be remembered that labelling right and left relatively to the frontal aspect of persons and objects is a *learned convention* rather than an intrinsic property of such stimuli.

6. Finally, there was some indication that, particularly among younger children, girls were more likely to lateralize the two figures disparately than were boys. Although the investigator can offer no cogent explanation for such a sex difference in performance, this finding should provide welcome support for some popular notions regarding female inconsistency!

The findings might have been clarified by asking contrary responders to account for the difference in the way they lateralized their self-drawing and the nonself-figure. However, due to young children's limited ability to explain their rationale, such a procedure would have been fraught with communication problems. It also might be fruitful to compare children's lateralizations of *real* self-reflections with their lateralizations of self-photographs, when both are comparably posed.

CONCLUSIONS AND DISCUSSION

Assuming the representativeness of the present sample, it has been shown that, without control of previous learning, elementary school children vary in lateralizing front-view figures of human beings. Investigators who use such material to study differential conceptions and attitudes regarding the two sides of the body should take such variations into account. Further, it has been demonstrated that the mirror-image or diagonal lateralization of human figures is not a matter of chance, but the result of a rather consistent individual disposition which is related to age, to the ability to imagine at least one other point of view, to intelligence, and to sex.

The exploration of the question that prompted this study led to the consideration of related problems with intriguing implications beyond the present context. Principally, these concern the mechanisms underlying the transposition of spatial relations. Among the issues encountered are the following:

1. What is the relation of learning particular rules (such as "the right hand of a person facing the self is diagonally across from one's own") to a pervasively relativistic approach to spatial frames of reference? Does the one precede, facilitate, or interfere with the other? And how is one to distinguish between the two?

2. Might differences in ability to make spatial transpositions be one aspect of a general cognitive style, such as Witkin *et al.'s* articulate-global dimension,[17] in addition to being related to intelligence and to sex?

3. What is the explanation for the significant sex differences found in the regression of diagonal designations on age? The present data are consistent with the hypothesis that females begin the transition from mirror-image to diagonal lateralization earlier than do males. Could this be a function of the frequently reported[14] (p. 577) superior language development of females in early childhood? As suggested by Benton[2] (p. 43), it is likely that language facility enhances the capacity to use rules and to resort to verbal mediation. Such an advantage could be related to learning the transposition of viewpoints. Although this hypothesis is persuasive, it should be noted that no significant sex differences in language development were observed among the younger subjects sampled.* It would be valuable to replicate this study with extension of the age range in both directions in order to test further for sex differences in the development of lateralization patterns.

---

*Vocabulary was measured by applying Cureton's Mental Age Equivalents[3] to the vocabulary test of the Stanford-Binet Intelligence Scale, Form M-L.

4. Feffer and Gourevitch[5] have suggested that the ability to shift spatial orientations, so that one can imagine the point of view of others, is a necessary antecedent of moving from social egocentrism to the capacity to assume various roles and "to put oneself into another person's shoes," generally. If this proved to be so, would training in making spatial transpositions enhance one's social perspicacity? Might the demonstration of such a connection provide a clue to the "missing link" between perception and personality?

5. It is interesting that neither handedness nor the ability to identify correctly one's own right and left hands, *per se,* bore a notable relationship to making either mirror-image or diagonal lateralizations. [The second finding contrasts with Benton's corresponding observations[2] p. 139).] However, confusing one's own right and left hands did occur significantly more frequently among contrary rather than consistent lateralizers—perhaps because such confusion coincided with unstabilized conceptions of sidedness in general.

Mention should be made of a potential source of confusion in connection with the now popular procedure of asking subjects to identify corresponding body parts on themselves and on other persons. Previous investigators occasionally have confounded their results by instructing subjects to identify "right" or "left" body parts on others, rather than by requiring that they merely indicate "which side on the other person they considered to correspond to each of their own." It is possible that the resulting responses were affected *both* by the ability to label "right" and "left" correctly from *any* perspective and by the capacity to shift viewpoints. The method used in the present lateralization tests eliminates such confounding of data by recording only whether the subject lateralizes the figure facing him in mirror-image or in diagonal fashion. (The subject's way of referring to his right and left hands is "accepted" whether it is correct or not, and his designation of the correspondingly named hand on the figure is recorded as mirror image or as diagonal, according to the designation signified.) Wider adoption of this procedure seems warranted, and particularly so, where deficient capacity to transpose orientations is considered clinically significant.

When the developmental course of particular behavior systems is scrutinized, two questions typically arise: first, "What is the *characteristic pattern* of such development throughout some or all of the life span—or even throughout the history of the species?" and second, "What are the *processes underlying transitions* with respect to the behavior under investigation?" By combining cross-sectional with longitudinal sampling, it has been possible to explore both of these questions in the present context. To implement this strategy, age-associated patterns and transitional phases first were charted cross-sectionally at successive age intervals. Then a more intensive, partially longitudinal examination of a transitional phase was made in an attempt to gain insight into the mental processes involved in the developmental shift from making mirror image to making diagonally oriented lateralizations.

SUMMARY

The concept of sidedness is integral to conventional communication about spatial relationships. In relation to human figures, this study demonstrates that lateralization, defined as the attribution of sides, becomes increasingly relativistic during childhood. A simple test was applied to indicate which side of a self-drawing children considered to correspond to the right or left of their actual body. The percentage lateralizing such figures in mirror-image fashion was nearly equal to the percentage who lateralized them in 180-degree rotation (diagonally). Type of lateralization was found to be a function of age, sex, intelligence, and ability to transpose orientation. Most children who considered the corresponding hands of nonself-figures to be diagonally across from their own, also lateralized self-drawings in such fashion. Exceptions to this trend were examined in order to gain insight into the normative transition process from making mirror-image to making diagonal lateralizations of frontview human figures.

REFERENCES

1. Belmont, L., and Birch, H. G. Lateral dominance and right-left awareness in normal children. *Child Develop., 34*:257-271, 1963.
2. Benton, A. L. *Right-Left Discrimination and Finger Localization.* New York, Hoeber, 1959.
3. Cureton, E. E. Mental age equivalents for the Revised Stanford-Binet Vocabulary Test. *J. Consult. Psychol., 18*:381-384, 1954,
4. Dubanoski, R. A. Inferring the Phenomenal Locus of the Perceiver from Responses to Tactile Stimulation. Paper read at American Psychological Association, Los Angeles, California, September, 1964.
5. Feffer, M. H., and Gourevitch, V. Cognitive aspects of role taking in children. *J. Personal., 28*:383-396, 1960.
6. Gellert, E. Children's conceptions of the content and functions of the human body. *Genet. Psychol. Monogr., 65*:293-405, 1962.
7. Gellert, E. The Development of Conceptions of the Body Image. Paper read at Society for Research in Child Development, Berkeley, California, April, 1963.
8. Gellert, E. The Development of Self-recognition from Anterior, Posterior, and Side Views of the Human Body. Paper read at Western Psychological Association, Portland, Oregon, April, 1964.
9. Gellert, E. The Transition from Mirror Image to Diagonal Sets in Children's Lateralizations of Human Figures. Paper read at Society for Research in Child Development, Minneapolis, Minnesota, March, 1965.
10. Gellert, E., and Stern, J. B. Age and Sex Differences in Children's Judgments of Their Height and Body Proportions. Paper read at American Psychological Association, Los Angeles, California, September, 1964.
11. Goodenough, F. L. *Measurement of Intelligence by Drawings.* New York, Harcourt, Brace, & World, 1926.
12. Hammer, E. F. House-Tree-Person (H-T-P) drawings as a projective technique with children. In A. J. Rabin and M. Haworth (Eds.), *Projective Techniques with Children.* New York, Grune & Stratton, 1960, pp. 257-272.
13. Harris, D. B. *Children's Drawings as Measures of Intellectual Maturity.* New York, Harcourt, Brace, & World, 1963.
14. McCarthy, D. Language development in children. In L. Carmichael (Ed.), *Manual of Child Psychology,* 2nd ed. New York, Wiley, 1954, pp. 492-630.
15. Machover, K. *Personality Projection in the Drawing of the Human Figure.* Springfield, Thomas, 1949.
16. Piaget, J. *Judgment and Reasoning in the Child.* London, Routledge & Paul, 1928, pp. 107-113.
17. Witkin, H. A.; Dyk, R. B.; Fatterson, H. F.; Goodenough, D. R., and Karp, S. A. *Psychological Differentiation.* New York, Wiley, 1962.

PART VIII

EMOTIONAL AND SOCIAL DEVELOPMENT

INFANTS AND CHILDREN spontaneously explore, play, experiment, and practice their skills because there is pleasure in "doing." However, not too many years ago, these same activities were viewed by some theorists as the sole behavioral consequents of physiological drives. Conversely, some other theorists argued that even after basic needs are met the organism is still an active, seeking creature. To explain this behavior, Dr. Robert White proposed a motivational model, called *effectance,* based on the principle of competence. Capability (competence) to deal with the environment develops as the organism produces effects (effectance) upon objects, and in so doing learns to deal with his world. Dr. White's model, rich in ideas, provides insight about the active, adaptive, and persistent behavior of the child. The following paper includes a discussion of the competence model, and an analysis of psychoanalytic and ego theory and their inadequacy as models of child behavior.

Chapter 21

Competence and the Psychosexual Stages of Development

ROBERT W. WHITE

T HE PURPOSE of this paper is to reconsider a part of psycho-analytic theory, the part that deals with stages of emotional development. It will be necessary first, however, to show why I think it important to look again at a theory that has survived nearly half a century of critical onslaught and that enjoys enduring high esteem among clinicians. This will require a short exposition of the concept of competence and of certain related concepts which I have discussed at length elsewhere (1959). As you will see, my use of these concepts puts me at variance with theories that make drive the necessary condition for activity and learning; at variance, therefore, with Freud's theory of instincts. The concept of competence, moreover, leads to an idea of the ego that is different from the one we usually find in discussion of psychosexual stages. Freud's theory of these stages undoubtedly occupies a secure historical position. It will stand in the history of thought as an astonishing first approximation to a theory of growth in its dynamic aspects. Nevertheless, I believe that the time has come when its continued use will only block further insights. The theory that illuminated us all as a first approximation may only hinder us in reaching those closer approximations that always mark the forward steps in a scientific pilgrimage.

In broadest outline, Freud's theory is that the most important features of childhood development, the ones that are fateful for emotional well-being and for the shape of personality, have their motive power in sexual energy or libido. Conceiving sexuality broadly to include the obtaining of pleasure from various zones of the body, he postulated a maturational sequence whereby first the mouth, then the anal zone, finally the genitals become the dominant source of libidinal gratification, Aggressive impulses, fused with libidinal ones, enter importantly during the anal stage and from then on, but the movement from one stage to another is determined biologically by the sequence of libidinal changes. The latency period and the final genital stage likewise come into existence through developments strictly in the sphere of sexual energy. Thus it is possible to speak of psychosexual stages, and Freud intended the double adjective to be taken quite literally. It is libido, he said, that makes demands upon the mind, that calls forth psychic activity, that constitutes the motivating force behind the development of the mental apparatus.[14-17]

The great virtue of this theory lies, of course, in its gathering and ordering of the confusingly diverse facts of development. For the first three and the last stages it provides us with a model or prototype of behavior: the infant at the breast, the child on the toilet, the phallic child concerned about genital impulses toward family members, the physically mature adult in the heterosexual relation. It tells us, moreover, that these prototypes are truly basic, that events in these situations are really the most important things that happen, so that if we know just these aspects of a person's history we know all that counts. Each prototype involves not only libidinal and aggressive energies but also frustrations, anxieties, defenses, ego developments, and relations with other people. But all these other things are brought to pass by the instincts, and we are thus permitted to place them in a subordinate relation to the central libidinal events. The theory thus achieves a heroic simplification. Right or wrong, it rescued us historically from a tangled mass of facts and made it possible for the first time to think coherently about emotional development.

Freud's ideas on this subject were completed nearly forty years ago. His ideas concerning the libido itself, a highly mobile and general source of energy, look anything but plausible in the light of recent research on motivation. Many psychoanalysts, however, retain the libido model as a working tool, finding that it greatly helps them to understand their patients' problems. Other workers have proposed more or less extensive revisions in the theory of development. In the writings of Horney,[30] Thompson,[54] and Fromm,[19] for instance, emphasis is shifted sharply from instinctual roots to human relations, especially those between child and parents. These neo-Freudians treat motivation in an offhand, pluralistic way, with perhaps special accent on security and anxiety. Development really turns, they believe, on a series of crises in parent-child relations, crises which arise because the parents, acting both for themselves and for the culture, make successive demands upon the infant that put the relation under strain. The libido model is thus displaced in favor of an interpersonal model.

One might suppose that this change of model would sweep away the prototypes provided by psychosexual theory. But the fact is that only Sullivan[52] has seriously attempted to revise the scheme of crises in strictly interpersonal terms. With most of the revisionists the oral, anal, phallic, and genital prototypes live on, either quite literally or in such guises as "neurotic trends" and "character orientations." The familiar stages, no longer libidinal, are still considered to be crucial. This situation is most clearly recognized by Silverberg,[49] who translates Freud's stages into *"areas of experience . . .* presented to the children of western civilization by parents performing the task of acculturating their offspring." Each area has its typical problem: deprivation in the oral area; obedience, conformity, and rebelliousness in the anal; rivalry and genitality in the phallic area. It is thus contended that the prototypes originally provided by libido theory are adequate models for the crucial events in the child's interpersonal development. Feeding, toilet training, and the Oedipal triangle are still the fateful battlefields of growth.

The thesis of this paper can be set forth at this point in the form of two propositions. I shall contend, first, that the child's emotional development cannot be adequately conceptualized by an exclusive libido model, no matter how liberally we interpret this concept. Second, I shall try to show that when the prototypes derived from libido theory are translated into interpersonal terms they still do not constitute adequate models for development. The best of these prototypes is undoubtedly the feeding child of the oral stage, who cuts a prominent figure even in Sullivan's revision, but from then on the models simply miss part of the significant problems of growth. In particular they fail to embody the development of competence, and they tend to direct attention away from certain crises in the growth of the child's sense of competence. This weakness is attested most eloquently by the lack of a clear-cut model for the latency period, when competence is a central theme. What is needed, I shall argue, is a clearly conceived *competence model* that can be used throughout the stages. Sexual and interpersonal models will be needed too, but we can never do justice to emotional development until we work up a competence model to put beside them.

COMPETENCE AND SENSE OF COMPETENCE

By presenting my theme in this way I have placed a great burden on the word "competence," and I must now give this concept a fuller introduction. Let me say at the outset that it is not something I have invented. It has been distilled from the writings of a great many workers in animal psychology, child development, research on personality, and psychopathology—workers whose only common quality is a certain disenchantment with prevailing concepts of drive. It is a way of saying what I believe many voices have been saying, especially during the last twenty years. Among those who have moved in this direction, it seems to me, are Erikson,[8-9] Hartmann,[25-26] and other workers who are trying to carry psychoanalytic ego psychology forward from the point at which Freud left it. I am therefore not trying to promote a novel idea, but rather to find suitable expression for a concept which, suppressed for a time by the immensely popular drive theories, has lately begun to throw out restless derivatives in every direction.

Competence means "fitness or ability." The competence of an organism means its fitness or ability to carry on those transactions with the environment which result in its maintaining itself, growing, and flourishing. Some parts of the environment must if possible be fought off, but other parts can safely be enjoyed, and still others can be ingested and transformed into materials for self-maintenance and growth. Some organisms are born more or less fully equipped with patterns of behavior that produce effective interactions with favorable surroundings. This is not the case with the higher animals, least of all with man, who has to learn almost everything that is useful in dealing with his world, yet who immeasurably surpasses all other living creatures in his ultimate ability to subdue and transform the environment to his own use. Man's prowess as a learner has long been an object of wonder. How does he do it, and when does he get it all done?

Theories in which drive is the central motivational concept deal quite simply with this problem. Drives arise from lacks and deficits. They are powerful and persistent internal stimuli which arouse the organism from homeostatic bliss and promote activities that ultimately eliminate the deficit, thus reducing the drive. Reduction of drive supplies the selective principle whereby patterns of behavior are retained or discarded. Our knowledge of the world and our competence in dealing with it are thus acquired in the course of satisfying our constantly recurring needs. We learn what helps us to reduce drives.

There have recently been some startling departures from this orthodoxy—not, as one might suppose, among soft-headed students of personality, but in the very heartland of hard-headedness, the animal laboratory. In a series of experiments Sheffield and others[46-48] have shown that instrumental learning can take place without drive reduction, indeed under circumstances where one can suppose only that drive level is being increased. Olds and Milner[41] have found a connection between reinforcement and the electrical stimulation of certain areas of the brain. A whole series of workers[2,4,24,38,40] have pointed out that animals show persistent tendencies toward activity, exploration, and manipulation even when all known primary drives have been satiated. Clearly the original drive model, based on hunger and other internal deficits, stands in need of extensive revision.

One way of accomplishing this revision is to postulate new drives not hitherto included in the list. In addition to hunger, sex, and the avoidance of pain we must attribute an exploratory drive and perhaps an activity drive to the higher animals, even a manipulative drive to those forms that have free use of the forelimbs. These new drives are like the older ones, it is argued, in that they provoke activity and lead to the reinforcement of instrumental learning. I find myself unable to climb aboard this drive bandwagon because I am so impressed by the differences between the old and new drives. Exploration and manipulation have nothing to do with deficits, they appear to arise in the nervous system without visceral stimulation, and they produce instrumental learning without any signs of consummatory response or drive reduction. Call them drives if you are fixated on the term, but remember that in doing so you have destroyed the original conception of drive, including Freud's conception of the instincts. Remember that you are separating drives from visceral deficits and somatic cravings, so that hunger and sex must be treated as special cases rather than as prototypes for the whole idea. But if you do remember these things, what good are you getting out of the concept of drive? I prefer to leave the word in its excellent original meaning so that we can look with a fresh eye at the adaptive significance of activity, manipulation, and exploration.

The theory that we learn what helps us to reduce our viscerogenic drives will not stand up if we stop to consider the whole range of what a child must learn in order to deal effectively with his surroundings. He has much to learn about visual forms, about grasping and letting go, about the coordination of hand and eye. He must work out the difficult problem of the constancy of objects. He must put together an increasingly varied repertory of skilled acts such as locomotion and the use of words. He must learn many facts about his world, building up a cognitive map that will afford guidance and structure for his behavior. It is not hard to see the biological advantage of an arrangement whereby these many learnings can get under way before they are needed as instruments for drive reduction or for safety. An animal that has thoroughly explored its environment stands a better chance of escaping from a sudden enemy or satisfying a gnawing hunger than one that merely dozes in the sun when its homeostatic crises are past. Seen in this light, the many hours that infants and children spend in play are by no means wasted or merely recuperative in nature. Play may be fun, but it is also a serious business in childhood. During these hours the child steadily builds up his competence in dealing with the environment.

Careful study of exploratory play, even in the first year of life, shows it to have the characteristics of directedness, selectivity, and persistence. Piaget's observations[43] make it plain that the child seeks opportunities to investigate his surroundings and will go to no little trouble to find them. My proposal is that activity, manipulation, and exploration, which are all pretty much of a piece in the infant, be considered together as aspects of competence, and that for the present we assume that one general motivational principle lies behind them. The word I have suggested for this motive is *effectance* because its most characteristic feature is seen in the production of effects upon the environment. At first these effects may consist of any changes in sensory input that follow upon activity or exertion, but before long the child becomes able to intend particular changes and to be content only with these. The experience that goes with producing such changes I have designated as the *feeling of efficacy*. Effectance is to be conceived as a neurogenic motive, in contrast to a viscerogenic one. It can be informally described as what the sensori-neuro-muscular system wants to do when it is not occupied with homeostatic business. Its adaptive significance lies in its promotion of spare-time behavior that leads to an extensive growth of competence well beyond what could be learned in connection with drive reduction.

This, then, is the new motivational base from which I want to reconsider the stages of psychosexual development. But I must make it clear that my procedure will not consist merely of introducing a neglected motive and fighting for its recognition against the claims of sexuality and aggression. If the problem could be so easily solved, it would have been solved long ago. The difficulty is that effectance does not pursue a separate life. It does not typically come into sharp, decisive conflict with drives. It can be mobilized alone, as in the child's play or in the adult's fascination with puzzles, but it is often mobilized in close connection with other needs. The feeling of efficacy can be experienced alone, but it is often merged with other satisfactions, as when, for example, a campus Don Juan reduces his sexual drive while also congratulating himself on the success of his technique of seduction. Because of this high tendency toward fusion it is not profitable to carry on the analysis of later development in terms of effectance and feelings of efficacy. Competence is built up out of all kinds of interactions with the environment, including those due to effectance alone and those due to much more complex patterns of motives. Our interest from here on will be in *competence* and its very important subjective aspect, which I am calling *sense of competence*. And we shall not find it profitable to look for the sense of competence as if it were a separate thing in personality; rather, we must become aware of the aspect of competence in a wide variety of actions and experiences.

Sense of competence can be seen as the cumulative product of one's history of efficacies and inefficacies. It comes to operate in new behavior as a kind of set: we judge whether or not we can jump over a brook or carry out a proposed task. It also comes to be much cherished, so that we feel truly elated at new proofs of our ability and deeply humiliated when we cannot do something we supposed was within our power. The sense of competence thus has strong motivational backing, doubtless from a variety of sources. Its importance in personality will be more readily apparent if we bear in mind that it applies to interactions with people as well as to dealings with the inanimate environment. Just as the child explores his physical surroundings, finding out what he can do with objects and what they will do to him, so he investigates his human environment, learning what he can make people do and what he can expect of them. Sense of social competence may well be the more important of the two, though I think we should beware of the current fashion of discussing personality as if it grew in a physical vacuum where tumbles and bumps, victories of locomotion, and struggles with refractory objects are held to exist only insofar as they elicit social responses. We do not live exclusively in a social environment, but we live there importantly, and it is often harder to develop a stable sense of one's social competence than to know what one can accomplish with material objects.

COMPETENCE AND EGO PSYCHOLOGY

I should like now to indicate the relation between these ideas and some of the recent advances in psychoanalytic ego psychology. As you will see, there is a great deal of similarity when we talk on the level of general concepts. There are also many common implications for the psychosexual stages, though only Erikson[8-9] has tried to reconsider these stages in a systematic way.

We start with Hartmann, whose important essay, *Ego Psychology and the Problem of Adaptation*,[25] came out in the year of Freud's death and is considered by many workers to be, somewhat paradoxically, both a turning point in psychoanalytic theory and a direct sequel to Freud's own work on the ego. In this essay Hartmann questioned the adequacy of instincts, at least in the human case, to bring about adaptive behavior. He did not believe that the mere collision between instinctual urge and frustrating circumstance could ever generate the reality principle. The pressures of the environment can be met only with the aid of an innate ego apparatus which has its own laws of development through maturation and learning. To indicate the autonomous nature of this development he spoke of it as taking place in good part in a "conflict-free sphere." Functions like locomotion or the mastery of language ripen in the course of time without necessarily being caught up in anxious conflicts over erotic and aggressive satisfactions. Following a suggestion of Freud's, Hartmann concluded that the energy behind ego development is intrinsic, independent of the instincts, and that growth in this sphere yields a pleasure of its own. He further proposed that events in the conflict-free sphere might have important consequences for the handling of conflicts: adaptive capacities learned in this sphere can be transferred to libidinal and aggressive battlegrounds.

The agreement between this theory and the one I have already described seems thus far sufficient to make me a follower of Hartmann. You will notice that in language which is only slightly different he says that drive reduction cannot account for the range and variety of our adaptive accomplishments, that an independent source of motivation must be assumed for the growth of competence, and that effectiveness or ego strength cannot be understood apart from this growth. But now something happens that prevents me from following in Hartmann's footsteps. Suddenly I run into him, stopped in his tracks. As I see it, he makes practically no further effort to develop the concept of an autonomous ego factor. Instead, in later writing,[26] he turns back to a notion apparently more favored by Freud, that of the neutralization of drive energies. According to this notion, ego development makes use of the energies of erotic and aggressive instincts, which energies, however, have become transformed or neutralized so that they no longer impel toward erotic or aggressive goals. This doctrine has its comforts, among them the removal of incentive to reconsider the psychosexual stages, for the instincts are neatly restored to their place of energic supremacy. But it seems to me a rather unfortunate attempt to hold the line at all costs for Freud's instinct theory, and I anticipate greater gains by pursuing the theme of autonomous ego development.

Other workers in psychoanalytic ego psychology have gone somewhat further with this theme. Hendrick,[27] for example, argued the case for an additional instinct, the *instinct to master,* and he produced in evidence a great many of the facts I have drawn together under the heading of competence. Calling mastery an instinct is open to the same objection as calling exploration or manipulation a drive; everyone jumped on Hendrick for using the concept in such a radically altered sense. Apart from this dubious bit of conceptual strategy, however, his ideas are in close accord with those I am advancing here. Let a single quotation suffice to indicate the similarity: "Primary pleasure is sought by the efficient use of the central nervous system for the performance of well-integrated ego functions which enable the individual to control and alter his environment."[28]

A somewhat different conceptualization, yet one much in the same direction is Mittelmann's proposal of a *motility urge.* Mittelmann[37] emphasizes the driven, persistent, time-consuming quality of motor activity. He points out its relation to reality testing, its service to ego development, and its vital role in the economy of self-esteem. During the second and third years of life, the

traditional anal stage, the motility urge is the dominant one in behavior, and Mittelmann accordingly suggests calling this period
"the motor level of ego and libido development." Although he
treats motility as an urge in its own right, he refers to it as a
"partial instinct," likens it to oral, excretory, and genital urges,
and does not propose further changes in the psychosexual stages.

It is in the work of Erikson[8,9] that one finds the most far-reach-
ing attempt to extend the range of ego psychology. Erikson's eight
stages in the development of the ego constitute, it seems to me, a
major advance in psychoanalytic theory. For the first time the latency period is given a significance of its own. Likewise for the
first time the problems of growth are seen as continuing beyond
young adulthood when haply the goal of genital primacy has been
achieved. But the most important step is the systematic relating of
the child's unfolding capacities to his encounters with the social
environment. Erikson sees early development as a process of
mutual regulation between child and parents. The child's changing capacities and the parents' changing demands lead to a series
of decisive encounters, the outcomes of which are fateful for future growth. Later on, these encounters involve the social environment more broadly conceived; in this way, Erikson achieves the
social relatedness that is the virtue of neo-Freudian theories without falling into their vice of losing touch with the biological roots
of behavior.

Erikson's description of development is remarkably inclusive.
In his concept of zones he retains the essence of libido theory,
though with a somewhat altered meaning. With the concept of
mutual regulation he draws in the best features of the interpersonal model. With his idea of modes he introduces competence,
describing at each stage the motor and cognitive capacities that determine the character of the crisis. Erikson's account therefore
seems to have everything the heart could desire. But it has one
thing I wish it did not have, namely, an implied close connection
between zones and modes which I think can lead only to confusion.

In recasting libido theory Erikson undertakes to avoid the scientific crudeness of Freud's formulation by a generous broadening

of the biological base. Zonal sensitivities are but part of the picture; the progression from oral to anal to phallic stages is determined by a general ripening of sensory-motor capacity as a whole. The concept of mode captures these broader possibilities. Thus the oral stage, called "oral-sensory," is dominated by the incorporative mode, which means that everything the infant does, even his visual and tactile exploration, has the character of a taking in of experience. The anal stage, renamed "muscular-anal," represents more advanced prowess in motor and manipulative control. It is dominated by the retentive and eliminative modes, which show themselves alike in bowel functions and in the familiar manipulative sequence characterized by grasping and a little later by letting go and throwing away. Likewise the "locomotor-genital" stage brings to full flower the intrusive mode, which includes "the intrusion into other bodies by physical attack; the intrusion into other people's ears and minds by aggressive talking; the intrusion into space by vigorous locomotion; the intrusion into the unknown by consuming curiosity"[8] (p. 83). Erogenous zones and neuromuscular competence are thus seen as strictly isomorphic, set in the same patterns of interaction with the environment.

My discontent with this idea comes from my belief that in trying to put the stages of development on a broader base Erikson has not sufficiently disengaged himself from the old libidinal prototypes. He wants to assign significance to the growth of competence, but he describes this growth in generalizations carried over directly from the original theory. Incorporation, retention, elimination, and intrusion precisely describe the zonal impulses demanded by straight libido theory. Erikson then asks us to believe that these modes successively characterize virtually all the important things a young child does in the course of growth. This seems to me rather dubious, and I prefer a different strategy for finding out about it. It seems to me safer to treat visual exploration, manipulation, locomotion, and the many other aspects of competence as functions developing in their own right, more or less autonomously, without any presumed relation to zonal pleasures or presumed similarity to zonal impulses. By using the competence model in this way we can protect ourselves from unwarranted generalizations while yet leaving the facts free to tumble back into the old psychosexual stages if that is how they really look.

Let us proceed to recxamine the stages in the light of what I have said about effectance, feeling of efficacy, competence, and sense of competence, and let us see what happens.

THE ORAL STAGE

The oral stage occupies approximately the first year of life. Following Abraham,[1] it is customarily divided into an early phase, in which pleasurable sucking is the predominant activity, and a later phase, often called "oral-sadistic," introduced by the eruption of teeth and the appearance of a strong urge to bite. According to psychoanalytic theory the oral zone during this stage is the chief seat of libidinal excitability. This means that it is the infant's main source of satisfaction and at the same time his principal point of contact with the environment. Ego development is therefore described in terms of the feeding model. The breast and then the mother become the first objects to be clearly discriminated. The infant's relation to the world, his basic trust or mistrust (as Erikson expresses it), is forever colored by his experience with these first objects. The consequences of oral experience for later development and for a possible psychotic outcome are well known to all students of Freud, and concepts such as oral dependence, oral receptivity, and oral aggression have become commonplace tools in clinical diagnosis.

The psychoanalytic theory of development is not confined to the dimensions of love and hate, but there is a strong tendency to relate all other trends to the feeding model. The infant's cognitive outlook, his knowledge of reality, and his discrimination between self and outer world are all described as taking place almost exclusively in relation to the food-providing mother. The defense mechanisms attributed to the first year, especially introjection and projection, are easily cast in feeding terms. Such accomplishments as visual fixation and manual grasping are made analogous to feeding in Erikson's concept of the incorporative mode. It is even held that the infant's interest in the inanimate environment is somehow mediated by the mother. Spitz[50] has argued that the child understands objects by analogy with food, so that his attitude toward toys can be considered a by-product of his attitude toward the mother and her more central gift.

It is of course a cardinal point in more orthodox psychoanalytic theory that the satisfactions involved in sucking and feeding are primarily libidinal satisfactions. On the basis of different assumptions about basic drives one could suppose that feeding involved primary satisfaction of the hunger drive and some undetermined amount of additional pleasure from stimulation of the sensitive oral zones. Sullivan,[52] who devoted many pages to the child at the breast, used the feeding model without any implication that its gratifications were libidinal. This issue, however, need not concern us here. Our problem is to try out the very different concept of competence.

Looking again at the familiar scene of the first year of life, we can see on the surface much that bespeaks the importance of feeding. Gesell's description of the feeding of the 16-week-old infant agrees closely with the picture painted by psychoanalytic writers.[21] This genial observer does full justice to the tremendous eagerness and overt signs of satisfaction during and after feeding, and he does not overlook the evidences of an independent urge to suck. The eagerness stays at high pitch up to eight months. It is apt to be expressed vocally when the breast, the bottle, or even the spoon comes in sight, and the infant may become highly impatient if he has to watch the preparation of a meal.

So far there is nothing to violate Freud's conception of the oral stage, but we must not forget that the feeding pattern undergoes a considerable change before the end of the first year. In part the change can still be captured in the psychosexual formula: libido theory has its explanation for the marked decline of the sucking need, shown in the fact that a year-old infant may want but one bottle a day and may toss it off in three or four minutes instead of the half hour that would have been required earlier. In part, however, the changes seem to me to imply that something else, some other need, is beginning to encroach upon pure oral gratification. For one thing, there are clear signs that additional entertainment is desired during a meal. The utensils are investigated, the behavior of spilled food is explored, toys are played with throughout the feeding. Gesell suggests that at one year of age a toy in each hand is the only guarantee that a meal will be completed without housekeeping disaster. A similar situation prevails during the bath, when water toys are needed and when the germ of scientific interest may express itself by "dabbling water onto the floor from the washcloth." More important, however, is the infant's growing enthusiasm for the doctrine of "do it yourself." He assists in his own nourishment by holding the bottle and by active finger feeding. Around one year there is likely to occur what Levy[35] calls "the battle of the spoon," the moment "when the baby grabs the spoon from the mother's hand and tries to feed itself." From Gesell's painstaking description of the spoon's "hazardous journey" from dish to mouth we can be sure that the child is not motivated at this point by increased oral gratification. He gets more food by letting mother do it, but doing it himself he gets more of another kind of satisfaction—a feeling of efficacy, and perhaps already a growth of the sense of competence.

Development in the sphere of competence can be observed more decisively if we turn to behavior that is not connected with feeding. Somehow the image has gotten into our minds that the infant's time is divided between eating and sleep. Peter Wolff[58] is now showing that this is not true even for newborn infants, who show distinct forerunners of what will later become playful exploratory activity. Gesell notes that at four weeks there is apt to be a waking time in the late afternoon during which visual experience begins to be accumulated. At 16 weeks this period may last for half an hour, and the times increase steadily up to one year, when Gesell's typical "behavior day" shows an hour of play before breakfast, two hours before lunch, an hour's carriage ride and another hour of social play during the afternoon, and perhaps still another hour after being put to bed. At the age of 12 months the child is already putting in a six-hour day of play, not to mention the overtime that occurs during meals and the bath.

What goes on during these increasingly long intervals of play? At first visual exploration is the most concentrated form of activity, though babbling and gross motor movements are also present. Halfway through the year comes what Gesell calls the "heyday of manipulation," when grasping is an "eager and intent business." Here is his description of play with a clothespin at 28 weeks:

> The child wants to finger the clothespin, to get the feel of it. He puts it in his mouth, pulls it out, looks at it, rotates it with a twist of the wrist, puts it back into his mouth, pulls it out, gives it another twist, brings up his free hand, transfers the clothespin from hand to hand, bangs it on the high chair tray, drops it, recovers it, retransfers it from hand to hand, drops it out of reach, leans over to retrieve it, fails, fusses a moment, then bangs the tray with his empty hand. . . He is never idle because he is under such a compelling urge to use his hands for manipulation and exploitation[21] (pp. 108-109).

Later in the year the child will become a creeper and may even rise for his first step or two by the first birthday. The creeper can be something of an adventurer; things might be easier for his mother if he did not expose himself to so much of his environment. In the cognitive sphere we can consult Piaget[43] for an account of what the infant does with his spare time. Five of the six stages in the development of "sensorimotor intelligence" were transversed by the three Piaget children, possibly a skewed sample, by the end of the first year. Active exploration of the environment, even to the extent of experimenting with the fall of objects from different positions, could be seen going on during the eleventh month, and quite early in the second year the children appeared to have mastered through experience the important concept of permanent substantial objects. Mind you, we are talking about the oral stage of development. The model of the feeding child does scant justice to Piaget's son, a youthful Galileo lying in his crib and dropping his celluloid swan from various positions overhead to see where it will fall.

If we look with similar attention at the realm of social competence we shall see once again that the infant's interest is not entirely confined to oral satisfaction. It is true that in exploring the properties of his mother, in finding out how to maximize gratifications and minimize neglect or punishment, he will be strongly influenced by her position as chief source of oral and affectionate supplies. Here the aspect of competence may be pretty well obscured by such powerful affects as love, anger, and anxiety. But there are other moments of social interaction that do not seem to be so mingled with basic drives. If we watch the child happily passing objects back and forth with another person, playing peek-a-boo, hiding behind chairs, or engaging in the hilarious pastime of being chased while creeping, it looks as if there were a good many quite different ways of having fun. I should not like to depreciate the affection that infants feel for those around them, but I am inclined to agree with Woodworth[56] that part of the fun in social play comes simply from "the opportunity to do something interesting in the environment." Young chimpanzees, according to observations made by Welker,[55] prefer to play with objects that are brightly colored, that light up, or that make sounds; objects, in other words, that provide a rich return of stimulation in response to effort expended. Similarly, young children like to play with those objects which, because they are animated, give them the most for their money.

In summary concerning the oral stage, let me say that if one is determined to use a single model for everything that happens during the first year, the model of the feeding child is clearly the proper choice. The delights of feeding, the pleasures of sucking, and the central position of the mother in emotional development are attested equally by direct superficial observation and by deep psychoanalytic interpretation. But are we obliged to use only one model? Does this result in the best possible conceptualization? I am proposing that we use at least two models for this period of development: the oral model, typified by the infant at the breast, and a competence model, represented by the child's exploratory play—the active interaction with his surroundings that starts as fun but that contributes steadily to the attainment of adult competence. The addition of the competence model I believe to be necessary here, and much more so at the later stages, if we are to do justice to the child's adaptive prowess and to the manner in which natural growth takes place from year to year. We need it if we are to have an effective ego psychology to go with instinct psychology.

The psychoanalytic hypothesis of oral libido requires us, first, to merge nutritional satisfaction with erotic satisfaction; second, to find the motivation of all the competence sequences in oral eroticism. Competence sequences such as manipulation or explor- ation can be considered erotic through association with feeding, through secondary reinforcement by feeding, through symbolism, or through the kind of developmental analogy that is implied in Erikson's incorporative mode. Connections of this kind assuredly exist. I have no intention to dispute what Erikson,[8] among others, has shown about symbolism in children's play and about the erotic and aggressive preoccupations that lead to play disruption. But we lose rather than gain, in my opinion, if we consider the child's *undisrupted* play, six hours a day, to be a continuous ex- pression of libidinal energy, a continuous preoccupation with the family drama, as if there could be no intrinsic interest in the prop- erties of the external world and the means of coming to terms with it. We lose rather than gain if we look only for an incorpora- tive element in the infant's cognitive and motor behavior, remem- bering, for instance, that he puts the clothespin in his mouth but forgetting that he uses it to bang on the chair. We lose rather than gain if we try to force upon the mother an exclusive part in in- teresting the child in his surroundings. The psychosexual theory of the oral stage involves us in a regrettable overgeneralization from a very sound core. It can be corrected only by a new discrimina- tion such as the one I am proposing here.

I believe that this correction makes important differences. One brief example must suffice. Weaning appears both in psychoanaly- tic theory and in learning (reinforcement) theory as an unmiti- gated evil and a potential trauma. It involves the replacement of a more gratifying method by a temporarily less gratifying method of securing nourishment. It can be endured only if the mother draws upon her accumulated capital of dependent affection and rewards the child for his sacrifices by expressions of love and ap- proval. In the absence of such capital the results are bound to be unfortunate. If at this point we add the competence model, we see at once that the process of weaning is very much assisted by the motive of effectance. It is aided by the infant's inherent satisfac- tion in mastering the cup and spoon, in bringing these parts of the environment under the governance of his own effort and initiative. He does not have to do it wholly for mother; as an active living being he has his own stake in growing up.

THE ANAL STAGE

The second main stage in psychosexual development, to which we now turn, comes when the libidinal excitability of the oral zone yields its primacy to the anal region. According to libido theory, the anal zone becomes increasingly erotized or libidinized during the second and third years, with the result that the child's emotional development turns more and more on events connected with excretion. The model for this stage may be expressed as the child on the toilet, but this phrase should imply that the child is being trained to use the toilet in scheduled adult fashion. Freud's conception is as always firmly instinctual. Libidinal pleasure is involved in the passing and retaining of bowel movements. Frustration and crisis lurk in the fact that the child is required to sacrifice some of this pleasure, or at least to subordinate it to cultural regulations imposed by the parents. Neo-Freudian revisionists generally reject the libido postulate but retain the idea of a struggle with discipline, and often enough they continue to use toilet training as the central model for this crisis in growth.[49,54]

As with the oral stage, Abraham[1] divided the "anal-sadistic stage," as he called it, into an early and late phase, characterized by predominant pleasure respectively in excretion and in retention. Erikson[8] points out that the anal zone "lends itself more than any other to the display of stubborn adherence to contradictory impulses because it is the modal zone of two conflicting modes of approach, which must become alternating, namely *retention* and *elimination*." The preoccupations of toilet training are held to radiate widely and to determine the course of emotional growth. Freud first postulated the anal stage when studying the ambivalences of adult compulsion neurotics, and he traced to it the famous "anal character" with its qualities of stubbornness, neatness, and parsimony. Fenichel[10] asserted that the pinching off of feces was perceived as a sadistic act and that, later on, "persons are treated as the feces previously were treated." By such extensions, the model of the child on the toilet is made equal to every aspect of growth during the second and third years.

Erikson,[9] in his still strictly parallel stages of ego development, describes the crisis of this period as a "battle for autonomy," the outcome of which is "decisive for the ratio between love and hate, for that between cooperation and willfulness, and for that between the freedom of self-expression and its suppression." If the child can weather the struggle and achieve "self-control without loss of self-esteem," he will emerge with "a lasting sense of autonomy and pride." If he is less fortunate, his legacy will be one of doubt and shame, his later character will probably be compulsive, and at the worst he may fall into the cruel grip of obsessional neurosis.

Clearly we are dealing with important problems of development, but is it correct to place the decisive struggle in the bathroom? Does the child in toilet training provide an adequate model, a sufficient interpretative nucleus, for all that is going on? Let us introduce again the competence model and see whether or not it can help us with the problems of this stage. It is worth noticing at the outset that direct observation does not give the libido theory the kind of support it provided in the oral stage. To be sure, there is plenty of evidence, even in the pages of the clean-minded Gesell, that children are interested in anal functions, that they play with feces, and that they experience frustration and conflict over the process of training. But direct observation would never suggest that these happenings were the central preoccupations of the second and third years, nor would introspection convince us that retaining and eliminating could have anything like the intensity of oral pleasures. The evidence for a stage of predominant anal libido thus rests heavily upon the reconstructions that occur in psychoanalytic treatment. On the other hand direct observation has long recognized a sharp and significant crisis in human relations, usually called two-year-old negativism. This could be, of course, a displacement from bowel training, but the competence model suggests another possibility. We may be dealing here with a profound *intrinsic* crisis in the growth of social competence.

Let us ask what the child accomplishes during the second and third years in the way of competent interactions with his environment. As regards locomotion he starts as an awkward toddler, but by the middle of the second year he becomes a restless runabout who not only gets into everything but also clearly experiments with his prowess by such stunts as walking backwards or pushing his own carriage. His first upright steps may have been wildly applauded, but his locomotor accomplishments soon become cause for parental despair and seem to continue without benefit of social reward. By the third birthday he may display his astonishing gains in coordination by starting to ride a tricycle. Parallel growth in manipulation is shown in those long stretches of time when he is quite happy to play by himself. One observes a constant activity of carrying objects about, filling and emptying containers, tearing things apart and fitting them together, lining up blocks and eventually building with them, digging and constructing in the sandbox. Such play may look idle to an adult, but it brings about a tremendous increase in the child's ability to deal with the physical world.

It is this picture of persistent, driven motor activity that led Mittelmann[37] to postulate a *motility urge*. The second and third years, he points out, show the most rapid growth of motility; he even asserts that at this stage the motor urge "dominates all other urges." Motility is seen by him as "one of the most important avenues for exercising such functions as mastery, integration, reality-testing, and control of impulses—usually referred to in analysis as ego functions." During the third year the child shows a desire to do things himself and may resent help. "There is an increasing emphasis now on motor accomplishment leading to self-esteem. Thus the evolution of self-assertiveness and self-esteem is intimately connected with motor development." In such fashion Mittelmann uses the idea that I am referring to as *sense of competence*.

Development in the sphere of motility seems important in its own right, and it helps us to understand the social crisis of negativism. The child busily tests his own growing capacities; he explores the properties of physical objects; he finds out the ways in which he can influence the environment and have effects upon it. In parallel fashion he begins new tests of his competence in the social sphere. Two developments introduce the crisis that has been so often described. In the first place, the span of consecutive action and intention reaches a point where interference before the end can be frustrating and successful completion can be rewarding. In the second place, the use of language advances to a point where commands can be attempted and where the consequences of the word "no," as uttered by oneself, begin to invite investigation. Behind these developments lies something a bit more inferential, described by Stern[51] in these words: "The child deports and realizes himself as a living entity, a one complete center of power"; thus for the first time "he wishes to affirm himself, his existence, his importance—and to increase it." Earlier, his effectance behavior has seemed more like a series of discrete stabs resulting in discrete feelings of efficacy. Now he begins to act more like a self, with a more organized sense of competence.

At some point, then, the child begins quite directly to try out his social competence. The sharp-eyed Sully[53] pointed out a "sudden emergence of self-will" around the age of two. Stern chose "wilfulness" as the proper term to characterize this phase of development. Words such as "obstinacy" and "defiance" are also common in the literature. Gesell, who sees these tendencies as reaching their peak at two and a half, feels certain that parents would vote this time "the most exasperating age in the preschool period," and he observes with disapproval that "the spanking curve comes to a peak at about this time." As an example of defiance and obstinacy, Stern, like Piaget and assiduous observer of his own children, chose a mealtime episode in which his little daughter Eva gave the command: "Father, pick up the spoon." A clash of wills followed because she had not said, and would not say, "please"; her obstinate refusal resulted in her having no dinner. Today we may be inclined to applaud Eva for her fight against excessive middle-class decencies, but in any event she illustrates the testing of social competence both by giving a command and by refusing to obey one.

The meaning of this early self-assertion and negativism has

been examined carefully in a recent paper by Levy.[35] He uses the term "oppositional behavior" for this and certain similar phenomena both earlier and later in life, including the infant's refusal to suck when awakened too quickly and the generalized negativism found in catatonic schizophrenia. Although he calls such forms of behavior "oppositional," Levy makes it clear that they do not start as expressions of aggression. Their true adaptive significance is that of resisting external influence. If behavior were allowed to be governed wholly from outside, there would be no scope for inner needs and no way to develop inner controls. "The oppositional behavior of the second year of life," Levy writes, "is a general movement towards the autonomy of the whole person . . . the first flowering of self-determination, of which the budding had long been in evidence." The two forms, "I do it myself," and "No, no," are aspects of the same trend toward autonomy; indeed, there is evidence[29] that children who have a marked stubborn period are more independent later on. While Levy does not use the word "competence," he is certainly employing a similar idea.

During the second and third years, then, the child, because of practiced maturing of general coordination and of verbal capacity, reaches a critical juncture in his ability to interact with his social environment. His attempts to exploit the new possibilities and to increase his sense of social competence are at first somewhat crude and uncompromising. In his inexperience he challenges rather forcefully his parents' sense of competence. These tests are exacting for the parents. The temptation to prevail at all costs will be powerful not only for parents who like to exercise authority but also for apostles of permissiveness who are startled to find such tyranny emerging in their young. How much sense of social competence can the child preserve in these crises? The outcome of his first concerted attempts to measure his efficacy against that of other people may leave quite a lasting mark upon his confidence.

You will notice that the competence model does not create any quarrel with Erikson's concept of a crisis in autonomy. There is agreement as to what constitutes the central problem in ego development at this stage. But the competence model, I maintain, is far better able to conceptualize this development than the model derived from libido theory. I do not want to make light of the child's excretory interests or to minimize his problems over bowel training. The analysis of children with psychosomatic complaints of the digestive tract attests the value of such concepts. My argument is that bowel training is not a correct prototype for the problem of autonomy. It is not the right model for those tryings and testings of the sense of competence that would have to go on anyway, even if bowel training were of no consequence at all.

The bowel training model is wrong, I think, in two ways. First, it concerns a function that is governed by autonomic nervous system, that never comes under direct voluntary control, and that does not carry the experience of initiative that goes with voluntary action. The child may be proud when he can meet parental expectations, but it will be pride in meeting a somewhat mysterious demand by a somewhat mysterious process of habit formation, not the pride of mastering things directly by trial and by effort expended, as when one learns to throw or to bat a ball. Second, it is a situation in which cultural requirements inevitably prevail. Every child is bowel trained. This is a far greater victory for authority than generally prevails elsewhere; in other matters the child preserves more freedom to resist, plead, cajole, and force compromises on his surrounding adults. In short, the bowel training model all but eliminates the initiative and versatility on the child's part that is an essential aspect of any true autonomy. The best outcome of the bowel training problem is that the child will come to will the inevitable. The best outcome of the struggle for social competence is that he will face the world with self-respect and a measure of confidence in his own strength.

As with the oral stage, I shall take but one example to show how the proposed competence model makes a real difference. I think it throws new light on the anal-erotic character. There can be no doubt that Freud hit upon a very real pattern when he formulated this idea, but there has always been something peculiar about its interpretation in anal-libidinal terms. Of the triad of traits, parsimony and stubbornness go well enough together, and it is possible to see them as two forms of opposition to the demand for timely performance on the toilet. The third trait, orderliness, does not seem to belong in the same picture. It is said to be a reaction-formation against disorderly desires, a surrender to cultural pressure. Why does the anal problem give rise so frequently to this pattern of two oppositional traits and one reaction-formation, when other combinations seem equally possible?

The competence model helps us out of this dilemma by shedding new light on orderliness. You have probably noticed that orderliness is a suspect trait these days. It is taken to signify neuroticism, compulsiveness, rigidity, and failure to appreciate what is important in life. I remember the trouble that ensued when one of my course assistants, happily liberated from obsessional symptoms such as bookkeeping, handed back to the students a set of graded examination papers and kept no record of the grades he had assigned. This incident may help to convince you of the point I now want to make, which is that orderliness has an adaptive function, that it is within certain limits a competent way of dealing with one's surroundings. Neatness is not just something the culture forces upon us. If we look closely at the development of competence in the child, we can see that tendencies toward orderliness emerge spontaneously during the second year and that they have a function in dealing with the environment. This function proves to be not at all incongruous with stubbornness and parsimony.

The function of orderliness was pointed out by Goldstein[23] in his account of brain-injured patients. Some of these patients were vehemently insistent that their belongings be always in the same place, so that when needed they could be found without difficult mental acts of remembering. The theme reappears in Kanner's work on autistic children,[32] who demand a ritualistic sameness in the physical environment. In Gesell's pages we notice the emergence of similar tendencies during the second year: an interest in putting things away, in where things belong, and in the possibility of calling some things "mine." All these trends can be understood as attempts to establish control over things so that they can be readily found and kept. At the same time the child shows tendencies toward ritual, making demands, for instance, for certain foods at certain times, served in certain ways. Here again the rigidities serve the cause of controlling the environment, including the people in it, and assuring oneself that accustomed satisfactions can be made to reappear. Orderliness serves to increase competence, and it is very definitely imposed upon adults at times as a means of making their behavior more predictable and controllable.

In these terms, then, stubbornness, parsimony, and orderliness are completely of a piece. They are ways of preventing oneself from being pushed around by the environment. They emerge when they do because they depend upon certain other developmental achievements: the constancy of objects, and a continuity of play interests from day to day. The fixation of the triad of traits happens when there is relative feeling of incompetence in relation to the environment, especially the human one: when toys are arbitrarily taken away by parents or other children, when gratifications seem to come whimsically, when demands are made without relation to inner inclinations—the demand for bowel regularity being one instance. A human environment that is not in good intuitive contact with the child's inclinations, one that is also fairly active with its demands, would seem most likely to evoke such a pattern. The "anal character" is a person who somewhat mistrusts his environment. His traits coherently express how he adapted to this mistrust during the second year. Reaction formation need not be assumed for any of them.

There is another kind of orderliness, however, which depends directly upon reaction formation. This kind of orderliness represents a docile response to parental requirements. In such children we would expect orderliness to appear without stubbornness or stinginess; it would be associated instead with other evidences of being a good, compliant child more or less on the side of parental values. Such children might have residual messy fantasies, but they would represent lost pleasures rather than a fighting issue. It would be a serious misdiagnosis to class them with "anal-erotic" characters in the other sense.

THE PHALLIC STAGE

According to Freud's theory of the libido, the third stage of psychosexual development comes about through a process of maturation whereby the genital organs become the chief seat of erotic excitability, overthrowing the primacy of the anal zone. As a consequence there is a marked increase of autoerotic activity, of erotic exploration and play, and of curiosity about the facts of reproductive life. There is also, Freud inferred, the beginning of a sexual feeling somewhat analogous to that of adults, sufficiently so to produce possessive love and jealousy and thus to give rise to that early cornerstone of psychoanalytic theory, the Oedipus complex. The ensuing emotional crisis he believed to be nuclear for neurosis and for development in general. The chances for a fearless outflow of libido after puberty, and for happiness in love and marriage, were very likely to be influenced by the outcome of this crucial first encounter. When later Freud conceived the idea of the superego, he related this agency directly to the Oedipus complex, which thereby assumed a central place in the processes of socialization and internal control. He believed that once the child had made his passage through this time of supreme trial the main outlines of his character were set for life.

Interpretation of the phallic stage according to an interpersonal model is made easy by the fact that Freud's own model included such specific interpersonal consequences. Though belittling the analogy between phallic and genital sexuality, the revisionists have been well satisfied to retain the Sophoclean prototype as a model for the interpersonal crisis of the period. But the issues are seen in somewhat different lights. Horney[30] believed that most of the attachments of a child to a parent at this time were of a clinging, dependent nature, mobilized by a compelling need for security. Fromm[18] emphasizes quite another aspect, the child's battle with irrational authority as represented by the parents and their prohibitions. Rivalry, jealousy, hostility are certainly all to be detected in these complex events. Erikson,[8] viewing the activities of the phallic stage as many-sided expressions of the intrusive mode, conceives the ego's crisis to be one of maintaing a sense of initiative. If fortunate, the child will continue to feel that his exuberant powers have a chance of asserting themselves. The danger of the stage is that guilt and anxiety will supervene so strongly that passive resignation or illness will become the only possible ways of life.

Erikson's formulation is actually very much in terms of our competence model. The child is brought nearer to his crisis, he says, by developments in three spheres of competence: locomotion, language, and imagination. Locomotion reaches the point of being a serviceable tool rather than a difficult stunt. The child can walk and run freely, covering a lot of territory, and he can use his tricycle to get about still more widely. He likes to race up and down stairs and perform spectacularly on the stair rail or jungle gym. Furthermore, he becomes able to saw and cut, to throw overhand, and to dress himself without any assistance. The emergence of these seemingly adult motor patterns make it possible for him to compare himself with grown-ups, yet to wonder about the differences in size. This is the time when dressing up in adult clothes and imitating grown-up behavior becomes popular. It is also the time when children pretend to be engineers and truck drivers, relishing the roles that imply remarkable power over the environment.

Language likewise reaches a stage of development at which it can support wider understanding and social exchange. Verbal humor and playing with rhymes attest and produce a growing mastery of speech, and the child begins to understand such subtleties as "might" and "could." The imperious "I" and "you" of the previous stage give place to "we," especially with family members. The important thing is that linguistic competence now opens ready channels for finding out about the world. Questions can be asked, as no parent will forget who has tried to bear up in the onrushing stream of 4-year-old interrogation. Unfortunately for exhausted parents, these sieges must be regarded as highly important to the child's growth. Besides extending his knowledge about the world, he is securing needed practice in expressing himself and in listening with comprehension to what others have to say.

Imagination is the third sphere of competence in which a marked development takes place during the fourth and fifth years. This is the time when the child can first maintain the fantasy of an imaginary companion. It is the time when he can begin to dramatize himself in different adult roles, when he can clothe plain objects like blocks with all the attributes of airplanes, vehicles, animals, and people, when he begins to have frightening dreams involving injury and pursuit by wolves. For, as Erikson[9] expresses it, "both language and locomotion permit him to expand his imagination over so many things that he cannot avoid frightening himself with what he himself has dreamed and thought up" (p. 75).

If we consider the bearing of these developments on social competence, it is clear that the child has reached a point of understanding where for the first time he can contemplate his place in the family and his relation to other people in general. To some extent he continues to experiment with crude social power, especially with other children whom he may boss, hit, and threaten in various ways. But he is also beginning to grasp the nature of roles. It is at this time that he learns his culture's definition of sex roles, and he experiments with a variety of adult roles. For the first time he is intellectually capable of asking those questions, so portentous in libido theory, about marrying the parent of the opposite sex. Up to a point, the culture encourages his ripening capacity to act in grown-up fashion. At about 4 he probably has graduated to an adult-sized bed and may be taking some of his meals at the family table. But he is not yet an adult, so his aspirations are bound to be frustrated in many ways, including his proposals of matrimony.

It is interesting that Erikson, at that point in his account of the "locomotor-genital" stage at which he wants to assign centrality to the Oedipus complex, continues to write in terms of the competence model. "The increased locomotor mastery," he says, "and the pride in being big now and *almost* as good as father and mother receives its severest setback in the clear fact that in the genital sphere one is vastly inferior; furthermore, it receives an additional setback in the fact that not even in the distant future is one ever going to be father in sexual relationship to mother, or mother in sexual relationship to father" (p. 77). But here I cannot help feeling that Erikson has mixed his models. From the point of view of competence, of pride in being big, genital inferiority is by no means greater than many other inferiorities such as stature, strength, speed of running, distance one can throw a ball. Father can start the power lawn mower and control it; he can drive the car; for the modern child these must be obvious and hopeless tokens of his superiority. If the genital comparison is to be made nuclear, it can hardly be in terms of the competence model. One must already have assumed that whatever is sexual is necessarily central.

I should make it clear at this point that I do not believe in using the competence model exclusively. Even if one hesitates a bit over the psychoanalytic evidence based on adult recollections of the phallic stage, it would be impossible to deny the direct evidence presented, for instance, by Susan Isaacs[31] from her nursery school or by Anna Freud and Dorothy Burlingham[13] from their wartime nurseries, not to mention what any observant person can notice in children of this age, that there is a clearly sexual flavor to some of the child's activities and interests. This must not be neglected, but neither should it be taken, I believe, as a matter so profound that the whole of emotional development hangs upon it. The growth of competence leads to intrinsic emotional and interpersonal crises. Perhaps the best way to make this clear is to imagine for the moment a child in the phallic stage who is normal in every way except that no increase in genital sensitivity takes place. This child would still make locomotor, linguistic, and imaginative progress, would become interested in being like adults, would make comparisons as to size, would be competitive and subject to defeats and humiliations, would be curious, ask endless questions and encounter rebuffs, would have bad dreams and guilt feelings over imagined assertive or aggressive actions, would learn about sex roles, would struggle to understand his relation to other family members, and might very well ask about marrying one of the parents. All of these things arise inescapably from progress in the growth of competence. They all have important emotional consequences. In all these situations there is a chance to maintain and strengthen a sense of initiative; in all there is also a chance that the environment will act so as to impose a burden of guilt.

If we now restore to our hypothetical child his genital sensitivity, his life may become yet more complicated, but it will still revolve around initiative and guilt. Oedipal wishes add an emotional dimension, but they do not completely change the nature of the interpersonal crisis. And it seems to me that the Oedipal prototype falls short as a general model for the phallic stage in just the way toilet training failed for the anal stage. Once again Freud selected as his central image a hopeless situation, one where defeat for the child is inevitable. The child must learn to renounce the whole Oedipal wish, just as he must learn to renounce any thought of not being bowel-trained. I submit the idea that if these were the true and determinative models it would be quite a problem to explain the survival of any sense of initiative. These models help us to understand why we have shame and guilt, but they do not give us much reason to suppose that we could emerge with autonomy and initiative. The competence model is not so harsh, though it certainly is not intended to gloss over the tragic features of childhood. By its help we can more easily see where the child fights less unequal battles, where he sometimes achieves compromise and sometimes prevails, where he is free to increase the scope of his activities and build up his sense of competence. We can discover, in short, some of the places where initiative is likely to be strengthened, thus making the inevitable renunciations less bitter and overwhelming.

As before, I shall mention but one specific problem that might benefit by introducing the competence model. I believe that we can now make a consistent systematic distinction between shame and guilt. These two words have become so confused in the psychological literature that they are often used interchangeably. They are confused in experience, too; very few people can distinguish sharply between being ashamed and feeling guilty. It has been proposed that there are wide cultural differences in the use of these two deterrents, so that one can properly speak of shame-cultures and guilt-cultures, but this suggestion has by no means won the applause of anthropologists as a whole. The neo-Freudians have made the confusion systematic by their emphasis on rejection and abandonment as the true basic anxiety that guides our lives. Shame and guilt alike are painful because they signify desertion, so there is no point in trying for a sharp distinction.

A determined attempt to rescue and separate the two concepts has been made in a recent monograph by Piers and Singer.[44] Structurally, they say, shame arises from tension between ego and ego-ideal; guilt from tension between ego and superego. This means that shame occurs when there is shortcoming or failure to reach a goal through lack of ability, whereas guilt implies touching or transgressing a moral boundary. In my own words I should say that shame is always connected with incompetence. It occurs when we cannot do something that either we or an audience thinks we should be able to do: when we cannot lift the weight, when we cannot hit the ball, when we offer to knock someone down and get knocked down ourselves. It means belittlement and loss of respect. In contrast, guilt does not imply that one is unable to do something; it signifies that one has done, or is thinking of doing, something within one's power that is forbidden.

The distinction can be illustrated straight from the classical Oedipus situation. The father or the mother can discourage the little boy's erotic pretensions in either of two ways. They may tell him that his advances are wrong and bad, indicating that they don't like badness and will punish him, but making no suggestion that he could not carry out his intentions. Or they may tell him that he is too young, that his penis is too small to please his mother, thus belittling him but not implying that the impossible act would be morally wrong. It is doubtless more common to combine these implications, thus strengthening the subjective confusion between shame and guilt. But in principle the distinction seems to me to be clear.

It is unfortunate, I think, that Piers and Singer try to connect shame with fear of abandonment. Belittlement means to the child, they claim, that the parent will walk away in disgust and leave his offspring in the grip of separation anxiety. This is completely at odds with Erikson's conception of shame, which emphasizes a sense of exposure on the child's part and a desire to hide. Indeed the experience of shame seems always to involve an impulse to run away, hide, or sink through the floor. If the basic fear were desertion, the basic response should be clinging, but in fact we want to get away from those who belittle us.

Shame, then, is a response to incompetence, not to moral violation. Its pain comes from a diminished sense of competence, from a lowering of respect and of self-respect. I must not digress from my theme at this point, but I can hardly say how important I think it is for dynamic psychology, which has operated so long with love, hate, and anxiety as its chief tools, to bring back into its ways of thinking the variable of respect. For this, the concept of competence is indispensable.

THE LATENCY PERIOD

We come now to a stage of life during which, according to libido theory, there is a relative quiescence in the erotic sphere. Believing that sexual energies actually declined between the phallic stage and puberty, Freud seems to have found the period something of a bore. Psychoanalysis, which was prepared to shock the world with the Oedipus complex and with its reanimation at puberty, had no startling disclosures to make about the intervening years when the problem was so well controlled that the ego could busy itself with the real world. It was perhaps on this account that the unfortunate word "latent" came to be applied, with its all-too-effective suggestion that nothing of importance could happen until Nature enlivened things again by dramatically strengthening the sexual impulses at puberty. Freud provided no picturesque model or prototype for the stage. It can be described, however, in terms of his later structural concepts. The superego, more or less introjected as an outcome of the Oedipal conflict, is now for the first time available to assist the ego in controlling the id. The ego thus finds itself possessed of surplus energies for problems of adaptation.

Freud's handling of the latency period was not one of his happier ventures. In the first place, his assumption about the quiescence of sexual energies seems to be simply wrong. Anthropological evidence and better observation in our own society have combined to cast grave doubt on the hypothesis of a biologically determined sexual latency. For once we can almost say that Freud underestimated the importance of sex. The mistake has serious consequences. By leading us to assume that there is less to contol, it falsifies our understanding of the problems of control that are so vital during these years. In the second place, Freud's gathering of six to eight years of the child's life under a single somewhat negative heading, in striking contrast to the fine discriminations upon which he insisted for the first five years, must be rated as one of those conceptualizations that tend to stifle research. Freud's attitude toward the latency period almost seems to imply that it is not worth investigating. Happily even his loyal followers have not always taken the hint, and the period has lately begun to receive a more searching scrutiny.

It is becoming clear that the latency period is not all of one piece. Hartmann, Kris, and Loewenstein[26] describe the evolution of the superego, which at the start is harsh, rigid, yet erratic, in the manner of a person unfamiliar with newly found authority. In time, and with intellectual growth, this primitiveness gives place to a greater flexibility, so that what Murray[39] calls the integration of ego and superego begins to take place. Bornstein[5] takes this development as a basis for distinguishing two phases of the latency period, with a division point at eight years. Even direct observations with no pretension of depth, such as those made by Gesell and Ilg,[22] show marked changes in emotional outlook at six, seven, and eight which are consistent with the idea that the Oedipus problem is not resolved, nor the superego formed in a short time. Staying entirely within the framework of Freud's theories, one must still allow for important dynamic progressions during the latency stage.

The interpersonal model has been applied to this period in illuminating fashion by Sullivan.[52] His description of the "juvenile era," the time from 6 to 12, is heavily based on the behavior of children with their contemporaries. Sullivan considered that the chief problems were *competition* and *compromise,* a pair of concepts that puts the emphasis on social competence rather than on affective gratifications. At school and on the playground the child finds himself in a competitive, unaffectionate society, with which it is possible to come to terms only by practicing new roles and learning new arts of participation, protection, and compromise. Sullivan's description of the "crudeness of interpersonal relations" at the beginning of the juvenile era matches the picture of the crude superego drawn by more orthodox workers. In terms of competence it is not surprising that crudeness should be characteristic of several kinds of complex behavior. Schoolwork from 6 to 8 undoubtedly merits the same description.

Erikson's account of the latency period adheres quite strictly to the competence model. The child reaches a point where he is no longer satisfied with just play and make-believe. In line with his interest in becoming an adult, he needs to feel useful and to be able to make things and deal with things that have significance in the adult world. He needs, in other words, a *sense of industry,* and he is now capable of the "steady attention and persevering diligence" that foster this sense. His efforts may be enhanced by "positive identification with those who *know* things and know how to *do* things." The dangers lie in the possibility that success will prove to be elusive and social encouragement too weak, in which case the legacy of the stage may be a lasting sense of inadequacy and inferiority.

I hope you will have observed how well the case for competence has been made for me without my speaking a word in its behalf. Erikson makes it central for dealings with the humanly significant objective world; Sullivan made it central for the social world. Once we open up the problems of emotional development in these terms, we can begin to make connections with the findings of workers outside the psychoanalytic tradition who have observed the upbuilding of competence in great detail. One thing that is certainly not latent is the growth of capacities in the realms of both action and of understanding. Think of the differences between a child of 6 and a child of 11—between first-graders and sixth-graders. What the child wants, what he dreads, where he runs into emotional crises, will be very much influenced by the level of his understanding and by the growth of sheer capacity for social interaction.

Let us take this last point to illustrate the benefits that come from using the competence model. Gesell tells us that at the age of nine the children in his sample begin to move in spontaneous groups or gangs that can be orderly and harmonious without adult supervision. Charlotte Bühler[6] reports that first-grade classes cannot act as a whole, that positions of leadership are highly transient, and that the children cannot put their classmates in a rank order of importance. In contrast, fifth-grade classes readily act as units under class leaders, and the children find it a simple task to rank the membership. These observations suggest that a marked growth in social action and understanding takes place somewhere around nine. The nature of this growth has been approached from another angle in Piaget's studies of rules and moral ideas.

Piaget[42] demonstrates that children of seven and eight are only just emerging from a conception of rules as something absolute and unchangeable, a finding which suggests that the early crudeness of the superego comes partly from immaturity of understanding. By the age of 9 the Geneva children had a good idea of reciprocity, realizing, for instance, that it is fair to change the rules provided everyone agrees and the new rules apply to all. But one must wait two or three years more for the emergence of a steady sense of equity, in which fairness is achieved by giving special concessions to handicapped players. This implies that the child has grasped the possibility that another child's need and outlook may be different from his own. He has transcended egocentrism, or, as Lerner[34] conceived it, he has attained the power to shift perspectives, a power manifested in Lerner's own experiment only at eleven or twelve. And it is between nine and twelve that Sullivan[52] locates the first emergence of true chumship in which the other child's feelings and interests become as important as one's own.

These facts suggest that there is a definite pattern in the growth of social competence. Between 6 and 9 the child has to find out how to get along with others in the sense of competing, compromising, protecting himself from hurt, and learning the rules of the game. He does this partly because he has to, being thrown with others at school, and partly because, as Woodworth[56] expresses it, other children "afford him the opportunity to do something interesting in the environment." During this time, however, dependent needs, security, and affection must still find their satisfaction almost entirely in the family circle. Only the most assertive members of juvenile society are likely to achieve a sense of security in their new world. At home, therefore, a good many of the problems that start in the phallic stage continue through several more years. Jealousy, desire for a favored place, guilt, and demands for affection still characterize the child's emotional life at home.

At about 9, however, social competence and understanding advance to the point that the world of contemporaries begins to compete with the family circle. Membership in a gang or on a team starts to have the emotional yield known as "we-feeling," and friendships may begin to supply some of the affective response hitherto obtainable only under one's own rooftree. As Helene Deutsch[7] has shown, these alliances serve the purpose of creating an alternative to the family world, thus opening the way for a new growth of independence.

Obviously there are crises along the route of these developments. The sense of competence is challenged on many fronts. The mastery of schoolwork and other adult tasks can build firm self-esteem and social approval, but it can also produce frustration and a deep sense of inferiority. The outcomes of competitive activity on the playground can yield superb self-confidence or painful feelings of inadequacy. Attempts to participate in groups, gangs, and team activities can confer the rewards of membership or the punishments of rejection and ridicule. The seeking of friendships can open avenues for warm and cherishing feelings, or it can lead to rebuffs and withdrawal into self. Are these crises of any lasting importance for the development of personality? Freud seems to have assigned little weight to any crisis that occurred after the age of six. Sullivan took the opposite view. The juvenile era, he said, was "the first developmental stage in which the limitations and peculiarities of the home as a socializing influence begin to be open to remedy." Even more influential, in his opinion, were preadolescent friendships, which under fortunate circumstances might rescue young people otherwise destined for emotional trouble and mental breakdown.

Does the competence model help us to deal with this problem on which the libidinal expert and the interpersonal expert so spectacularly disagree? I think it does, because it leads us to look for the aspect of competence in behavior and for the vicissitudes of the sense of competence. In thinking about characteristics of adult behavior it leads us to consider what part is played by competence, and this makes us more likely to detect the effects of the latency stage, when the sense of competence faces some of its most significant crises. So I take sides with Sullivan and propose the hypothesis that the effects of the first five years can be substantially changed by developments during later childhood. Mildly unfortunate residues of infancy can become increased to neurotic proportions because competence fares badly, so that the child dares not chip away at his old anxieties or branch out into new regions of satisfaction. Contrariwise, a badly troubled first five years can lead to a relatively healthy outcome when latency encourages a rich growth for the sense of competence in many directions.

One example must suffice here to make clear my meaning. And to be strictly classical, though something else would probably be more convincing, let this example again be the Oedipus complex. When insufficiently renounced, the Oedipus complex becomes a hazard in adolescence by charging heterosexual interests with all the urgencies and inhibitions acquired during the phallic stage. The young man, for instance, is drawn to girls who in some significant way resemble his mother, and from the start the relation is ill-starred. The search for intimacy founders because of childlike demandingness and jealousy, and sexual fulfillment is under a cloud of anxiety. We can attribute this to a fixation that has lain unchanged during latency, but the competence model suggests a more refined analysis. The young man of our instance is also exhibiting passivity and lack of initiative: he does nothing to find interesting companionship with girls and waits until his hand is forced, so to speak, by an irresistible unconscious attraction, at which point he proceeds with the unpracticed skill of a 5-year-old. The inability to be interested in girls other than mother-surrogates is a distinctive feature of many such cases.

Suppose, however, that the latency period has encouraged initiative and a firm sense of competence. Suppose that events have conferred self-confidence in juvenile society, brought prominence in school life, included some fortunate chumships, and begotten a self-assured friendliness with girls. It may be that this young man will have one or more love affairs which will still be spoiled by Oedipal residues, but he will not be without alternative resources. No timid novice in social realtions, he may be able to see and modify his demandingness and jealousy; or, if this fails, he will not find it impossible to explore the contentment that may be found with girls who are not like his mother. The young man, in other words, has acquired during latency a number of characteristics which are now available to give him a wide range of confident activity and keep him from being bound to the single type of relation that always ends in frustration. If this happens, the young man will not appear as a patient. It is conceivable, however, that he might appear as a candidate for training in psychoanalysis, and the study of training analyses, especially by analysts who see possible merit in the competence model, may prove to be a very good way to shed light on these problems.

The pictures I have drawn can be expressed in psychoanalytic terms. The two young men differ with respect to ego strength. But this is not saying much unless we have ideas about how ego strength develops. The competence model, as I have shown, can give us ideas on just this point.

THE FINAL GENITAL STAGE

We come now to the last stage in psychosexual development, the stage at which newly strengthened sexual impulses bring about the possibility of genital primacy. In view of the great length of this paper you will be happy to hear that I shall have few words to say about the final stage. The plot is already clear. A prolonged fifth act would add little to whatever impact it may already have made. Obviously I would have words of praise for the more orthodox description of adolescence as given, for instance, by Anna Freud,[11,12] Bernfeld,[3] and Helene Deutsch.[7] Obviously there is great illumination in the treatment of this period as a time of increased instinctual drive and threat to established patterns of ego control. Certainly it is fruitful to look upon some aspects of adolescent behavior as a struggle to maintain and expand one's defenses. You would expect me also to mention some merit in the interpersonal model as developed, for instance, by Sullivan,[52] who described the task of late adolescence as that of establishing "a fully human or mature repertory of interpersonal relations." But then you would predict complaints on my part about the neglect of competence and the failure of the two models to capture whole ranges of behavior that are essential for full understanding. To spell out what you can so easily anticipate would be a bad anticlimax, and it would be a pity to lend an air of anticlimax to anything as dramatic as adolescence and genital primacy.

Perhaps the one thing I should do is to indicate the kinds of havior in adolescence that I consider important, well handled by a competence model, and neglected by libido and interpersonal models. Since the adolescent is reaching adult size, strength, and mental development, the behavior in question lies in the realm of serious accomplishment—serious in the terms either of the youth culture or of adult society. I am referring to the adolescent equivalent of what Erikson calls a *sense of industry* in the latency period, and I see this problem as continuing rather more strongly after puberty than seems to be implied in Erikson's account. No doubt I bring to this judgment an occupational bias different from that of a therapist. My professional life is spent among late adolescents whose sexual problems and social relations have for the most part not overwhelmed them. We talk together about their plans for study, their abilities and limitations, their struggles with materials to be learned and skills to be attained, their occupational leanings, career plans, and concerns about modern society as the scene of their future endeavors. We talk, in other words, mostly about their competence, and I do not believe that understanding is fostered by interpreting these concerns too much as displacements of instinctual drives, defense mechanisms, or interpersonal relations. They are real.

Adolescents today learn how to drive cars. Some of them learn to compete against adult records in sports, occasionally breaking them. Some of them become part of the football, band, and cheer-leader complex that plays such an important part in community entertainment. Some of them try their hands at building work-able radio sets, at scientific exploration, at editing newspapers, at writing stories and verse, at musical and dramatic performances, at political activity. Some of them with fewer opportunities or talents put their maturing bodies to heavy work or their matur-ing minds to white-collar office jobs. All this belongs in the sphere of work, and work, as Schilder[45] so cogently argued, is importantly a phenomenon of competence. These happenings create many crises, many defeats, many victories for the sense of competence. Once again there are large spheres in which the adolescent can be suffering losses or making gains in ego strength. In theorizing about the subject we must not foreclose the possibility that these developments significantly affect what happens in the erotic and interpersonal realms.

I shall say no more about this stage of development except to launch my last complaint against the models bequeathed us by psychosexual theory. The model proffered by libido theory is that of heterosexual relations, and their ideal form is embodied in the concept of genital primacy. It is not argued, of course, that we all successfully become genital primates, but the ideal type serves to indicate the problems of the period. The sexual act itself plays a prominent part in genital primacy, reminding us that Freud's oft-mentioned broadened conception of sex sometimes touched base again in what no one has ever denied to be sexual. In libidinal terms, the regular discharge of genital tensions serves also to drain some of the energy from pregenital tensions, thus making a con-trol and sublimation of the latter an easy problem for the ego. Erikson[8] prefers "to put it more situationally: the total fact of finding, via the climactic turmoil of the orgasm, a supreme ex-perience of the mutual regulation of two beings in some way breaks the point off the hostilities and potential rages caused by the oppositeness of male and female, of fact and fancy, of love and hate. Satisfactory sex relations thus make sex less obsessive, over-compensation less necessary, sadistic controls superfluous." Erikson's further account of what "the utopia of genitality" should in-clude—mutual trust and a willingness to share lives in the interest of securing a happy development for the children—is something I commend to you all as an uncommonly beautiful statement of what we should aspire to in family life. It is an interpersonal statement as well as a libidinal one. I like it so well that I am sor-ry to point out that it has only the slightest relation to compe-tence and to that other sphere of human concern—work.

Unfortunately the climactic turmoil of the orgasm is com-pletely the wrong model for work. This is not to say that good sexual relations may not sometimes free a person from gnawing hates and doubts that have interfered with his capacity to work. But the emphasis of the idea of orgastic potency and mutuality is on an essential loss of ego, a drowning of all other considerations in the immense involuntary experience of the sexual relation. He who takes the ego to bed with him will never get a gold star for genital primacy. The orgastic model has virtue for certain human activities requiring a temporary submergence of self, such as in-spiration, creative imagination, and thoroughly relaxed play. But it will never do for the serious, stable, lasting concerns of human life, the realm that I am trying to designate as work. This is the sphere in which the ego must always keep a firm hand on the helm.

Work requires a certain constancy of effort. There must be sustained endeavor with control of wayward impulses that distract from the requirements of external reality and social roles. There must be a capacity for persistent return to tasks, sometimes dull in themselves, that form part of the job requirement or that belong in a long-range plan to achieve remote goals. There must be a quality of reliability, so that one keeps promises and lives up to the obligations one has assumed. Even the fashion for being spon-taneous and natural, even the bright vision of self-fulfilling work in Fromm's sane society,[20] even Marcuse's fantasy of a nonrepressive civilization in which all work becomes libidinal pleasure[36] cannot exorcize the true and somewhat stern nature of reality. And even Ernst Kris,[33] no enemy of psychoanalytic theory, reminded us that artistic creation required, in addition to a phase of inspiration, a second phase characterized by "the experience of purposeful organization and the intent to solve a problem." When we call an artist "merely competent" it is a weak form of praise, but if he were "merely inspired," without a certain rather high minimum of competence, we would never even see or hear his products.

I should like to close with a short coda on the words "merely competent." I particularly do not want to be misunderstood concerning the part to be assigned to competence and the sense of competence in human development. As a simple and sovereign concept it will never do. A person developed wholly along lines of competence, with no dimensions of passion, love, or friendliness, would never qualify for maturity. Competence is not intended to describe such experiences as enjoying food, immersing oneself in a sexual relation, loving children, cherishing friends, being moved by natural beauty or great works of art; nor is it designed to swallow up the problems created by aggression and anxiety. This is what I meant by saying that the competence model must always be used in conjunction with other models that do full justice to such things as hunger, sexuality, and aggression. It may hurt one's desire for logical simplicity to suppose that several models are needed to understand a problem. Yet I think no one can claim a probability that human nature was designed in the interests of logic.

It is my conviction, in short, that Freud's discoveries were of epoch-making importance, that psychoanalytic ego psychology has taken effective steps to fill out some of the undeveloped parts of Freud's theories, and that Erikson in particular has accomplished a synthesis that promises good things for future understanding of the growth of personality. But I also believe that our understanding cannot be rounded out by stretching Freud's concepts in a vain attempt to cover everything, or by calling everything interpersonal as if body and material world did not exist. We should add to the picture a meticulous consideration, at every level, of the growth of the child's capacity both for action and for understanding. We should try to be as shrewd in detecting the vicissitudes of the sense of competence as Freud was with sexuality, aggression, and defense. It is to encourage such a development that I have had so much to say about the concept of competence.

SUMMARY

Even an idea as monumental as Freud's theory of the psychosexual stages of development can come to have an adverse effect upon scientific progress if it is believed too literally too long. Libido theory provided a series of models for critical phases in emotional growth: feeding, toilet training, the Oedipus situation, latency, and the adult heterosexual relation. These models are largely preserved in revisions of Freud, though changed to interpersonal terms, and they continue to dominate the thinking of workers in psychoanalytic ego psychology. In this paper it is maintained that the models are in certain respects inadequate and misleading. In particular, they encourage us to neglect a range of facts which is ordered here under the concept of competence. If these facts are slighted, it is held, there can be little hope of further progress in psychoanalytic ego psychology or in closing the gap between this and other theories of development.

The concept of competence subsumes the whole realm of learned behavior whereby the child comes to deal effectively with his environment. It includes manipulation, locomotion, language, the building of cognitive maps and skilled actions, and the growth of effective behavior in relation to other people. These acquisitions are made by young animals and children partly through exploratory and manipulative play when drives such as hunger and sex are in abeyance. The directed persistence of such behavior warrants the assumption of a motivation independent of drives, here called effectance motivation, which has its immediate satisfaction in a feeling of efficacy and its adaptive significance in the growth of competence. Effectance motivation can be likened to independent ego energies in the psychoanalytic scheme. The child's actual competence and his sense of competence are built up from his history of efficacies and inefficacies, and sense of competence is held to be a crucial element in any psychology of the ego.

It is proposed that libidinal and interpersonal models for critical points in development be supplemented by a competence model. For the oral stage this means taking serious account of the growth of manipulative prowess and experimentation as seen both in the child's many hours of play and in his zeal for self-help in feeding. For the anal stage it means attributing importance to negativism in the sphere of giving and receiving commands, an early crisis in social competence, and to the enormous growth of motility with its constant influence upon self-esteem. Neither development is adequately implied in the anal-erotic model. For the phallic stage it means detecting the consequences of growth in locomotion, linguistic understanding, and imagination; it also means noticing the child's waxing ability to comprehend and try out various social roles, in many of which he receives encouragement. The Oedipus model, with its foreordained inexplicable defeat, cannot be considered typical for the period. During latency the chief developments are in the sphere of competence; this is clear in Erikson's account of the sense of industry and Sullivan's of competition and compromise. For the final genital stage the competence model invites us to take seriously the adolescent's continuing concern with sense of industry and with social competence, problems that confront him with new crises in their own right. The heterosexual relation does not provide an adequate model for all the serious concerns of this stage of life, nor can they be fully conceptualized in terms of instinctual drive and defense.

In short, the competence model is held to supplement in significant ways the models of development derived from psychoanalysis. By directing attention to action and its consequences and to the vicissitudes of the sense of competence, it should help to speed the construction of an adequate ego psychology.

REFERENCES

1. Abraham, K. *Selected Papers on Psychoanalysis..* London, Hogarth, 1927.
2. Berlyne, D. E. Novelty and curiosity as determinants of exploratory behavior. *Brit. J. Psychol., 41*:68-80, 1950.

3. Bernfeld, S. Types of adolescence. *Psychoanal. Quart., 7*:243-253, 1938.

4. Butler, R. A. Exploratory and related behavior: A new trend in animal research. *J. Indiv. Psychol., 14*:111-120, 1958.

5. Bornstein, B. On latency. *Psychoanal. Stud. Child, 6*:279-285, 1951.

6. Bühler, C. The social behavior of the child. In C. Murchison, (Ed.), *A Handbook of Child Psychology.* Worcester, Mass., Clark Univer. Press, 1931, pp. 392-431.

7. Deutsch, Helene. *The Psychology of Women.* Vol. I. New York, Grune & Stratton, 1944.

8. Erikson, E. H. *Childhood and Society.* New York, Norton, 1950.

9. Erikson, E. H. Identity and the life cycle: selected papers. *Psychol. Issues,* 1959, Monograph 1.

10. Fenichel, O. *The Psychoanalytic Theory of Neurosis.* New York, Norton, 1945.

11. Freud, Anna. *The Ego and the Mechanisms of Defence.* (Trans. by C. Baines.) London, Hogarth, 1937.

12. Freud, Anna. Adolescence. *Psychoanal. Stud. Child, 13*:255-278, 1958.

13. Freud, Anna, and Burlingham, D. T. *Infants Without Families.* New York, International Univ. Press, 1944.

14. Freud, S. *Three Contributions to the Theory of Sex* (1905). (Trans. by A. A. Brill.) New York and Washington, Nerv. and Ment. Dis. Pub. Co., 1930.

15. Freud, S. Character and anal erotism (1908). *Collected Papers.* (Trans. under supervision of J. Riviere.) New York, Basic Books, 1959, Vol. II, pp. 45-50.

16. Freud, S. The predisposition to obsessional neurosis (1913). *Collected Papers.* (Trans. under supervision of J. Riviere.) New York, Basic Books, 1959, Vol. II. pp. 122-131.

17. Freud, S. The infantile genital organization of the libido (1923). *Collected Papers.* (Trans. under supervision of J. Riviere.) New York, Basic Books. Vol. II, 244-249.

18. Fromm, E. Individual and social origins of neurosis. *Amer. Sociol. Rev., 9*:380-384, 1944.

19. Fromm, E. *Man for Himself.* New York, Rinehart, 1947.

20. Fromm, E. *The Sane Society.* New York, Rinehart, 1955.

21. Gesell, A., and Ilg, Frances L. *Infant and Child in the Culture of Today.* New York, Harper, 1943.

22. Gesell, A. and Ilg, Frances L. *The Child from Five to Ten.* New York, Harper, 1946.

23. Goldstein, K. *Human Nature in the Light of Psychopathology.* Cambridge, Mass., Harvard Univ. Press, 1940.

24. Harlow, H. F. Mice, monkeys, men, and motives. *Psychol. Rev., 60*:23-32, 1953.

25. Hartmann, H. *Ego Psychology and the Problem of Adaptation.* (Trans. by D. Rapaport.) New York, International Univ. Press, 1958.

26. Hartmann, H., Kris, E. and Loewenstein, R. Notes on the theory of aggression. *Psychoanal. Stud. Child, 3/4*:9-36, 1949.

27. Hendrick, I. Instinct and the ego during infancy. *Psychoanal. Quart., 11:* 33-58, 1942.

28. Hendrick, I. Work and the pleasure principle. *Psychoanal. Quart., 12:* 311-329, 1943.

29. Hetzer, H. Entwicklungsbedingte Erziehungsschwierigkeiten. *Z. Pädagog. Psychol., 30:*77-85, 1929.

30. Horney, Karen. *New Ways in Psychoanalysis.* New York, Norton, 1939.

31. Isaacs, Susan. *Social Development in Young Children.* London, Routledge, 1933.

32. Kanner, L. The conception of wholes and parts in early infantile autism. *Amer. J. Psychiat., 108:*23-26, 1951.

33. Kris, E. *Psychoanalytic Explorations in Art.* New York, International Univ. Press, 1952.

34. Lerner, E. The problem of perspective in moral reasoning. *Amer. J. Sociol., 43:*249-269, 1937.

35. Levy, D. M. Oppositional syndromes and oppositional behavior. In P. H. Hoch and J. Zubin (Eds.), *Psychopathology of Childhood.* New York, Grune & Stratton, 1955, pp. 204-226.

36. Marcuse, H. *Eros and Civilization. Boston,* Beacon Press, 1955.

37. Mittelmann, B. Motility in infants, children, and adults. *Psychoanal. Stud. Child, 9:*142-177, 1954.

38. Montgomery, K. C. The role of the exploratory drive in learning. *J. Comp. Physiol. Psychol., 47:*60-64, 1954.

39. Murray, H. A. *Explorations in Personality.* New York, Oxford Univ.. Press, 1938.

40. Myers, A. K., and Miller, N. E. Failure to find a learned drive based on hunger; evidence for learning motivated by "exploration." *J. Comp. Physiol. Psychol., 47:*428-436, 1954.

41. Olds, J., and Milner, P. Positive reinforcement produced by electrical stimulation of septal area and other regions of rat brain. *J. Comp. Physiol. Psychol., 47:*419-427, 1954.

42. Piaget, J. *The Moral Judgment of the Child.* (Trans. by M. Gabain.) New York, Harcourt, Brace, 1932.

43. Piaget, J. *The Origins of Intelligence in Children.* (Trans. by M. Cook.) New York, International Univ. Press, 1952.

44. Piers, G., and Singer, M. B. *Shame and Guilt.* Springfield, Thomas, 1953.

45. Schilder, P. *Goals and Desires of Men.* New York, Columbia Univ. Press, 1942.

46. Sheffield, F. D., and Roby, T. B. Reward value of a non-nutritive sweet taste. *J. Comp. Physiol. Psychol., 43:*471-481, 1950.

47. Sheffield, F. D.; Roby, T. B., and Campbell, B. A. Drive reduction vs. consummatory behavior as determinants of reinforcement. *J. Comp. Physiol. Psychol., 47:*349-354, 1954.

48. Sheffield, F. D.; Wulff, J. J., and Backer, R. Reward value of copulation without sex drive reduction. *J. Comp. Physiol. Psychol., 44:*3-8, 1951.

49. Silverberg, W. V. *Childhood Experience and Personal Destiny.* New York, Springer, 1952.

50. Spitz, R. A. Anaclitic depression. *Psychoanal. Stud. Child, 2:*313-342, 1946.

51. Stern, W. *Psychology of Early Childhood,* 2nd ed. (Trans. by A. Barwell.) New York, Holt, 1930.

52. Sullivan, H. S. *The Interpersonal Theory of Psychiatry.* New York, Norton, 1953.

53. Sully, J. *Studies of Childhood.* London and New York, Appleton, 1896.

54. Thompson, C. *Psychoanalysis: Evolution and Development.* New York, Hermitage, 1950.

55. Welker, W. L. Some determinants of play and exploration in chimpanzees. *J. Comp. Physiol. Psychol., 49:*84-89, 1956.

56. Woodworth, R. S. *Dynamics of Behavior.* New York, Holt, 1958.

57. White, R. W. Motivation reconsidered: The concept of competence. *Psychol. Rev., 66:*297-333, 1959.

58. Wolff, P. H. Observations on newborn infants. *Psychosomat. Med. 21:* 110-118, 1959.

IN ANY culture a major challenge of childhood is to become socialized, that is, to behave according to the expectations of society. Most societies are complex entities with subgroups that rigidly control some aspects of behavior and allow wide latitude in others. The asocial neonate must learn, in time, what is acceptable behavior and what is not. It is a slow, tortuous process, sometimes leading to stressful periods between child and caretaker. Some theorists have proposed that the child has a passive role and is shaped and molded into a social being by manipulation of drives and carefully administered reinforcement. That, however, is not the perspective of Dr. Lois B. Murphy. In the discussion below, she suggests that learning to cope with the self and the environment requires an adapting, active participant. Dr. Murphy also recognizes the marked individual differences that characterize infants and children, as well as the varied kinds of experiences which affect how the individual copes with his milieu.

Chapter 22

Adaptational Tasks in Childhood
in Our Culture

Lois B. Murphy

I N THE MORE than one hundred years since *The Origin of Species*
an increasingly balanced understanding of adaptational processes
in human beings has gradually emerged. The concept of phylogenetic evolution with its insight into the prerequisites for survival of a given organism in a specific environment was followed by
a series of steps in the understanding of ontogenetic development.
It is not surprising that different streams of scientific work had
to continue to be separate for half a century. Those initiated by
Freud's contributions to the understanding of epigenesis of drive[1]
and aspects of mental functioning influenced by drives remained
relatively remote from the successive discoveries of experimental
and developmental psychology of the universities. This was true
despite the interest of G. Stanley Hall—founder of child psychology—in Freud's work, and later, the interest of Susan Isaacs[2] as
early as the twenties in contributions from experimental work.

Only when Freud's own formulations regarding the ego were
followed by Hartmann's monograph[3] on the ego and the problem
of adaptation was the way opened for more spontaneous rap-
prochement of the two broad streams of investigations. The
later work of Piaget on the development of intelligence[4] has
captured the interest of a large body of workers, some of whom
have also been interested in analyzing parallels and differences
between Piaget and Freud.[5] But there is room for much more

Reprinted with permission from the *Bulletin of the Menninger Clinic, 28:*309-
22, 1964. Copyright 1964 by the Menninger Foundation.

This paper is based in part on a series of studies of 60 normal children. The
investigations were supported by Public Health Service Research Grants No. MH-27,
M-680 and M-4093 from the National Institute of Mental Health.

work toward an integrated dynamic view of the adaptational process. This discussion of basic tasks of adaptation is one step in this direction—a step taken in response to stimulation by new reports of Soviet psychology, recent developments in Western psychology, and also by data from our own research.

DEVELOPMENT IN INFANCY

The first and most basic task of human development, as well as the one which lasts the longest, in fact for the lifetime of the individual, is to survive. For the very young baby in the critical early weeks of postnatal life this is a matter of achieving adequate integration in the basic vegetative functions such as breathing, feeding and digesting, eliminating, resting, and sleeping. Achievement of smooth organic functioning is important not only in its own right, but also as a prerequisite for the stable positive mood-level sometimes described as bliss or narcissistic pleasure. Without a dependable experience of feeling good within himself the infant has little basis for attributing goodness to the external world. Moreover, when difficulties in oral and gastrointestinal functioning, lack of skin comfort, or other primitive gratifications, contribute to overwhelming and persistent distress with autonomic flooding, the autonomous development of perceptual and other cognitive functions is jeopardized. However, mild discomforts, within the range of the infant's capacity to handle through motor coping devices, can stimulate adaptive efforts.

Broadly speaking, survival implies another basic task of the infant: to grow up at a pace consistent with optimal functioning of his own equipment and development of his capacities, in cooperation with appropriate stimulus, support and protection from the environment. Thus *stimulus management* is another basic task: in relation to (1) evoking enough and sufficiently relevant stimulation for the development of specific aspects of perceptual-motor and other cognitive functioning; (2) protecting oneself against excessive or painful stimulation which could interfere with optimal development of perception, memory, image formation and their use in differentiation of the self from the external world and interacting with it; (3) selecting the stimuli needed for development of integrative functions of the ego. The latter include the organized orientation (cognitive map building) to the environment; the selection of relevant gratifiers or means of gratifying ends; the mobilization of motor resources in goal-directed action; and developing both the capacity to accept substitutes at times, to wait at times, as well as to use both the environment and the self for stimulation.

Active participation in the evolution of basic relationships to other persons as differentiated individuals (with or without exclusive attachment to the mother) is another major task of the first year. This uses the infant's capacity to evoke satisfying action from the caretaker in times of need, mutually responsive communication, and affective exchange, and the related foundations of basic identification. Closely related to the above are the complex capacities to cope with separation, loss, change. The latter implies adequate development and use of imagery and fantasy and anticipation of future gratification.

Emergence of Functions

"Sensitive phases" or "critical phases"[6] are sometimes differentially referred to the period of emergence and still incomplete integration of new evolving functions, and the time period when stimulation is required specifically for consolidation of a new process or function, as in the critical phase for imprinting as discussed by ethologists.[7] With infants, the first days after birth may be considered a critical phase for the integration of feeding mechanisms; but the whole first year (during which the infant triples his weight) is a period when oral needs are intense, although no more important than the infant's *need for contact,* for adequate *stimulation* (nutriment) for all the basic sensorimotor functions, and for the establishment of basic human *relationships*.

That is, a series of sensitive phases may be seen in the first year of life as new functions are emerging, functions involved in handling the tasks outlined above; these may be roughly summarized as follows, with the proviso that wide individual differences in timing of the emergence of function have been documented in many investigations.[8]

1. The first weeks after birth are critical for organic integration and the related sense of well-being, as mentioned above.

2. At about 8 weeks the emergence of more focused, sustained and selective looking and listening presents a sensitive phase for perception, with a danger of overstimulation and fixation of defenses against this, or the danger of apathy in the case of understimulation. (This does not mean that perception "begins" at this time; early precursors in the "orienting reflex" which from birth may even interrupt feeding, visual fixation, response to auditory stimulus, are all evidence of the gradual integration of perceptual capacities.) The emergence of the "smile of recognition" in response to the human face parallels this increased organization of visual and auditory perception. Infants need stimuli of some degree of complexity.

3. At about 4 months or later, differing with different infants, the beginning emergence of differentiation between self and the external world is a sensitive phase for the consolidation of both objectivity and a delighted response to stimulation as opposed to a confused or suspicious, affectively loaded perception of the external world. Normally at this stage we see a peak of joyful, eager response to stimulation and beginnings of deliberate if still vague affectomotor behavior to evoke interaction with other persons.[9] The suspicious or hostile orientation may become patterned or fixed when persistent acute distress (presumably accompanied by autonomic upheaval and flooding of the brain with chemical by-products) prevents adequately neutral or serene perceptual development. This can be seen most vividly in cases of unreachable, frantic, disorganized children who are not merely "emotionally disturbed" at a later stage but do not have foundations for dependably satisfying perceptions. To them the world can cause only distress.

The development of discrimination between self and the world is supported by the emergence of more active sensorimotor interactions with major objects in the environment. Now the infant has the task of extending his repertoire of resources for making something (pleasurable) happen. Objects capable of providing pleasure—the breast or the bottle—are recognized at this time.

Parallel with the basic self-object differentiation is the discrimination between factors relevant and irrelevant to pain or pleasure. Memory of painful inoculations is global during the early months; anxiety regarding anticipated inoculation is aroused by perception of the doctor's office or the doctor in a white coat in contrast to the only gradually differentiated association of anxiety specifically with the inoculating needle.[10] The task of learning exactly what to blame or to be anxious about thus involves increasing differentiation of threatening parts in an experience-whole, which generally develops only from 6 months on.

4. At 6 to 8 months differentiated recognition of mother in contrast to strangers[11] has emerged or is emerging, although some infants show this much earlier. We find now a sensitive phase for separation anxiety[12] regarding the strangers. Some infants are able to cope with the task of mastering this anxiety within a few weeks, and C. Buhler[13] included this capacity as an 8-months developmental test. For other infants these sources of anxiety remain acute through the second year of life or until autonomy in basic functions has provided added security. A variety of coping devices may be developed to deal with anxiety regarding strangers, including strategic or self-protective withdrawal, and the elaboration of multiple ways of maximizing contact with the mother (turning toward, running to, climbing onto her lap, clutching at her skirt).

5. Meantime, parallel with the increasing perceptual organization of the environment and discrimination between self and environment is the increasing awareness of and cathexis of self, which has to proceed to a point of clarity about what one can manage alone before separation from mother (as protector and buffer against the world) can be tolerated. This blossoms during the second year, intensified by the vivid consciousness of control of the body as toilet training is accomplished, and also control of the environment.

6. Fundamental for these basic tasks of achieving secure and gratifying differentiation between self and the world, and the sense of control of both, are the motor developments (standing, creeping, beginning to walk) which present a multitude of

challenges to the infant, new sources of information about the world, ways of using it, and both potential gratification and potential pain to be encountered in his explorations. He has to learn the rudiments of how to be safe and avoid collisions at this stage, as well as what satisfactions are provided by what sources.

7. Continuing through the second year, although beginning in the first half-year, is the mastery of many specific ways of using the body and parts of the body, from early learning to roll over, to sitting up; then to stand, creep, walk, and later to climb and to jump. The major body achievement of a vertical position (standing, walking) often brings the first open expressions of triumphant mastery. The achievements contribute to new dimensions of the sense of well-being, which arises not only from the sensations associated with good vegetative functioning, but also from striped muscle sensations involved in the practice of the new coordination. These experiences of delight in mastery, or triumph, are doubtless very important in motivating the further effort needed to move on to new stages of control, and of integration of basic skills with more complex interactions with the personal and the impersonal world. The period of first emergence of any of these skills may be a sensitive phase: Shirley[14] and others have noted instances of inhibition of walking after it had begun, following painful encounters or falls doubtless at a time of sensitization increased by other factors.

8. Another task which also goes along with those mentioned above is the development of the *capacity for communication of wants,* needs, frustrations, pleasure and unhappiness. This actually begins after birth with crying, at first a reflex, but soon used as an expression of discomfort or need for attention. More differentiated expressions of protest, demand or interest, hunger, or pain, as well as expressions of comfort and joy, develop during the first six months. By the age of 8 months babies have been observed to differentiate between different emotional expressions from the mother[13] although even earlier some babies can be inhibited by controlling words expressed by the mother such as "Ssh" or "No, no."[15] The expression of needs and of both pleasure and displeasure, insofar as it evokes appropriate and helpful responses

from the environment, also brings a new dimension to the sense of well-being: trust,[16] security, confidence,[17] or perhaps we could say a feeling of attunement between one's self and the world. This does not mark an entirely new development of interaction between cathexis of the self and the environment, but rather a culmination and integration of positive feelings responding to good interactions with the environment.

Any new phase in communication is similarly "sensitive," in that adequate response from mother or caretaker is needed for the promotion of communication. Maternally deprived babies are not only emotionally apathetic[18] but lacking in the signaling resources developed by others who are adequately mothered.

9. After the first year of life come increasing societal demands for autonomy, control of sphincters and of aggression, and modulation of both aggression and erotic responses. Perhaps there are simple practical reasons for the earlier response to toilet training demanded in temperate climates where the small child has to wear more clothes; when clothes are unnecessary in early childhood, soiling is less of a problem. When demands from adults for *conformity* to toilet training coincide with the burst of *autonomy* awareness which accompanies motor achievements, an intense conflict between the child and the environment may ensue. However, when this conflict is avoided, sphincter control adds another dimension to autonomy. Thus the second year is recognized as a critical phase for the constructive integration of autonomy.[16]

Increasing capacities for self-help, in self-feeding, as well as in keeping clean, and also the expression of needs in speech rather than nonspecific crying or gestures, further this growing autonomy. Teasing, humorous or provocative defiance, escape from and experimental imitation of adults are among the expressions of new self-awareness in the second year of life, as each child solves the problem of becoming an "I" in his own way. Illness or other gross interference with emerging autonomy at this sensitive stage may retard or prevent adequate progress through this developmental phase. But favorable progress contributes to gradual outgrowing of infantile comfort devices.

10. Mastery of three-dimensional space, as increasingly encountered by the more skilled body, is followed by beginning mastery of time problems ("soon," "later") which contribute steadily to management of frustration, tolerance of change, newness, and deviations from routine. These complex aspects of ego-functioning also develop out of interaction with the environment, and are vulnerable at this stage of insecure autonomy. In this period, extreme frustration is apt to lead to regression.

11. Increasing capacity for spontaneous relations with peers, and the ability to use one's own ideas in beginning to carry on cooperative and imaginative play activities, begin to flower after such integrative developments reflected in mastering of space and time.

12. Mastery of three-dimensional space and time (past and future) contributes further to the capacity to plan, to forestall danger, to anticipate, wait for, or work toward future gratification. Closely related to these are the extended capacities for fantasy which provide new resources for both solitary and group play. Thus the two main gross areas of functioning—within the organism and in its intercourse with the environment—may be seen as involving the task of maintaining sufficient internal integration on the one hand, and developing a style of interchange with the environment which supports the development of mutually satisfying relations between the individual and the environment.

To summarize thus far: In early infancy, if surviving and growing proceed smoothly, they are accompanied by a more or less vivid sense of well-being and narcissistic pleasure in each area of one's own functioning; then gradually, as the sense of self is differentiated and integrated, pleasure in one's self. Good oral experience, digestion and gastrointestinal functioning generally are one major zone, but also good management of stimulation so as to experience positive satisfaction from all of the senses, and a gradual increase in motor coordination and integration of motility with sensory functions, all contribute a share to gratification and, in turn, to ease in response to others.

At least relative serenity and freedom from strain, anxiety, and the kind of distress which after the early months can be felt as localized pain are important for the maintenance of the autonomy of emerging functions such as perception and locomotion and their integration with other aspects of functioning of the infant—his desires and his relations with the environment. Consequently the maintenance of a sense of well-being, referred to by van der Waals[37] as healthy narcissism, can be regarded as one of the major tasks of infancy, and a prerequisite for the emergence and organization of early ego functions at an optimal level. Capacities for organization of one's perceptions of the environment and oneself into integrated unitary wholes, for grasping sequences of events and also capacities for control or management of one's body and impulses, along with developing useful interaction patterns with the environment, are all involved here.

That is, on the heels of the emerging perceptual and motor functions with their integrations is the early discovery of the body and the self as distinct from the environment and the separation out of most significant figures in the environment, such as mother, from the rest. Only after the differentiation and separation of self from others and of mother as an important other from the rest of the people in the environment, is it possible for the baby to develop that special relation with the mother in which he is aware of needing her and becomes anxious when she leaves. As part of this process he differentiates the familiar from the strange; then a next step is the mastery of or getting used to the strange, by developing ways of managing strangeness and coming to terms with it, as well as finding new joy in the familiar.

By the age of 3 in our culture, then, we expect most children to have mastered the following basic adaptational tasks:

1. *Good vegetative functioning* including satisfying eating and elimination, and management of the drives and impulses involved in these.

2. *Perceptual orientation* to and familiarization with the environment of home and skills for orienting to a new environment.

3. *Motor skills* for exploring and using the spaces and objects of the environment in a satisfying way which leads to self-help, self-feeding, and increasing self-selection of stimuli from the environment.

4. *Communication* skills including both speech and expressions of feeling through face, body and voice, to implement needs and to share experiences.

5. *Emotional organization* including the capacity for attachment to and response to affective support and stimulus from adults and children and the capacity for love and anger toward major objects.

6. *Sphincter control* and capacity to keep clean along with other controls.

7. The beginning of *concepts of time, number, space* which help to organize the here-and-now, the recent past, and the near future.

THE LATER PRESCHOOL STAGE

New energy resources appear to be released in many children both by these rich early achievements in the preschool years and by the new psychosexual interests which are combined with and stimulated by growing perceptual differentiation of size, sex differences, growth and time. The 4-year-old phase in Western culture at least has been referred to as "the first adolescence."[19] It shares with the teen-age period a lively sense of sex roles and vivid heterosexual feelings, along with intense feelings about newly perceived size and adequacy. These parallel awarenesses of size, sex differences, growth, time, age, increasing skills—verbal, motor, and conceptual ("Remember last year, Miss B., when I didn't understand?" asked one 4-year-old) —and the push of new erotic drive and emotional expressiveness, all contribute to the 4-year-old's dramatic expressions of love (in our culture) and thoughts of marrying his mother when he grows up.

Competition with father, older siblings, peers, and the need to combat the inevitable disappointments resulting from encounters with limits, all lead to elaborations of problems and to their possible solutions in fantasy which now becomes a major resource for dealing with problems at this stage. Oedipal conflicts turn into idiosyncratic dramas played out on the peer stage.

Aggressive vigor (fed probably by hormone changes, by energy released from the preoccupation with mastering basic motor skills, and by frustrations arising from the clash between new capacities and environmental restrictions) also becomes available for directed exploitation against competitors and adversaries, in some children, especially boys. Aggression parallels social sensitivity expressed in cooperation and even sympathy[20] at this stage.

Difficulties or failure in one or more of the developmental areas contributing to autonomy may be expressed in lack of progress in mastering strangeness and reducing dependence upon the mother; in anxiety, in extreme immaturities, and in failure to develop frustration tolerance, capacity to share with peers, and the flexible coping resources typical of this age. Symptoms such as prolonged bed-wetting, sucking, extreme dependence on blanket or bottle, extreme inhibition or immobilization may be related to failures or delays in one or more of the developmental tasks, as well as to difficulties in resolving conflicts regarding the need to retain possession of the parent. However, temporary interruption or slowness in mastery of the preschool developmental tasks does not necessarily imply permanent danger to the integration of the child if progress is being made.

Behavior at a given stage cannot be evaluated without knowledge of the experiences through which the child has come at each phase, his individual equipment with its varying possibilities of minor or major defect or damage,[21] intrinsic difficulties in integration, the residua of preschool or infantile illness, or predispositions to anxiety[38] emerging from disturbances of infancy. A majority of our study group[22] had some symptoms at the preschool stage, chiefly enuresis and speech difficulties which for the most part were largely "outgrown" in the next few years, or modulated to the tolerance level of the subculture.

LATER TASKS: ENTRANCE TO SCHOOL

At latency, entrance to school demands further final mastery of separation anxiety; new levels of relationship to a neutral teacher-object; capacity to accept new types of stereotyped structuring in the school situation, with its use of "rules" and combined appeal to conscience or "honor" and respect for external control; capacity to focus on autonomous ego functioning with minimal or only periodic opportunity for impulse expression; capacity to transfer investments and interest to the peer group, and to tolerate much less absolute acceptance than may have been characteristic within the family at the infancy and preschool level even for children exposed to taunts and rejection by peers.

Mastery of the new challenges greatly strengthens the child's capacity to let go of intense involvements with parents, and acceptance of rules which organize peer relationships helps acceptance of home rules. Where illness, developmental defects or imbalances interfere with typical latency achievements, realistic dependence on the mother continues and, with it, persistent Oedipal conflicts as well.

Difficulties and failures to achieve the further levels and areas of integration, and resources for coping with the environment and with inner needs and conflicts, may be expressed in new forms or intensity of separation anxiety (school phobia), severe psychosomatic reactions or other disturbances of physiological functioning and control, as in enuresis, or disturbances of cognitive functioning even reflected in decline in tested intelligence scores.[23]

At the same time, for the majority of normal children who manage these shifts ("We have to sit still and be quiet, and listen to the teacher—and I'm the best one!"), new rewards of increased cognitive and motor skills participation in organized games, along with external recognition (marks, school offices), support new gratifications. Optimally the child learns to learn and to like learning, to be a member of a class and to have pride in his group.

At the prepuberty stage the child moves into junior high school with a shift from one major teacher to teaching situations which change from one teacher to another, involving the relinquishment now of a stable teacher object and demand for still more autonomy and responsibility on the part of the child. Many children are anxious about the shift to junior high[24] and some have difficulty after it occurs, especially when previous difficulties in space orientation, or familiarizing oneself in new situations or those involving frequent change, have persisted. Disequilibria and disorientations associated with the growth spurt and the peak of body tension contribute to anxiety at this stage. Sex-role identification has to be crystallized as a precondition for smooth heterosexual interactions, and in the present generation can present a crisis even at this early stage. Shifts in body configurations, appearance and the fitting into cultural stereotypes for attractiveness, difficulties such as acne, precocity or delay, emergence of primary or secondary sex characteristics, marked deviations in growth rate (slowest or fastest) or sudden changes expressed in dramatic shifts in height or weight, may all involve threats to narcissism—however well-rooted the child's early psychosexual progress and latency achievement—and to security in peer-group relationships. Further adverse effects on sex-role crystallization and efforts to consolidate identity are apt to accompany this narcissistic crisis at puberty.

These multiple threats and the resulting disequilibrium contribute to the upsurge of dependency needs and pre-Oedipal problems already noted by Anna Freud[25] and others. At the same time, the increased anxiety about and often apparently neurotic dependence on peer-group acceptance involves not only increasing conflict with parent objects (and sometimes also teacher objects) but also a sense of loss and new forms of separation anxiety which in turn further reinforce the upsurge of dependency needs.

Deviations in the pattern of physiological maturation contribute special problems with peer-group isolation, which in turn also deprives the child of resources to outgrow dependency needs and intimacy with the mother, especially for girls. We know that unresloved conflicts from pre-Oedipal or infantile levels tend to be revived or exacerbated in this phase of precarious integration; this is especially true under conditions of biological deviation. These problems may of course be increased by any recent or concurrent illnesses which add to the task of integration. Concurrent disturbances, either physical or emotional, in the parent tend moreover to make the child feel guilty about rebellion or even normal separation. The coincidence of maternal menopause with adolescent problems in the daughter or son makes resolution of these conflicts especially hard.

CONCLUSION

When we investigate the ways in which more or less normal children cope with everyday developmental problems, we see that many of these are related to difficulties or (external or internal) conflicts in meeting basic needs in ways consistent with the sensitivities, capacities, drives, of the individual child—needs for adequate vegetative functioning and a sense of well-being, nutriment for every growing function as well as for communication, relationship and a place in the group.

Implied throughout this review of adaptational tasks are the contributions of (1) emerging drives and maturation of cognitive, motor,[26] and affective[27] capacities; (2) the simultaneous operation of functions contributing to the formation of structures[4] and a variety of learning processes including classical Pavlovian conditioning,[28] operant conditioning, and trial and error learning. Affectomotor functions[9] and integrative functions of the ego[3,16,29] are shaped in functional interaction of drive and autonomous ego factors.

Individual differences in every aspect of equipment and drive, as well as differences in stimulation, demand from and frustrations by the environment, will affect the patterning of complex adaptational styles which evolve from the successive efforts of the child to deal with his environment.[15,30-36]

REFERENCES

1. Freud, Sigmund. *Three Contributions to the Theory of Sex,* 4th ed. New York, Nervous and Mental Disease Publishing Company, 1930.
2. Isaacs, Susan. *Social Development in Young Children.* London, Routledge, 1937.
3. Hartmann, Heinz (1939). *Ego Psychology and the Problem of Adaptation.* David Rapaport, translator. New York, International Universities, 1958. See also papers in *Psa. Study of the Child,* 1950, 1952.
4. Piaget, Jean. *The Origins of Intelligence in Children.* New York, International Universities, 1952.
5. Wolff, P. H. The developmental psychologies of Jean Piaget and psychoanalysis. *Psychol. Issues,* Vol. 2, No. 1, 1960.
6. Erikson, Erik H. Problems of infancy and early childhood. In George M.

Piersol (Ed.), *Cyclopedia of Medicine, Surgery and Specialties.* Philadelphia, F. A. Davis, 1945.

7. Hess, E. H. The relationship between imprinting and motivation. In M. R. Jones (Ed.), *Nebraska Symposium on Motivation.* Lincoln, University of Nebraska, 1959.

8. Stone, L. J., and Church, Joseph. *Childhood and Adolescence.* New York, Random House, 1957.

9. Mittelmann, Bela. Motility in infants, children and adults: patterning and psychodynamics. *Psa. Study of the Child, 9:*142-177, 1954.

10. Levy, David. The infant's earliest memory of inoculation: a contribution to public health procedures. *J. Genet. Psychol., 96:*3-46, 1960.

11. Yarrow, L. J. Separation from parents during childhood. *Review of Child Development Research.* Vol. I. New York, Russell Sage Foundation, 1954.

12. Bowlby, John. Separation anxiety. *Int. J. Psa., 41:*89-113, 1960.

13. Buhler, Charlotte. *The First Year of Life.* New York, John Day, 1930.

14. Shirley, Mary Margaret. *The First Two Years.* Minneapolis, University of Minnesota, 1931-33.

15. Escalona, Sibylle K., and Leitch, Mary. *Earliest Phases of Personality Development: A Non-Normative Study of Infant Behavior,* Child Research Monograph No. 17. Evanston, Ill., Child Development Publications, 1953. See also Infant Records (Filed at Topeka Kansas, The Menninger Foundation).

16. Erikson, Erik H. *Childhood and Society.* New York, Norton, 1950.

17. Benedek, Therese. Psychobiological aspects of mothering. *Amer. J. Orthopsychiat., 26:*272-278, 1956.

18. Spitz, René. Hospitalism: an inquiry into the genesis of psychiatric conditions in early childhood. *Psa. Study of the Child, 1:*53-74, 1945; 2:113-117, 1946.

19. Gesell, Arnold. *The First Five Years.* New York, Harper, 1940.

20. Murphy, Lois B. *Social Behavior and Child Personality.* New York, Columbia University, 1937.

21. Pasamanick, Benjamin; Rogers, M. E., and Lilienfeld, A. M. Pregnancy experience and the development of behavior disorder in children. *Amer. J. Psychiat., 112:*613-618, 1956.

22. Murphy, Lois B.; Moriarty, Alice E., and Raine, Walter. *The Development of Adaptational Style.* (To be published).

23. Moriarty, Alice E. Continuity and Change: A Clinical View of Relationships Between Tested Intelligence and Personality. (In press).

24. Murphy, Lois B., and Moriarty, Alice E. *The Quiet Transition.* (To be published).

25. Freud, Anna. *The Ego and the Mechanisms of Defence.* New York, International Universities, 1946.

26. McGraw, Myrtle. *Growth: A Study of Johnny and Jimmy.* New York, Appleton-Century-Croft, 1935.
27. Bridges, K. M. B. Emotional development in early infancy. *Child Develop., 3:*324-341, 1932.
28. Hilgard, E. R. *Theories of Learning.* New York, Appleton-Century-Croft, 1958.
29. Freud, Sigmund (1925-1926). Inhibitions, symptoms and anxiety. *Standard Edition, 20:*77-175, 1959.
30. Alpert, Augusta; Neubauer, P. B., and Weil, A. P. Unusual variations in drive endowment. *Psa. Study of the Child, 11:*125-163, 1956.
31. Escalona, Sibylle K. Patterns of infantile experience and the developmental process. *Psa. Study of the Child, 18:*197-244, 1963.
32. Heider, Grace: Vulnerability in infants and young children: a pilot study. *Genetic Psychol. Monogr.,* (In press).
33. Murphy, Lois B. Psychoanalysis and child development. *Bull. Menninger Clin., 21:*177-188, 248-258, 1957.
34. Yarrow, Leon J. The development of object relationships during infancy. *Amer. Psychol., 11:*423, 1956. (abstract)
35. Fries, Margaret, and Woolf, Paul J. Some hypotheses on the role on the congenital activity type in personality development. *Psa. Study Child, 8:*48-62, 1953.
36. Caldwell, Bettye M. Assessment of infant personality. *Merrill Palmer Quart., 8:*71-81, 1962.
37. van der Waals, H. G. Le narcissisme. *Revue Française Psychanalyse, 13:* 501-525, 1949.
38. Greenacre, Phyllis. *Trauma, growth and personality.* New York, Norton, 1952.

ADULTS HAVE a complex and relatively unsystematic pattern of rewards and penalties for modifying the behavior of infants and children. We have begun to isolate some of the factors which account for this behavioral modification but as yet we do not have a theoretical model which ties these factors together. In addition, there may be subtle interaction of variables which have not emerged in studies. Another limiting factor is that laboratory studies may not be directly applicable to behavior seen in natural settings. However, even with these limitations, we can observe how learning is affected by social reinforcement. The following review by Dr. Frances Horowitz analyzes some experimental studies on reinforcement and discusses how the type of reinforcement, age, sex, and personality of the child relate to the effectiveness of a particular reinforcer. A point not mentioned in the review but one that is currently provoking considerable interest is the mutual influence system of parent and child. It is suggested that certain characteristics of children, such as appearance, sex, and activity level affect parent behavior leading to differential interaction patterns and then to differential patterns of social reinforcement. Future research will specify this system in more detail.

Chapter 23

Social Reinforcement Effects
on Child Behavior

FRANCES DEGEN HOROWITZ

ALMOST everyone who has interacted with a young child knows that if you laugh at something he does, there is a good chance he will do it again. The adult's laugh serves as a response which has the effect of encouraging the child to repeat his behavior. In this obvious way and in many more subtle ways, adults' responses may encourage children to repeat, change, or stop what they are doing.

The cumulative effects of parent and teacher responses to children's behaviors are considered major determinants of complex social and intellectual characteristics. Both colloquial and professional points of view tend to accept this. Reliable evidence, however, on just how adults affect children's behavior has not always been available to support or disprove these assumptions or their implications. Indeed, the long-standing controversies on methods of guidance and discipline reflect the paucity of our knowledge.

In the more technical vocabulary of psychologists, parents and teachers act as reinforcers in responding positively, negatively or neutrally to what children do and say. They are, in this sense, social reinforcers. In its broadest meaning a social reinforcer is the action of one individual that maintains, modifies, or inhibits the behavior of another individual. In a still broader sense, social

Reprinted with permission from *The Young Child: Reviews of Research.* Copyright 1967, National Association for the Education of Young Children, 1834 Connecticut Avenue, N.W., Washington, D. C. 20009.

Dr. Horowitz wrote this article and conducted her research reported here while holding a U. S. Public Health Service Postdoctoral Research Fellowship. She wishes to acknowledge partial support for the research given by a Sigma Xi-RESA grant-in-aid of research.

reinforcers form a subclass of the larger category of social stimulation. At the early developmental stages it is not always clear exactly when social stimulation is social reinforcement. The entire problem of terminology concerning social stimulation and social reinforcement is beyond the scope of this discussion.

For our purposes, social reinforcement is defined by the behavior of one person that has the effect of shaping the behavior of another person. In the studies to be discussed here an adult is the social reinforcer to a child. It is possible that social reinforcement is a two-way track. A child can act as a social reinforcer to an adult. And peers, too, can operate in this capacity. There has been little investigation of these last two areas.

Interestingly enough, in this currently popular research area theories have played a less prominent part than in many other research areas. While theories have sometimes directly stimulated research and are often brought into discussions of research findings, the bulk of the work on social reinforcement has been more empirical than theoretical. That is, the research questions asked are often not formally derived from theoretical hypotheses. Instead, they reflect direct curiosity about how children behave and learn when adults respond in given ways; what conditions enhance and what conditions hinder adult effectiveness.

Such empirical approaches sometimes have the value of encouraging the researcher to look at behavior with fewer assumptions. But they can also spawn a body of evidence that is diverse and difficult to integrate. At the end of this article the reader is likely to be left with the feeling that while much is known, little is understood.

The studies of social reinforcement to be included in this review range widely. For the sake of organization they have been grouped into three sections: (1) effects of social stimulation and reinforcement on the social responsiveness of young infants; (2) effects of social deprivation on subsequent behavior under conditions of social reinforcement; (3) effects of various kinds of social reinforcements on learning.

SOCIAL RESPONSIVENESS IN YOUNG INFANTS

It is common to regard the newborn infant as making almost no sense out of his environment and of being little influenced by people or objects around him except as they fulfill his biological needs. In the early days of life the newborn eats, sleeps, eliminates, cries, and makes seemingly random movements. Adults react to these behaviors with little expectation that the newborn will make any direct social responses in return.

Very Young Infants

Recent evidence suggests that the newborn infant is not all this passive. He can discriminate forms in the early days of life and prefers to look at more complex and interesting stimuli.[12] Very young infants spend much of their waking moments regarding people and things. The newborn also demonstrates ability to learn to turn in the appropriate direction to be fed when held by its mother.[3] But it is not until the appearance of the smile that adults become acutely aware that the child is responding directly to them.

Studies of the development of smiling generally agree that smiling does not usually occur much before the age of one month[1,2,17,26,32] Thereafter, developmental trends are notable both in the increase in frequency of the smiling response and in the nature of the stimuli required to elicit smiling. Smiling increases in frequency up to about the age of 6 months.[2,26] The human face is the most effective stimulus for eliciting smiles and some evidence shows that with increasing age the infant must see more and more of the adult before he will smile. At 2 months the appearance of the eyes and forehead is sufficient to elicit a smile; at 3 months the eyes, forehead and nose must be visible; at 4 and 5 months the full face and shoulders are required; After 5 months the full face and upper torso are necessary to elicit smiling.[1]

The eyes seem to be necessary at all stages. If the eyes of the adult are covered while a baby is smiling the smiling ceases immediately.[2] It has been suggested that the human face is shiny, complex, and mobile. As an interesting stimulus it might thus be capable of attracting and holding the infant's attention.[23] This fits well with data that indicate infants prefer to look at complex, varied, and patterned stimuli.[11] In light of the evidence that the eyes are necessary for eliciting smiling at the human face it is interesting to speculate that the eyes are the most shiny, complex, and mobile parts of the human face, and this factor may account for the importance of these stimuli in eliciting and maintaining social responses in infants.

Why Infants Smile

Exactly why smiling initially appears is unknown. It is thought to be an innate, maturational phenomenon. Once it occurs, it probably does come under partial control of social reinforcement factors. The specific conditions which control smiling are not clear.

During the first twenty-six weeks of life infants smile to adults whether or not adults respond to the smile.[8] But, some affect of adult response has been noted. In one experimental study[4] an adult socially reinforced 3-month-old infants every time they smiled. The babies increased their rate of smiling to a stable level. When this point had been reached the adult changed her behavior for half of the infants and responded only every other time they smiled for a period of time. Then the adult ceased to respond to the infants.

After the adult ceased responding, those infants who had received social reinforcement every time they smiled declined in their rate of smiling faster than those who had received social reinforcement every other time they smiled. In other words, the influence of the presence of the adult figure is only one variable. The ratio of reinforcement to response also makes a difference in the subsequent behavior of the infant.

Social reinforcement factors are thought to be important in the general development of what is loosely referred to as social responsiveness. However, it is difficult to identify those specific reinforcement factors which affect social responsiveness. One approach was the comparison of the social stimulation and reinforcement present in the institutional setting with those found in the home setting. Rheingold[23] reported that 3- and 4-month-old infants in the home received more stimulation in all caretaking areas when compared with infants in an institution except in the number of adults present. But, the institution infants exhibited more social responsiveness to a stranger than the home-reared children.

This was contrary to expectation. Since the routinization of care in an institution is assumed to provide less social reinforcement than would be available in the more informal home atmosphere, institutionalized infants were expected to show less social responsiveness. In the study just cited this was not the case. Some explanation of this finding may be provided by another study of two groups of infants over a period of time. Infants at home and in an institution were followed from eight weeks of age to 26 weeks of age.[2]

In this extended comparison smiling increased to a peak of responsiveness and then declined. For the home infants this peak was reached at about 13 weeks of age; for the institution infants the peak was not reached until about 20 weeks of age. There was a period, after the home infants had reached their peak and before the institution infants had reached theirs when institution infants were more responsive to a stranger than home infants. Thus, the timing of the developmental pattern in social responsiveness may be a function of the amount and kind of social reinforcement typically offered by environmental conditions.

Four 6-Month-Old Infants

An attempt to study the effect of environmental conditions which might affect social responsiveness was made in an experimental modification of such conditions in an institution.[22] Two groups of four 6-month-old infants in an institution were "mothered" by an experimenter for a period of eight weeks. These infants were compared with comparable infants in the same institution who remained under the regular routines. The mothered infants were cared for personally by one individual much as a mother might care for them in a home.

When these mothered infants were compared with the children who had remained under routine schedule the mothered infants showed a significant increase in social responsiveness and in the amount of vocalizing.

One year later, however, after all the infants had left the institution and gone to their own or adoptive homes, the mothered infants showed no more social responsiveness than the non-mothered ones. The only difference between the two groups was that the mothered infants exhibited more vocalization.

The increased social responsiveness resulting from the mothering experience lends support to the importance of social stimulation and social reinforcement in the child's environment. The knowledge that the effects were not measurable a year later may suggest that eight weeks of mothering was too short a period to get persistent effects.

It is also possible that the developmental period at which the experiment was conducted was not one most sensitive to such an experience. The infants might not have reached or might have passed that period when the most lasting effects would have resulted. It is possible that the effects of stimulation and reinforcement for vocalizations did occur at an optimal period in language development and thus resulted in durable effects. An experimental study demonstrated that social reinforcement significantly increased vocalizations of 3-month-old institutional infants.[25]

Thus, we see that social responsiveness can be affected by environmental conditions. Whether this class of behavior is shaped by the summated cumulative effects of experiences, or by specific experiences coming at sensitive periods in development, or whether it is a complex interaction of the two factors is not known. Further evidence should help integrate and explain the present findings.

DEPRIVATION AND SOCIAL REINFORCEMENT

We turn now to a series of experimental laboratory studies in which children experience minimal social contact or lack of social contact for a period of time. They then participate in a task where correct responses are socially reinforced by an adult. The studies are concerned with effects of a period of social deprivation on task performance when social reinforcement is used.

These manipulations represent attempts to isolate some of the factors that enhance the effects of adult approval. The use of a period of social deprivation is analgous to the use of states such as hunger or thirst. For instance, if a person is deprived of food for a sufficient amount of time we know he becomes hungry; if deprived of liquids we know he becomes thirsty.

Primary Drives

In these instances, primary or unlearned drives are aroused. We speak of a hunger drive, or a thirst drive. Behavior under these conditions is said to be so motivated that the organism is more sensitized to stimuli related to the drive state. In the case of a hunger drive behavior which results in the acquisition of food increases and behavior which results in the withholding of food decreases; similarly for the thirst drive.

Analogously, a period of isolation or social deprivation is thought to arouse a social drive. Under these conditions behavior which results in the acquisition of social interaction or social approval should increase; behavior which results in the withholding of social interaction or approval should decrease. Another way of saying this is that a period of social deprivation should enhance the effectiveness of social reinforcers in subsequent task experiences.

To study this, preschool children have been left alone for a period of twenty minutes while waiting for "the game to be fixed."[13] Following this they dropped marbles in one of two holes. The adult indicated approval only when the child dropped a marble in the hole initially least preferred. The child's performance was compared with performance on the same task when, instead of social deprivation, he had experienced twenty minutes of interaction with the adult prior to the task.

It was found that the choice of the approved hole showed greater increase after a period of deprivation than after a period of interaction. The effect was more pronounced for boys when the approving adult was a female and somewhat more pronounced for girls when the approving adult was a male.

In accord with these findings are the results indicating that the effectiveness of social reinforcement with first and second graders also is differentially influenced by prior experience.[14] In the same task as that used with the preschool children, social reinforcement was most effective when used following a twenty-minute period of social deprivation; was intermediately effective when no specific interaction period or waiting period preceded the game; was least effective when the game was preceded by twenty minutes of interaction. With first and second graders no sex differences were found.

Some argue that social isolation does not necessarily arouse a specific social drive but arouses general anxiety which has the effect of making any reinforcer more effective in a subsequent task. While some research has attempted to provide evidence for this argument,[29-31] a recent test of the notion suggests that deprivation enhances the effectiveness of a social reinforcer but not of a marble reinforcer.[10]

Sixth grade children were given either twenty minutes of social deprivation or twenty minutes of interaction with an adult. During a subsequent task they were presented with pairs of nouns, one animate and one inanimate. They were reinforced by either a marble or social approval for choosing the animate nouns.

Marble Versus Social Reinforcement

If social deprivation aroused general anxiety then both the marble and the social approval should have been equally effective as reinforcers. If the deprivation experience aroused a social drive then the social reinforcer should have been effective but the marble reinforcer relatively ineffective in increasing the reinforced choices. Given twenty minutes of interaction prior to the task, marble and social reinforcement should have been equally as effective and totally less effective than under the deprivation condition.

The findings supported the notion that social deprivation arouses a social drive rather than general anxiety. Children under social deprivation conditions performed much better when given a social reinforcement than when given a marble reinforcement, while under the interaction condition marble and social reinforcement were equally effective. Overall social deprivation and social reinforcement led to better performance.

Individual Differences

The studies just cited do not take into account the individual differences each child brings into an experimental situation. The cumulative history of the child probably interacts importantly with experimental experiences. It has been suggested that the child's initial degree of dependency will partially determine the effectiveness of social deprivation and subsequent social reinforcement.

In one study,[15] preschool children were rated for dependency. High and low dependent boys and girls were given either ten minutes of interaction with an adult (nurturance) or five minutes interaction and five minutes of deprivation (nurturance withdrawal).

In the subsequent tasks, regardless of dependency status, girls who had experienced the deprivation performed better in a socially reinforced situation than girls who had experienced the ten minutes of interaction. For boys, deprivation enhanced the effects of social reinforcement only in cases of high dependency. Low dependency boys performed better under a social reinforcer when the period of interaction preceded the task.

In another study,[9] high and moderately dependent preschool children were found to voluntarily remain in a socially reinforced task longer than low dependent children. Evidence suggests that the degree of dependency is a factor in enhancing social reinforcer effectiveness. Studies cited in the following section give further evidence that individual differences affect behavior under social reinforcement conditions.

The evidence just reviewed strongly indicates that the effectiveness of social reinforcers in performance tasks is partially determined by experiences just prior to the task situation. There are interesting sex differences and individual differences. Here, too, further research may more clearly delineate conditions which determine how effective social reinforcers will be.

SOCIAL REINFORCEMENT AND LEARNING

Is reward a more effective means of teaching than punishment? While this time-worn question has been debated by "experts" and parents alike, the answer is not presently available from research evidence. Two basic questions are involved. The first is in terms of a given learning experience. "What is the most effective way to teach a child to do or not to do something under given conditions?" That is, in the short run, what will do the job most efficiently?

The second question is more complex. "What are the cumulative effects of given reinforcement conditions on learning, not only in terms of specific responses being taught at the time but with reference to a rather broad range of responses that are incidentally learned over a period of time?"

Evidence now available on the relative effects of reward and punishment on learning is the result of attempts to answer the first, more simple question. The studies involve children in single learning experiments. They do not concern themselves with the effects of an extended series of experiences under given reinforcement conditions.

We do not have experimental evidence relative to the long-term effects of successive experiences under specific reinforcement conditions, and our evidence only deals with a limited range of kinds of rewards and punishments. For obvious reasons, punishment such as spanking and other forms of physical attack have not been the subject of laboratory studies.

Present investigations on the relative effectiveness of social reward and punishment on learning have used limited definitions of the reinforcement conditions. Reward is usually defined as indicating verbal approval. The child is told when he is right. Punishment is defined as indicating disapproval by telling a child when he is wrong.

A number of such studies have been reported.[5,7,19,20,28] The results indicate that the combination of reward and punishment, or punishment only, tend to be most effective as reinforcement conditions. The reward-only condition tends to be, relatively, the least effective reinforcement condition. If punishment is defined more severely as a loud, noxious tone[21] then learning under the punishment-only condition is clearly superior.

There is also some evidence that children come to look upon an adult's silence as meaning the opposite of the verbalized reinforcement condition.[6] That is, silence takes on approval when paired with verbal criticism and it takes on disapproval when paired with verbal praise.

The effectiveness of a social reinforcer is not only a function of reward or punishment. The age of the child, the sex of the child relative to the sex of the experimenter, and the child's own history of experience, are all variables which help determine the effectiveness of a social reinforcer on learning.

If children are asked their preferences for rewards, younger children choose value objects such as candy and money more frequently than older children. But by the time a child is 10 or 12 he says that he prefers a social reward.[33] Experimental studies of learning do not always bear this out. There is some evidence that verbal rewards are less influential with older children than younger children.[18]

In recent studies just completed at the Bureau of Child Research preschool through sixth grade children were given some discrimination tasks. Half of the children were given a social reinforcement. They were told they were correct when they made the right choice. The other half of the children heard a buzzer every time they made the right choice.

Age Trend

There is a definite age trend in our findings (see Fig. 23-1). Looking at the relative differences between performance under buzzer and social reinforcement at the preschool level (3 to 5 years) the buzzer reinforcement condition yielded somewhat better learning. At kindergarten the difference is slight. At first grade and through fourth grade the children performed better under social reinforcement than under buzzer reinforcement but

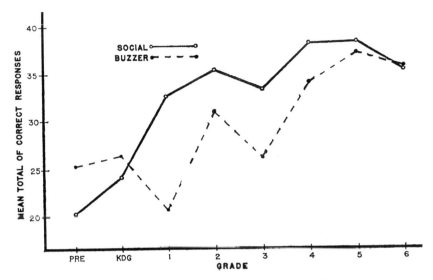

Figure 23-1. Mean number of correct responses in discrimination learning under social and buzzer reinforcement.

at the fifth and sixth grades there is again no difference between the two conditions.

Thus, a verbal reinforcer is relatively more effective than a buzzer reinforcer for children in grades one through four. We also have some evidence that the social reinforcer makes relatively more difference in the early stages of learning than in the later stages of learning.

Cross-Sex Factor

The sex of the person delivering the social reinforcer relative to the sex of the child is an important factor. A strong cross-sex factor appears to be involved. Girls do better when males are delivering the social reinforcer and boys do better when females are delivering the social reinforcer.[13,14,16,27]

Chronological age probably affects this. In our study we used a male experimenter. We found that girls performed better only at the second and third grade level. At all other grade levels there was no difference. At the preschool level the direction was slightly opposite. That is, boys at the preschool level performed better than girls with a male experimenter. Our data partially agree with the suggestion that the greatest cross-sex effect is to be found between the ages of 5 and 8.

As seen above, degree of dependency appears to bear importantly on the effectiveness of a social reinforcer. With older elementary school children anxiety level also suggests itself as an important factor. We have found that fourth grade children who score high on the Children's Manifest Anxiety scale learn much better when given a social reinforcer than when given a buzzer reinforcer. But low-anxiety fourth graders do equally as well under social or buzzer reinforcement. For low-anxious children, then, reinforcement condition makes little difference in performance, while for high-anxious children there is a significant difference.

It becomes apparent from this summary of evidence that the learning process is directly influenced by social reinforcement. The type of social reinforcer, the age and sex of the child and the personality characteristics of the child all relate to the eventual effectiveness of a social reinforcer. The cumulative history of experiences enters into the learning situation and partially determines the outcome. A body of research evidence comparing the effectiveness of social reinforcement with retarded and normal children somewhat amplifies this point.[34]

SUMMARY AND CONCLUSIONS

The reader was warned at the outset that the abundance of evidence belies the fact that our degree of understanding about social reinforcement is limited. It is obvious that social stimulation (and social reinforcement as a subclass of social stimulation) effectively modifies infant behavior, particularly in the broad area labeled social responsiveness. The experimental evidence suggests that deprivation of social stimulation enhances the effectiveness of subsequent social reinforcement. And, there is a substantial amount of evidence that a number of current and historical variables interact with the effectiveness of social reinforcers in the learning process.

Until more evidence is available, particularly that relating to the cumulative effects of reinforcement conditions, any attempt at explanation represents speculation. While omitting such speculation has the probable effect of leaving the reader somewhat frustrated, it does at least leave the author somewhat safely off the limb. But such conservatism is not the only consideration.

At this point, particularly when dealing with complex behavioral phenomena, a solid scientific understanding of human behavior may have more to gain from "I don't know" than from premature speculative integration. Perhaps twenty years from now another article appearing in this journal will be able to offer the reader a review of evidences that provides such an explanation (s) .

REFERENCES

1. Ahrens, R. Z. *Exp. Angew. Psychologie, 2* (3) :445, 1954. (Cited in Ambrose, 1961.)
2. Ambrose, J. A. The development of the smiling response in early infancy. In Foss, B. M. (Ed.) , *Determinants of Infants Behavior*. New York, Wiley, 1961, pp. 179-201.
3. Blauvelt, H., and McKenna, J. Mother-neonate interaction: Capacity of the human newborn for orientation. In Foss, B. B. (Ed.) , *Determinants of Infant Behavior*. New York, Wiley, 1961, pp. 3-35.
4. Brackbill, Y. Extinction of the smiling response as a function of reinforcement schedule. *Child Develop., 29*:115-124, 1958.
5. Brackbill, Y., and Ohara, J. The relative effectiveness of reward and punishment for discrimination learning in children. *J. Comp. Physiol. Psychol, 51*:747-751, 1958.
6. Crandall, V. C.; Good, S., and Crandall, V. J. The reinforcement effects of adult reactions and non-reactions on children's achievement expectations: A replication study. *Amer. Psychol., 17*:299, 1962.
7. Curry, C. Supplementary report: The effects of verbal reinforcement combination on learning in children. *J. Exp. Psychol., 59*:434, 1960.
8. Dennis, W. An experimental test of two theories of social smiling in infants. *J. Soc. Psychol., 6*:214-223, 1936.
9. Endsley, R. C., and Hartup, W. W. Dependency and performance by preschool children on a socially reinforced task. *Amer. Psychol., 15*: 399, 1960.
10. Erikson, N. T. The effects of social deprivation and satiation on verbal conditioning in children. *J. Comp. Physiol. Psychol., 55*:953-957, 1962.
11. Fantz, R. L. The origins of form perception. *Scientific Amer.*, May, 1961.

12. Fantz, R. L. Pattern vision in newborn infants. *Science,* 1963, 1940, 296-297.
13. Gewirtz, J., and Baer, D. The effect of brief social deprivation on behaviors for a social reinforcer. *J. Abnorm. Soc. Psychol., 56:*49-56, 1958.
14. Gewirtz, J., and Baer, D. Deprivation and satiation of social reinforcers as drive conditions. *J. Abnorm. Soc. Psychol., 57:*165-172, 1958.
15. Hartup, W. W. Nurturance and nurturance withdrawal in relation to the dependency behavior of preschool children. *Child Develop., 29:*191-201, 1958.
16. Hartup, W. W. Sex and social reinforcement effects with children. *Amer. Psychol., 16:*363, 1961.
17. Kaila, E. *Anals Univ., Aboensen. B. Humania,* 1932. (Cited in Spitz, 1946.)
18. McCullers, J. C., and Stevenson, H. W. Effects of verbal reinforcement in a probability learning situation. *Psychol. Rep., 7:*439-445, 1960.
19. Meyer, W. J., and Seidman, S. B. Relative effectiveness of different reinforcement combinations on concept learning of children at two developmental levels. *Child Develop., 32:*117-127, 1961.
20. Meyer, W. J., and Seidman, S. B. Age differences in the effectiveness of different reinforcement conditions on the acquisition and extinction of a simple concept learning problem. *Child Develop., 31:*419-429, 1960.
21. Penney, R. K., and Lupton, A. A. Children's discrimination learning as a function of reward and punishment. *J. Comp. Physiol. Psychol., 54:* 449-451, 1961.
22. Rheingold, H. L. The modification of social responsiveness of institutional babies. *Monogr. Soc. Res. Child Develop.,* Vol. XXI, Ser. No. 63, No. 2, 1956.
23. Rheingold, H. L. The effect of environmental stimulation upon social and exploratory behavior in the human infant. In Foss, B. M. (Ed.), *Determinants of Infant Behavior.* New York, Wiley, 1961.
24. Rheingold, H. L., and Bayley, N. The later effects of an experimental modification of mothering. *Child Develop., 30:*363-372, 1959.
25. Rheingold, H. L.; Gewirtz, J., and Ross, H. W. Social conditioning of vocalizations in the infant. *J. Comp Physiol. Psychol., 52:*68-72, 1959.
26. Spitz, R. A. The smiling response: A contribution to the ontogenesis of social relations. *Genet. Psychol. Monogr., 34:*57-125, 1946.
27. Stevenson, H. W. Social reinforcement with children as a function of CA, sex of E and sex of S. *J. Abnorm. Soc. Psychol., 63:*147-154, 1961.
28. Sullivan, P. W. The effects of verbal reward and verbal punishment on concept elicitation in children. *Amer. Psychol., 15:*401, 1960.
29. Walters, R. W., and Ray, E. Anxiety, social isolation, and reinforcer effectiveness. *J. Personal., 28:*358-367, 1960.

30. Walters, R. H., and Karal, P. Social deprivation and verbal behavior. *J. Personal., 28:*89-107, 1960.

31. Walters, R. H.; Marshall, W. E., and Shooter, J. R. Anxiety, social isolation, and susceptibility to social influence. *J. Personal., 28:*518-529, 1960.

32. Washburn, R. A study of smiling and laughing of infants in the first year of life. *Genet. Psychol. Monogr., 6:*399-537, 1929.

33. Witryol, S., and Ornsby, E. L. Age Trends in Children's Incentives Scaled by Paired Comparisons. Paper given at 1961 meetings of the Eastern Psychological Association.

34. Zigler, E., and Williams, J. Institutionalization and the effectiveness of social reinforcement. *J. Abnorm. Soc. Psychol., 66:*197-205, 1963.

Author Index

Subject Index

561